D0147452

The Editor

CARLA KAPLAN is the Davis Distinguished Professor of American Literature at Northeastern University and the Chair of the Editorial Board of *Signs: A Journal of Women in Culture and History.* She is the author of *The Erotics of Talk: Women's Writing and Feminist Paradigms, Zora Neale Hurston: A Life in Letters,* and *Miss Anne in Harlem: The White Women of the Black Renaissance,* as well as a forthcoming biography of the muckraker and activist Jessica Mitford. She is also editor of Nella Larsen's *Passing: A Norton Critical Edition,* as well as *Every Tongue Got to Confess: Negro Folk Tales from the Gulf States* by Zora Neale Hurston, and *Dark Symphony and Other Works* by Elizabeth Laura Adams.

A NORTON CRITICAL EDITION

Nella Larsen
QUICKSAND

AUTHORITATIVE TEXT
BACKGROUNDS AND CONTEXTS
CRITICISM

Edited by

CARLA KAPLAN
NORTHEASTERN UNIVERSITY

W · W · NORTON & COMPANY · *New York* · *London*

W. W. Norton & Company has been independent since its founding in 1923, when William Warder Norton and Mary D. Herter Norton first published lectures delivered at the People's Institute, the adult education division of New York City's Cooper Union. The firm soon expanded its program beyond the Institute, publishing books by celebrated academics from America and abroad. By midcentury, the two major pillars of Norton's publishing program—trade books and college texts—were firmly established. In the 1950s, the Norton family transferred control of the company to its employees, and today—with a staff of five hundred and hundreds of trade, college, and professional titles published each year—W. W. Norton & Company stands as the largest and oldest publishing house owned wholly by its employees.

Library of Congress Cataloging-in-Publication Data

Names: Larsen, Nella, author. | Kaplan, Carla, editor.
Title: Quicksand : authoritative text, backgrounds and contexts,
    criticism / Nella Larsen ; edited by Carla Kaplan.
Description: First edition. | New York : W. W. Norton & Company,
    [2020] | Series: A Norton critical edition | Includes bibliographical
    references.
Identifiers: LCCN 2019019859 | ISBN 9780393932423 (paperback)
Subjects: LCSH: Larsen, Nella. Quicksand. | African Americans—
    Fiction. | African American women—Fiction. | Racially mixed
    people—Fiction. | Danish American women—Fiction. | Young
    women—Fiction. | Harlem (New York, N.Y.)—Fiction. |
    Copenhagen (Denmark) —Fiction.
Classification: LCC PS3523.A7225 Q55 2020 | DDC 813/.52—dc23
LC record available at https://lccn.loc.gov/2019019859

W. W. Norton & Company, Inc., 500 Fifth Avenue, New York, NY 10110
wwnorton.com

W. W. Norton & Company Ltd., 15 Carlisle Street, London W1D 3BS

1 2 3 4 5 6 7 8 9 0

Contents

Introduction: A "Queer Dark Creature"[1]

I. Achievement's Lift: "Harlem . . . filled her only with restlessness"[2]

Slim first novels rarely enjoy the success which *Quicksand* did on its publication by Alfred A. Knopf, "the preeminent American publisher of modern fiction,"[3] in March 1928. Prior to that publication, Nella Larsen was familiar in Harlem, but little known as a writer. Her output was too small. *Quicksand* propelled her into celebrity as one of only two black women—Jessie Fauset was the other—considered major fiction writers.[4] W. E. B. Du Bois, arguably the most important black man in America, singling out *Quicksand* as "the best piece of fiction that Negro America has produced since the heyday of [Charles] Chesnutt," praised the novel's "subtle comprehension of the curious cross currents that swirl about the black American."[5] Almost overnight, Larsen became a celebrated, public personality. Given the novel's anger, and its attitude toward Harlem, the position it gave to Nella Larsen could not have been anticipated. *Quicksand* is one of the grimmest novels in modern black letters, a "queer dark creature" unequalled (until Richard Wright's *Native Son*, in 1940) in its pessimism. Yet, for a while, the novel lifted Larsen's life.

Born on April 13, 1891, Larsen had led a lonely Chicago childhood, the only mixed-race child of a white Danish mother whose second, white, husband may have wished her gone (her father was a

1. Nella Larsen, *Quicksand*, originally published New York: Knopf, 1928 (New York: Collier, 1971), 123 [61, 43]. Future page references in brackets will refer to this Norton Critical Edition based on the 1928 Knopf edition.
2. Larsen, *Quicksand*, 90 [43]
3. George Hutchinson, *In Search of Nella Larsen: A Biography of the Color Line* (Cambridge: Belknap, 2006), p. 223.
4. Larsen and Fauset were often paired. See, for example, "Bids for Literary Laurels," *Chicago Defender* (May 12, 1928): A1, included in the "Contemporary Reviews" section of this edition, and Ann duCille, "Blues Notes on Black Sexuality: Sex and the Texts of Jessie Fauset and Nella Larsen," *Journal of the History of Sexuality*, 3.3 (1993): 418–44, excerpted in the "Criticism" section of this volume.
5. W. E. B. Du Bois, "Two Novels," *The Crisis* (June 1928). Du Bois's review is included in the "Contemporary Reviews" section of this volume.

black or mixed-race West Indian).[6] Often the only person of color in all-white schools or neighborhoods, young Nella, then known as Nellie, developed defensive strategies of self-erasure and silence.[7] As a young child, she visited Denmark with her mother and sister. Nella attended Moseley and Colman primary schools, graduated from Wendell Phillips High School, and studied briefly at Fisk. Between 1909 and 1912, she made other trips back to Denmark, where her mother's family lived. In 1892, a younger sister, Anna, was born to parents Mary Hansen Walker and Peter Walker. Where Nella's birth certificate marked her as "colored," the rest of the family appears in census records as white. Self-reliance was forced upon her as the only person of color in a white family which many believe tried to distance itself from its one non-white member.

Taking advantage of an emerging profession offering respectable work, Larsen trained as a nurse, enrolling in a newly accredited program at New York's Lincoln Hospital in 1912. Lincoln was one of the few places in the nation open to black nurses[8] (but not to black doctors; all of Larsen's supervisors at Lincoln were white). Nurses were urged to put "unselfish commitment to the care of others" above individual concerns and to put the ideal of healing the race above all else.[9] The school's motto was "Gladly My Service." Larsen received her license, as a Registered Nurse, in 1915.

In the fall of 1915, a few months after her graduation, Larsen took the position of Head Nurse at Tuskegee Institute. The position asked a great deal of a newly graduated professional and Larsen was miserable at Tuskegee, overwhelmed by a workload which added heavy administration and teaching to already substantial nursing duties. Larsen chafed under Tuskegee's rigid conduct codes and was appalled by the constant surveillance which dogged Tuskegee's

---

6. For speculation that this second husband may have been Larsen's original father, now passing for white, see Thadious M. Davis, *Nella Larsen: Novelist of the Harlem Renaissance: A Woman's Life Unveiled* (Baton Rouge: Louisiana UP, 1994), especially pp. 47–50.
7. In the absence of an archive or robust public record—Larsen disappeared from public view for decades before her death—dedicated biographers have successfully reconstructed much of Larsen's life, beginning with Charles Larson's *Invisible Darkness: Jean Toomer & Nella Larsen* (Iowa City: U of Iowa P, 1993). Thadious Davis's biography offers particular insight into the intersectional oppressions a black woman without family faced in Larsen's time. George Hutchinson's more recent biography, *In Search of Nella Larsen: A Biography of the Color Line* (Cambridge: Harvard UP, 2006), fills in gaps in Larsen's chronology and offers particular insight into the challenges of biracial and mixed-racial identity, especially at a time when Americans were offered no such option. See also his essay, "Nella Larsen and the Veil of Race," *American Literary History* 9.2 (1997): 329–49, for a scholarly challenge to the long-standing idea that Larsen may have exaggerated, or invented, her time in Scandinavia.
8. According to Davis, there were approximately sixteen such institutions in the nation (76). On nursing as a profession for black women, see also Darlene Clark Hine, *Black Women in White: Racial Conflict and Cooperation in the Nursing Profession, 1890–1950* (Bloomington: Indiana UP, 1989).
9. Davis, *Nella Larsen*, p. 87.

female employees. She opposed founder Booker T. Washington's methods of courting white support and philanthropy. Like other black, northern progressives, she had a keen sense of the many draw-backs of practical accommodation to the South. She found that she opposed both Washington's vocational mission and his racial philos-ophy of self-help. The discipline Tuskegee imposed on students and teachers struck her as nothing short of tyranny (which she later depicted in *Quicksand*).[1] At Tuskegee, women were given special responsibility for racial "uplift," an ideology that charged educated blacks with helping to lift the rest of the race. Uplift demanded both sacrifice and service. But Larsen, as George Hutchinson notes, "disdained . . . uplift."[2]

Larsen left Tuskegee as soon as she could, resigning in October of 1916 and returning to New York. She worked for the New York City Department of Health, in its Bureau of Preventable Diseases. This meant working long hours and caring for some of the city's poorest residents. She worked hard, joined a visiting nurse association, and volunteered through the Circle for Negro War Relief. But even in New York, nursing provided little access to the social circles she craved. That access came, in large measure, through Elmer S. Imes, whom Larsen met in 1918 and to whom *Quicksand* is dedicated.

Nella's only certainty about her family was that she could expect little from them. But Elmer came from a close family, which cher-ished its history (free blacks on his father's side and survivors of slav-ery on his mother's), had proud traditions of education at Fisk, and was part of the African American elite, having achieved professional status in medicine, music, science, and the church. Born in 1883, Elmer was ten years older than Nella and considerably more estab-lished. When they met, he had just completed his PhD at the Uni-versity of Michigan—making him the nation's second black physicist and one of only thirty-nine black PhDs in the country.[3] His work in

---

1. See Washington's "Atlanta Exposition Address" and W. E. B. Du Bois's response, "Of Mr. Booker T. Washington and Others," both excerpted in the "Cultural Contexts" section of this volume. For a description of Tuskegee, see Susan Reverby's "Hallowed Ground," excerpted in the "Criticism" section of this volume. While many Harlem intellectuals, such as Du Bois, criticized Washington, not until Ralph Ellison's *Invisible Man* was there another fictional portrait as critical of Tuskegee as *Quicksand* (nor has Ellison's evident debt to *Quicksand* been adequately addressed). Larsen may also have objected to Southern perceptions of nursing, often viewed not professionally, but instead "classed with personal service and associated with the traditional role of the black 'Mammy,'" as Hutchinson explains. Washington, Hutchinson writes, put nurses at the "bottom of the totem pole, next to laborers and laundresses." See Hutchinson, *Search*, pp. 92–93. On the cultural stereotype of the black "Mammy," see Chandler Owen, "Black Mam-mies," included in the "Cultural Contexts" section of this volume.
2. Hutchinson, *Search*, p. 166. On uplift ideology and *Quicksand*, see also Daylanne English, "W. E. B. Du Bois's Family Crisis," *American Literature: A Journal of Literary History, Criticism, and Bibliography*, 72.2 (2000): 291–319.
3. Davis, *Nella Larsen*, p. 722.

infrared spectroscopy, electromagnetic radiation, and quantum theory was highly regarded in scientific circles.

While Nella was emotional and impulsive, Elmer was both "methodical" and cool. Evidently his family found Nella "unrefined and irreligious" and they disapproved of his choice. But Elmer was taken with Nella's looks and intelligence. Elmer was not especially handsome. He had a small chin, receding hairline, and overly large round glasses gave him an owlish look. But Larsen was very attractive. He had enormous confidence, which Nella lacked. His career and credentials opened doors, whereas "Larsen's work" as a nurse, Thadious Davis explains, "limited her to a lower social sphere."[4] Elmer, Hutchinson notes, was "well connected to the national black elite."[5] They shared an interest in Harlem's many cultural activities, and he supported Nella's writing ambitions. Elmer's brother, William Lloyd Imes, married them on May 3, 1919, in Union Theological Seminary.

Relying on the Danish heritage of her mother and on her own travels to Denmark[6] to meet her mother's family, Larsen published "Three Scandinavian Games" in 1920. That publication was followed by two short stories under a pseudonym (one about a woman trapped by the sexual double standard and a very Edith Wharton-esque tale about a man doomed by his own selfishness), as well as a review, in her own name, of Walter White's passing novel *Flight*. She also published a spirited defense of White in the press. There were occasional other literary reviews as well, in which Larsen took on white writers and, in one case, boldly called them out for racist "twaddle."[7]

In 1921, as the Harlem Renaissance took off, Nella met white librarian Ernestine Rose.[8] Rose directed the library, operating it as Harlem's de facto community center. As historian David Levering Lewis put it, at the library, "the intellectual pulse of Harlem throbbed."[9] Larsen worked with Rose on a "Negro art" exhibit for the library. Prior to library work, Rose had done settlement work with immigrant communities. She carried philosophies of community self-expression, learned there, into Harlem with her. At the library, she

4. Davis, *Nella Larsen*, pp. 120, 121.
5. Hutchinson, *Search*, p. 123.
6. While some critics and biographers questioned Larsen's claim to international travel, George Hutchinson has demonstrated that Larsen did indeed travel to Denmark at least twice, once in 1909 and once in 1912. *Quicksand*'s descriptions of Helga Crane's time in Scandinavia draw from these travels.
7. See Larsen's review of T. Bowyer Campbell's novel *Black Sadie*, included in the "Nella Larsen's Writings" section of this volume.
8. Rose was named after, but not related to, suffragist and abolitionist Ernestine Louise Rose, who died in 1892.
9. David Levering Lewis, *When Harlem Was in Vogue* (New York: Oxford UP, 1929), p. 105.

encouraged exhibitions of local artists, reading groups on black history and literature, symposia, and extensive adult educational programming, especially in African American literature and history. She hired black staff, when there were few interracial models available for institutional staffing. Believing in both integration and black pride, Rose argued that "race knowledge must be stimulated and guided."[1] She had faith in what she called "the inevitable democratizing tendency of good books."[2] "Atomic changes" in racial attitudes, she predicted, would "sink all differences" to create "common ground."[3] According to Hutchinson, Rose "hand-picked" Larsen to break the profession's race barrier.[4] At the library, Larsen witnessed the power of culture to change social attitudes. Its impact on Larsen was profound. She saw the central role that a library could play.

With Rose's support and also Elmer's, Larsen became the first professionally trained and credentialed black librarian in the large New York system. It was the sort of professional gamble that her marriage to Imes made possible. As Davis writes, "after more than a decade being on her own, and often a lonely outsider, she had both a home and companionship."[5] On receiving her library certificate, she was able to get a coveted position as Children's Librarian at the 135th Street library. This was an exciting time for such work. Children's literature was gaining importance and librarians often counseled publishers to help more of it reach the public. It was an especially exciting time to work at the 135th Street branch, thanks to the library's rich calendar of lectures, readings, round tables, classes, receptions, club meetings, rehearsals, political meetings, book parties, readings, and after-theater parties.

In focusing on the arts and making the library so important to Harlem, Rose was unusual among whites, but in those views she aligned well with the black community's values. Literature was the social currency of public debate in Harlem. Activists such as Du Bois saw art as the "one true method of gaining sympathy and human interest."[6] Black artists and intellectuals, historian Nathan Huggins notes, "promoted poetry, prose, painting and music as if

---

1. Ernestine Rose, "Serving New York's Black City." *Library Journal* 46 (March 1921).
2. Ernestine Rose, "Books and the Color Line." *Survey Graphic* 48 (April 15, 1922). Included in the "Cultural Contexts" section of this volume.
3. Ernestine Rose, "A Librarian in Harlem." *Opportunity* (July 1923), p. 207, included in the "Cultural Contexts" section of this volume. This essay proved controversial when some readers expressed concern that Rose seemed supportive of segregated white and black libraries, an almost inevitable misreading of any white writer's attempt to advocate a black "race consciousness." See also Ernestine Rose, "Where White and Black Meet," *The Southern Workman* 51 (October 1922).
4. Hutchinson, *Search*, p. 8.
5. Davis, *Nella Larsen*, p. 123.
6. W. E. B. Du Bois, "Criteria of Negro Art," *The Crisis* (October 1926).

their lives depended on it."[7] Indeed, activists such as James Weldon Johnson believed that "through his artistic efforts the Negro is smashing the race barriers faster than he has ever done with any other method."[8] Cultural achievement was understood as essential to fostering race pride. And "race pride," as Alain Locke, sometimes called the midwife of the movement, put it, "was the mainspring of Negro life" in Harlem.[9]

Larsen came to Harlem already persuaded of literature's "potential to shape ideas and policies on a national scale."[1] Her growing perception that racism and sexism were linked, however, and institutionally reproduced, complicated available ideas of race pride and race loyalty, and her intersectional insights put her somewhat at odds with the ways "race pride" anchored the political and aesthetic movement.

Harlem's complex social networks contributed to making Nella and Elmer anxious about Harlem's networks. They understood how critical the right connections were, and it disturbed them not to be central to what George Hutchinson calls "High Harlem" and to be "left off some of the guest lists" that counted.[2] Harlem centrality meant hosting or contributing writing, art, or political leadership to the growing movement. But friends who did not drive couldn't get to their New Jersey home. Larsen was shy in large gatherings. And Elmer was seen as both "haughty" and "caustic."[3] Elmer's writing was not the sort that Harlem was looking for, and Nella's work was still, largely, promise.[4] Larsen was in her twenties, when promise suffices, but Elmer was in his thirties, when accomplishments begin to be tallied, and he was ambitious for success.

Through the library, as well as through Harlem's famous parties and cabarets, the Imeses met black artists and intellectuals such as Rudolph Fisher, Walter White, Frank Horne, Zora Neale Hurston, James Weldon Johnson, Dorothy Peterson, Gwendolyn Bennett, and Eric Walrond. They made friends with white "Negrotarians" such

7. Nathan Irvin Huggins, *The Harlem Renaissance*, rev. ed. (New York: Oxford UP, 2007), p. 9.
8. James Weldon Johnson, "Preface," *The Book of American Negro Poetry*, rev. ed. (New York: Harcourt Brace Jovanovich, 1931), p. 9. For more on the arts and the Harlem Renaissance, see Carla Kaplan, *Miss Anne in Harlem: The White Women of the Black Renaissance* (New York: Harper, 2013).
9. Alain Locke, "The New Negro," in Locke, ed., *The New Negro: Voices of the Harlem Renaissance* (1925; rpr. New York: Atheneum, 1992), p. 11.
1. Karin Roffman, "Nella Larsen: Librarian at 135th Street," *From the Modernist Annex: American Women Writers in Museums and Libraries* (Tuscaloosa: U of Alabama P, 2010).
2. Hutchinson, *Search*, p. 168.
3. Mrs. John (Edith) Work, Interview with Thadious Davis, March 8, 1987, as cited by Davis, *Nella Larsen*, p. 333.
4. Imes published papers on such topics as infrared absorption of diatomic gases and the "Fine-structure of Gases HCl, HBr, and HF." Occasionally Larsen provided copies to those she hoped to impress.

as Carl Van Vechten, Fania Marinoff, Eddie Wasserman, Harry Block, and Blanche and Alfred Knopf.[5] They were frequent guests at the interracial parties hosted by Gladys White, Dorothy Peterson, Grace and James Weldon Johnson, and Fania Marinoff and Carl Van Vechten, to whom Larsen became especially close.[6] Van Vechten was a powerful tastemaker and the most loyal of friends. But he was a controversial figure, especially following the publication of the 1926 novel *Nigger Heaven*, which had ignited a critical firestorm for its title and its racy depictions of black cabaret life.[7] Larsen defended Van Vechten's right to write about blacks, his risky subject matter, and his title—meant ironically. In taking his side, she allied herself with the modernists against the traditionalists, and with full artistic freedom of expression, against restraint. It was a daring alliance.

Larsen later claimed that *Quicksand* was written in only six weeks.[8] This claim glossed over her many revisions and rewrites and ignored the fact that she'd begun work on the novel as early as 1925. But she did work quickly on the novel, weighing, as she worked, the comparable advantages of the major publishers interested in black fiction at the time. In the summer of 1926 she told Van Vechten that she had decided on Knopf but might consider Viking as a backup.[9] She was also reading voraciously. A fall letter to Van Vechten shows her working her way through the Blue Jade series of books, which appealed to readers' interest in the exotic and included *Saïd the*

---

5. "Negrotarian," coined by Zora Neale Hurston, referred to white supporters of the Harlem Renaissance.
6. According to Davis, the parties Larsen attended in Harlem "bolstered her self-confidence and alleviated the sense of rejection that was one of the scars from her youth"—wounds inflicted on the only dark child of a white, immigrant family, for whom she was a distinct inconvenience (*Nella Larsen*, p. 56). More than just confidence-building, those parties also provided the professional networking that enabled success. White editors such as the Knopfs, Harry Block, a senior editor at Knopf, and T. R. Smith, a senior editor at Boni & Liveright, were anxious to publish black literature. But they often felt insecure about their ability to judge what seemed to them a very new field. They leaned heavily on the advice of white advisers and favored the writers those advisers brought to them and whom they had come to know socially. Alfred and Blanche Knopf especially depended on white writer Carl Van Vechten to tell them what to pursue. For more on how socializing helped advance careers in Harlem, see George Hutchinson, *The Harlem Renaissance in Black and White* (Cambridge: Belknap, 1995), and Carla Kaplan, *Miss Anne in Harlem: White Women of the Black Renaissance* (New York: Harper, 2013).
7. Carl Van Vechten's *Nigger Heaven*, published in 1926, divided many of Harlem's "literati." Du Bois and others detested the book and called Van Vechten a traitor for trading on his many black friendships to gain access to black culture which he then, in Du Bois's view, depicted at its worst. But Larsen was steadfast in her support of Van Vechten and even dedicated *Passing* to him and Fania Marinoff. I discuss the controversy over *Nigger Heaven* at greater length in "Nella Larsen's Erotics of Race," the "Introduction" to *Passing: A Norton Critical Edition*, ed. Carla Kaplan (New York: W. W. Norton and Company, 2007).
8. Interview with Thelma Berlack, "New Author Unearthed Right Here in Harlem," in *Passing*, ed. Carla Kaplan.
9. Nella Larsen to Carl Van Vechten, Wednesday 21st [July 1926], included in the "Correspondence" section of this volume.

Fisherman, the Middle Eastern novel Helga Crane reads as *Quicksand* opens.[1] She was enthusiastic about the idea of a Harlem bookstore. A summer 1927 attempt to host a tea for renowned singer Ethel Waters (who failed to show up) demonstrates growing social confidence, as does asking Gertrude Stein, modernism's most formidable woman, for a reading of *Quicksand*.[2]

In 1927, largely through Van Vechten, Nella Larsen attended numerous parties with the Knopfs. In the spring, she attended a party at the Van Vechten-Marinoffs, where Blanche Knopf was present, and only four days later another party where both Knopf editors Harry Block and Blanche Knopf were present. Nine days after that she joined a group that included photographer Nicholas Muray and writers Louise Bryant, James Weldon Johnson, Zelda and F. Scott Fitzgerald, Walter White, Rebecca West, and Paul Morand at yet another party. That same month, March 1927, the Knopfs, encouraged by Van Vechten, accepted *Quicksand*.

One month later, in April 1927, Nella and Elmer moved into Harlem, taking a five-room fifth-floor walk-up apartment at 236 W. 135th Street, walking distance from the library. Larsen's letters from this period reveal growing confidence about her place in literary culture. She trusted that she could reinvent herself as a "novelist," as she put it in a letter to her friend Dorothy Peterson.[3] She now took her success as a matter of course and counseled others on theirs. She assessed, astutely, that the "vogue"[4] for blackness, drawing both tourists and publishers to Harlem, could not last. "I've met a man from Macmillans," she wrote her friend Dorothy Peterson, in 1927, "who asked me to look out for any Negro stuff and send them to him." Write "something," quickly, she urged Peterson.[5] "It may be just a fad on their part," she added, "but I think it's an awfully good fad."[6]

Quicksand gave Larsen a footing. She was now such a notable figure in black New York's literary circles that reporters noted where

1. Nella Larsen to Carl Van Vechten, Wednesday 29th [September 1926], included in the "Correspondence" section of this volume.
2. See Larsen's letters to Carl Van Vechten, [June 29]; Nella Larsen to Gertrude Stein, February 1, 1928; and Nella Larsen to Gertrude Stein, February 26, [1931?], included in the "Correspondence" section of this volume.
3. Nella Larsen to Dorothy Peterson, Tuesday 2nd [August 1927], James Weldon Johnson Collection, Beinecke Library, Yale University. From the Dorothy Peterson Collection, Yale Collection of American Literature, Beinecke Rare Book and Manuscript Library.
4. Langston Hughes, "When the Negro Was in Vogue," *The Big Sea* (New York: Hill and Wang, 1940), p. 228.
5. Nella Larsen to Dorothy Peterson, Thursday 21st [July 1927]. James Weldon Johnson Collection, Beinecke Library, Yale University. This letter is reproduced in full in Kaplan, ed., *Passing: A Norton Critical Edition*, pp. 164–65.
6. Nella Larsen interview with Marion L. Starkey, "Negro Writers Come into Their Own." Unpublished MS. in the Alfred A. Knopf Collection, Harry Ransom Research Center, University of Texas. As cited by Hutchinson, *Search*, pp. 322–23.

she traveled, whom she dined with, what awards she garnered, the political positions she took, and even how a case of flu was progressing.[7] Her picture was included, in April 1928, along with portraits of Paul Robeson, James Weldon Johnson, Langston Hughes, Walter White, Alain Locke, Carl Van Vechten, and others, in a much-touted exhibition of works by famed photographer James L. Allen, at the 135th Street library.[8] Reviews began appearing in May 1928, two months after the novel appeared. Partly on the strength of the success *Quicksand* seemed to augur, Nella and Elmer moved to the Dunbar apartments, one of Harlem's toniest addresses, where their neighbors included Rudolph Fisher, W. E. B. Du Bois, and Paul Robeson, among others. Now they were in the heart of Harlem, just when Harlem was still the seat of the nation's "New Negro Renaissance." Rents at the Dunbar apartments were high. At $64.50 for four rooms and $99 a month for six rooms and two baths, they were almost double what was then typical for New York. But everyone in Harlem paid higher rents.

Harlem's symbolic importance is hard to overstate. As Adam Clayton Powell Sr., the pastor of the Abyssinian Baptist Church, put it, Harlem was "the symbol of liberty and the Promised Land to Negroes everywhere."[9] For black people all over the nation—and, in fact, the world—Harlem was as much idea and ideal as it was a physical place. It represented self-definition and pride, refuge and, for some, a "foretaste of paradise."[1] It is "nearly ideal," Walter White declared.[2] Harlem was so beloved that the radical journal *The Messenger* gave a yearly prize for the best essay written by "New York Negroes" on why they liked Harlem. The 1927 winner, who lived a block over from Nella and Elmer, wrote that Harlem "is black life perfected."[3] Langston Hughes, who came to Harlem from the Midwest, "was in love with Harlem long before I got there."[4]

7. See, for example, "Intimate Talk on Theater," *New York Times*, December 6, 1928; "12 Negroes Honored for Achievement," *New York Times*, January 3, 1929; "Guggenheim Fund Makes 85 Grants," *New York Times*, March 24, 1930; "Writers Appeal to Roosevelt," *New York Times*, December 3, 1932; "Improving," *New York Amsterdam News*, February 6, 1929; "Novelist Here," *Chicago Defender*, September 23, 1933, p. 4; "Books for Vacation," *Chicago Defender*, July 1928, p. A2; and Thelma E. Berlack, "New Author Unearthed Right Here in Harlem," in *Passing: A Norton Critical Edition*, ed. Carla Kaplan, pp. 149–50. In the "Contemporary Articles" section of this volume, see "Random Thoughts" and "[H]onor Author of *Quicksand* at Tea."
8. Hutchinson, *Search*, p. 276.
9. Adam Clayton Powell Sr., as quoted by Jervis Anderson, *This Was Harlem: A Cultural Portrait, 1900–1950* (New York: Farrar, 1982), p. 61.
1. Arna Bontemps, Preface, *Personals* (London: Breman, 1973).
2. Walter White, "Color Lines," *Survey Graphic VI* (March 1925): 681.
3. Ira D. A. Reid, "Why I Like Harlem." *The Messenger* (January 1927). Indeed, one popular expression went: "I'd rather be a lamppost in Harlem, than the Governor of Georgia." Nearly 100,000 new black migrants came into Harlem in the 1920s, according to Alain Locke. See his "Enter the New Negro," in Locke, ed., *The New Negro*.
4. Langston Hughes, "My Early Days in Harlem." *Freedomways* 3 (Summer 1963): 312.

Yet, *Quicksand* criticizes Harlem. Helga Crane[5] moves unhappily through five different representative environments: Naxos/Georgia, Chicago, Harlem, Copenhagen, Harlem, and Alabama. Only Harlem is visited twice.[6] Only Harlem has two chances to make Helga happy. And only Harlem fails Helga twice. As Charles Larson notes, "the extensive episodes set in Harlem are the most important" ones in the novel.[7] They respond to Harlem's vaunted status with a fierce critique of its cultural and sexual politics. *Quicksand* endorses almost none of Harlem's ideas of uplift, literary advocacy, black pride, or the arts. Marriage, which had given Larsen both social prestige and economic stability, fares even worse. Harlem fails *Quicksand*'s protagonist. Marriage destroys her.

II. Rage's Pull: "angry . . . Angry . . . Angry"[8]

The "New Negro" spirit which energized the Harlem Renaissance was not gender neutral. Pressure to prove the "manhood" denied by slavery helped animate the Harlem Renaissance. The galvanizing return of Harlem's triumphant 369th Regiment of the American Expeditionary Forces, also known as the "Harlem Hellfighters," saturated the movement with militant ideals of fighting valor. Du Bois called on "New Negroes" to "return from fighting" and "return fighting" the enemy at home.[9] Claude McKay's widely reprinted poem, "If We Must Die" admonished black men to die "fighting back."[1] This fighting spirit coded race pride, Locke's "mainspring of Negro life,"[2] as male. As Davis writes, "the leading figures and the most influential ones in the literary movement were all males . . . Women were largely excluded from decision-making circles."[3] Many of Harlem's male writers adopted this ethos and embedded it into their aesthetics.

Where did this fighting spirit and masculinist imperative leave women's anger and Harlem's women writers? What was their route, if any, to valor's wellspring of "race pride"? Uplift was one arena

---

5. The name "Helga" derives from the Old Norse word "Helge" for "blessed."
6. In Claude McKay's *Home to Harlem*, Jessie Fauset's *Plum Bun*, and Wallace Thurman's *The Blacker the Berry*, characters also move in and out of Harlem. I am grateful to Rafia Zafar for an exchange on these patterns.
7. Larson, *Invisible Darkness*, p. 68. For an excellent example of how the work of cultural geography can trace one racialized body's movement through space, history, and language, see Laura Tanner, "Intimate Geography: The Body, Race, and Space in Larsen's *Quicksand*," *Texas Studies in Literature and Language*, 51.2 (Summer 2009): 179–202.
8. Larson, *Quicksand*, p. 59 [27].
9. W. E. B. Du Bois, "Fighting Soldiers," *The Crisis* (May 1919): 13.
1. Claude McKay, "If We Must Die," *The Liberator* (July 1919): 21; reprinted in *The Messenger* (September 1919) and Claude McKay, *Harlem Shadows* (New York: Harcourt, Brace, Jovanovich, 1922).
2. Alain Locke, "The New Negro," in Locke, ed., *The New Negro*, p. 11. See also Du Bois, "Race Pride," included in the "Cultural Contexts" section of this volume.
3. Davis, *Nella Larsen*, p. 159.

where women's leadership predominated. In 1927, one year before Larsen's novel appeared, *The Messenger* published a three-month symposium called "Negro Womanhood's Greatest Needs."[4] Conducted by "leading Negro clubwomen" (often the foundation of "uplift"), the symposium promised to expose the "special" difficulties black women faced. As one writer noted simply, the black woman "needs everything. . . . She has steadily marched forward with torn and bleeding feet, head often bowed down in sorrow and a breaking heart. She has had to fight foes within and foes without." Yet the contributors did not call for militancy or encourage anger. They called on other black women "not to flare up as a meteor . . . but be cautious."[5] They urged service. Through service, another club member wrote, we "must help others to rise." "The work of the Negro woman," another contributor wrote, "is in lifting up that portion of the American people that suffers at least a half-century of handicap."[6] Uplift was urged on women writers as well.

As Larsen knew only too well, "overpowering conditions . . . circumscribe[d]" black women's lives.[7] Employment opportunities were clustered in domestic service, with jobs such as housecleaner, laundress, maid, and cook accounting for more than half the work black women could find, even as white women were entering into clerical work, bookkeeping, retail sales, and journalism. When middle-class black women did break into nursing, teaching, and library work, they were paid less. Infant and maternal mortality rates were nearly double what they were for whites.[8] Sterilization was often forced upon black women as population control. White women could expect to live, on average, thirteen years longer than black women (whose average life expectancy was only forty-seven years).[9] Hence, women such as Helga Crane found themselves caught between "the racism of birth control rhetoric and the sexism of racial uplift discourse," with motherhood sometimes promoted as a racial

---

4. Portions of this symposium are reprinted in the "Cultural Contexts" section of this volume.
5. (Mrs.) Bonnie Bogle, April 1927, Symposium.
6. Ethel Minor Gavin, May 1927, Symposium.
7. See McDougald, "The Task of Negro Womanhood," included in the "Cultural Contexts" section of this volume.
8. Du Bois lambasted the price black women paid for motherhood; see his "Damnation of Women" excerpted in the "Cultural Contexts" section of this volume. Alice Dunbar-Nelson worried over racist forms of birth control and declining birth rates. See her essay, "Woman's Most Serious Problem," *The Messenger* 9 (March 1927): 73, 86. Marita Bonner lamented the fact that even faced with unfair standards and impossible stereotypes, black women were encouraged to be patient and even-tempered. See her essay, "On Being Young—a Woman—and Colored," in the "Cultural Contexts" section of this volume.
9. Most of these statistics are based on U.S. census reports and on statistics compiled by the Pew Research Center. I am grateful to my research assistant, Sarah Payne, for compiling these for me.

obligation.[1] In *Quicksand*, uplift is derided and race pride is depicted as an acid constraint. Unlike her protagonist, Nella Larsen never had children. She concentrated on her writing.

Although the arts were at the forefront of the Harlem Renaissance, women's artistic expression, like their labor, was subject to the demands of uplift and the pressures of what is now known as the politics of respectability.[2] In 1928, then-radical black journalist George Schuyler published his "Instructions for Contributors" to his periodicals. He echoed widespread sentiments in warning would-be writers that "nothing that casts the least reflection on contemporary moral or sex standards will be allowed. . . . Keep away from the erotic! Contributions must be clean and wholesome. . . . The color problem is bad enough without adding any fuel to the fire."[3] Male writers such as Claude McKay were given latitude on sexual representation. Women writers were not. Faced with both a militancy they could not model and with a responsibility for respectably representing the race, many black women, even in the midst of an emancipatory movement, felt trapped. In that context, *Quicksand* is especially bold. Neither Jessie Fauset nor Zora Neale Hurston, for example, approached sexuality as directly at this time. As Charles Larson puts it, *Quicksand* shows that all too often "educated black women— sophisticated and cultured black women, middle-class black women— are trapped in life with no satisfying alternatives."[4]

Nevertheless, the novel attempts to refuse the entrapment it depicts. Helga's sexuality is a—perhaps the—central facet of her character. As Hazel Carby puts it, Helga is "the first truly sexual black female protagonist in Afro-American fiction."[5] *Quicksand* indicts all facets of society—white or black, straight or queer—which deny black women's sexual selves.[6] Being more than one race, as

---

1. Lynne Parish Craig, "'That Means Children to Me': The Birth Control Movement in Nella Larsen's *Quicksand*," *Gender Scripts in Medicine and Narrative*, eds. Marcelline Block, Angela Laflen, and Rita Charon (Newcastle upon Tyne, England: Cambridge Scholars, 2010).
2. See Evelyn Brooks Higginbotham, *Righteous Discontent: The Women's Movement in the Black Baptist Church* (Cambridge: Harvard UP, 1994).
3. George S. Schuyler, "Instructions for Contributors." Illustrated Feature Section. Reprinted and circulated by Eugene Gordon, "Negro Fictionist[s] in America," *The Saturday Evening Quill* (April 1929). These "Instructions" are included in the "Cultural Contexts" section of this volume.
4. Larson, *Invisible Darkness*, p. 72.
5. Hazel Carby, *Reconstructing Womanhood: The Emergence of the Afro-American Woman Novelist* (New York: Oxford UP, 1987), p. 174.
6. In 1937, well after the Harlem Renaissance was over, Zora Neale Hurston also issued a scathing, but subtle, critique of its masculinist prohibitions against black female sexuality. Hurston's novel *Their Eyes Were Watching God* (1937) takes the oldest form of storytelling we have—the quest romance—and rewrites that as a young black woman's search for sexual fulfillment—the orgasm she has witnessed in the "ecstatic shiver" of a "creaming" pear tree which is "frothing with delight" (11). Instead of keeping "away from the erotic," as Schuyler and others advised, Hurston penned one of the most compelling and explicit descriptions of orgasm in American letters. Janie finally

Helga is (and Larsen was), does not afford Helga racial choice. Under the nation's one-drop rule of "hypodescent," she is classified as black, regardless of the complexities of her heritage. This makes Helga one of the first truly "intersectional" figures of women's literature, a character for whom the various strands of race, gender, class, and sexuality can never be disentangled (since all contribute to her misery).[7]

Quicksand's scope was also bold, especially for a first novel. In a kind of microhistory of black America, Helga's travels map modern African American life. She traverses the Great Migration from the South, black industrial education, black cultural institutions, the historic debates between Tuskegee founder Booker T. Washington and northern intellectual W. E. B. Du Bois over Harlem as black America's "Mecca," the lure of Europe, the fate of black arts, the role of the growing black church, the plight of black women, and the pressures of motherhood. The novel also traverses a wide literary terrain, referencing other works of literature from many traditions and countries, and from realism to modernism.[8] *Quicksand* revisits and revises the trope of the tragic mulatto(a)—the biracial figure with no possible home[9]—to give it a distinctly modern, more

---

achieves satisfaction not in Harlem, not in any of the uplift organizations which Hurston (like Larsen) sneered at, nor in the radical literary circles which Hurston helped create. Instead, Janie satisfies her "oldest human longing" (for "self-revelation") with only one other person, her "kissing" friend, Pheobe Watson (7). For more on Hurston's critique of the Harlem Renaissance, see Carla Kaplan, *The Erotics of Talk: Women's Writing and Feminist Paradigms* (New York: Oxford UP, 1996).

7. As Claudia Tate puts it, "both racism and sexism are culpable in her tragedy" (240). See Tate, "Desire and Death in *Quicksand*," *American Literary History* 7.2 (1995): 234–60. On intersectionality as intersecting vectors of oppression such as gender, race, class, and sexuality, see especially Kimberlé Crenshaw, "Demarginalizing the Intersection of Race and Sex: A Black Feminist Critique of Antidiscrimination Doctrine, Feminist Theory, and Antiracist Politics," *University of Chicago Legal Forum* 40 (1989): 139–67 and "Mapping the Margins: Intersectionality, Identity Politics, and Violence against Women of Color," *Stanford Law Review* 43.6 (July 1991): 1241–99; Patricia Hill Collins, "Intersectionality's Definitional Dilemmas," *Annual Review of Sociology* 41 (2015): 1–20 and *Black Feminist Thought: Knowledge, Consciousness, and the Politics of Empowerment* (New York: Routledge, 1990); and Brittney Cooper, "Intersectionality" *The Oxford Handbook of Feminist Theory*, ed. Lisa Disch and Mary Hawkesworth (New York: Oxford UP, 2016). On the intersectionality of *Quicksand*, see especially, Cheryl Wall, *Women of the Harlem Renaissance* (Bloomington: Indiana UP, 1995). Larsen leans heavily on the word "queer"—already in use by 1928 to mean sexually non-normative—to express a range of counter-normal ideas and behaviors. "Queer" appears thirteen times in the novel. In its intersectional representation of the oppressive crosscurrents that combine to afflict black women, *Quicksand* also anticipates philosophical and cultural issues much discussed today, including cultural constructions of identity, agency, compulsory heterosexuality, and queerness. On the novel's ability to anticipate our own current debates, see especially Chandan Reddy, "Nella Larsen's *Quicksand*: Black Literary Publics During the Interwar Years," *Freedom with Violence: Race, Sexuality, and the US State* (Durham: Duke UP, 2011), pp. 90–133.

8. See Anna Brickhouse, "Nella Larsen and the Intertextual Geography of *Quicksand*," *African American Review* 35.4 (2001): 533–60, for a comprehensive explanation of the literary ground Larsen covers.

9. For an example of this trope in poetry, see Langston Hughes, "Cross," included in the "Backgrounds and Contexts" section of this volume. Short samples of various "Tragic

racially complex, and gendered, twist. *Quicksand* also represents, and
genders, most of the central ideological African American debates
of its day, including primitivism, race loyalty, race pride, sexuality,
double consciousness, double audience, black aesthetics, uplift, col-
orism, interracial marriage, and miscegenation.[1]

Part of the novel's force comes from its combination of expansive
subject matter and claustrophobic plot. Since there are no options
for the "happiness" (26) [15] Helga seeks, the text moves widely, and
then stops cold, over and over again, engaging the reader in Helga's
futile movements.[2] Helga "swirls"—to use Du Bois's term. Trying to
choose amid equally impossible choices, she remains blind to the
fact that it is meaningful choice, or agency itself, which her social
conditions, and her character, preclude.[3] Helga's flailing is personal,
but it is not *just* personal. Her failures critique, and indict, the myriad ways that non-white women are denied.

Hence, Helga's "restlessness" is also a symbolic history.[4] Her movements track the (im)possibility she faces. She is denied, everywhere,
the two freedoms fundamental to American liberalism: freedom
from and freedom *to*. Naxos is notorious for forcefully denying both.
Through the details of Helga's room at Naxos—"furnished with rare
and intensely personal taste"—Larsen unpacks and ironizes "taste"
as the measure of personal choice that we might imagine it to be.
Helga experiences her room as a "small oasis in a desert of darkness."
But this carefully furnished and "tasteful" room is not purely personal. Helga furnishes her room to oppose Naxos's drab décor,
letting Naxos define her likes and dislikes in the negative. And her
"intensely personal" taste—colorful flowers, an oriental stool,

---

Mulatto(a)" stories from different time periods are also included in the "Tragic
Mulatto(a)" section of Kaplan, ed., *Nella Larsen, Passing: A Norton Critical Edition.*
1. On primitivism, see especially Zora Neale Hurston, "The 'Pet Negro' System," *American
Mercury* 56 (May 1943): 593–600. On race loyalty and race pride, see especially Du
Bois, "Race Pride"; on sexuality, see especially Schuyler, "Instructions for Contributors" and Du Bois, "The Damnation of Women"; on double consciousness (a phrase
introduced by Du Bois in *The Souls of Black Folk* [Chicago: McClurg, 1903]) and double audience, see Johnson, "The Dilemma of the Negro Author"; and on uplift, see
"Negro Womanhood's Greatest Needs," included in the "Cultural Contexts" section of
this volume.
2. Ann Hostetler describes the "narrative style" of the novel as a repeated "dynamic"
wherein "time and again Helga finds herself trapped in a particular social setting and
responds with flight." See Ann E. Hostetler, "The Aesthetics of Race and Gender in
Nella Larsen's *Quicksand*," *PMLA* 105.1 (January 1990), pp. 36–37.
3. Larsen's biographers have noted that many of Helga's constricting and intersecting
conditions were also faced by Larsen: "Larsen Imes's movement through various institutions, places, and jobs in a relatively short period," Thadious Davis writes, gave her
an especially acute "outsider's perspective" on the "limitations placed on the individual
female by the environment in which she existed" (*Larsen*, 172, 171). Many have wondered if the novel's tragedy foretold or predicted the sadness and loneliness that dogged
its author's life.
4. Her "dilemma is symptomatic," as Jacquelyn McClendon puts it. See "Social Nightmare
in *Quicksand*," *The Politics of Color in the Fiction of Jessie Fauset and Nella Larsen*
(Charlottesville: UP of Virginia, 1995), p. 90.

brocade mules, a tapestry chair, and a "blue Chinese carpet" (24) [7], even her reading material, *Saïd the Fisherman*—were already clichés by 1928. Her "intensely personal" taste is a consumption-driven Orientalism fashionable among the upper-class.[5] Through that taste, she is rendered both sympathetic and unreliable.

In a moment of heavy-handed foreshadowing, her "slender, frail glass vase" falls from the windowsill "with a tingling crash" and Helga feels beset both by "hot anger" and "an overpowering desire for action of some sort" (27) [10]. In what soon becomes the novel's repeated pattern, Helga decides to flee. She imagines her formal resignation letter: a "Plea for Color." Helga is struck by the "dull attire" Naxos forces on its women. And she is struck that the women accept it: "drab colors, mostly navy blue, black, brown, unrelieved save for a scrap of white or tan about the hands and neck." This attire responds modestly and cautiously to racism: "Bright colors are vulgar—Black, gray, brown, and navy blue are the most becoming colors for colored people." But dark colors, Helga notes, "actually destroyed the luminous tones lurking in their dusky skins" (46–47) [21]. Her imaginary and unvoiced "Plea for Color" would argue that uplift ideology ignores women's needs and that uplift is achieved at their expense.[6] Her unspoken "Plea for Color" would have advanced both her own case and that of women, more generally, since the "careless cruelties" of the "smug . . . machine" (28–29) [10–11] of Naxos would "smudge" (30) [11] out any woman's striving or desire, she saw. Dr. Anderson nearly seduces Helga into uplift but he also reveals that she would have to pay its price: "Service is like clean white linen," he says, "even the tiniest speck shows" (51) [23]. Still holding out for both individuality and pleasure, Helga is overtaken by "angry thoughts which scurried here and there like trapped rats." His appeal precipitates her flight. "I don't belong here. I shall be leaving at once. This afternoon. Good morning" (52) [24].

When we next see Helga, she is trapped in the Jim Crow car of a northbound train, as a white man spits into the only drinking water blacks are allowed. This time Helga pays a literal price—$10 for the berth that should cost her $5—for her own racial oppression, a cost also mandated by class and gender rules which decree it improper for a genteel woman to sit up all night. The chapter ends with the train rolling forward and with Helga feeling "angry. . . . Angry. . . .

---

5. Larsen *Quicksand*, p. 24 [7]. On "Orientalism," see especially Cherene Sherrard-Johnson, "'A Plea for Color': Nella Larsen's Iconography of the Mulatta," *American Literature* 76.4 (2004): 833–69, excerpted in the "Criticism" section of this volume. I am grateful to Carla Peterson, who is writing a book on African American taste, for our discussions of taste in black literature.

6. Hostetler writes, "the emphasis on color advances a thematics of race. . . . Themes of race merge with concerns of gender, for Helga's destiny is shaped as much by her sex as by the problematics of race" p. 35.

Angry" (59) [29]. Helga's anger is underscored by the novel's epi-graph. While Hughes's title "Cross" can mean crossroads, it also means angry: to feel cross, to be crossed or cheated by others. Such anger, like taste, is a social emotion. One of the most suffocating aspects of racism is the demand that the oppressed not burden their oppressors with anger. Helga cannot, and will not, control her anger.

Like thousands of African Americans traveling north in the Great Migration, Helga arrives in Chicago, also home to a black literary renaissance but "grey" to Helga. Without references she cannot get even a housecleaning job. When she finally does land a temporary job, as personal assistant to the "race woman" Mrs. Hayes-Rore, she receives the endorsement which her angry outburst at Anderson has cost her: "anyway, she would have a reference. . . . She began hap-pily to paint the future in vivid colors" (74) [35]. Again on a train, and now heading farther north, Mrs. Hayes-Rore elicits Helga's story: "passionately, tearfully, incoherently, the final words tumbled from her quivering petulant lips" (79) [38]. Mrs. Hayes-Rore does not respond to the anger she elicits: "During the little pause that fol-lowed Helga's recital, the faces of the two women, which had been bare, seemed to harden. It was almost as if they had slipped on masks" (79) [38]. There is no place for the kind of anger Helga feels.

When Helga steps into Harlem, she is initally entranced. "The continuously gorgeous panorama of Harlem fascinated her, thrilled her" (87) [42]. She lands on 139th Street, not far from one of Nella Larsen's early Harlem addresses, in the home of the aptly named Anne Grey,[7] niece of Mrs. Hayes-Rore. Anne's taste, like Helga's, runs to modern Orientalism, with "Chinese tea chests . . . a lac-quered jade-green settee . . . lustrous Eastern rugs," and "Japanese prints" (86) [41–42]. For a year, Helga is "happy" there, with secre-tarial work, acquaintances, friends, and most importantly, a feel-ing of belonging—"that magic sense of having come home" and of "seeming at last to belong somewhere" (84–85) [40–41]. She even experiences a "sense of freedom, a release from the feeling of small-ness which had hedged her in" (89) [43]. But Helga's Harlem happi-ness, of course, "didn't last" (89–90) [43].

Increasingly, Helga feels repulsed by the myriad ways race con-sciousness thwarts individuality. Anne Grey cannot appreciate Flor-ence Mills, Taylor Gordon, or Paul Robeson. Her tastes are formed by her aversion, on the one hand, to doing what whites expect of her, and, on the other hand, by ready-made definitions of what she should and shouldn't enjoy.[8] A surprise encounter with Dr. Anderson

---

7. Anne, or Miss Anne, is a pseudonym for any white woman. Grey, of course, is a mix of black and white.
8. On "ready-mades," see also Judith Butler, *Gender Trouble: Feminism and the Subversion of Identity* (New York: Routledge, 1990). See also Allison Berg, "Fatal Contractions:

reignites Helga's repressed sexuality and exacerbates her discontent. She finds herself beset by "vague yearning" and "indefinite longings" (95–96) [46–47]. Just before she abandons Harlem for Copenhagen, the text's most important minor character is introduced: sensual, ambiguously raced Audrey Denney.[9]

Audrey Denney appears exactly halfway through the novel, operating like a pivot. She represents the road that Helga will not, or cannot, take. Before introducing Denney, the novel sets a very deliberate stage. Helga has joined a group which has gone "cabareting" at a Harlem nightclub where blackness is commercialized as a primitive jungle essence. Dancing "ecstatically to a thumping of unseen tom-toms," the revelers gyrate to "savage" music in a "fantastic motley" of human colors which make a gorgeous and sensual "moving mosaic" (107–108) [53]. Helga is "drugged, lifted, sustained" by it all, "blown out, ripped out, beaten out" (108) [53]. Moved by what she has been trained to despise, Helga tries to regain genteel, middle-class ground: "She wasn't, she told herself, a jungle creature." While struggling to feel "contemptuous" (108) [53] of the jazz which delights her, she spots Dr. Anderson and Audrey Denney.

Denney resembles Helga. She is mixed-race, slim, lovely, and highly sexual. But Denney is unlike Helga in important ways. She refuses to play with a deck stacked against her. She lives not in Harlem, but downtown in Greenwich Village, which better suits her taste. She does not care about the harsh judgments of others, such as Anne, who pronounces her "disgusting," "obscene," and "treacherous" and declares that she "ought to be ostracized" (110) [54] for refusing to choose between races. And Audrey, unlike Helga, appears white and could pass if she chose. Audrey Denney knows what she likes. She is neither angry nor restless. Helga feels "not contempt, but envious admiration" for her. She does not think Denney betrays black Harlem by having the "courage" to "placidly . . . ignore racial

---

Nella Larsen's *Quicksand* and the New Negro Mother," *Mothering the Race: Women's Narratives of Reproduction, 1890–1930* (Urbana: U of Illinois P, 2002), p. 129. In *Invisible Man* (New York: Vintage, 1989), Ralph Ellison makes a similar point in a striking passage where the narrator discovers, to his surprise, that he loves the taste of yams: "I no longer felt ashamed of the things I had always loved. . . . What and how much had I lost by trying to do only what was expected of me instead of what I myself had wished to do?" (266). He concludes by proclaiming, proudly, "I yam what I am" without recognizing the irony that he lacks first principles, that he doesn't know if he once loved yams because he, himself, loved yams, or because loving yams was expected of him. Nor does he know, in rediscovering the yams, if he rediscovers an actual personal taste, a preference, or just the nostalgia for a lost moment of his history which, as with all nostalgias, may not have been real, even then.

9. On the importance of "minor" characters in literature, see Alex Woloch, *The One vs. the Many: Minor Characters and the Space of the Protagonist in the Novel* (Princeton: Princeton UP, 2003). Davis identifies Audrey Denney as based on socialite Blanche Dunn. Hutchinson believes she is based on light-skinned model and writer Anita Thompson, a modernist who lived in Greenwich Village and was a distant cousin of Langston Hughes.

barriers and give her attention to people, as individuals." But before Helga can seriously contemplate what Denney's choices and evident privileges mean, she feels a resurgence of the sexual desire which Anderson (she believes) arouses. She runs from the scene "panting, confused . . . cold, unhappy, misunderstood, and forlorn" (112) [55]. It never occurs to Helga that Denney, not Anderson, arouses her desire. But the implication is clear.[1]

Helga runs to Copenhagen next. Needless to say, it satisfies only briefly. While appreciated there, Helga is displayed to fit Danish ideas of an "exotic," sensual, primitive, "savage"—"like nothing so much as some new and strange species of pet dog being proudly exhibited" (122–24) [60–61].[2] It does not take her long to tire of being "a curiosity, a stunt, at which people came and gazed" (126) [63]. Before leaving Denmark, she attends a minstrel performance where racist stereotypes enchant the white audience while shaming her. Feeling betrayed, repulsed, and angry, her "suspensive conflict" (143–44) [72] draws her compulsively to view what pains her most.

At this moment, dashing, racist, and sexist Axel Olsen proposes first a sexual liaison and, failing that, a marriage. Recognizing that Axel can only see her through a scrim of received racist images (some exalting her and others denigrating her), Helga turns him down. That rejection is textual as well as personal. It spurns the standard narrative resolution of women's unhappy lives: "Reader, I married him," as Jane famously declares in *Jane Eyre*. His proposal and her rejection extend the narrative formula of Helga's desperate (and failed) attempts to find good choices to make. Few options exist.

At this point, Helga feels the "growing nostalgia" (146) [73] for blackness and Harlem that is a stock element of black stories of passing, a "moment of regret"[3] which passing characters inevitably feel and which usually leads to their choosing black culture over white. In Helga's nostalgia, Larsen's readers would have recognized the many echoes of James Weldon Johnson's passing novel, *Autobiography of an Ex-Colored Man* (1912), especially in *Quicksand*'s Copenhagen circus scenes. In *Autobiography*, the mixed-race narrator suddenly finds himself "possessed by a strange longing for my mother's people" after many years of living as a white man. It is a "strange longing" because the narrator believes that he does not believe in race. There should be nothing for him to miss. And it is a strange longing because the

---

1. On Larsen's homoerotic subtexts, see especially Deborah E. McDowell, "'That Nameless . . . Shameful Impulse': Sexuality in Nella Larsen's *Quicksand* and *Passing*," and Laura Doyle, "Queering Freedom's Theft in Nella Larsen," both excerpted in the "Criticism" section of this volume. On Denney as representing "an element of Helga's own character," see Davis, *Larsen*, p. 212.
2. See especially, Hurston, "The 'Pet Negro' System."
3. On this "moment of regret," see also Kaplan, "Introduction: Nella Larsen's Erotics of Race," in *Passing: A Norton Critical Edition*.

sudden desire to be among "his people" is so forceful, threatening to upend all the security his painful choices have provided him.[4] His longing is sparked, in part, by hearing black spirituals, or "sorrow songs," and by wanting to preserve their legacy, ideally in a modern form—to do just what Antonín Dvořák had done with the "New World Symphony," which Helga had gone to hear in Copenhagen and which sparked her "strange longing" as well.[5]

Such "strange longing" restores the protagonist to blackness in most black-authored passing fiction (though not, curiously, in Johnson's text). In so doing, that longing validates the race. Helga now returns to Harlem a second time. Following the formula, Harlem should now satisfy her. With its "miraculous joyousness" and its promise of belonging—"<u>These</u> were her people" (162) [81]—Harlem, indeed, seems poised to do just that. But once again, Audrey Denney appears. And once again Helga is flooded with "irrepressible longing" (177) [89] and "long-hidden, half-understood desire" (174) [88]. Helga again associates her desires with Anderson and returns to her "prim hotel bed" (176) [88] alone and "angry . . . Angry . . . Angry" (59) [27]. Harlem has failed her, again. That failure spurs the "mental quagmire" (177) [89] from which she never emerges. In giving Harlem two chances, Larsen sends a coded message, legible to anyone aware of Harlem's symbolic weight.[6] Here, Harlem is not restorative.

Helga's final choice—Reverend Green, the church, marriage, Alabama, children, religion, service, and sacrifice—is no choice at all. "Helga Crane was not religious" (71) [33]. She is not maternal. She is not interested in uplift. Or in living in the South. Poverty does not draw her. She makes anti-choices in a fog of sexual frustration and in the absence of options. Clearly this new life will suffocate her.

The novel's title points to the inevitability of its outcome. As a medium, quicksand seems to defy natural laws. It is neither fully solid, nor fully liquid. It cannot support weight. Quicksand is a property overwhelmed; it forms when an agitated liquid medium, such as water, takes on so much solid matter, such as sand, that the water can no longer flow. Quicksand is neither one thing nor another: uncanny and out of category. Struggling in quicksand displaces its suspended particles, causing a deeper drag or pull. To remove even one foot stuck in quicksand, physicists say, requires the force that

---

4. See James Weldon Johnson, *The Autobiography of an Ex-Colored Man* (New York: Penguin, 1990), p. 153.
5. Larsen gives an even stronger version of the "strange longing" to Clare Kendry, in *Passing*. On the "sorrow songs," see W. E. B. Du Bois, "Of the Sorrow Songs," *The Souls of Black Folk*, and Alain Locke, "The Negro Spirituals," in Locke, ed., *The New Negro*.
6. On "double audience," see especially James Weldon Johnson, "The Dilemma of the Negro Author," in the "Cultural Contexts" section of this volume.

would be necessary to lift a car. This is why quicksand is so difficult to escape and why struggling against it is so counterproductive.[7] Only by behaving counterintuitively, by not struggling and allowing oneself to drift, can a body survive.[8] Quicksand, a down-pull, is uplift's opposite, and a metaphor for Helga's discovery that struggling against her circumstances only worsens them. But not acting is hardly viable.

Death is both in *Quicksand*'s title and in its epigraph, from Langston Hughes's poem "Cross."[9] The typical "tragic mulatto(a)" is homeless because s/he is welcome nowhere. The question is always where he or she can live. But Hughes's lines pose a different question: where can such a figure die? "I wonder where I'm gonna die / Being neither white nor black." Emphasizing death points toward the role that mixed-race people play as social scapegoats (nailed, as it were, to bigotry's cross). The question "Cross" asks is the question that the hopeless—not the homeless—might ask.

Nothing is spared *Quicksand*'s fatalism. By the end of the novel, having exhausted every possible option, Helga tries not choosing. She attempts inaction through extreme conformity. Allowing others to choose for her, she gives in to her circumstances, embraces all she'd rejected and stops struggling. But as we see, that cessation of

7. Keguro Macharia notes that "recent scientific research has shown that human bodies do not actually sink in quicksand. Instead, they float, remain suspended, and eventually are forced to the surface of the medium, they can escape by slowly moving sideways, as one would in a rip tide. Those who struggle, however, remain suspended, and can die of exposure or starvation if they are not rescued by others. See Keguro Macharia, "Queering Helga Crane: Black Nativism in Nella Larsen's *Quicksand*," *Modern Fiction Studies* 57.2 (2011): 273.

8. Quicksand is a common literary trope and was prominent, before Larsen's novel, in both Victor Hugo's *Les Miserables* (1862) and Robert Louis Stevenson's *Pavilion in the Links* (1880). Edith Wharton also used it in her short story "The Quicksand," which appeared in *Harper's* in 1902 and was widely reprinted in subsequent years. Hutchinson argues that Larsen was not only a victim of racism but very prescient about the institutional sources of her psychological woes. Unlike Helga, who lacks insight into herself, Larsen was "highly self-critical," as Hutchinson notes (167). Helga, by contrast, is, as Mary Esteve writes, the "suspensive conflict" in which she finds herself. See Mary Esteve, "Nella Larsen's 'Moving Mosaic': Harlem, Crowds, and Anonymity," *American Literary History* 9.2 (Summer 1997): 268–86. While arguing that Helga is both "*of* quicksand and *as* quicksand" (282), Esteve maintains that Larsen uses the properties of crowds to afford Helga possibilities of subjectivity—of "anonymity" (284)—not usually available in modernity. This allows us to see the novel's ending as suspended, Esteve argues, and allows for the possibility that Helga "may indeed resurface" (282).

9. Like Larsen, and many members of the Harlem Renaissance, Langston Hughes was mixed-race, the grandson of numerous white grandfathers and black grandmothers, as well as of French, Native American, and Scottish ancestry. Like Larsen, Hughes attempted to live between categories, especially available sexual categories, which did not suit him. A fierce proponent of "black pride," especially in essays such as "The Negro Artist and the Racial Mountain," Hughes also refused most of the then-available ideas about blackness. Like Larsen, Hughes was close to Carl Van Vechten, and defended Van Vechten's right to "cross" both into Harlem and into representing blackness as well. "Cross" was first published in *The Weary Blues* in 1926. The full text of the poem is included in the "Cultural Contexts" section of this volume.

struggle does not free her—as it might from actual quicksand—it only sinks her deeper. Her strength has been sapped both by her conditions *and* by her efforts to fight them.

In short order Larsen offers Helga all the options which would have been available to a black woman in her circumstances. She exhausts them, to no good outcome. The only option *Quicksand* leaves unexplored is passing, or crossing, into whiteness. This, Larsen reserves for *Passing*, published one year later.

It took about a month after publication of *Quicksand* for reviews and notices to appear, but ultimately the book garnered a good deal of attention, especially for a first novel. On the whole, reviews were "generally enthusiastic," as Charles Larson notes, even in the white press.[1] The *New York Times* called the novel "articulate, sympathetic."[2] And the *Boston Evening Transcript* praised its "tragedy."[3] The *Saturday Review of Literature* praised the novel's "well-mannered" style.[4] Margery Latimer (who married multiracial writer Jean Toomer in 1931) offered high praise. "The book makes you want to read everything that Nella Larsen will ever write."[5] But some white reviewers saw only what they wanted to see. T. S. Matthews, in *The New Republic*, for example, used the novel as a foil for racist pronouncements about black character.[6] Predictably, many reviews focused on the question of whether the novel was autobiographical. And a number of reviewers, women especially, praised Larsen's psychosocial complexity and what white NAACP founder Mary White Ovington called the book's "keen insight."[7] Some reviewers commented on how modern the novel was. One—Eda Walton—noted how brave Larsen was to attempt a full representation of female sexual desire. Some thought the novel was merely another "tragic mulatto(a)" story. Some praised Larsen for elegant style. Others accused her of the self-conscious writing which often plagues first novels. Most faulted the novel's ending—as inconsistent with Helga's character.

1. Larson, *Invisible Darkness*, 75.
2. "A Mulatto Girl," *New York Times Book Review,* April 8, 1928: 16–17.
3. H. W. R., *"Quicksand:* A Story of the Revolt of a Negro School Teacher," *Boston Evening Transcript,* June 20, 1928: 2, included in the "Contemporary Reviews" section of this volume.
4. "The New Books," *Saturday Review of Literature* (May 19, 1928): 895–96, included in the "Contemporary Reviews" section of this volume.
5. Margery Latimer, "Nella Larsen's 'Quicksand,'" *New York World,* July 22, 1928: 7M, included in the "Contemporary Reviews" section of this volume.
6. T. S. Matthews, "What Gods! What Gongs!" *The New Republic* (May 30, 1928): 50–51, included in the "Contemporary Reviews" section of this volume.
7. Mary White Ovington, "Book Chat," NAACP Press Release, August 3, 1928. Davis, however, feels that "contemporary reviewers failed to apprehend the psychological drama reproduced in *Quicksand"* and that "its complexity was not perceived" (*Larsen*, pp. 252, 277).

Often paired with McKay's *Home to Harlem* (1927, which outsold *Quicksand* by a considerable margin) or with *Nigger Heaven* (1926), which still stirred controversy two years after it first appeared, the novel divided black reviewers who were "partisans of the 'cabaret school' and those who identified with racial uplift."[8] An anonymous review in the black paper, *Afro-American*, declared it "refreshing" that "there is something else in Negro life besides jazz and cabarets."[9] "Many folks," Larsen's friend Gwendolyn Bennett maintained, "will be interested to hear that this book does not set as its tempo that of the Harlem cabaret—this is the story of the struggle of an interesting and cultured Negro woman against her environment. Negroes will be relieved that Harlem night-life is more or less submerged by this author in the psychological struggle of the heroine."[1] Schuyler praised *Quicksand*, in spite of Larsen's refusal of his "Instructions for Contributors."[2] Alain Locke pronounced the novel "a social document of importance," and Arthur Huff Fauset called it "a step forward."[3] Du Bois mused that Larsen's refusal of Van Vechten's or Claude McKay's path might keep down her sales. "It is not near nasty enough for New York columnists," he wrote.[4] Black novelist Wallace Thurman, on the other hand, felt Larsen had entirely missed the mark. He faulted her for avoiding the "half world" of "cabaret hounds" and reported—mistakenly, but dismissively—that "her negroes are all of the upper class."[5] Eugene Gordon was critical of the ending.[6]

Only one black reviewer took note of Larsen's handling of Harlem. Writing in the *New York Amsterdam News*, one of the most important black papers in the country, that reviewer expressed surprise that Helga wasn't pleased with Harlem. "The reader," the reviewer wrote, "wonders if there is any place this side of heaven, or in heaven, where she will be contented."[7] White reviewers, however, seem to have noticed no criticism of Harlem. To Katharine Shepard

---

8. Hutchinson, *Search*, p. 285.
9. "Book a Week," *Baltimore Afro-American*, May 15, 1928: 6, included in the "Contemporary Reviews" section of this volume.
1. Gwendolyn B. Bennett, "The Ebony Flute," *Opportunity* (May 30, 1928): 153, included in the "Contemporary Reviews" section of this volume.
2. See George S. Schuyler, "Views and Reviews," *Pittsburgh Courier*, April 14, 1928: 2.8, included in the "Contemporary Reviews" section of this volume.
3. Alain Locke, "1928: A Retrospective Review." *Opportunity* 7 (January 1929), 8–11; Arthur Huff Fauset, "*Quicksand*," *Black Opals* (June 1928), 19–20, both included in the "Contemporary Reviews" section of this volume.
4. W. E. B. Du Bois, "Two Novels," *The Crisis* (June 1928): 202–11, included in the "Contemporary Reviews" section of this volume.
5. Wallace Thurman, "High, Low, Past, and Present" *Harlem* (November 1928): 32.
6. Eugene Gordon, "Negro Fictionist[s] in America," *Saturday Evening Quill* 2 (April 1929): 18–19. See the "Contemporary Reviews" section of this volume.
7. "Miscegenation? Bah!" *New York Amsterdam News*, May 16, 1928: 16. See the "Contemporary Reviews" section of this volume.

Hayden, for example, "the pictures of Harlem are tremendously interesting, full of color and delightful detail."[8]

In addition to the reviews, and the money to move into enviable Harlem housing, *Quicksand* brought rewards such as a prestigious Harmon Awards Bronze Medal and a May 1928 honorary tea sponsored by the Women's Auxiliary of the NAACP and attended by over one hundred people. The novel led quickly to the writing and publication of Larsen's second novel, *Passing*, which appeared on April 26, 1929. In 1930, Larsen received a much-coveted Guggenheim fellowship and published the short story "Sanctuary," included in the section of Larsen's writing in this volume.

But in spite of all these successes, things went badly for Larsen. Her marriage to Elmer collapsed. According to Davis, Elmer felt "eclipsed by Nella's sudden literary success," and in 1928 he began an affair with a white Fisk staff member, Ethel Bedient Gilbert, who often traveled to New York to raise funds for Fisk, a role she performed so successfully that much of the campus adored her.[9] After accepting a position at Fisk in 1929, Elmer did little to hide his affair with Gilbert, who was his constant escort to Fisk functions, while Nella was home in New York. Elmer's affair was doubly scandalous, because of his marriage and because of Gilbert's race. We do not know exactly when Nella discovered the affair. But we do know Elmer enjoined her to the strictest secrecy, on the grounds that gossip would cost Elmer his job and, hence, Nella's financial security. Under intense pressure to protect her security and not violate codes of racial loyalty, Nella fell apart.

She was accused of plagiarizing "Sanctuary" from a story called "Mrs. Adis" (1922) by Sheila Kaye-Smith (included in the "Cultural Contexts" section of this volume).[1] Her third novel, *Mirage*, was rejected in 1931. Larsen was peripatetic in 1931 and 1932, moving between Europe, North Africa, and New York. She attempted, in 1932, to live with Elmer in Nashville, largely to assuage the anxieties of Fisk president Thomas E. Jones, who built the Imeses a beautiful home in hopes of saving their marriage. The tension of living with Elmer, under the circumstances, broke Larsen. She began to lose her hair, to behave erratically, and probably to drink. Although, as Davis writes, "divorce among her class of African-American peers

8. Katharine Shepard Hayden, review, *Annals of the American Academy of Political and Social Science* (November 8, 1928): 344–45. See the "Contemporary Reviews" section of this volume.
9. Davis, *Nella Larsen*, p. 333.
1. For scholarly treatments of the plagiarism scandal, see the essays by Cohen, Doyle, Haviland, Hochman, Hoeller, Larson (Kelli), Mafe, and Williams (Erika) listed in the Selected Bibliography of this volume. Larsen addressed the plagiarism charges in print. See "The Author's Explanation," reprinted in Kaplan, ed., *Passing: A Norton Critical Edition*.

was unthinkable," Nella divorced Elmer in 1933. For the press, she claimed that they had parted "amicably."[2] But nothing could be further from the truth, although the financial settlement for Nella was a generous one. Nella believed that Ethel was pregnant and that she and Elmer would wed just days after the divorce was finalized.[3] She never again spoke to Elmer or allowed him to know where she was living. All payments and communications were directed to a bank address.

After divorcing Elmer in 1933, Nella withdrew from Harlem. She returned to New York, traveled to Chicago, and returned to New York again, joining a multiracial circle of artists, many of them gay, who used Olivia Wyndham's Connecticut farm as a kind of home base. In 1937 she turned her back on that social circle and returned to nursing. For decades, she lived alone in New York, entirely removed socially from her former friends in Harlem, but often only walking distance from many of them. Nella Larsen died alone, at home, on March 30, 1964. Her books and papers were destroyed. Her one living relative denied any knowledge of her. And she was buried, largely for expediency's sake, in the family plot of a co-worker. A small notice of her death appeared in the *New York Times*. It said, merely: "Imes—Nella Larsen, died March 30, 1964, sister of Anna Larsen Gardener of Calif."[4]

Larsen is now widely seen as one of the central figures of the Harlem Renaissance, as well as one of the few early black women to write openly about sexuality and one of the few black writers of the 1920s to cross into high modernist forms and aesthetics. With more than 125 scholarly articles on *Quicksand* alone, and at least 79 dissertations which discuss the novel in at least one chapter (see the Selected Bibliography), Larsen's status among early twentieth-century black women writers is rivaled only by Zora Neale Hurston's, in spite of a much smaller literary output. Her work is hailed for helping create modernist psychological interiority, expanding our uses of irony and unreliable narration, challenging marriage and middle-class domesticity, complexly interrogating the intersections of gender, race, class, and sexual identity, and for redeploying traditional tropes—such as passing and the Tragic Mulatto(a)—with a contemporary, critical twist. Most importantly, Larsen's work is now prized for its portrayal of black, female subjectivity, its depiction of the consequences of repressing women's sexuality, and for its

---

2. "Love Triangle Behind Fisk Divorce," *Baltimore Afro-American*, October 21, 1933, p. 1.
3. Neither Davis nor Hutchinson could locate records of either a baby or a marriage. Gilbert did stay with Elmer until his death, from cancer, in 1941. His will left everything he had to her.
4. Obituary, *New York Times*, April 7, 1964, p. 35.

representation of the social and psychological vertigo caused when identity categories break down.

Given that status, it is not surprising that *Quicksand* has attracted a wide array of critical approaches. These include literary influence and intertextuality; psychoanalytic readings; and historical readings that contextualize the novel's representations of Harlem, Scandinavia, motherhood, miscegenation, the church, birth control, black education, eugenics, consumer culture, and uplift. Interdisciplinary critics apply the lens of cultural geography to Larsen's cosmopolitanism, the visual arts to her treatment of portraiture, and jazz studies to her structure and treatment of time. Literary critics map her aesthetics, narrative strategies, and influences.[5]

The richness of that criticism, and the richness of the biographical work on Larsen, made choosing selections of criticism for this Norton Critical Edition particularly challenging. Included here is a small selection of critical pieces that discuss the novel's sexuality, its queerness, its depiction of race, its relationship to other arts, and its relationship to other places and publics. Ann duCille's essay offers a black feminist recuperation of a writer too easily dismissed for not fitting existing models. Lori Harrison-Kahan's essay puts the novel in the context of African American musical traditions, arguing that Helga's restlessness can be seen as a blues trope. Arne Lunde and Anna Westerstahl Stenport take their cues from Paul Gilroy's influential study *The Black Atlantic* (1993) to inquire into Larsen's depiction of Scandinavian society and to make a case that Larsen belongs as much in the Scandinavian tradition as she does in the African American literary tradition. Deborah McDowell's essay remains, in many ways, the gold standard for Larsen's treatment of sexuality, as well as offering a strong example of close reading put to the service of social analysis. The essay by Hanna Musiol, who teaches in Scandinavia, offers a deeply theorized analysis of Larsen's cosmopolitanism, part of recent scholarship on cultural migration that challenges traditional periodizations and borders and that opens onto work in cultural geography such as Laura Tanner's work on *Quicksand* (see the Selected Bibliography). Susan M. Reverby, one

---

5. Those interested in Larsen's depiction of Harlem, for example, might consult the essays by Balshaw, English, Esteve, and Howard listed in the Selected Bibliography. Many of Larsen's best critics have focused on her treatment of sexuality, as in the essays by duCille, McDowell, Monda, and Tate listed in the Selected Bibliography. Among the many critics writing on Larsen and primitivism are the essays by DeFalco and Silverman listed in the Selected Bibliography. Those interested in Larsen's depiction of motherhood might consult the essays by Ahad, Berg, Calloway, Craig, and Gallego listed in the Selected Bibliography. Not surprisingly, *Quicksand* has interested many critics who focus on consumer culture, as in the essays by Goldsmith, Karl, Lutes, Muzak, Rhodes, Rosenblum, and Zackodnick listed in the Selected Bibliography. Those interested in the intertextual connections between Larsen and Wharton might consult the essays by Bromell, Dittmar, Goldsmith, and Orlando listed in the Selected Bibliography.

of the premier social and medical historians of Tuskegee, gives us a glimpse of the Institute, and its cultural meanings, during the time that Larsen took the post of Head Nurse. And Cherene Sherrard-Johnson's essay combines literary analysis with the emerging field of visual culture to broaden the ways in which we look at literary imagery, especially Orientalism and images of the mulatta, or mixed-race woman. Other critical works are cited throughout the Introduction to help suggest the range of critical approaches and analytic questions that *Quicksand* continues to attract.

As well as providing readers with a sense of critical approaches to the novel, this Norton Critical Edition aims to help them situate *Quicksand* in an historical and cultural context. Readers interested in Larsen's relation to debates of her day might consult "Cultural Contexts." Readers interested in the novel's reception (an index to racial, sexual, and aesthetic ideas of the time) might consult the "Contemporary Reviews" (the originals of which are very hard to locate in their original sources; hence the reviews are included in their entirety here). Readers interested in articles about Nella Larsen might consult both "Contemporary Articles" and the Selected Bibliography. A Chronology is included in this volume, and readers are also encouraged to consult the excellent biographies by Davis and Hutchinson. Additional writings by Nella Larsen are included here, as well as a short selection of her correspondence. As this volume goes to press, numerous new works on *Quicksand* are no doubt in process. The Selected Bibliography for this Norton Critical Edition includes those essays of which the bibliographers and the editor were able to obtain copies up to 2016 when this volume began to go into production.

Acknowledgments

I would like to acknowledge, once again, the extraordinary community of scholars who work on Nella Larsen and, more generally, on African American women's writing; this volume would be impossible without the excellent work of these critics, historians, and biographers. I am grateful to my students for their insights into this novel, across many different graduate and undergraduate classes, at Northeastern University, and elsewhere. For precious time to conduct the background research for this volume, and various forms of support, I especially thank the Hutchins Center for African and African American Research and the National Endowment for the Humanities "Public Scholar" Program. At Norton I was lucky to continue working with Carol Bemis, and also with Rachel Goodman. My agent, Brettne Bloom, and my husband, Steve Larsen, continue, as Hurston would say, to prop me up on every leaning side. I am grateful to the scholars who read and commented on the Introduction, especially George Hutchinson, Carla Peterson, and Rafia Zafar, and to my two wonderful writing groups for all of their feedback. Most particularly I wish to thank the superb research assistants without whose work, background research, and review of existing criticism this volume could not have been completed and without whose cheerfulness, good spirits, and persistence I would not have wanted to work on it: Hanna Musiol, who originally prepared the excellent Selected Bibliography of scholarship on Larsen, Aleks Galus, Lauren Kuryloski and Sarah Payne, who updated it and helped with the background research (huzzahs to Lauren for all the updating and to Sarah for McDougald, Rose, Locke, Owen, Washington, and other headnotes, endnote work, and detailed edition comparisons), and Abbie Levesque, who joined this project at the end, tolerated the tedium of proofreading aloud, and was immeasurably helpful in myriad textual, technological, editorial, and intellectual ways.

A Note on the Text

Originally entitled "Cloudy Amber," *Quicksand* was published by Knopf on March 30, 1928. The text of this Norton Critical Edition is based on the first edition of that original printing. Larsen's original spelling and punctuation have been retained throughout this text. Originally priced at $2.50 (the price of *Passing* was lowered to $2), *Quicksand* was handsomely printed, on high-quality paper and bound in a bright orange cloth, with a light green dust jacket, banded with orange and black. It was advertised as "wholly free from the curse of propaganda." The front flap described the book as "a human, not a sociological, tragedy." While sales figures for *Quicksand* were not particularly high, they were sufficient for Larsen and her husband, physicist Elmer Imes, to move into a larger, better, apartment. Larsen claimed to have drafted the novel in only six weeks, but there is evidence that she wrote and rewrote it carefully, and at much greater length, beginning in 1926. *Quicksand* was well reviewed and it garnered notices, awards, fellowships, and other publications. Its success led Larsen to publish *Passing* only one year later, in 1929. In spite of those successes, Larsen dropped out of the literary world after *Passing*. She died alone, in the small New York apartment she inhabited for more than twenty years, in 1964, after decades spent as a nurse. On March 30, the day that *Quicksand* first appeared thirty-six years earlier, her body was found, and a nursing colleague arranged for her funeral. None of the many papers scattered in Larsen's home at the time of her death were kept. No known copy of Larsen's original *Quicksand* manuscript has yet come to light, and there is no Nella Larsen archive. Numerous editions of *Quicksand* have been published, none previously identical to the original. Significant variations from that edition have been noted in the footnotes that accompany this text.

The Text of
QUICKSAND

FOR E. S. I.[1]

---

1. Elmer Samuel Imes, Larsen's husband, a physicist. Nella and Elmer met in 1918 and married, in the chapel of Union Theological Seminary, in 1918. While Imes was initially supportive of Larsen and her literary ambitions, the marriage began to fail in 1928, when Larsen was finishing her second novel, *Passing*. By 1929, the Imeses were beginning to lead somewhat separate lives, with Elmer working as the Head of the Physics Department at Fisk University and Larsen traveling and applying for a fellowship to support more travel. At Fisk, Elmer began an affair with a white colleague, Ethel Gilbert. In 1933 Larsen divorced Imes, in Tennessee, on the grounds of "cruelty." The *Baltimore Afro-American* reported on the Larsen/Imes/Gilbert triangle in October of 1933. This dedication is missing in DoVeanna Fulton's edition.

My old man died in a fine big house.
My ma died in a shack.
I wonder where I'm gonna die,
Being neither white nor black?
LANGSTON HUGHES[2]

2. These are the last four lines of Langston Hughes's poem "Cross," published in 1926 in *The Weary Blues*. The full text of the poem appears in the "Cultural Contexts" section of this volume.

ONE

HELGA CRANE sat alone in her room, which at that hour, eight in the evening, was in soft gloom. Only a single reading lamp, dimmed by a great black and red shade, made a pool of light on the blue Chinese carpet, on the bright covers of the books which she had taken down from their long shelves, on the white pages of the opened one selected, on the shining brass bowl crowded with many-colored nasturtiums beside her on the low table, and on the oriental silk[1] which covered the stool at her slim feet. It was a comfortable room, furnished with rare and intensely personal taste,[2] flooded with Southern sun in the day, but shadowy just then with the drawn curtains and single shaded light. Large, too. So large that the spot where Helga sat was a small oasis in a desert of darkness. And eerily quiet. But that was what she liked after her taxing day's work, after the hard classes, in which she gave willingly and unsparingly of herself with no apparent return. She loved this tranquillity, this quiet, following the fret and strain of the long hours spent among fellow members of a carelessly unkind and gossiping faculty, following the strenuous rigidity of conduct required in this huge educational community of which she was an insignificant part. This was her rest, this intentional isolation for a short while in the evening, this little time in her own attractive room with her own books. To the rapping of other teachers, bearing fresh scandals, or seeking information, or other more concrete favors, or merely talk, at that hour Helga Crane never opened her door.

An observer would have thought her well fitted to that framing of light and shade. A slight girl of twenty-two years, with narrow, sloping shoulders and delicate, but well-turned, arms and legs, she had, none the less, an air of radiant, careless health. In vivid green and gold negligee and glistening brocaded mules, deep sunk in the big high-backed chair, against whose dark tapestry her sharply cut face, with skin like yellow satin, was distinctly outlined, she was—to use a hackneyed word—attractive. Black, very broad brows over soft, yet penetrating, dark eyes, and a pretty mouth, whose sensitive and sensuous lips had a slight questioning petulance and a tiny dissatisfied

---

1. Larsen describes an Orientalism, or fascination with Eastern culture as imagined through Western eyes, which was not uncommon in the 1920s. Fascination with Asia and the East was fed by a growing, global, consumer culture which allowed shoppers to purchase "exotic" goods.
2. Taste can be thought of either as highly individual and individuated or as determined by group and cultural preferences. Helga's understanding of her own Orientalism as "rare and intensely personal" both raises questions about the relationship between individuals and groups and begins to suggest that Helga's view of herself may not be entirely reliable.

droop, were the features on which the observer's attention would fasten; though her nose was good,[3] her ears delicately chiseled, and her curly blue-black hair plentiful and always straying in a little wayward, delightful way. Just then it was tumbled, falling unrestrained about her face and on to her shoulders.

Helga Crane tried not to think of her work and the school as she sat there. Ever since her arrival in Naxos[4] she had striven to keep these ends of the days from the intrusion of irritating thoughts and worries. Usually she was successful. But not this evening. Of the books which she had taken from their places she had decided on Marmaduke Pickthall's *Saïd the Fisherman*.[5] She wanted forgetfulness, complete mental relaxation, rest from thought of any kind. For the day had been more than usually crowded with distasteful encounters and stupid perversities. The sultry hot Southern spring had left her strangely tired, and a little unnerved. And annoying beyond all other happenings had been that affair of the noon period, now again thrusting itself on her already irritated mind.

She had counted on a few spare minutes in which to indulge in the sweet pleasure of a bath and a fresh, cool change of clothing. And instead her luncheon time had been shortened, as had that of everyone else, and immediately after the hurried gulping down of a heavy hot meal the hundreds of students and teachers had been herded into the sun-baked chapel to listen to the banal, the patronizing, and even the insulting remarks of one of the renowned white preachers of the state.

Helga shuddered a little as she recalled some of the statements made by that holy white man of God to the black folk sitting so respectfully before him.[6]

---

3. Attention to such so-called "good" features such as "good" hair and a "good" nose were signals, often used ironically, of mixed racial heritage and aesthetic standards of whiteness.
4. "Saxon" spelled backward; the school is modeled on Tuskegee Institute, founded by Booker T. Washington in 1881, where Larsen worked in 1915. Naxos is also a Greek island where Ariadne was abandoned by Theseus.
5. British writer and translator Marmaduke Pickthall (1875–1936) was a renowned Islamic scholar, especially noted for his translation of the Qur'an and for his conversion from Christianity to Islam. *Saïd the Fisherman*, a very popular semi-historical novel set in Syria and Egypt in the nineteenth century (1860–82), tells the story of a hero who leaves home to seek his fortune and dies as an Islamic martyr.
6. During slavery, many white ministers, some of whom later became involved in industrial education, had worked to justify slavery on Christian or biblical grounds, maintaining that God had made the races both separate and unequal, and that inequality was enshrined in the Bible, especially in the story of Ham. Numerous historically black colleges and universities were founded by southern whites, some of them connected to the church, who believed in both segregation and industrial training for blacks. The "Hampton Model," founded by northern General Samuel Chapman Armstrong (1839–1893), was dedicated to practical work, manual labor, and Christian morals. Armstrong firmly opposed to blacks being involved in either politics or higher education of a nonvocational sort. Booker T. Washington was a protégé of Armstrong and helped to make Hampton particularly influential throughout the South; it was the model for Tuskegee. Many northern philanthropists joined southern whites in

This was, he had told them with obvious sectional pride, the finest school for Negroes anywhere in the country, north or south; in fact, it was better even than a great many schools for white children. And he had dared any Northerner to come south and after looking upon this great institution to say that the Southerner mistreated the Negro. And he had said that if all Negroes would only take a leaf out of the book of Naxos and conduct themselves in the manner of the Naxos products, there would be no race problem, because Naxos Negroes knew what was expected of them. They had good sense and they had good taste. They knew enough to stay in their places, and that, said the preacher, showed good taste. He spoke of his great admiration for the Negro race, no other race in so short a time had made so much progress, but he had urgently besought them to know when and where to stop. He hoped, he sincerely hoped, that they wouldn't become avaricious and grasping, thinking only of adding to their earthly goods, for that would be a sin in the sight of Almighty God. And then he had spoken of contentment, embellishing his words with scriptural quotations and pointing out to them that it was their duty to be satisfied in the estate to which they had been called, hewers of wood and drawers of water.[7] And then he had prayed.

Sitting there in her room, long hours after, Helga again felt a surge of hot anger and seething resentment. And again it subsided in amazement at the memory of the considerable applause which had greeted the speaker just before he had asked his God's blessing upon them.

The South. Naxos. Negro education. Suddenly she hated them all. Strange, too, for this was the thing which she had ardently desired to share in, to be a part of this monument to one man's genius and vision. She pinned a scrap of paper about the bulb under the lamp's shade, for, having discarded her book in the certainty that in such a mood even *Saïd* and his audacious villainy could not charm her, she wanted an even more soothing darkness. She wished it were vacation, so that she might get away for a time.

"No, forever!" she said aloud.

The minutes gathered into hours, but still she sat motionless, a disdainful smile or an angry frown passing now and then across her face. Somewhere in the room a little clock ticked time away. Somewhere outside, a whippoorwill wailed. Evening died. A sweet smell of early Southern flowers rushed in on a newly-risen breeze which suddenly

---

constructing an educational model designed to perpetuate, rather than challenge, black subordination.

7. Biblical reference, from Genesis 9:20, to slavery; prefigures Booker T. Washington's Atlanta Exposition Address, which urged African Americans to accept their social station.

parted the thin silk curtains at the opened windows. A slender, frail glass vase fell from the sill with a tingling crash,[8] but Helga Crane did not shift her position. And the night grew cooler, and older.

At last she stirred, uncertainly, but with an overpowering desire for action of some sort. A second she hesitated, then rose abruptly and pressed the electric switch with determined firmness, flooding suddenly the shadowy room with a white glare of light. Next she made a quick nervous tour to the end of the long room, paused a moment before the old bow-legged secretary that held with almost articulate protest her school-teacher paraphernalia of drab books and papers. Frantically Helga Crane clutched at the lot and then flung them violently, scornfully toward the wastebasket. It received a part, allowing the rest to spill untidily over the floor. The girl smiled ironically, seeing in the mess a simile of her own earnest endeavor to inculcate knowledge into her indifferent classes.

Yes, it was like that; a few of the ideas which she tried to put into the minds behind those baffling ebony, bronze, and gold faces reached their destination. The others were left scattered about. And, like the gay, indifferent wastebasket, it wasn't their fault. No, it wasn't the fault of those minds back of the diverse colored faces. It was, rather, the fault of the method, the general idea behind the system. Like her own hurried shot at the basket, the aim was bad, the material drab and badly prepared for its purpose.

This great community, she thought, was no longer a school. It had grown into a machine. It was now a show place in the black belt,[9] exemplification of the white man's magnanimity, refutation of the black man's inefficiency. Life had died out of it. It was, Helga decided, now only a big knife with cruelly sharp edges ruthlessly cutting all to a pattern, the white man's pattern. Teachers as well as students were subjected to the paring process, for it tolerated no innovations, no individualisms. Ideas it rejected, and looked with open hostility on one and all who had the temerity to offer a suggestion or ever so mildly express a disapproval. Enthusiasm, spontaneity, if not actually suppressed, were at least openly regretted as unladylike or ungentlemanly qualities. The place was smug and fat with self-satisfaction.

A peculiar characteristic trait, cold, slowly accumulated unreason in which all values were distorted or else ceased to exist, had with surprising ferociousness shaken the bulwarks of that self-restraint which was also, curiously, a part of her nature. And now that it had

8. This prefiguring symbol of the protagonist's fate could be compared to the cigarette that goes out in *Passing*.
9. The agricultural area of the South with significant black populations that reach back to slavery (especially Mississippi, Alabama, and Georgia).

waned as quickly as it had risen, she smiled again, and this time the smile held a faint amusement, which wiped away the little hardness which had congealed her lovely face. Nevertheless she was soothed by the impetuous discharge of violence, and a sigh of relief came from her.

She said aloud, quietly, dispassionately: "Well, I'm through with that," and, shutting off the hard, bright blaze of the overhead lights, went back to her chair and settled down with an odd gesture of sudden soft collapse, like a person who had been for months fighting the devil and then unexpectedly had turned round and agreed to do his bidding.

Helga Crane had taught in Naxos for almost two years, at first with the keen joy and zest of those immature people who have dreamed dreams of doing good to their fellow men. But gradually this zest was blotted out, giving place to a deep hatred for the trivial hypocrisies and careless cruelties which were, unintentionally perhaps, a part of the Naxos policy of uplift. Yet she had continued to try not only to teach, but to befriend those happy singing children, whose charm and distinctiveness the school was so surely ready to destroy. Instinctively Helga was aware that their smiling submissiveness covered many poignant heartaches and perhaps much secret contempt for their instructors. But she was powerless. In Naxos between teacher and student, between condescending authority and smoldering resentment, the gulf was too great, and too few had tried to cross it. It couldn't be spanned by one sympathetic teacher. It was useless to offer her atom of friendship, which under the existing conditions was neither wanted nor understood.

Nor was the general atmosphere of Naxos, its air of self-rightness and intolerant dislike of difference, the best of mediums for a pretty, solitary girl with no family connections. Helga's essentially likable and charming personality was smudged out. She had felt this for a long time. Now she faced with determination that other truth which she had refused to formulate in her thoughts, the fact that she was utterly unfitted for teaching, even for mere existence, in Naxos. She was a failure here. She had, she conceded now, been silly, obstinate, to persist for so long. A failure. Therefore, no need, no use, to stay longer. Suddenly she longed for immediate departure. How good, she thought, to go now, tonight!—and frowned to remember how impossible that would be. "The dignitaries," she said, "are not in their offices, and there will be yards and yards of red tape to unwind, gigantic, impressive spools of it."

And there was James Vayle to be told, and much-needed money to be got. James, she decided, had better be told at once. She looked at the clock racing indifferently on. No, too late. It would have to be tomorrow.

She hated to admit that money was the most serious difficulty. Knowing full well that it was important, she nevertheless rebelled at the unalterable truth that it could influence her actions, block her desires. A sordid necessity to be grappled with. With Helga it was almost a superstition that to concede to money its importance magnified its power. Still, in spite of her reluctance and distaste, her financial situation would have to be faced, and plans made, if she were to get away from Naxos with anything like the haste which she now so ardently desired.

Most of her earnings had gone into clothes, into books, into the furnishings of the room which held her. All her life Helga Crane had loved and longed for nice things. Indeed, it was this craving, this urge for beauty which had helped to bring her into disfavor in Naxos—"pride" and "vanity" her detractors called it.

The sum owing to her by the school would just a little more than buy her ticket back to Chicago. It was too near the end of the school term to hope to get teaching-work anywhere. If she couldn't find something else, she would have to ask Uncle Peter for a loan. Uncle Peter was, she knew, the one relative who thought kindly, or even calmly, of her. Her step-father, her step-brothers and sisters, and the numerous cousins, aunts, and other uncles could not be even remotely considered. She laughed a little, scornfully, reflecting that the antagonism was mutual, or, perhaps, just a trifle keener on her side than on theirs. They feared and hated her. She pitied and despised them. Uncle Peter was different. In his contemptuous way he was fond of her. Her beautiful, unhappy mother had been his favorite sister. Even so, Helga Crane knew that he would be more likely to help her because her need would strengthen his oft-repeated conviction that because of her Negro blood she would never amount to anything, than from motives of affection or loving memory. This knowledge, in its present aspect of truth, irritated her to an astonishing degree. She regarded Uncle Peter almost vindictively, although always he had been extraordinarily generous with her and she fully intended to ask his assistance. "A beggar," she thought ruefully, "cannot expect to choose."

Returning to James Vayle, her thoughts took on the frigidity of complete determination. Her resolution to end her stay in Naxos would of course inevitably end her engagement to James. She had been engaged to him since her first semester there, when both had been new workers, and both were lonely. Together they had discussed their work and problems in adjustment, and had drifted into a closer relationship. Bitterly she reflected that James had speedily and with entire ease fitted into his niche. He was now completely "naturalized," as they used laughingly to call it.[1] Helga, on the other hand, had never quite achieved the unmistakable Naxos mold, would never achieve it, in spite of much trying. She could neither conform, nor be happy in her unconformity. This she saw clearly now, and with cold anger at all the past futile effort. What a waste! How pathetically she had struggled in those first months and with what small success. A lack somewhere. Always she had considered it a lack of understanding on the part of the community, but in her present new revolt she realized that the fault had been partly hers. A lack of acquiescence. She hadn't really wanted to be made over. This thought bred a sense of shame, a feeling of ironical disillusion. Evidently there were parts of her she couldn't be proud of. The revealing picture of her past striving was too humiliating. It was as if she had deliberately planned to steal an ugly thing, for which she had no desire, and had been found out.

Ironically she visualized the discomfort of James Vayle. How her maladjustment had bothered him! She had a faint notion that it was behind his ready assent to her suggestion anent a longer engagement than, originally, they had planned. He was liked and approved of in Naxos and loathed the idea that the girl he was to marry couldn't manage to win liking and approval also. Instinctively Helga had known that secretly he had placed the blame upon her. How right he had been! Certainly his attitude had gradually changed, though he still gave her his attentions. Naxos pleased him and he had become content with life as it was lived there. No longer lonely, he was now one of the community and so beyond the need or the desire to discuss its affairs and its failings with an outsider. She was, she knew, in a queer indefinite way, a disturbing factor. She knew too that a something held him, a something against which he was powerless. The idea that she was in but one nameless way necessary to him filled her with a sensation amounting almost to shame. And yet his mute helplessness against that ancient appeal by which she held him pleased her and fed her vanity—gave her a feeling of power. At the same time she shrank away from it, subtly aware of possibilities she herself couldn't predict.

Helga's own feelings defeated inquiry, but honestly confronted, all pretense brushed aside, the dominant one, she suspected, was relief. At least, she felt no regret that tomorrow would mark the end of any claim she had upon him. The surety that the meeting would be a clash annoyed her, for she had no talent for quarreling—when possible she preferred to flee. That was all.

---

1. Naturalization was the process of making foreigners citizens. Many forms of anti-immigrant legislation in the 1920s created obstacles to naturalization for immigrants. Those who were allowed to naturalize were also encouraged to assimilate.

The family of James Vayle, in near-by Atlanta, would be glad. They had never liked the engagement, had never liked Helga Crane. Her own lack of family disconcerted them. No family. That was the crux of the whole matter. For Helga, it accounted for everything, her failure here in Naxos, her former loneliness in Nashville. It even accounted for her engagement to James. Negro society, she had learned, was as complicated, and as rigid in its ramifications as the highest strata of white society. If you couldn't prove your ancestry and connections, you were tolerated, but you didn't "belong." You could be queer, or even attractive, or bad, or brilliant, or even love beauty and such nonsense if you were a Rankin, or a Leslie, or a Scoville; in other words, if you had a family. But if you were just plain Helga Crane, of whom nobody had ever heard, it was presumptuous of you to be anything but inconspicuous and conformable.

To relinquish James Vayle would most certainly be social suicide, for the Vayles were people of consequence. The fact that they were a "first family" had been one of James's attractions for the obscure Helga.[2] She had wanted social background, but—she had not imagined that it could be so stuffy.

She made a quick movement of impatience and stood up. As she did so, the room whirled about her in an impish, hateful way. Familiar objects seemed suddenly unhappily distant. Faintness closed about her like a vise. She swayed, her small, slender hands gripping the chair arms for support. In a moment the faintness receded, leaving in its wake a sharp resentment at the trick which her strained nerves had played upon her. And after a moment's rest she got hurriedly into bed, leaving her room disorderly for the first time.

Books and papers scattered about the floor, fragile stockings and underthings and the startling green and gold negligee dripping about on chairs and stool, met the encounter of the amazed eyes of the girl who came in the morning to awaken Helga Crane.

TWO

SHE woke in the morning unrefreshed and with that feeling of half-terrified apprehension peculiar to Christmas and birthday mornings. A long moment she lay puzzling under the sun streaming in a golden flow through the yellow curtains. Then her mind returned to the night before. She had decided to leave Naxos. That was it.

---

2. For the black middle and upper middle class, family genealogy was as important as it was to white upper-class families who used their lineage as leverage against the encroachment of others. James Vayle's people are a "first family," that is, people of importance who can trace their descendancy, something often denied to black people under slavery.

Sharply she began to probe her decision. Reviewing the situation carefully, frankly, she felt no wish to change her resolution. Except— that it would be inconvenient. Much as she wanted to shake the dust of the place from her feet forever, she realized that there would be difficulties. Red tape. James Vayle. Money, Other work. Regretfully she was forced to acknowledge that it would be vastly better to wait until June, the close of the school year. Not so long, really. Half of March, April, May, some of June. Surely she could endure for that much longer conditions which she had borne for nearly two years. By an effort of will, her will, it could be done.

But this reflection, sensible, expedient, though it was, did not reconcile her. To remain seemed too hard. Could she do it? Was it possible in the present rebellious state of her feelings? The uneasy sense of being engaged with some formidable antagonist, nameless and un-understood,[1] startled her. It wasn't, she was suddenly aware, merely the school and its ways and its decorous stupid people that oppressed her. There was something else, some other more ruthless force, a quality within herself, which was frustrating her, had always frustrated her, kept her from getting the things she had wanted. Still wanted.

But just what did she want? Barring a desire for material security, gracious ways of living, a profusion of lovely clothes, and a goodly share of envious admiration, Helga Crane didn't know, couldn't tell. But there was, she knew, something else. Happiness, she supposed. Whatever that might be. What, exactly, she wondered, was happiness. Very positively she wanted it. Yet her conception of it had no tangibility. She couldn't define it, isolate it, and contemplate it as she could some other abstract things. Hatred, for instance. Or kindness.

The strident ringing of a bell somewhere in the building brought back the fierce resentment of the night. It crystallized her wavering determination.

From long habit her biscuit-coloured feet had slipped mechanically out from under the covers at the bell's first unkind jangle. Leisurely she drew them back and her cold anger vanished as she decided that, now, it didn't at all matter if she failed to appear at the monotonous distasteful breakfast which was provided for her by the school as part of her wages.

In the corridor beyond her door was a medley of noises incident to the rising and preparing for the day at the same hour of many schoolgirls—foolish giggling, indistinguishable snatches of merry conversation, distant gurgle of running water, patter of slippered feet, low-pitched singing, good-natured admonitions to hurry, slamming

---

1. This appears as "understood" in DoVeanna Fulton's edition.

of doors, clatter of various unnamable articles, and—suddenly—calamitous silence.

Helga ducked her head under the covers in the vain attempt to shut out what she knew would fill the pregnant silence—the sharp sarcastic voice of the dormitory matron. It came.

"Well! Even if every last one of you did come from homes where you weren't taught any manners, you might at least try to pretend that you're capable of learning some here, now that you have the opportunity. Who slammed the shower-baths door?"

Silence.

"Well, you needn't trouble to answer. It's rude, as all of you know. But it's just as well, because none of you can tell the truth. Now hurry up. Don't let me hear of a single one of you being late for breakfast. If I do there'll be extra work for everybody on Saturday. And *please* at least try to act like ladies and not like savages from the backwoods."[2]

On her side of the door, Helga was wondering if it had ever occurred to the lean and desiccated Miss MacGooden that most of her charges had actually come from the backwoods. Quite recently too. Miss MacGooden, humorless, prim, ugly, with a face like dried leather, prided herself on being a "lady" from one of the best families—an uncle had been a congressman in the period of the Reconstruction. She was therefore, Helga Crane reflected, perhaps unable to perceive that the inducement to act like a lady, her own acrimonious example, was slight, if not altogether negative. And thinking on Miss MacGooden's "ladyness," Helga grinned a little as she remembered that one's expressed reason for never having married, or intending to marry. There were, so she had been given to understand, things in the matrimonial state that were of necessity entirely[3] too repulsive for a lady of delicate and sensitive nature to submit to.

Soon the forcibly shut-off noises began to be heard again, as the evidently vanishing image of Miss MacGooden evaporated from the short memories of the ladies-in-making. Preparations for the intake of the day's quota of learning went on again. Almost naturally.

"So much for that!" said Helga, getting herself out of bed.

She walked to the window and stood looking down into the great quadrangle below, at the multitude of students streaming from the six big dormitories which, two each, flanked three of its sides, and assembling into neat phalanxes preparatory to marching in military order to the sorry breakfast in Jones Hall on the fourth side. Here

2. MacGooden here repeats the racist presumptions that would have oppressed her black students.
3. The first edition printed "en-entirely."

and there a male member of the faculty, important and resplendent in the regalia of an army officer, would pause in his prancing or strutting, to jerk a negligent or offending student into the proper attitude or place. The massed phalanxes increased in size and number, blotting out pavements, bare earth, and grass. And about it all was a depressing silence, a sullenness almost, until with a horrible abruptness the waiting band blared into "The Star Spangled Banner." The goose-step began. Left, right. Left, right. Forward! March! The automatons moved. The squares disintegrated into fours. Into twos. Disappeared into the gaping doors of Jones Hall.[4] After the last pair of marchers had entered, the huge doors were closed. A few unlucky latecomers, apparently already discouraged, tugged half-heartedly at the knobs, and finding, as they had evidently expected, that they were indeed barred out, turned resignedly away.

Helga Crane turned away from the window, a shadow dimming the pale amber loveliness of her face. Seven o'clock it was now. At twelve those children who by some accident had been a little minute or two late would have their first meal after five hours of work and so-called education. Discipline, it was called.

There came a light knocking on her door.

"Come in," invited Helga unenthusiastically. The door opened to admit Margaret Creighton, another teacher in the English department and to Helga the most congenial member of the whole Naxos faculty. Margaret, she felt, appreciated her.

Seeing Helga still in night robe seated on the bedside in a mass of cushions, idly dangling a mule across bare toes like one with all the time in the world before her, she exclaimed in dismay: "Helga Crane, do you know what time it is? Why, it's long after half past seven. The students—"

"Yes, I know," said Helga defiantly, "the students are coming out from breakfast. Well, let them. I, for one, wish that there was some way that they could forever stay out from the poisonous stuff thrown at them, literally thrown at them, Margaret Creighton, for food. Poor things."

Margaret laughed. "That's just ridiculous sentiment, Helga, and you know it. But you haven't had any breakfast, yourself. Jim Vayle asked if you were sick. Of course nobody knew. You never tell anybody anything about yourself. I said I'd look in on you."

"Thanks awfully," Helga responded, indifferently. She was watching the sunlight dissolve from thick orange into pale yellow. Slowly it crept across the room, wiping out in its path the morning shadows. She wasn't interested in what the other was saying.

---

4. *into fours. Into twos. Disappeared into the gaping*: These lines are missing from Adelaide Cromwell Hill's edition.

"If you don't hurry, you'll be late to your first class. Can I help you?" Margaret offered uncertainly. She was a little afraid of Helga. Nearly everyone was.

"No. Thanks all the same." Then quickly in another, warmer tone: "I do mean it. Thanks, a thousand times, Margaret. I'm really awfully grateful, but—you see, it's like this, I'm not going to be late to my class. I'm not going to be there at all."

The visiting girl, standing in relief, like old walnut against the buff-colored wall, darted a quick glance at Helga. Plainly she was curious. But she only said formally: "Oh, then you *are* sick." For something there was about Helga which discouraged questionings.

No, Helga wasn't sick. Not physically. She was merely disgusted. Fed up with Naxos. If that could be called sickness. The truth was that she had made up her mind to leave. That very day. She could no longer abide being connected with a place of shame, lies, hypocrisy, cruelty, servility, and snobbishness. "It ought," she concluded, "to be shut down by law."

"But, Helga, you can't go now. Not in the middle of the term." The kindly Margaret was distressed.

"But I can. And I am. Today."

"They'll never let you," prophesied Margaret.

"*They* can't stop me. Trains leave here for civilization every day. All that's needed is money," Helga pointed out.

"Yes, of course. Everybody knows that. What I mean is that you'll only hurt yourself in your profession. They won't give you a reference[5] if you jump up and leave like this now. At this time of the year. You'll be put on the black list.[6] And you'll find it hard to get another teaching-job. Naxos has enormous influence in the South. Better wait till school closes."

"Heaven forbid," answered Helga fervently, "that I should ever again want work anywhere in the South! I hate it." And fell silent, wondering for the hundredth time just what form of vanity it was that had induced an intelligent girl like Margaret Creighton to turn what was probably nice live crinkly hair, perfectly suited to her smooth dark skin and agreeable round features, into a dead straight, greasy, ugly mass.

Looking up from her watch, Margaret said: "Well, I've really got to run, or I'll be late myself. And since I'm staying— Better think it

---

5. Ralph Ellison put the difficulty of getting references, for blacks who do not conform, at the heart of his novel *Invisible Man* (1952), where negative letters of recommendation are a recurring trope.
6. The list of those to be shunned and denied opportunities for political reasons or political revenge. This term came into wide use in the 1950s to refer to communists or socialists who were blacklisted, or shut out, of employment and other opportunities. In recent years, so-called black lists of liberal professors have been proliferating on the Internet.

over, Helga. There's no place like Naxos, you know. Pretty good sal-
aries, decent rooms, plenty of men, and all that. Ta-ta." The door
slid to behind her.

But in another moment it opened. She was back. "I do wish you'd
stay. It's nice having you here, Helga. We all think so. Even the dead
ones. We need a few decorations to brighten our sad lives." And again
she was gone.

Helga was unmoved. She was no longer concerned with what anyone in Naxos might think of her, for she was now in love with the
piquancy of leaving. Automatically her fingers adjusted the Chinese-
looking pillows on the low couch that served for her bed. Her mind
was busy with plans for departure. Packing, money, trains, and—
could she get a berth?

THREE

ON one side of the long, white, hot sand road that split the flat green,
there was a little shade, for it was bordered with trees. Helga Crane
walked there so that the sun could not so easily get at her. As she
went slowly across the empty campus she was conscious of a vague
tenderness for the scene spread out before her. It was so incredibly
lovely, so appealing, and so facile. The trees in their spring beauty
sent through her restive mind a sharp thrill of pleasure. Seductive,
charming, and beckoning as cities were, they had not this easy
unhuman loveliness. The trees, she thought, on city avenues and
boulevards, in city parks and gardens, were tamed, held prisoners
in a surrounding maze of human beings. Here they were free. It
was human beings who were prisoners. It was too bad. In the midst
of all this radiant life. They weren't, she knew, even conscious of its
presence. Perhaps there was too much of it, and therefore it was less
than nothing.

In response to her insistent demand she had been told that
Dr. Anderson could give her twenty minutes at eleven o'clock. Well,
she supposed that she could say all that she had to say in twenty minutes, though she resented being limited. Twenty minutes. In Naxos,
she was as unimportant as that.

He was a new man, this principal, for whom Helga remembered
feeling unaccountably sorry, when last September he had first been
appointed to Naxos as its head.[1] For some reason she had liked him,
although she had seen little of him; he was so frequently away on

---

1. Numerous critics believe that Dr. Anderson is based on Booker T. Washington's Tuskegee successor, Robert Russa Moton, who was seen as less of an accommodationist than
   Washington on racial matters.

publicity and money-raising tours. And as yet he had made but few
and slight changes in the running of the school. Now she was a little
irritated at finding herself wondering just how she was going to tell
him of her decision. What did it matter to him? Why should she
mind if it did? But there returned to her that indistinct sense of sympathy for the remote silent man with the tired gray eyes, and she
wondered again by what fluke of fate such a man, apparently a
humane and understanding person, had chanced into the command
of this cruel educational machine. Suddenly, her own resolve loomed
as an almost direct unkindness. This increased her annoyance
and discomfort. A sense of defeat, of being cheated of justification,
closed down on her. Absurd!

She arrived at the administration building in a mild rage, as unreasonable as it was futile, but once inside she had a sudden attack of
nerves at the prospect of traversing that great outer room which was
the workplace of some twenty odd people. This was a disease from
which Helga had suffered at intervals all her life, and it was a point
of honor, almost, with her never to give way to it. So, instead of turning away, as she felt inclined, she walked on, outwardly indifferent.
Half-way down the long aisle which divided the room, the principal's secretary, a huge black man, surged toward her.

"Good-morning, Miss Crane, Dr. Anderson will see you in a few
moments. Sit down right here."

She felt the inquiry in the shuttered eyes. For some reason this
dissipated her self-consciousness and restored her poise. Thanking
him, she seated herself, really careless now of the glances of the ste-
nographers, book-keepers, clerks. Their curiosity and slightly veiled
hostility no longer touched her. Her coming departure had released
her from the need for conciliation which had irked her for so long.
It was pleasant to Helga Crane to be able to sit calmly looking out
of the window on to the smooth lawn, where a few leaves quite pre-
maturely fallen dotted the grass, for once uncaring whether the frock
which she wore roused disapproval or envy.

Turning from the window, her gaze wandered contemptuously
over the dull attire of the women workers. Drab colors, mostly navy
blue, black, brown, unrelieved, save for a scrap of white or tan about
the hands and necks.[2] Fragments of a speech made by the dean of
women floated through her thoughts—"Bright colors are vulgar"—
"Black, gray, brown, and navy blue are the most becoming colors for

---

2. Alice Walker's *The Color Purple* (1982) responds to this passage in its title, and in its
    character's wish for "somethin purple, maybe little red in it too" when all that is avail-
    able to her is "brown, maroon, or navy blue." Eventually the main character paints
    "everything in [her] room purple and red cept the floor." See Alice Walker, *The Color
    Purple* (Boston: Mariner Books, 1992), pp. 20–21 and 284 especially. Walker does
    write the "Plea for Color" that Helga soon requests.

colored people"—"Dark-complected people shouldn't wear yellow, or green or red."—The dean was a woman from one of the "first families"—a great "race" woman;[3] she, Helga Crane, a despised mulatto, but something intuitive, some unanalyzed driving spirit of loyalty to the inherent racial need for gorgeousness told her that bright colours *were* fitting and that dark-complexioned people *should* wear yellow, green, and red. Black, brown, and gray were ruinous to them, actually destroyed the luminous tones lurking in their dusky skins. One of the loveliest sights Helga had ever seen had been a sooty black girl decked out in a flaming orange dress, which a hor-rified matron had next day consigned to the dyer. Why, she won-dered, didn't someone write *A Plea for Color*?

These people yapped loudly of race, of race consciousness, of race pride, and yet suppressed its most delightful manifestations, love of color, joy of rhythmic motion, naïve, spontaneous laughter. Har-mony, radiance, and simplicity, all the essentials of spiritual beauty in the race they had marked for destruction.

She came back to her own problems. Clothes had been one of her difficulties in Naxos. Helga Crane loved clothes, elaborate ones. Nevertheless, she had tried not to offend. But with small success, for, although she had affected the deceptively simple variety, the hawk eyes of dean and matrons had detected the subtle difference from their own irreproachably conventional garments. Too, they felt that the colors were queer; dark purples, royal blues, rich greens, deep reds, in soft, luxurious woolens, or heavy, clinging silks. And the trimmings—when Helga used them at all—seemed to them odd. Old laces, strange embroideries, dim brocades. Her faultless, slim shoes made them uncomfortable and her small plain hats seemed to them positively indecent. Helga smiled inwardly at the thought that whenever there was an evening affair for the fac-ulty, the dear ladies probably held their breaths until she had made her appearance. They existed in constant fear that she might turn out in an evening dress. The proper evening wear in Naxos was afternoon attire. And one could, if one wished, garnish the hair with flowers.

Quick, muted footfalls sounded. The secretary had returned.

"Dr. Anderson will see you now, Miss Crane."

She rose, followed, and was ushered into the guarded sanctum, without having decided just what she was to say. For a moment she felt behind her the open doorway and then the gentle impact of its closing. Before her at a great desk her eyes picked out the figure of

3. A race woman or race man dedicated her or his life to uplifting the race and was com-mitted to "service." Race women and men did often talk about "race pride." Here Helga accuses them of hypocrisy for imposing white aesthetic and social standards.

a man, at first blurred slightly in outline in that dimmer light. At his "Miss Crane?" her lips formed for speech, but no sound came. She was aware of inward confusion. For her the situation seemed charged, unaccountably, with strangeness and something very like hysteria. An almost overpowering desire to laugh seized her. Then, miraculously, a complete ease, such as she had never known in Naxos, possessed her. She smiled, nodded in answer to his questioning salutation, and with a gracious "Thank you" dropped into the chair which he indicated. She looked at him frankly now, this man still young, thirty-five perhaps, and found it easy to go on in the vein of a simple statement.

"Dr. Anderson, I'm sorry to have to confess that I've failed in my job here. I've made up my mind to leave. Today."

A short, almost imperceptible silence, then a deep voice of peculiarly pleasing resonance, asking gently: "You don't like Naxos, Miss Crane?"

She evaded. "Naxos, the place? Yes, I like it. Who wouldn't like it? It's so beautiful. But I—well—I don't seem to fit here."

The man smiled, just a little. "The school? You don't like the school?"

The words burst from her. "No, I don't like it. I hate it!"

"Why?" The question was detached, too detached.

In the girl blazed a desire to wound. There he sat, staring dreamily out of the window, blatantly unconcerned with her or her answer. Well, she'd tell him. She pronounced each word with deliberate slowness.

"Well, for one thing, I hate hypocrisy. I hate cruelty to students, and to teachers who can't fight back. I hate backbiting, and sneaking, and petty jealousy. Naxos? It's hardly a place at all. It's more like some loathsome, venomous disease. Ugh! Everybody spending his time in a malicious hunting for the weaknesses of others, spying, grudging, scratching."

"I see. And you don't think it might help to cure us, to have someone who doesn't approve of these things stay with us? Even just one person, Miss Crane?"

She wondered if this last was irony. She suspected it was humor and so ignored the half-pleading note in his voice.

"No, I don't! It doesn't do the disease any good. Only irritates it. And it makes me unhappy, dissatisfied. It isn't pleasant to be always made to appear in the wrong, even when I know I'm right."

His gaze was on her now, searching. "Queer," she thought, "how some brown people have gray eyes. Gives them a strange, unexpected appearance. A little frightening."

The man said, kindly: "Ah, you're unhappy. And for the reasons you've stated?"

"Yes, partly. Then, too, the people here don't like me. They don't think I'm in the spirit of the work. And I'm not, not if it means suppression of individuality and beauty."

"And does it?"

"Well, it seems to work out that way."

"How old are you, Miss Crane?"

She resented this, but she told him, speaking with what curtness she could command only the bare figure: "Twenty-three."

"Twenty-three. I see. Some day you'll learn that lies, injustice, and hypocrisy are a part of every ordinary community. Most people achieve a sort of protective immunity, a kind of callousness, toward them. If they didn't, they couldn't endure. I think there's less of these evils here than in most places, but because we're trying to do such a big thing, to aim so high, the ugly things show more, they irk some of us more. Service is like clean white linen, even the tiniest speck shows." He went on, explaining, amplifying, pleading.

Helga Crane was silent, feeling a mystifying yearning which sang and throbbed in her. She felt again that urge for service, not now for her people, but for this man who was talking so earnestly of his work, his plans, his hopes. An insistent need to be a part of them sprang in her. With compunction tweaking at her heart for even having entertained the notion of deserting him, she resolved not only to remain until June, but to return next year. She was shamed, yet stirred. It was not sacrifice she felt now, but actual desire to stay, and to come back next year.

He came, at last, to the end of the long speech, only part of which she had heard. "You see, you understand?" he urged.

"Yes, oh yes, I do."

"What we need is more people like you, people with a sense of values, and proportion, an appreciation of the rarer things of life. You have something to give which we badly need here in Naxos. You mustn't desert us, Miss Crane."

She nodded, silent. He had won her. She knew that she would stay. "It's an elusive something," he went on. "Perhaps I can best explain it by the use of that trite phrase, 'You're a lady.' You have dignity and breeding."

At these words turmoil rose again in Helga Crane. The intricate pattern of the rug which she had been studying escaped her. The shamed feeling which had been her penance evaporated. Only a lacerated pride remained. She took firm hold of the chair arms to still the trembling of her fingers.

"If you're speaking of family, Dr. Anderson, why, I haven't any. I was born in a Chicago slum."

The man chose his words, carefully he thought. "That doesn't at all matter, Miss Crane. Financial, economic circumstances can't destroy tendencies inherited from good stock. You yourself prove that!"

Concerned with her own angry thoughts, which scurried here and there like trapped rats, Helga missed the import of his words. Her own words, her answer, fell like drops of hail.

"The joke is on you, Dr. Anderson. My father was a gambler who deserted my mother, a white immigrant. It is even uncertain that they were married. As I said at first, I don't belong here. I shall be leaving at once. This afternoon. Good-morning."

FOUR

LONG, soft white clouds, clouds like shreds of incredibly fine cotton, streaked the blue of the early evening sky. Over the flying landscape hung a very faint mist, disturbed now and then by a languid breeze. But no coolness invaded the heat of the train rushing north. The open windows of the stuffy day coach, where Helga Crane sat with others of her race, seemed only to intensify her discomfort. Her head ached with a steady pounding pain. This, added to her wounds of the spirit, made traveling something little short of a medieval torture. Desperately she was trying to right the confusion in her mind. The temper of the morning's interview rose before her like an ugly mutilated creature crawling horribly over the flying landscape of her thoughts. It was no use. The ugly thing pressed down on her, held her. Leaning back, she tried to doze as others were doing. The futility of her effort exasperated her.

Just what had happened to her there in that cool dim room under the quizzical gaze of those piercing gray eyes? Whatever it was had been so powerful, so compelling, that but for a few chance words she would still be in Naxos. And why had she permitted herself to be jolted into a rage so fierce, so illogical, so disastrous, that now after it was spent she sat despondent, sunk in shameful contrition? As she reviewed the manner of her departure from his presence, it seemed increasingly rude.

She didn't, she told herself, after all, like this Dr. Anderson. He was too controlled, too sure of himself and others. She detested cool, perfectly controlled people. Well, it didn't matter. He didn't matter. But she could not put him from her mind. She set it down to annoyance because of the cold discourtesy of her abrupt action. She disliked rudeness in anyone.

She had outraged her own pride, and she had terribly wronged her mother by her insidious implication. Why? Her thoughts lingered with her mother, long dead. A fair Scandinavian girl in love with life, with love, with passion, dreaming, and risking all in one blind surrender.[1] A cruel sacrifice. In forgetting all but love she had forgotten, or had perhaps never known, that some things the world never forgives. But as Helga knew, she had remembered, or had learned in suffering and longing all the rest of her life. Her daughter hoped she had been happy, happy beyond most human creatures, in the little time it had lasted, the little time before that gay suave scoundrel, Helga's father, had left her.[2] But Helga Crane doubted it. How could she have been? A girl gently bred, fresh from an older, more polished civilization, flung into poverty, sordidness, and dissipation. She visualized her now, sad, cold, and—yes, remote. The tragic cruelties of the years had left her a little pathetic, a little hard, and a little unapproachable.

That second marriage, to a man of her own race, but not of her own kind—so passionately, so instinctively resented by Helga even at the trivial age of six—she now understood as a grievous necessity.[3] Even foolish, despised women must have food and clothing; even unloved little Negro girls must be somehow provided for. Memory, flown back to those years following the marriage, dealt her torturing stabs. Before her rose the pictures of her mother's careful management to avoid those ugly scarifying quarrels which even at this far-off time caused an uncontrollable shudder, her own childish self-effacement, the savage unkindness of her stepbrothers and sisters, and the jealous, malicious hatred of her mother's husband. Summers, winters, years, passing in one long, changeless stretch of aching misery of soul. Her mother's death, when Helga was fifteen. Her rescue by Uncle Peter, who had sent her to school, a school for Negroes, where for the first time she could breathe freely, where she discovered that because one was dark, one was not necessarily loathsome, and could, therefore, consider oneself without repulsion.

Six years. She had been happy there, as happy as a child unused to happiness dared be. There had been always a feeling of strangeness, of outsideness, and one of holding her breath for fear that it wouldn't last. It hadn't. It had dwindled gradually into eclipse of painful isolation. As she grew older, she became gradually aware of a difference between herself and the girls about her. They had mothers, fathers, brothers, and sisters of whom they spoke frequently, and who sometimes visited them. They went home for the vacations which Helga spent in the city where the school was located.

1. While little information is available about Larsen's mother, Mary Hansen, a white Dane who immigrated to the United States from Denmark in the late 1880s, many have noted the apparently autobiographical details of this passage.
2. Little information is available about Larsen's father, Peter Walker, a "colored" man from the Danish West Indies, who died or left the family when Nella was very young. Many have noted the apparently autobiographical details of this passage.
3. Nella's mother's second marriage, when Nella was either just an infant or not yet born, was to a white man, Peter Larsen.

They visited each other and knew many of the same people. Discontent for which there was no remedy crept upon her, and she was glad almost when these most peaceful years which she had yet known came to their end. She had been happier, but still horribly lonely.

She had looked forward with pleasant expectancy to working in Naxos when the chance came. And now this! What was it that stood in her way? Helga Crane couldn't explain it, put a name to it. She had tried in the early afternoon in her gentle but staccato talk with James Vayle. Even to herself her explanation had sounded inane and insufficient; no wonder James had been impatient and unbelieving. During their brief and unsatisfactory conversation she had had an odd feeling that he felt somehow cheated. And more than once she had been aware of a suggestion of suspicion in his attitude, a feeling that he was being duped, that he suspected her of some hidden purpose which he was attempting to discover.

Well, that was over. She would never be married to James Vayle now. It flashed upon her that, even had she remained in Naxos, she would never have been married to him. She couldn't have married him. Gradually, too, there stole into her thoughts of him a curious sensation of repugnance, for which she was at a loss to account. It was new, something unfelt before. Certainly she had never loved him overwhelmingly, not, for example, as her mother must have loved her father, but she *had* liked him, and she had expected to love him, after their marriage. People generally did love then, she imagined. No, she had not loved James, but she had wanted to. Acute nausea rose in her as she recalled the slight quivering of his lips sometimes when her hands had unexpectedly touched his; the throbbing vein in his forehead on a gay day when they had wandered off alone across the low hills and she had allowed him frequent kisses under the shelter of some low-hanging willows. Now she shivered a little, even in the hot train, as if she had suddenly come out from a warm scented place into cool, clear air. She must have been mad, she thought; but she couldn't tell why she thought so. This, too, bothered her.

Laughing conversation buzzed about her. Across the aisle a bronze baby, with bright staring eyes, began a fretful whining, which its young mother essayed to silence by a low droning croon. In the seat just beyond, a black and tan young pair were absorbed in the eating of a cold fried chicken, audibly crunching the ends of the crisp, browned bones. A little distance away a tired laborer slept noisily. Near him two children dropped the peelings of oranges and bananas on the already soiled floor.[4] The smell of stale food and ancient

4. Helga is forced to ride in a segregated or "Jim Crow" train car, legal in the United States under the "separate but equal" terms of *Plessy v. Ferguson* (May 18, 1896). Separate, of

tobacco irritated Helga like a physical pain. A man, a white man, strode through the packed car and spat twice, once in the exact centre of the dingy door panel, and once into the receptacle which held the drinking-water. Instantly Helga became aware of stinging thirst. Her eyes sought the small watch at her wrist. Ten hours to Chicago. Would she be lucky enough to prevail upon the conductor to let her occupy a berth, or would she have to remain here all night, without sleep, without food, without drink, and with that disgusting door panel to which her purposely averted eyes were constantly, involuntarily straying?

Her first effort was unsuccessful. An ill-natured "No, you know you can't," was the answer to her inquiry. But farther on along the road, there was a change of men. Her rebuff had made her reluctant to try again, but the entry of a farmer carrying a basket containing live chickens, which he deposited on the seat (the only vacant one) beside her, strengthened her weakened courage. Timidly, she approached the new conductor, an elderly gray-mustached man of pleasant appearance, who subjected her to a keen, appraising look, and then promised to see what could be done. She thanked him, gratefully, and went back to her shared seat, to wait anxiously. After half an hour he returned, saying he could "fix her up," there was a section she could have, adding: "It'll cost you ten dollars." She murmured: "All right. Thank you." It was twice the price, and she needed every penny, but she knew she was fortunate to get it even at that, and so was very thankful, as she followed his tall, loping figure out of that car and through seemingly endless others, and at last into one where she could rest a little.

She undressed and lay down, her thoughts still busy with the morning's encounter. Why hadn't she grasped his meaning? Why, if she had said so much, hadn't she said more about herself and her mother? He would, she was sure, have understood, even sympathized. Why had she lost her temper and given way to angry half-truths?— Angry half-truths— Angry half—

FIVE

GRAY Chicago seethed, surged, and scurried about her. Helga shivered a little, drawing her light coat closer. She had forgotten how cold March could be under the pale skies of the North. But she liked it, this blustering wind. She would even have welcomed snow, for it would more clearly have marked the contrast between this freedom

---

course, was rarely—if ever—equal. And black travelers, especially in the South, were routinely denied any place to sleep or eat when they traveled.

and the cage which Naxos had been to her. Not but what it was marked plainly enough by the noise, the dash, the crowds.

Helga Crane, who had been born in this dirty, mad, hurrying city, had no home here. She had not even any friends here. It would have to be, she decided, the Young Women's Christian Association.[1] "Oh dear! The uplift.[2] Poor, poor colored people. Well, no use stewing about it. I'll get a taxi to take me out, bag and baggage, then I'll have a hot bath and a really good meal, peep into the shops—mustn't buy anything—and then for Uncle Peter. Guess I won't phone. More effective if I surprise him."

It was late, very late, almost evening, when finally Helga turned her steps northward, in the direction of Uncle Peter's home. She had put it off as long as she could, for she detested her errand. The fact that that one day had shown her its acute necessity did not decrease her distaste. As she approached the North Side,[3] the distaste grew. Arrived at last at the familiar door of the old stone house, her confidence in Uncle Peter's welcome deserted her. She gave the bell a timid push and then decided to turn away, to go back to her room and phone, or, better yet, to write. But before she could retreat, the door was opened by a strange red-faced maid, dressed primly in black and white. This increased Helga's mistrust. Where, she wondered, was the ancient Rose, who had, ever since she could remember, served her uncle.

The hostile "Well?" of this new servant forcibly recalled the reason for her presence there. She said firmly: "Mr. Nilssen, please."

"Mr. Nilssen's not in," was the pert retort. "Will you see Mrs. Nilssen?"

Helga was startled. "Mrs. Nilssen! I beg your pardon, did you say Mrs. Nilssen?"

"I did," answered the maid shortly, beginning to close the door.

"What is it, Ida?" A woman's soft voice sounded from within.

"Someone for Mr. Nilssen, m'am." The girl looked embarrassed.

In Helga's face the blood rose in a deep-red stain. She explained: "Helga Crane, his niece."

"She says she's his niece, m'am."

"Well, have her come in."

1. Founded in 1887, the Young Women's Christian Association, or YWCA, was devoted to the betterment of young women. The YWCA of Chicago opened a wide range of services—from employment to recreation—to black women beginning in 1915. Many of the jobs that the YWCA helped black women to locate were service jobs, such as housecleaning or child care.
2. Racial uplift was based on the belief that educated blacks, sometimes called "the Talented Tenth," after Du Bois, were responsible to help "lift" the rest of the race, to help them better their condition, and that the rest of the black population needed assistance in racial self-help to raise their social station.
3. A wealthy and then a largely white section of Chicago spanning the lakefront.

There was no escape. She stood in the large reception hall, and was annoyed to find herself actually trembling. A woman, tall, exquisitely gowned, with shining gray hair piled high, came forward murmuring in a puzzled voice: "His niece, did you say?"

"Yes, Helga Crane. My mother was his sister, Karen Nilssen. I've been away. I didn't know Uncle Peter had married." Sensitive to atmosphere, Helga had felt at once the latent antagonism in the woman's manner.

"Oh, yes! I remember about you now. I'd forgotten for a moment. *Well,* he isn't exactly your uncle, is he? Your mother wasn't married, was she? I mean, to your father?"

"I—I don't know," stammered the girl, feeling pushed down to the uttermost depths of ignominy.

"Of course she wasn't." The clear, low voice held a positive note. "Mr. Nilssen has been very kind to you, supported you, sent you to school. But you mustn't expect anything else. And you mustn't come here any more. It—well, frankly, it isn't convenient. I'm sure an intelligent girl like yourself can understand that."

"Of course," Helga agreed, coldly, freezingly, but her lips quivered. She wanted to get away as quickly as possible. She reached the door. There was a second of complete silence, then Mrs. Nilssen's voice, a little agitated: "And please remember that my husband is not your uncle. No indeed! Why, that, that would make me your aunt! He's not—"

But at last the knob had turned in Helga's fumbling hand. She gave a little unpremeditated laugh and slipped out. When she was in the street, she ran. Her only impulse was to get as far away from her uncle's house, and this woman, his wife, who so plainly wished to dissociate herself from the outrage of her very existence. She was torn with mad fright, an emotion against which she knew but two weapons: to kick and scream, or to flee.

The day had lengthened. It was evening and much colder, but Helga Crane was unconscious of any change, so shaken she was and burning. The wind cut her like a knife, but she did not feel it. She ceased her frantic running, aware at last of the curious glances of passersby. At one spot, for a moment less frequented than others, she stopped to give heed to her disordered appearance. Here a man, well groomed and pleasant-spoken, accosted her. On such occasions she was wont to reply scathingly, but, tonight, his pale Caucasian face struck her breaking faculties as too droll. Laughing harshly, she threw at him the words: "You're not my uncle."

He retired in haste, probably thinking her drunk, or possibly a little mad.

Night fell, while Helga Crane in the rushing swiftness of a roaring elevated train sat numb. It was as if all the bogies and goblins that had beset her unloved, unloving, and unhappy childhood had come to life with tenfold power to hurt and frighten. For the wound was deeper in that her long freedom from their presence had rendered her the more vulnerable. Worst of all was the fact that under the stinging hurt she understood and sympathized with Mrs. Nilssen's point of view, as always she had been able to understand her mother's, her stepfather's, and his children's points of view. She saw herself for an obscene sore in all their lives, at all costs to be hidden. She understood, even while she resented. It would have been easier if she had not.

Later in the bare silence of her tiny room she remembered the unaccomplished object of her visit. Money. Characteristically, while admitting its necessity, and even its undeniable desirability, she dismissed its importance. Its elusive quality she had as yet never known. She would find work of some kind. Perhaps the library. The idea clung. Yes, certainly the library. She knew books and loved them.

She stood intently looking down into the glimmering street, far below, swarming with people, merging into little eddies and disengaging themselves to pursue their own individual ways. A few minutes later she stood in the doorway, drawn by an uncontrollable desire to mingle with the crowd. The purple sky showed tremulous clouds piled up, drifting here and there with a sort of endless lack of purpose. Very like the myriad human beings pressing hurriedly on. Looking at these, Helga caught herself wondering who they were, what they did, and of what they thought. What was passing behind those dark molds of flesh. Did they really think at all? Yet, as she stepped out into the moving multi-colored crowd, there came to her a queer feeling of enthusiasm, as if she were tasting some agreeable, exotic food—sweetbreads, smothered with truffles and mushrooms—perhaps. And, oddly enough, she felt, too, that she had come home. She, Helga Crane, who had no home.

SIX

HELGA woke to the sound of rain. The day was leaden gray, and misty black, and dullish white. She was not surprised, the night had promised it. She made a little frown, remembering that it was today that she was to search for work.

She dressed herself carefully, in the plainest garments she possessed, a suit of fine blue twill faultlessly tailored, from whose left pocket peeped a gay kerchief, an unadorned, heavy silk blouse, a small, smart, fawn-colored hat, and slim, brown oxfords, and chose a brown umbrella. In a near-by street she sought out an appealing little restaurant, which she had noted in her last night's ramble through the neighborhood, for the thick cups and the queer dark silver of the Young Women's Christian Association distressed her.

After a slight breakfast she made her way to the library, that ugly gray building, where was housed much knowledge and a little wisdom, on interminable shelves. The friendly person at the desk in the hall bestowed on her a kindly smile when Helga stated her business and asked for directions.

"The corridor to your left, then the second door to your right," she was told.

Outside the indicated door, for half a second she hesitated, then braced herself and went in. In less than a quarter of an hour she came out, in surprised disappointment. "Library training"—"civil service"—"library school"—"classification"—"cataloguing"—"training class"—"examination"[1]—"probation period"—flitted through her mind.

"How erudite they must be!" she remarked sarcastically to herself, and ignored the smiling curiosity of the desk person as she went through the hall to the street. For a long moment she stood on the high stone steps above the avenue, then shrugged her shoulders and stepped down. It *was* a disappointment, but of course there were other things. She would find something else. But what? Teaching, even substitute teaching, was hopeless now, in March. She had no business training, and the shops didn't employ colored clerks or sales-people, not even the smaller ones. She couldn't sew, she couldn't cook. Well, she *could* do housework, or wait on table, for a short time at least. Until she got a little money together. With this thought she remembered that the Young Women's Christian Association maintained an employment agency.

"Of course, the very thing!" She exclaimed, aloud. "I'll go straight back."

But, though the day was still drear, rain had ceased to fall, and Helga, instead of returning, spent hours in aimless strolling about the hustling streets of the Loop district.[2] When at last she did retrace her steps, the business day had ended, and the employment office was closed. This frightened her a little, this and the fact that she had spent money, too much money, for a book and a tapestry purse, things which she wanted, but did not need and certainly could not afford. Regretful and dismayed, she resolved to go without her dinner, as a self-inflicted penance, a[s] well as an economy—and

---

1. *"training class"—"examination"*: These are omitted in McDowell's edition.
2. Chicago's central business district received the name of "the Loop" for the cable cars and elevated railways that defined the area. It was named around the time when Larsen was born and living in Chicago. In 1908, just after Larsen left Chicago, the Loop was made the official center for all Chicago addresses, dividing them into North, South, East, or West.

she would be at the employment office the first thing tomorrow morning.

But it was not until three days more had passed that Helga Crane sought the Association, or any other employment office. And then it was sheer necessity that drove her there, for her money had dwindled to a ridiculous sum. She had put off the hated moment, had assured herself that she was tired, needed a bit of vacation, was due one. It had been pleasant, the leisure, the walks, the lake, the shops and streets with their gay colors, their movement, after the great quiet of Naxos. Now she was panicky.

In the office a few nondescript women sat scattered about on the long rows of chairs. Some were plainly uninterested, others wore an air of acute expectancy, which disturbed Helga. Behind a desk two alert young women, both wearing a superior air, were busy writing upon and filing countless white cards. Now and then one stopped to answer the telephone.

"Y. W. C. A. employment. . . . Yes. . . . Spell it, please. . . . Sleep in or out? Thirty dollars? . . . Thank you, I'll send one right over."

Or, "I'm awfully sorry, we haven't anybody right now, but I'll send you the first one that comes in."

Their manners were obtrusively business-like, but they ignored the already embarrassed Helga. Diffidently she approached the desk. The darker of the two looked up and turned on a little smile.

"Yes?" she inquired.

"I wonder if you can help me? I want work," Helga stated simply.

"Maybe. What kind? Have you references?"

Helga explained. She was a teacher. A graduate of Devon.[3] Had been teaching in Naxos.

The girl was not interested. "Our kind of work wouldn't do for you," she kept repeating at the end of each of Helga's statements. "Domestic mostly."

When Helga said that she was willing to accept work of any kind, a slight, almost imperceptible change crept into her manner and her perfunctory smile disappeared. She repeated her question about the reference. On learning that Helga had none, she said sharply, finally: "I'm sorry, but we never send out help without references."

With a feeling that she had been slapped, Helga Crane hurried out. After some lunch she sought out an employment agency on State Street. An hour passed in patient sitting. Then came her turn to be interviewed. She said, simply, that she wanted work, work of any kind. A competent young woman, whose eyes stared frog-like from

3. Devon appears to be modeled after Fisk University, in Nashville, Tennessee, which Larsen attended briefly, in 1907, and from which she may have been expelled, along with others, for violating dress codes.

great tortoise-shell-rimmed glasses, regarded her with an appraising look and asked for her history, past and present, not forgetting
the "references." Helga told her that she was a graduate of Devon,
had taught in Naxos. But even before she arrived at the explanation
of the lack of references, the other's interest in her had faded.

"I'm sorry, but we have nothing that you would be interested in,"
she said and motioned to the next seeker, who immediately came
forward, proffering several much worn papers.

"References," thought Helga, resentfully, bitterly, as she went out
the door into the crowded garish street in search of another agency,
where her visit was equally vain.

Days of this sort of thing. Weeks of it. And of the futile scanning
and answering of newspaper advertisements. She traversed acres of
streets, but it seemed that in that whole energetic place nobody
wanted her services. At least not the kind that she offered. A few
men, both white and black, offered her money, but the price of the
money was too dear. Helga Crane did not feel inclined to pay it.

She began to feel terrified and lost. And she was a little hungry
too, for her small money was dwindling and she felt the need to
economize somehow. Food was the easiest.

In the midst of her search for work she felt horribly lonely too.
This sense of loneliness increased, it grew to appalling proportions,
encompassing her, shutting her off from all of life around her.
Devastated she was, and always on the verge of weeping. It made
her feel small and insignificant that in all the climbing massed city
no one cared one whit about her.

Helga Crane was not religious. She took nothing on trust. Nevertheless on Sundays she attended the very fashionable, very high services in the Negro Episcopal church on Michigan Avenue.[4] She
hoped that some good Christian would speak to her, invite her to
return, or inquire kindly if she was a stranger in the city. None did,
and she became bitter, distrusting religion more than ever. She was
herself unconscious of that faint hint of offishness which hung about
her and repelled advances, an arrogance that stirred in people a
peculiar irritation. They noticed her, admired her clothes, but that
was all, for the self-sufficient uninterested manner adopted instinctively as a protective measure for her acute sensitiveness, in her child
days, still clung to her.

An agitated feeling of disaster closed in on her, tightened. Then,
one afternoon, coming in from the discouraging round of agencies
and the vain answering of newspaper wants to the stark neatness of

---

4. Probably St. Thomas Church, now located on Wabash Street and formerly on South
Michigan Avenue. St. Thomas was founded in 1878 as the first black Episcopal Church in
Chicago and is referred to as the "Mother Church of African American Episcopalians."

her room, she found between door and sill a small folded note. Spreading it open, she read:

> Miss Crane:
> *Please come into the employment office as soon as you return.*
>   Ida Ross

Helga spent some time in the contemplation of this note. She was afraid to hope. Its possibilities made her feel a little hysterical. Finally, after removing the dirt of the dusty streets, she went down, down to that room where she had first felt the smallness of her commercial value. Subsequent failures had augmented her feeling of incompetence, but she resented the fact that these clerks were evidently aware of her unsuccess. It required all the pride and indifferent hauteur she could summon to support her in their presence. Her additional arrogance passed unnoticed by those for whom it was assumed. They were interested only in the business for which they had summoned her, that of procuring a traveling-companion for a lecturing female on her way to a convention.

"She wants," Miss Ross told Helga, "someone intelligent, someone who can help her get her speeches in order on the train. We thought of you right away. Of course, it isn't permanent. She'll pay your expenses and there'll be twenty-five dollars besides. She leaves tomorrow. Here's her address. You're to go to see her at five o'clock. It's after four now. I'll phone that you're on your way."

The presumptuousness of their certainty that she would snatch at the opportunity galled Helga. She became aware of a desire to be disagreeable. The inclination to fling the address of the lecturing female in their face stirred in her, but she remembered the lone five-dollar bill in the rare old tapestry purse swinging from her arm. She couldn't afford anger. So she thanked them very politely and set out for the home of Mrs. Hayes-Rore on Grand Boulevard,[5] knowing full well that she intended to take the job, if the lecturing one would take her. Twenty-five dollars was not to be looked at with nose in air when one was the owner of but five. And meals—meals for four days at least.

Mrs. Hayes-Rore proved to be a plump lemon-colored woman with badly straightened hair and dirty finger-nails. Her direct, penetrating

---

5. Known originally as Forrestville, an area south of the Loop along Grand Boulevard in Chicago was settled by blacks as early as the 1890s. By 1930, blacks were almost 95 percent of the population of the area, which later became known as the center of Chicago's "Bronzeville." With a wealth of churches and large desirable homes, Grand Boulevard was a highly desirable section of the city. Most of the neighborhood was later incorporated into Hyde Park. *Mrs. Hayes-Rore*: Thadious Davis believes that Mrs. Hayes-Rore is modeled on Eva Jennifer-Rice, who founded the Chicago South Side YWCA in 1914 and was active in the black women's club movement.

gaze was somewhat formidable. Notebook in hand, she gave Helga the impression of having risen early for consultation with other harassed authorities on the race problem, and having been in conference on the subject all day. Evidently, she had had little time or thought for the careful donning of the five-years-behind-the-mode garments which covered her, and which even in their youth could hardly have fitted or suited her. She had a tart personality, and prying. She approved of Helga, after asking her endless questions about her education and her opinions on the race problem, none of which she was permitted to answer, for Mrs. Hayes-Rore either went on to the next or answered the question herself by remarking: "Not that it matters, if you can only do what I want done, and the girls at the 'Y' said that you could. I'm on the Board of Managers, and I know they wouldn't send me anybody who wasn't all right." After this had been repeated twice in a booming, oratorical voice, Helga felt that the Association secretaries had taken an awful chance in sending a person about whom they knew as little as they did about her.

"Yes, I'm sure you'll do. I don't really need ideas, I've plenty of my own. It's just a matter of getting someone to help me get my speeches in order, correct and condense them, you know. I leave at eleven in the morning. Can you be ready by then? . . . That's good. Better be here at nine. Now, don't disappoint me. I'm depending on you."

As she stepped into the street and made her way skillfully through the impassioned human traffic, Helga reviewed the plan which she had formed, while in the lecturing one's presence, to remain in New York. There would be twenty-five dollars, and perhaps the amount of her return ticket. Enough for a start. Surely she could get work there. Everybody did. Anyway, she would have a reference.

With her decision she felt reborn. She began happily to paint the future in vivid colors. The world had changed to silver, and life ceased to be a struggle and became a gay adventure. Even the advertisements in the shop windows seemed to shine with radiance.

Curious about Mrs. Hayes-Rore, on her return to the "Y" she went into the employment office, ostensibly to thank the girls and to report that that important woman would take her. Was there, she inquired, anything that she needed to know? Mrs. Hayes-Rore had appeared to put such faith in their recommendation of her that she felt almost obliged to give satisfaction. And she added: "I didn't get much chance to ask questions. She seemed so—er—busy."

Both the girls laughed. Helga laughed with them, surprised that she hadn't perceived before how really likable they were.

"We'll be through here in ten minutes. If you're not busy, come in and have your supper with us and we'll tell you about her," promised Miss Ross.

SEVEN

HAVING finally turned her attention to Helga Crane, Fortune now seemed determined to smile, to make amends for her shameful neglect. One had, Helga decided, only to touch the right button, to press the right spring, in order to attract the jade's notice.

For Helga that spring had been Mrs. Hayes-Rore. Ever afterwards on recalling that day on which with wellnigh empty purse and apprehensive heart she had made her way from the Young Women's Christian Association to the Grand Boulevard home of Mrs. Hayes-Rore, always she wondered at her own lack of astuteness in not seeing in the woman someone who by a few words was to have a part in the shaping of her life.

The husband of Mrs. Hayes-Rore had at one time been a dark thread in the soiled fabric of Chicago's South Side politics, who, departing this life hurriedly and unexpectedly and a little mysteriously, and somewhat before the whole of his suddenly acquired wealth had had time to vanish, had left his widow comfortably established with money and some of that prestige which in Negro circles had been his. All this Helga had learned from the secretaries at the "Y." And from numerous remarks dropped by Mrs. Hayes-Rore herself she was able to fill in the details more or less adequately.

On the train that carried them to New York, Helga had made short work of correcting and condensing the speeches, which Mrs. Hayes-Rore as a prominent "race" woman and an authority on the problem was to deliver before several meetings of the annual convention of the Negro Women's League of Clubs, convening the next week in New York.[1] These speeches proved to be merely patchworks of others' speeches and opinions. Helga had heard other lecturers say the same things in Devon and again in Naxos. Ideas, phrases, and even whole sentences and paragraphs were lifted bodily from previous orations and published works of Wendell Phillips, Frederick Douglass, Booker T. Washington,[2] and other doctors of the race's ills. For variety Mrs. Hayes-Rore had seasoned hers with a peppery

1. Committed to racial uplift, social service, and the betterment of black lives, the National Federation of Afro-American Women and the National League of Colored Women—the two most important women's clubs in the nation—merged in 1896, at a national convention in Boston. Predating either the NAACP or the Urban League, the black women's club movement was enormously influential in helping set a national agenda for civil rights struggles. In Chicago there was a Chicago Federation of Colored Women's Clubs to which Larsen may here refer.
2. Washington (1856–1915) was most famous as the founder of Tuskegee and as a race leader and educator who championed industrial education and self-help. See the Washington excerpt in the "Cultural Contexts" section of this volume. *Wendell Phillips* (1811–1884), Boston-based abolitionist with broad national influence. *Frederick Douglass* (1817–1895), former slave and a famous orator and abolitionist, as well as an editor, journalist, and statesman.

dash of Du Bois[3] and a few vinegary statements of her own. Aside from these it was, Helga reflected, the same old thing.

But Mrs. Hayes-Rore was to her, after the first short, awkward period, interesting. Her dark eyes, bright and investigating, had, Helga noted, a humorous gleam, and something in the way she held her untidy head gave the impression of a cat watching its prey so that when she struck, if she so decided, the blow would be unerringly effective. Helga, looking up from a last reading of the speeches, was aware that she was being studied. Her employer sat leaning back, the tips of her fingers pressed together, her head a bit on one side, her small inquisitive eyes boring into the girl before her. And as the train hurled itself frantically toward smoke-infested Newark, she decided to strike.

"Now tell me," she commanded, "how is it that a nice girl like you can rush off on a wildgoose chase like this at a moment's notice. I should think your people'd object, or'd make inquiries; or something."

At that command Helga Crane could not help sliding down her eyes to hide the anger that had risen in them. Was she to be forever explaining her people—or lack of them? But she said courteously enough, even managing a hard little smile: "Well you see, Mrs. Hayes-Rore, I haven't any people. There's only me, so I can do as I please."

"Ha!" said Mrs. Hayes-Rore.

Terrific, thought Helga Crane, the power of that sound from the lips of this woman. How, she wondered, had she succeeded in investing it with so much incredulity.

"If you didn't have people, you wouldn't be living. Everybody has people, Miss Crane. Everybody."

"*I* haven't, Mrs. Hayes-Rore."

Mrs. Hayes-Rore screwed up her eyes. "Well, that's mighty mysterious, and I detest mysteries." She shrugged, and into those eyes there now came with alarming quickness an accusing criticism.

"It isn't," Helga said defensively, "a mystery. It's a fact and a mighty unpleasant one. Inconvenient too," and she laughed a little, not wishing to cry.

Her tormentor, in sudden embarrassment, turned her sharp eyes to the window. She seemed intent on the miles of red clay sliding past. After a moment, however, she asked gently: "You wouldn't like to tell me about it, would you? It seems to bother you. And I'm interested in girls."

---

3. W. E. B. Du Bois (1868–1963) was one of the leading black intellectuals of his time. An author, editor, educator, and leader, he was a founder of the NAACP, a pan-Africanist, and the creator of numerous race concepts, such as "double consciousness," which remain influential. See the Du Bois excerpts in the "Cultural Contexts" section of this edition. Like Phillips, Douglass, and Washington, Du Bois was a great orator.

Annoyed, but still hanging, for the sake of the twenty-five dollars, to her self-control, Helga gave her head a little toss and flung out her hands in a helpless, beaten way. Then she shrugged. What did it matter? "Oh, well, if you really want to know. I assure you, it's nothing interesting. Or nasty," she added maliciously. "It's just plain horrid. For me." And she began mockingly to relate her story.

But as she went on, again she had that sore sensation of revolt, and again the torment which she had gone through loomed before her as something brutal and undeserved. Passionately, tearfully, incoherently, the final words tumbled from her quivering petulant lips.

The other woman still looked out of the window, apparently so interested in the outer aspect of the drab sections of the Jersey manufacturing city through which they were passing that, the better to see, she had now so turned her head that only an ear and a small portion of cheek were visible.

During the little pause that followed Helga's recital, the faces of the two women, which had been bare, seemed to harden. It was almost as if they had slipped on masks. The girl wished to hide her turbulent feeling and to appear indifferent to Mrs. Hayes-Rore's opinion of her story. The woman felt that the story, dealing as it did with race intermingling and possibly adultery, was beyond definite discussion.[4] For among black people, as among white people, it is tacitly understood that these things are not mentioned—and therefore they do not exist.

Sliding adroitly out from under the precarious subject to a safer, more decent one, Mrs. Hayes-Rore asked Helga what she was thinking of doing when she got back to Chicago. Had she anything in mind?

Helga, it appeared, hadn't. The truth was she had been thinking of staying in New York. Maybe she could find something there. Everybody seemed to. At least she could make the attempt.

Mrs. Hayes-Rore sighed, for no obvious reason. "Um, maybe I can help you. I know people in New York. Do you?"

"No."

"New York's the lonesomest place in the world if you don't know anybody."

"It couldn't possibly be worse than Chicago," said Helga savagely, giving the table support a violent kick.

They were running into the shadow of the tunnel. Mrs. Hayes-Rore murmured thoughtfully: "You'd better come uptown and stay with me a few days. I may need you. Something may turn up."

4. "Miscegenation," as it was then still known and used offensively, or "race intermingling," was illegal in many U.S. states and frowned upon by many blacks, including Du Bois, in some of his early published writings.

It was one of those vicious mornings, windy and bright. There seemed to Helga, as they emerged from the depths of the vast station, to be a whirling malice in the sharp air of this shining city. Mrs. Hayes-Rore's words about its terrible loneliness shot through her mind. She felt its aggressive unfriendliness. Even the great buildings, the flying cabs, and the swirling crowds seemed manifestations of purposed malevolence. And for that first short minute she was awed and frightened and inclined to turn back to that other city, which, though not kind, was yet not strange. This New York seemed somehow more appalling, more scornful, in some inexplicable way even more terrible and uncaring than Chicago. Threatening almost. Ugly. Yes, perhaps she'd better turn back.

The feeling passed, escaped in the surprise of what Mrs. Hayes-Rore was saying. Her oratorical voice boomed above the city's roar. "I suppose I ought really to have phoned Anne from the station. About you, I mean. Well, it doesn't matter. She's got plenty of room. Lives alone in a big house, which is something Negroes in New York don't do. They fill 'em up with lodgers usually. But Anne's funny. Nice, though. You'll like her, and it will be good for you to know her if you're going to stay in New York. She's a widow, my husband's sister's son's wife. The war, you know."

"Oh," protested Helga Crane, with a feeling of acute misgiving, "but won't she be annoyed and inconvenienced by having me brought in on her like this? I supposed we were going to the 'Y' or a hotel or something like that. Oughtn't we really to stop and phone?"

The woman at her side in the swaying cab smiled, a peculiar invincible, self-reliant smile, but gave Helga Crane's suggestion no other attention. Plainly she was a person accustomed to having things her way. She merely went on talking of other plans. "I think maybe I can get you some work. With a new Negro insurance company.[5] They're after me to put quite a tidy sum into it. Well, I'll just tell them that they may as well take you with the money," and she laughed.

"Thanks awfully," Helga said, "but will they like it? I mean being made to take me because of the money."

"They're not being made," contradicted Mrs. Hayes-Rore. "I intended to let them have the money anyway, and I'll tell Mr. Darling so—after he takes you. They ought to be glad to get you. Colored organizations always need more brains as well as more money. Don't worry. And don't thank me again. You haven't got the job yet, you know."

There was a little silence, during which Helga gave herself up to the distraction of watching the strange city and the strange crowds,

5. Black-owned insurance companies for black clients were one of the most important early black businesses. Most were started in the early 1900s.

trying hard to put out of her mind the vision of an easier future which her companion's words had conjured up; for, as had been pointed out, it was, as yet, only a possibility.

Turning out of the park into the broad thoroughfare of Lenox Avenue, Mrs. Hayes-Rore said in a too carefully casual manner: "And, by the way, I wouldn't mention that my people are white, if I were you. Colored people won't understand it, and after all it's your own business. When you've lived as long as I have, you'll know that what others don't know can't hurt you. I'll just tell Anne that you're a friend of mine whose mother's dead. That'll place you well enough and it's all true. I never tell lies. She can fill in the gaps to suit herself and anyone else curious enough to ask."

"Thanks," Helga said again. And so great was her gratitude that she reached out and took her new friend's slightly soiled hand in one of her own fastidious ones, and retained it until their cab turned into a pleasant tree-lined street and came to a halt before one of the dignified houses in the center of the block. Here they got out.

In after years Helga Crane had only to close her eyes to see herself standing apprehensively in the small cream-colored hall, the floor of which was covered with deep silver-hued carpet; to see Mrs. Hayes-Rore pecking the cheek of the tall slim creature beautifully dressed in a cool green tailored frock; to hear herself being introduced to "my niece, Mrs. Grey" as "Miss Crane, a little friend of mine whose mother's died, and I think perhaps a while in New York will be good for her"; to feel her hand grasped in quick sympathy, and to hear Anne Grey's pleasant voice, with its faint note of wistfulness, saying: "I'm so sorry, and I'm glad Aunt Jeanette brought you here. Did you have a good trip? I'm sure you must be worn out. I'll have Lillie take you right up." And to feel like a criminal.

EIGHT

A YEAR thick with various adventures had sped by since that spring day on which Helga Crane had set out away from Chicago's indifferent unkindness for New York in the company of Mrs. Hayes-Rore. New York she had found not so unkind, not so unfriendly, not so indifferent. There she had been happy, and secured work, had made acquaintances and another friend. Again she had had that strange transforming experience, this time not so fleetingly, that magic sense of having come home. Harlem, teeming black Harlem, had welcomed her and lulled her into something that was, she was certain, peace and contentment.

The request and recommendation of Mrs. Hayes-Rore had been sufficient for her to obtain work with the insurance company in which that energetic woman was interested. And through Anne it had been possible for her to meet and to know people with tastes and ideas similar to her own. Their sophisticated cynical talk, their elaborate parties, the unobtrusive correctness of their clothes and homes, all appealed to her craving for smartness, for enjoyment. Soon she was able to reflect with a flicker of amusement on that constant feeling of humiliation and inferiority which had encompassed her in Naxos. Her New York friends looked with contempt and scorn on Naxos and all its works. This gave Helga a pleasant sense of avengement. Any shreds of self-consciousness or apprehension which at first she may have felt vanished quickly, escaped in the keenness of her joy at seeming at last to belong somewhere. For she considered that she had, as she put it, "found herself."

Between Anne Grey and Helga Crane there had sprung one of those immediate and peculiarly sympathetic friendships. Uneasy at first, Helga had been relieved that Anne had never returned to the uncomfortable subject of her mother's death so intentionally mentioned on their first meeting by Mrs. Hayes-Rore, beyond a tremulous brief: "You won't talk to me about it, will you? I can't bear the thought of death. Nobody ever talks to me about it. My husband, you know." This Helga discovered to be true. Later, when she knew Anne better, she suspected that it was a bit of a pose assumed for the purpose of doing away with the necessity of speaking regretfully of a husband who had been perhaps not too greatly loved.

After the first pleasant weeks, feeling that her obligation to Anne was already too great, Helga began to look about for a permanent place to live. It was, she found, difficult. She eschewed the "Y" as too bare, impersonal, and restrictive. Nor did furnished rooms or the idea of a solitary or a shared apartment appeal to her. So she rejoiced when one day Anne, looking up from her book, said lightly: "Helga, since you're going to be in New York, why don't you stay here with me? I don't usually take people. It's too disrupting. Still, it *is* sort of pleasant having somebody in the house and I don't seem to mind you. You don't bore me, or bother me. If you'd like to stay— Think it over."

Helga didn't, of course, require to think it over, because lodgment in Anne's home was in complete accord with what she designated as her "æsthetic sense." Even Helga Crane approved of Anne's house and the furnishings which so admirably graced the big cream-colored rooms. Beds with long, tapering posts to which tremendous age lent dignity and interest, bonneted old highboys, tables that might be by Duncan Phyfe, rare spindle-legged chairs, and others whose ladder backs gracefully climbed the delicate wall panels. These historic things mingled harmoniously and comfortably with brass-bound Chinese tea-chests, luxurious deep chairs and davenports, tiny tables of gay color, a lacquered jade-green settee with gleaming black satin cushions, lustrous Eastern rugs, ancient copper, Japanese prints, some fine etchings, a profusion of precious bric-a-brac, and endless shelves filled with books.[1]

Anne Grey herself was, as Helga expressed it, "almost too good to be true." Thirty, maybe, brownly beautiful, she had the face of a golden Madonna, grave and calm and sweet, with shining black hair and eyes. She carried herself as queens are reputed to bear themselves, and probably do not. Her manners were as agreeably gentle as her own soft name. She possessed an impeccably fastidious taste in clothes, knowing what suited her and wearing it with an air of unconscious assurance. The unusual thing, a native New Yorker, she was also a person of distinction, financially independent, well connected and much sought after. And she was interesting, an odd confusion of wit and intense earnestness; a vivid and remarkable person. Yes, undoubtedly, Anne was almost too good to be true. She was almost perfect.

Thus established, secure, comfortable, Helga soon became thoroughly absorbed in the distracting interests of life in New York. Her secretarial work with the Negro insurance company filled her day. Books, the theater, parties, used up the nights. Gradually in the charm of this new and delightful pattern of her life she lost that tantalizing oppression of loneliness and isolation which always, it seemed, had been a part of her existence.

But, while the continuously gorgeous panorama of Harlem fascinated her, thrilled her, the sober mad rush of white New York failed entirely to stir her. Like thousands of other Harlem dwellers, she patronized its shops, its theaters, its art galleries, and its restaurants, and read its papers, without considering herself a part of the monster. And she was satisfied, unenvious. For her this Harlem was enough. Of that white world, so distant, so near, she asked only indifference. No, not at all did she crave, from those pale and powerful people, awareness. Sinister folk, she considered them, who had stolen her birthright. Their past contribution to her life, which had been but shame and grief, she had hidden away from brown folk in a locked closet, "never," she told herself, "to be reopened."

Some day she intended to marry one of those alluring brown or yellow men who danced attendance on her. Already financially successful, any one of them could give to her the things which she had now come to desire, a home like Anne's, cars of expensive makes

---

1. Anne's Orientalist aesthetic resembles Helga's in her room at Naxos. *Duncan Phyfe*: Highly regarded American cabinetmaker (1768–1854). A Phyfe table would indicate that Anne either collects antiques or comes from a long line of people with both taste and money.

such as lined the avenue, clothes and furs from Bendel's and Revillon Frères',[2] servants, and leisure.

Always her forehead wrinkled in distaste whenever, involuntarily, which was somehow frequently, her mind turned on the speculative gray eyes and visionary uplifting plans of Dr. Anderson. That other, James Vayle, had slipped absolutely from her consciousness. Of him she never thought. Helga Crane meant, now, to have a home and perhaps laughing, appealing dark-eyed children in Harlem. Her existence was bounded by Central Park, Fifth Avenue, St. Nicholas Park, and One Hundred and Forty-fifth street.[3] Not at all a narrow life, as Negroes live it, as Helga Crane knew it. Everything was there, vice and goodness, sadness and gayety, ignorance and wisdom, ugliness and beauty, poverty and richness. And it seemed to her that somehow of goodness, gayety, wisdom, and beauty always there was a little more than of vice, sadness, ignorance, and ugliness. It was only riches that did not quite transcend poverty.

"But," said Helga Crane, "what of that? Money isn't everything. It isn't even the half of everything. And here we have so much else—and by ourselves. It's only outside of Harlem among those others that money really counts for everything."

In the actuality of the pleasant present and the delightful vision of an agreeable future she was contented,[4] and happy. She did not analyze this contentment, this happiness, but vaguely, without putting it into words or even so tangible a thing as a thought, she knew it sprang from a sense of freedom, a release from the feeling of smallness which had hedged her in, first during her sorry, unchildlike childhood among hostile white folk in Chicago, and later during her uncomfortable sojourn among snobbish black folk in Naxos.

NINE

BUT it didn't last, this happiness of Helga Crane's.

Little by little the signs of spring appeared, but strangely the enchantment of the season, so enthusiastically, so lavishly greeted by the gay dwellers of Harlem, filled her only with restlessness. Somewhere, within her, in a deep recess, crouched discontent. She began to lose confidence in the fullness of her life, the glow began to fade from her conception of it. As the days multiplied, her need of something, something vaguely familiar, but which she could not

2. High-end furrier; *Bendel's*: high-end department store.
3. The boundaries of Harlem.
4. This appears as "she was contended" in Davis's edition.

put a name to and hold for definite examination, became almost intolerable. She went through moments of overwhelming anguish. She felt shut in, trapped. "Perhaps I'm tired, need a tonic, or something," she reflected. So she consulted a physician, who, after a long, solemn examination, said that there was nothing wrong, nothing at all. "A change of scene, perhaps for a week or so, or a few days away from work," would put her straight most likely. Helga tried this, tried them both, but it was no good. All interest had gone out of living. Nothing seemed any good. She became a little frightened, and then shocked to discover that, for some unknown reason, it was of herself she was afraid.

Spring grew into summer, languidly at first, then flauntingly. Without awareness on her part, Helga Crane began to draw away from those contacts which had so delighted her. More and more she made lonely excursions to places outside of Harlem. A sensation of estrangement and isolation encompassed her. As the days became hotter and the streets more swarming, a kind of repulsion came upon her. She recoiled in aversion from the sight of the grinning faces and from the sound of the easy laughter of all these people who strolled, aimlessly now, it seemed, up and down the avenues. Not only did the crowds of nameless folk on the street annoy her, she began also actually to dislike her friends.

Even the gentle Anne distressed her. Perhaps because Anne was obsessed by the race problem and fed her obsession. She frequented all the meetings of protest, subscribed to all the complaining magazines, and read all the lurid newspapers spewed out by the Negro yellow press. She talked, wept, and ground her teeth dramatically about the wrongs and shames of her race. At times she lashed her fury to surprising heights for one by nature so placid and gentle. And, though she would not, even to herself, have admitted it, she reveled in this orgy of protest.

"Social equality," "Equal opportunity for all," were her slogans, often and emphatically repeated. Anne preached these things and honestly thought that she believed them, but she considered it an affront to the race, and to all the vari-colored peoples that made Lenox and Seventh Avenues the rich spectacles which they were, for any Negro to receive on terms of equality any white person.

"To me," asserted Anne Grey, "the most wretched Negro prostitute that walks One Hundred and Thirty-fifth Street is more than any president of these United States, not excepting Abraham Lincoln." But she turned up her finely carved nose at their lusty churches, their picturesque parades, their naïve clowning on the streets. She would not have desired or even have been willing to live in any section outside the black belt, and she would have refused scornfully, had they been tendered, any invitation from white folk.

She hated white people with a deep and burning hatred, with the kind of hatred which, finding itself held in sufficiently numerous groups, was capable some day, on some great provocation, of bursting into dangerously malignant flames.

But she aped their clothes, their manners, and their gracious ways of living. While proclaiming loudly the undiluted good of all things Negro, she yet disliked the songs, the dances, and the softly blurred speech of the race. Toward these things she showed only a disdainful contempt, tinged sometimes with a faint amusement. Like the despised people of the white race, she preferred Pavlova to Florence Mills, John McCormack to Taylor Gordon, Walter Hampden to Paul Robeson.[1] Theoretically, however, she stood for the immediate advancement of all things Negroid, and was in revolt against social inequality.

Helga had been entertained by this racial ardor in one so little affected by racial prejudice as Anne, and by her inconsistencies. But suddenly these things irked her with a great irksomeness and she wanted to be free of this constant prattling of the incongruities, the injustices, the stupidities, the viciousness of white people. It stirred memories, probed hidden wounds, whose poignant ache bred in her surprising oppression and corroded the fabric of her quietism. Sometimes it took all her self-control to keep from tossing sarcastically at Anne Ibsen's remark about there being assuredly something very wrong with the drains, but after all there were other parts of the edifice.

It was at this period of restiveness that Helga met again Dr. Anderson. She was gone, unwillingly, to a meeting, a health meeting, held in a large church—as were most of Harlem's uplift activities—as a substitute for her employer, Mr. Darling. Making her tardy arrival during a tedious discourse by a pompous saffron-hued physician, she was led by the irritated usher, whom she had roused from a nap in which he had been pleasantly freed from the intricacies of Negro health statistics, to a very front seat. Complete silence ensued while she subsided into her chair. The offended doctor looked at the ceiling, at the floor, and accusingly at Helga, and finally continued his lengthy discourse. When at last he had ended and Helga had dared to remove her eyes from his sweating face and look about, she saw with a sudden thrill that Robert Anderson was among her nearest neighbors. A peculiar, not wholly disagreeable, quiver ran down her

---

1. Pavlova, McCormack, and Hampden were white. Mills, Gordon, and Robeson were black. *Anna Pavlova*: classical ballet dancer (1881–1931). *John Francis McCormack*: Irish opera singer (1884–1945). *Walter Hampden*: Shakespearean actor (1879–1955). *Florence Mills*: singer, activist and dancer (1896–1927). *Taylor Gordon*: singer (1893–1971). *Paul Robeson*: singer, activist, and actor (1898–1976) especially celebrated both in Harlem and throughout the nation.

spine. She felt an odd little faintness. The blood rushed to her face. She tried to jeer at herself for being so moved by the encounter.

He, meanwhile, she observed, watched her gravely. And having caught her attention, he smiled a little and nodded.

When all who so desired had spouted to their hearts' content—if to little purpose—and the meeting was finally over, Anderson detached himself from the circle of admiring friends and acquaintances that had gathered around him and caught up with Helga halfway down the long aisle leading out to fresher air.

"I wondered if you were really going to cut me. I see you were," he began, with that half-quizzical smile which she remembered so well.

She laughed. "Oh, I didn't think you'd remember me." Then she added: "Pleasantly, I mean."

The man laughed too. But they couldn't talk yet. People kept breaking in on them. At last, however, they were at the door, and then he suggested that they share a taxi "for the sake of a little breeze." Helga assented.

Constraint fell upon them when they emerged into the hot street, made seemingly hotter by a low-hanging golden moon and the hundreds of blazing electric lights. For a moment, before hailing a taxi, they stood together looking at the slow moving mass of perspiring human beings. Neither spoke, but Helga was conscious of the man's steady gaze. The prominent gray eyes were fixed upon her, studying her, appraising her. Many times since turning her back on Naxos she had in fancy rehearsed this scene, this re-encounter. Now she found that rehearsal helped not at all. It was so absolutely different from anything that she had imagined.

In the open taxi they talked of impersonal things, books, places, the fascination of New York, of Harlem. But underneath the exchange of small talk lay another conversation of which Helga Crane was sharply aware. She was aware, too, of a strange ill-defined emotion, a vague yearning rising within her. And she experienced a sensation of consternation and keen regret when with a lurching jerk the cab pulled up before the house in One Hundred and Thirty-ninth Street. So soon, she thought.

But she held out her hand calmly, coolly. Cordially she asked him to call some time. "It is," she said, "a pleasure to renew our acquaintance." Was it, she was wondering, merely an acquaintance?

He responded seriously that he too thought it a pleasure, and added: "You haven't changed. You're still seeking for something, I think."

At his speech there dropped from her that vague feeling of yearning, that longing for sympathy and understanding which his presence evoked. She felt a sharp stinging sensation and a recurrence of that anger and defiant desire to hurt which had so seared her on that past morning in Naxos. She searched for a biting remark, but, finding none venomous enough, she merely laughed a little rude and scornful laugh and, throwing up her small head, bade him an impatient good-night and ran quickly up the steps.

Afterwards she lay for long hours without undressing, thinking angry self-accusing thoughts, recalling and reconstructing that other explosive contact. That memory filled her with a sort of aching delirium. A thousand indefinite longings beset her. Eagerly she desired to see him again to right herself in his thoughts. Far into the night she lay planning speeches for their next meeting, so that it was long before drowsiness advanced upon her.

When he did call, Sunday, three days later, she put him off on Anne and went out, pleading an engagement, which until then she had not meant to keep. Until the very moment of his entrance she had had no intention of running away, but something, some imp of contumacy, drove her from his presence, though she longed to stay. Again abruptly had come the uncontrollable wish to wound. Later, with a sense of helplessness and inevitability, she realized that the weapon which she had chosen had been a boomerang,[2] for she herself had felt the keen disappointment of the denial. Better to have stayed and hurled polite sarcasms at him. She might then at least have had the joy of seeing him wince.

In this spirit she made her way to the corner and turned into Seventh Avenue.[3] The warmth of the sun, though gentle on that afternoon, had nevertheless kissed the street into marvelous light and color. Now and then, greeting an acquaintance, or stopping to chat with a friend, Helga was all the time seeing its soft shining brightness on the buildings along its sides or on the gleaming bronze, gold, and copper faces of its promenaders. And another vision, too, came haunting Helga Crane; level gray eyes set down in a brown face which stared out at her, coolly, quizzically, disturbingly. And she was not happy.

The tea[4] to which she had so suddenly made up her mind to go she found boring beyond endurance, insipid drinks, dull conversation, stupid men. The aimless talk glanced from John Wellinger's lawsuit for discrimination because of race against a downtown restaurant and the advantages of living in Europe, especially in France, to the significance, if any, of the Garvey movement.[5] Then it sped to

---

2. The boomerang is one of the central metaphors in Ralph Ellison's *Invisible Man* (1952).
3. In 1929 Nella Larsen lived at 2588 Seventh Avenue.
4. During Prohibition, "tea" sometimes meant tea and sometimes meant a cocktail party. Sometimes the invitee couldn't be sure which it would be until he or she arrived.
5. Jamaican-born Marcus Garvey (1887–1940) founded the Universal Negro Improvement Association and edited *Negro World,* both dedicated to supporting his "Back to Africa" movement, which garnered huge support and many followers in New York, briefly becoming the largest mass movement in black history. Sometimes mocked by

a favorite Negro dancer who had just then secured a foothold on the stage of a current white musical comedy, to other shows, to a new book touching on Negroes. Thence to costumes for a coming masquerade dance, to a new jazz song, to Yvette Dawson's engagement to a Boston lawyer who had seen her one night at a party and proposed to her the next day at noon. Then back again to racial discrimination.

Why, Helga wondered, with unreasoning exasperation, didn't they find something else to talk of? Why must the race problem always creep in? She refused to go on to another gathering. It would, she thought, be simply the same old thing.[6]

On her arrival home she was more disappointed than she cared to admit to find the house in darkness and even Anne gone off somewhere. She would have liked that night to have talked with Anne. Get her opinion of Dr. Anderson.

Anne it was who the next day told her that he had given up his work in Naxos; or rather that Naxos had given him up. He had been too liberal, too lenient, for education as it was inflicted in Naxos. Now he was permanently in New York, employed as welfare worker by some big manufacturing concern, which gave employment to hundreds of Negro men.

"Uplift," sniffed Helga contemptuously, and fled before the onslaught of Anne's harangue on the needs and ills of the race.

TEN

WITH the waning summer the acute sensitiveness of Helga Crane's frayed nerves grew keener. There were days when the mere sight of the serene tan and brown faces about her stung her like a personal insult. The care-free quality of their laughter roused in her the desire to scream at them: "Fools, fools! Stupid fools!" This passionate and unreasoning protest gained in intensity, swallowing up all else like some dense fog. Life became for her only a hateful place where one lived in intimacy with people one would not have chosen had one been given choice. It was, too, an excruciating agony. She was continually out of temper. Anne, thank the gods! was away, but her nearing return filled Helga with dismay.

Arriving at work one sultry day, hot and dispirited, she found waiting a letter, a letter from Uncle Peter. It had originally been sent to Naxos, and from there it had made the journey back to Chicago to

---

other black leaders for his self-made uniforms and his grandiose manner, Garvey was deported in 1927.

6. George Hutchinson believes that this passage refers to the well-known teas hosted at Jessie Fauset's home, on Seventh Avenue.

the Young Women's Christian Association, and then to Mrs. Hayes-Rore. That busy woman had at last found time between conventions and lectures to readdress it and had sent it on to New York. Four months, at least,[1] it had been on its travels. Helga felt no curiosity as to its contents, only annoyance at the long delay, as she ripped open the thin edge of the envelope, and for a space sat staring at the peculiar foreign script of her uncle.

715 Sheridan Road[2]
Chicago, Ill.

Dear Helga:
It is now over a year since you made your unfortunate call here. It was unfortunate for us all, you, Mrs. Nilssen, and myself. But of course you couldn't know. I blame myself. I should have written you of my marriage.

I have looked for a letter, or some word from you; evidently, with your usual penetration, you understood thoroughly that I must terminate my outward relation with you. You were always a keen one.

Of course I am sorry, but it can't be helped. My wife must be considered, and she feels very strongly about this.

You know, of course, that I wish you the best of luck. But take an old man's advice and don't do as your mother did. Why don't you run over and visit your Aunt Katrina? She always wanted you. Maria Kirkeplads,[3] No. 2, will find her.

I enclose what I intended to leave you at my death. It is better and more convenient that you get it now. I wish it were more, but even this little may come in handy for a rainy day.

Best wishes for your luck.

Peter Nilssen

Beside the brief, friendly, but none the less final, letter there was a check for five thousand dollars.[4] Helga Crane's first feeling was one of unreality. This changed almost immediately into one of relief, of liberation. It was stronger than the mere security from present financial worry which the check promised. Money as money was still not very important to Helga. But later, while on an errand in the big general office of the society, her puzzled bewilderment fled. Here the inscrutability of the dozen or more brown faces, all cast from

---

1. This appears as "Four months, at last" in McDowell's edition.
2. Runs along the expensive, largely-white, and fashionable lake-front districts of Chicago's North Side. In *Passing* Larsen also uses a letter as a crucial turning point in the story.
3. Street in the center of Copenhagen's Latin Quarter.
4. $5,000 in 1928 is equivalent to almost $73,000 in 2018.

the same indefinite mold, and so like her own, seemed pressing forward against her. Abruptly it flashed upon her that the harrowing
irritation of the past weeks was a smoldering hatred. Then, she was
overcome by another, so actual, so sharp, so horribly painful, that
forever afterwards she preferred to forget it. It was as if she were
shut up, boxed up, with hundreds of her race, closed up with that
something in the racial character which had always been, to her,
inexplicable, alien. Why, she demanded in fierce rebellion, should
she be yoked to these despised black folk?

Back in the privacy of her own cubicle, self-loathing came upon
her.[5] "They're my own people, my own people," she kept repeating
over and over to herself. It was no good. The feeling would not be
routed. "I can't go on like this," she said to herself. "I simply
can't."

There were footsteps. Panic seized her. She'd have to get out. She
terribly needed to. Snatching hat and purse, she hurried to the narrow door, saying in a forced, steady voice, as it opened to reveal her
employer: "Mr. Darling, I'm sorry, but I've got to go out. Please, may
I be excused?"

At his courteous "Certainly, certainly. And don't hurry. It's much
too hot," Helga Crane had the grace to feel ashamed, but there was
no softening of her determination. The necessity for being alone was
too urgent. She hated him and all the others too much.

Outside, rain had begun to fall. She walked bare-headed, bitter
with self-reproach. But she rejoiced too. She didn't, in spite of her
racial markings, belong to these dark segregated people. She was different. She felt it. It wasn't merely a matter of color. It was something broader, deeper, that made folk kin.

And now she was free. She would take Uncle Peter's money and
advice and revisit her aunt in Copenhagen. Fleeting pleasant memories of her childhood visit there flew through her excited mind. She
had been only eight, yet she had enjoyed the interest and the admiration which her unfamiliar color and dark curly hair, strange to
those pink, white, and gold people, had evoked. Quite clearly now
she recalled that her Aunt Katrina had begged for her to be allowed
to remain. Why, she wondered, hadn't her mother consented? To
Helga it seemed that it would have been the solution to all their problems, her mother's, her stepfather's, her own.

At home in the cool dimness of the big chintz-hung living-room,
clad only in a fluttering thing of green chiffon, she gave herself up
to day-dreams of a happy future in Copenhagen, where there were
no Negroes, no problems, no prejudice, until she remembered with

---

5. Helga's self-loathing resonates with Harlem Renaissance discussions of internalized
   racism.

perturbation that this was the day of Anne's return from her vacation at the sea-shore. Worse. There was a dinner-party in her honor that very night. Helga sighed. She'd have to go. She couldn't possibly get out of a dinner-party for Anne, even though she felt that such an event on a hot night was little short of an outrage. Nothing but a sense of obligation to Anne kept her from pleading a splitting headache as an excuse for remaining quietly at home.

Her mind trailed off to the highly important matter of clothes. What should she wear? White? No, everybody would, because it was hot. Green? She shook her head, Anne would be sure to. The blue thing. Reluctantly she decided against it; she loved it, but she had worn it too often. There was that cobwebby black net touched with orange, which she had bought last spring in a fit of extravagance and never worn, because on getting it home both she and Anne had considered it too *décolleté*, and too *outré*. Anne's words: "There's not enough of it, and what there is gives you the air of something about to fly," came back to her, and she smiled as she decided that she would certainly wear the black net. For her it would be a symbol. She was about to fly.

She busied herself with some absurdly expensive roses which she had ordered sent in, spending an interminable time in their arrangement. At last she was satisfied with their appropriateness in some blue Chinese jars of great age. Anne *did* have such lovely things, she thought, as she began conscientiously to prepare for her return, although there was really little to do; Lillie seemed to have done everything. But Helga dusted the tops of the books, placed the magazines in ordered carelessness, re-dressed Anne's bed in fresh-smelling sheets of cool linen, and laid out her best pale-yellow pajamas of *crêpe de Chine*. Finally she set out two tall green glasses and made a great pitcher of lemonade, leaving only the ginger-ale and claret to be added on Anne's arrival. She was a little conscience-stricken, so she wanted to be particularly nice to Anne, who had been so kind to her when first she came to New York, a forlorn friendless creature. Yes, she was grateful to Anne; but, just the same, she meant to go. At once.

Her preparations over, she went back to the carved chair from which the thought of Anne's home-coming had drawn her. Characteristically she writhed at the idea of telling Anne of her impending departure and shirked the problem of evolving a plausible and inoffensive excuse for its suddenness. "That," she decided lazily, "will have to look out for itself; I can't be bothered just now. It's too hot."

She began to make plans and to dream delightful dreams of change, of life somewhere else. Some place where at last she would be permanently satisfied. Her anticipatory thoughts waltzed and

eddied about to the sweet silent music of change. With rapture
almost, she let herself drop into the blissful sensation of visualizing
herself in different, strange places, among approving and admiring
people, where she would be appreciated, and understood.

ELEVEN

IT was night. The dinner-party was over, but no one wanted to go
home. Half-past eleven was, it seemed, much too early to tumble into
bed on a Saturday night. It was a sulky, humid night, a thick furry
night, through which the electric torches shone like silver fuzz—
an atrocious night for cabareting,[1] Helga insisted, but the others
wanted to go, so she went with them, though half unwillingly. After
much consultation and chatter they decided upon a place and
climbed into two patiently waiting taxis, rattling things which jerked,
wiggled, and groaned, and threatened every minute to collide with
others of their kind, or with inattentive pedestrians. Soon they pulled
up before a tawdry doorway in a narrow crosstown street and stepped
out. The night was far from quiet, the streets far from empty. Clang-
ing trolley bells, quarreling cats, cackling phonographs, raucous
laughter, complaining motor-horns, low singing, mingled in the
familiar medley that is Harlem. Black figures, white figures, little
forms, big forms, small groups, large groups, sauntered, or hurried
by. It was gay, grotesque, and a little weird. Helga Crane felt singularly apart from it all. Entering the waiting doorway, they descended
through a furtive, narrow passage, into a vast subterranean room.
Helga smiled, thinking that this was one of those places characterized by the righteous as a hell.

A glare of light struck her eyes, a blare of jazz split her ears. For
a moment everything seemed to be spinning round; even she felt that
she was circling aimlessly, as she followed with the others the black
giant who led them to a small table, where, when they were seated,
their knees and elbows touched. Helga wondered that the waiter,
indefinitely carved out of ebony, did not smile as he wrote their
order—"four bottles of White Rock,[2] four bottles of ginger-ale."
Bah! Anne giggled, the others smiled and openly exchanged knowing glances, and under the tables flat glass bottles were extracted
from the women's evening scarfs and small silver flasks drawn from
the men's hip pockets. In a little moment she grew accustomed to the
smoke and din.

---

1. Touring Harlem's famous cabarets and nightclubs.
2. One of the nation's most popular soft drink and mineral water companies—White
   Rock's logo used an image of Psyche, wife of Eros; "psyche" means "soul" (Greek).

They danced, ambling lazily to a crooning melody, or violently twisting their bodies, like whirling leaves, to a sudden streaming rhythm, or shaking themselves ecstatically to a thumping of unseen tomtoms. For the while, Helga was oblivious of the reek of flesh, smoke, and alcohol, oblivious of the oblivion of other gyrating pairs, oblivious of the color, the noise, and the grand distorted childishness of it all. She was drugged, lifted, sustained, by the extraordinary music, blown out, ripped out, beaten out, by the joyous, wild, murky orchestra. The essence of life seemed bodily motion. And when suddenly the music died, she dragged herself back to the present with a conscious effort; and a shameful certainty that not only had she been in the jungle, but that she had enjoyed it, began to taunt her. She hardened her determination to get away. She wasn't, she told herself, a jungle creature. She cloaked herself in a faint disgust as she watched the entertainers throw themselves about to the bursts of syncopated jangle, and when the time came again for the patrons to dance, she declined. Her rejected partner excused himself and sought an acquaintance a few tables removed. Helga sat looking curiously about her as the buzz of conversation ceased, strangled by the savage strains of music, and the crowd became a swirling mass. For the hundredth time she marveled at the gradations within this oppressed race of hers. A dozen shades slid by. There was sooty black, shiny black, taupe, mahogany, bronze, copper, gold, orange, yellow, peach, ivory, pinky white, pastry white. There was yellow hair, brown hair, black hair; straight hair, straightened hair, curly hair, crinkly hair, woolly hair. She saw black eyes in white faces, brown eyes in yellow faces, gray eyes in brown faces, blue eyes in tan faces. Africa, Europe, perhaps with a pinch of Asia, in a fantastic motley of ugliness and beauty, semi-barbaric, sophisticated, exotic, were here. But she was blind to its charm, purposely aloof and a little contemptuous, and soon her interest in the moving mosaic waned.

She had discovered Dr. Anderson sitting at a table on the far side of the room, with a girl in a shivering apricot frock. Seriously he returned her tiny bow. She met his eyes, gravely smiling, then blushed, furiously, and averted her own. But they went back immediately to the girl beside him, who sat indifferently sipping a colorless liquid from a high glass, or puffing a precariously hanging cigarette. Across dozens of tables, littered with corks, with ashes, with shriveled sandwiches, through slits in the swaying mob, Helga Crane studied her.

She was pale, with a peculiar, almost deathlike pallor. The brilliantly red, softly curving mouth was somehow sorrowful. Her pitch-black eyes, a little aslant, were veiled by long, drooping lashes and surmounted by broad brows, which seemed like black smears. The short dark hair was brushed severely back from the wide forehead. The extreme *décolleté* of her simple apricot dress showed a skin of unusual color, a delicate, creamy hue, with golden tones. "Almost like an alabaster," thought Helga.

Bang! Again the music died. The moving mass broke, separated. The others returned. Anne had rage in her eyes. Her voice trembled as she took Helga aside to whisper: "There's your Dr. Anderson over there, with Audrey Denney."

"Yes, I saw him. She's lovely. Who is she?"

"She's Audrey Denney, as I said, and she lives downtown. West Twenty-second Street.[3] Hasn't much use for Harlem any more. It's a wonder she hasn't some white man hanging about. The disgusting creature! I wonder how she inveigled Anderson? But that's Audrey! If there is any desirable man about, trust her to attach him.[4] She ought to be ostracized."

"Why?" asked Helga curiously, noting at the same time that three of the men in their own party had deserted and were now congregated about the offending Miss Denney.

"Because she goes about with white people," came Anne's indignant answer, "and they know she's colored."

"I'm afraid I don't quite see, Anne. Would it be all right if they didn't know she was colored?"

"Now, don't be nasty, Helga. You know very well what I mean." Anne's voice was shaking. Helga didn't see, and she was greatly interested, but she decided to let it go. She didn't want to quarrel with Anne, not now, when she had that guilty feeling about leaving her. But Anne was off on her favorite subject, race. And it seemed, too, that Audrey Denney was to her particularly obnoxious.

"Why, she gives parties for white and colored people together. And she goes to white people's parties. It's worse than disgusting, it's positively obscene."

"Oh, come, Anne, you haven't been to any of the parties, I know, so how can you be so positive about the matter?"

"No, but I've heard about them. I know people who've been."

"Friends of yours, Anne?"

Anne admitted that they were, some of them.

"Well, then, they can't be so bad. I mean, if your friends sometimes go, can they? Just what goes on that's so terrible?"

"Why, they drink, for one thing. Quantities, they say."

"So do we, at the parties here in Harlem," Helga responded. An idiotic impulse seized her to leave the place, Anne's presence, then, forever. But of course she couldn't. It would be foolish, and so ugly.

---

3. This puts Denney just north of Greenwich Village, in the current Chelsea neighborhood.
4. This appears as "attack him" in Adelaide Cromwell Hill's edition.

"And the white men dance with the colored women. Now you know, Helga Crane, that can mean only one thing." Anne's voice was trembling with cold hatred. As she ended, she made a little clicking noise with her tongue, indicating an abhorrence too great for words.

"Don't the colored men dance with the white women, or do they sit about, impolitely, while the other men dance with their women?" inquired Helga very softly, and with a slowness approaching almost to insolence. Anne's insinuations were too revolting. She had a slightly sickish feeling, and a flash of anger touched her. She mastered it and ignored Anne's inadequate answer.

"It's the principle of the thing that I object to. You can't get round the fact that her behavior is outrageous, treacherous, in fact. That's what's the matter with the Negro race. They won't stick together. She certainly ought to be ostracized. I've nothing but contempt for her, as has every other self-respecting Negro."

The other women and the lone man left to them—Helga's own escort—all seemingly agreed with Anne. At any rate, they didn't protest. Helga gave it up. She felt that it would be useless to tell them that what she felt for the beautiful, calm, cool girl who had the assurance, the courage, so placidly to ignore racial barriers and give her attention to people, was not contempt, but envious admiration. So she remained silent, watching the girl.

At the next first sound of music Dr. Anderson rose. Languidly the girl followed his movement, a faint smile parting her sorrowful lips at some remark he made. Her long, slender body swayed with an eager pulsing motion. She danced with grace and abandon, gravely, yet with obvious pleasure, her legs, her hips, her back, all swaying gently, swung by that wild music from the heart of the jungle. Helga turned her glance to Dr. Anderson. Her disinterested curiosity passed. While she still felt for the girl envious admiration, that feeling was now augmented by another, a more primitive emotion. She forgot the garish crowded room. She forgot her friends. She saw only two figures, closely clinging. She felt her heart throbbing. She felt the room receding. She went out the door. She climbed endless stairs. At last, panting, confused, but thankful to have escaped, she found herself again out in the dark night alone, a small crumpled thing in a fragile, flying black and gold dress. A taxi drifted toward her, stopped. She stepped into it, feeling cold, unhappy, misunderstood, and forlorn.

TWELVE

HELGA CRANE felt no regret as the cliff-like towers faded. The sight thrilled her as beauty, grandeur, of any kind always did, but that was all.

The liner drew out from churning slate-colored waters of the river into the open sea. The small seething ripples on the water's surface became little waves. It was evening. In the western sky was a pink and mauve light, which faded gradually into a soft gray-blue obscurity. Leaning against the railing, Helga stared into the approaching night, glad to be at last alone, free of that great superfluity of human beings, yellow, brown, and black, which, as the torrid summer burnt to its close, had so oppressed her. No, she hadn't belonged there. Of her attempt to emerge from that inherent aloneness which was part of her very being, only dullness had come, dullness and a great aversion.

Almost at once it was time for dinner. Somewhere a bell sounded. She turned and with buoyant steps went down. Already she had begun to feel happier. Just for a moment, outside the dining-salon, she hesitated, assailed with a tiny uneasiness which passed as quickly as it had come. She entered softly, unobtrusively. And, after all, she had had her little fear for nothing. The purser, a man grown old in the service of the Scandinavian-American Line, remembered her as the little dark girl who had crossed with her mother years ago, and so she must sit at his table. Helga liked that. It put her at her ease and made her feel important.

Everyone was kind in the delightful days which followed, and her first shyness under the politely curious glances of turquoise eyes of her fellow travelers soon slid from her. The old forgotten Danish of her childhood began to come, awkwardly at first, from her lips, under their agreeable tutelage. Evidently they were interested, curious, and perhaps a little amused about this Negro girl on her way to Denmark alone.

Helga was a good sailor, and mostly the weather was lovely with the serene calm of the lingering September summer, under whose sky the sea was smooth, like a length of watered silk, unruffled by the stir of any wind. But even the two rough days found her on deck, reveling like a released bird in her returned feeling of happiness and freedom, that blessed sense of belonging to herself alone and not to a race. Again, she had put the past behind her with an ease which astonished even herself. Only the figure of Dr. Anderson obtruded itself with surprising vividness to irk her because she could get no meaning from that keen sensation of covetous exasperation that had so surprisingly risen within her on the night of the cabaret party. This question Helga Crane recognized as not entirely new; it was but a revival of the puzzlement experienced when she had fled so abruptly from Naxos more than a year before. With the recollection of that previous flight and subsequent half-questioning a dim disturbing notion came to her. She wasn't, she couldn't be, in love with the man. It was a thought too humiliating, and so quickly dismissed. Nonsense! Sheer nonsense! When one is in love, one strives to please. Never, she decided, had she made an effort to be pleasing to Dr. Anderson. On the contrary, she had always tried, deliberately, to irritate him. She was, she told herself, a sentimental fool.

Nevertheless, the thought of love stayed with her, not prominent, definite; but shadowy, incoherent. And in a remote corner of her consciousness lurked the memory of Dr. Anderson's serious smile and gravely musical voice.

On the last morning Helga rose at dawn, a dawn outside old Copenhagen.[1] She lay lazily in her long chair watching the feeble sun creeping over the ship's great green funnels with sickly light; watching the purply gray sky change to opal, to gold, to pale blue. A few other passengers, also early risen, excited by the prospect of renewing old attachments, of glad home-comings after long years, paced nervously back and forth. Now, at the last moment, they were impatient, but apprehensive fear, too, had its place in their rushing emotions. Impatient Helga Crane was not. But she *was* apprehensive. Gradually, as the ship drew into the lazier waters of the dock, she became prey to sinister fears and memories. A deep pang of misgiving nauseated her at the thought of her aunt's husband, acquired since Helga's childhood visit. Painfully, vividly, she remembered the frightened anger of Uncle Peter's new wife, and looking back at her precipitate departure from America, she was amazed at her own stupidity. She had not even considered the remote possibility that her aunt's husband might be like Mrs. Nilssen. For the first time in nine days she wished herself back in New York, in America.

The little gulf of water between the ship and the wharf lessened. The engines had long ago ceased their whirring, and now the buzz of conversation, too, died down. There was a sort of silence. Soon the welcoming crowd on the wharf stood under the shadow of the great sea-monster, their faces turned up to the anxious ones of the passengers who hung over the railing. Hats were taken off, handkerchiefs were shaken out and frantically waved. Chatter. Deafening shouts. A little quiet weeping. Sailors and laborers were yelling and rushing about. Cables were thrown. The gangplank was laid.

Silent, unmoving, Helga Crane stood looking intently down into the gesticulating crowd. Was anyone waving to her? She couldn't tell.

1. For the many details of Larsen's descriptions of Copenhagen which accurately reflect the city in 1908–12, see George Hutchinson, *In Search of Nella Larsen,* pp. 69ff.

She didn't in the least remember her aunt, save as a hazy pretty lady. She smiled a little at the thought that her aunt, or anyone waiting there in the crowd below, would have no difficulty in singling her out. But—had she been met? When she descended the gangplank she was still uncertain and was trying to decide on a plan of procedure in the event that she had not. A telegram before she went through the customs? Telephone? A taxi?

But, again, she had all her fears and questionings for nothing. A smart woman in olive-green came toward her at once. And, even in the fervent gladness of her relief, Helga took in the carelessly trailing purple scarf and correct black hat that completed the perfection of her aunt's costume, and had time to feel herself a little shabbily dressed. For it was her aunt; Helga saw that at once, the resemblance to her own mother was unmistakable. There was the same long nose, the same beaming blue eyes, the same straying pale-brown hair so like sparkling beer. And the tall man with the fierce mustache who followed carrying hat and stick must be Herr Dahl, Aunt Katrina's husband. How gracious he was in his welcome, and how anxious to air his faulty English, now that her aunt had finished kissing her and exclaimed in Danish: "Little Helga! Little Helga! Goodness! But how you have grown!"

Laughter from all three.

"Welcome to Denmark, to Copenhagen, to our home," said the new uncle in queer, proud, oratorical English. And to Helga's smiling, grateful "Thank you," he returned: "Your trunks? Your checks?" also in English, and then lapsed into Danish.

"Where in the world are the Fishers? We must hurry the customs."

Almost immediately they were joined by a breathless couple, a young gray-haired man and a fair, tiny, doll-like woman. It developed that they had lived in England for some years and so spoke English, real English, well. They were both breathless, all apologies and explanations.

"So early!" sputtered the man, Herr Fisher, "We inquired last night and they said nine. It was only by accident that we called again this morning to be sure. Well, you can imagine the rush we were in when they said eight! And of course we had trouble in finding a cab. One always does if one is late." All this in Danish. Then to Helga in English: "You see, I was especially asked to come because Fru Dahl didn't know if you remembered your Danish, and your uncle's English—well—"

More laughter.

At last, the customs having been hurried and a cab secured, they were off, with much chatter, through the toy-like streets, weaving perilously in and out among the swarms of bicycles.

It had begun, a new life for Helga Crane.

THIRTEEN

SHE liked it, this new life. For a time it blotted from her mind all else. She took to luxury as the proverbial duck to water. And she took to admiration and attention even more eagerly.

It was pleasant to wake on that first afternoon, after the insisted-upon nap, with that sensation of lavish contentment and well-being enjoyed only by impecunious sybarites waking in the houses of the rich. But there was something more than mere contentment and well-being. To Helga Crane it was the realization of a dream that she had dreamed persistently ever since she was old enough to remember such vague things as day-dreams and longings. Always she had wanted, not money, but the things which money could give, leisure, attention, beautiful surroundings. Things. Things. Things.

So it was more than pleasant, it was important, this awakening in the great high room which held the great high bed on which she lay, small but exalted. It was important because to Helga Crane it was the day, so she decided, to which all the sad forlorn past had led, and from which the whole future was to depend. This, then, was where she belonged. This was her proper setting. She felt consoled at last for the spiritual wounds of the past.

A discreet knocking on the tall paneled door sounded. In response to Helga's "Come in" a respectful rosy-faced maid entered and Helga lay for a long minute watching her adjust the shutters. She was conscious, too, of the girl's sly curious glances at her, although her general attitude was quite correct, willing and disinterested. In New York, America, Helga would have resented this sly watching. Now, here, she was only amused. Marie, she reflected, had probably never seen a Negro outside the pictured pages of her geography book.

Another knocking. Aunt Katrina entered, smiling at Helga's quick, lithe spring from the bed. They were going out to tea, she informed Helga. What, the girl inquired, did one wear to tea in Copenhagen, meanwhile glancing at her aunt's dark purple dress and bringing forth a severely plain blue *crêpe* frock. But no! It seemed that that wouldn't at all do.

"Too sober," pronounced Fru Dahl. "Haven't you something lively, something bright?" And, noting Helga's puzzled glance at her own subdued costume, she explained laughingly: "Oh, I'm an old married lady, and a Dane. But you, you're young. And you're a foreigner, and different. You must have bright things to set off the color of your lovely brown skin. Striking things, exotic things. You must make an impression."

"I've only these," said Helga Crane, timidly displaying her wardrobe on couch and chairs. "Of course I intend to buy here. I didn't want to bring over too much that might be useless."

"And you were quite right too. Umm. Let's see. That black there, the one with the cerise and purple trimmings. Wear that."

Helga was shocked. "But for tea, Aunt! Isn't it too gay? Too— too—*outré?*"

"Oh dear, no. Not at all, not for you. Just right." Then after a little pause she added: "And we're having people in to dinner tonight, quite a lot. Perhaps we'd better decide on our frocks now." For she was, in spite of all her gentle kindness, a woman who left nothing to chance. In her own mind she had determined the role that Helga was to play in advancing the social fortunes of the Dahls of Copenhagen, and she meant to begin at once.

At last, after much trying on and scrutinizing, it was decided that Marie should cut a favorite emerald-green velvet dress a little lower in the back and add some gold and mauve flowers, "to liven it up a bit," as Fru Dahl put it.

"Now that," she said, pointing to the Chinese red dressing-gown in which Helga had wrapped herself when at last the fitting was over, "suits you. Tomorrow we'll shop. Maybe we can get something that color. That black and orange thing there is good too, but too high. What a prim American maiden you are, Helga, to hide such a fine back and shoulders. Your feet are nice too, but you ought to have higher heels—and buckles."

Left alone, Helga began to wonder. She was dubious, too, and not a little resentful. Certainly she loved color with a passion that perhaps only Negroes and Gypsies know. But she had a deep faith in the perfection of her own taste, and no mind to be bedecked in flaunting flashy things. Still—she had to admit that Fru Dahl was right about the dressing-gown. It did suit her. Perhaps an evening dress. And she knew that she had lovely shoulders, and her feet *were* nice.

When she was dressed in the shining black taffeta with its bizarre trimmings of purple and cerise, Fru Dahl approved her and so did Herr Dahl. Everything in her responded to his "She's beautiful; beautiful!" Helga Crane knew she wasn't that, but it pleased her that he could think so, and say so. Aunt Katrina smiled in her quiet, assured way, taking to herself her husband's compliment to her niece. But a little frown appeared over the fierce mustache, as he said, in his precise, faintly feminine voice: "She ought to have earrings, long ones. Is it too late for Garborg's? We could call up."

And call up they did. And Garborg, the jeweler, in Fredericksgaarde[1] waited for them. Not only were ear-rings bought, long ones

1. One of Copenhagen's central, and most fashionable, streets.

brightly enameled, but glittering shoe-buckles and two great bracelets. Helga's sleeves being long, she escaped the bracelets for the
moment. They were wrapped to be worn that night. The ear-rings,
however, and the buckles came into immediate use and Helga felt
like a veritable savage as they made their leisurely way across the
pavement from the shop to the waiting motor. This feeling was intensified by the many pedestrians who stopped to stare at the queer
dark creature, strange to their city. Her cheeks reddened, but both
Herr and Fru Dahl seemed oblivious of the stares or the audible
whispers in which Helga made out the one frequently recurring word
"*sorte*," which she recognized as the Danish word for "black."

Her Aunt Katrina merely remarked: "A high color becomes you,
Helga. Perhaps tonight a little rouge—" To which her husband nod-
ded in agreement and stroked his mustache meditatively. Helga
Crane said nothing.

They were pleased with the success she was at the tea, or rather
the coffee—for no tea was served—and later at dinner. Helga herself felt like nothing so much as some new and strange species of
pet dog being proudly exhibited. Everyone was very polite and very
friendly, but she felt the massed curiosity and interest, so discreetly
hidden under the polite greetings. The very atmosphere was tense
with it. "As if I had horns, or three legs," she thought. She was really
nervous and a little terrified, but managed to present an outward
smiling composure. This was assisted by the fact that it was taken
for granted that she knew nothing or very little of the language. So
she had only to bow and look pleasant. Herr and Fru Dahl did the
talking, answered the questions. She came away from the coffee
feeling that she had acquitted herself well in the first skirmish. And,
in spite of the mental strain, she had enjoyed her prominence.

If the afternoon had been a strain, the evening was something
more. It was more exciting too. Marie had indeed "cut down" the
prized green velvet, until, as Helga put it, it was "practically nothing but a skirt." She was thankful for the barbaric bracelets, for the
dangling ear-rings, for the beads about her neck. She was even
thankful for the rouge on her burning cheeks and for the very powder on her back. No other woman in the stately pale-blue room was
so greatly exposed. But she liked the small murmur of wonder and
admiration which rose when Uncle Poul brought her in. She liked
the compliments in the men's eyes as they bent over her hand. She
liked the subtle half-understood flattery of her dinner partners. The
women too were kind, feeling no need for jealousy. To them this girl,
this Helga Crane, this mysterious niece of the Dahls, was not to be
reckoned seriously in their scheme of things. True, she was attractive, unusual, in an exotic, almost savage way, but she wasn't one of
them. She didn't at all count.

Near the end of the evening, as Helga sat effectively posed on a
red satin sofa, the center of an admiring group, replying to questions about America and her trip over, in halting, inadequate Danish, there came a shifting of the curious interest away from herself.
Following the others' eyes, she saw that there had entered the room
a tallish man with a flying mane of reddish blond hair. He was wearing a great black cape, which swung gracefully from his huge shoulders, and in his long, nervous hand he held a wide soft hat. An artist,
Helga decided at once, taking in the broad streaming tie. But how
affected! How theatrical!

With Fru Dahl he came forward and was presented. "Herr Olsen,
Herr Axel Olsen." To Helga Crane that meant nothing. The man,
however, interested her. For an imperceptible second he bent over
her hand. After that he looked intently at her for what seemed to
her an incredibly rude length of time from under his heavy drooping lids. At last, removing his stare of startled satisfaction, he wagged
his leonine head approvingly.

"Yes, you're right. She's amazing. Marvelous," he muttered.

Everyone else in the room was deliberately not staring. About
Helga there sputtered a little staccato murmur of manufactured
conversation. Meanwhile she could think of no proper word of
greeting to the outrageous man before her. She wanted, very badly,
to laugh. But the man was as unaware of her omission as of her
desire. His words flowed on and on, rising and rising. She tried to
follow, but his rapid Danish eluded her. She caught only words,
phrases, here and there. "Superb eyes . . . color . . . neck column . . . yellow . . . hair . . . alive . . . wonderful . . ." His speech
was for Fru Dahl. For a bit longer he lingered before the silent girl,
whose smile had become a fixed aching mask, still gazing apprais-
ingly, but saying no word to her, and then moved away with Fru
Dahl, talking rapidly and excitedly to her and her husband, who
joined them for a moment at the far side of the room. Then he was
gone as suddenly as he had come.

"Who is he?" Helga put the question timidly to a hovering young
army officer, a very smart captain just back from Sweden. Plainly
he was surprised.

"Herr Olsen, Herr Axel Olsen, the painter. Portraits, you know."

"Oh," said Helga, still mystified.

"I guess he's going to paint you. You're lucky. He's queer. Won't
do everybody."

"Oh, no. I mean, I'm sure you're mistaken. He didn't ask, didn't
say anything about it."

The young man laughed. "Ha ha! That's good! He'll arrange that
with Herr Dahl. He evidently came just to see you, and it was plain
that he was pleased." He smiled, approvingly.

"Oh," said Helga again. Then at last she laughed. It was too funny. The great man hadn't addressed a word to her. Here she was, a curiosity, a stunt, at which people came and gazed. And was she to be treated like a secluded young miss, a Danish *frøkken,* not to be consulted personally even on matters affecting her personally? She, Helga Crane, who almost all her life had looked after herself, was she now to be looked after by Aunt Katrina and her husband? It didn't seem real.

It was late, very late, when finally she climbed into the great bed after having received an auntly kiss. She lay long awake reviewing the events of the crowded day. She was happy again. Happiness covered her like the lovely quilts under which she rested. She was mystified too. Her aunt's words came back to her. "You're young and a foreigner and—and different." Just what did that mean, she wondered. Did it mean that the difference was to be stressed, accented? Helga wasn't so sure that she liked that. Hitherto all her efforts had been toward similarity to those about her.

"How odd," she thought sleepily, "and how different from America!"

FOURTEEN

THE young officer had been right in his surmise. Axel Olsen was going to paint Helga Crane. Not only was he going to paint her, but he was to accompany her and her aunt on their shopping expedition. Aunt Katrina was frankly elated. Uncle Poul was also visibly pleased. Evidently they were not above kotowing[1] to a lion. Helga's own feelings were mixed; she was amused, grateful, and vexed. It had all been decided and arranged without her, and, also, she was a little afraid of Olsen. His stupendous arrogance awed her.

The day was an exciting, not easily to be forgotten one. Definitely, too, it conveyed to Helga her exact status in her new environment. A decoration. A curio. A peacock. Their progress through the shops was an event; an event for Copenhagen as well as for Helga Crane. Her dark, alien appearance was to most people an astonishment. Some stared surreptitiously, some openly, and some stopped dead in front of her in order more fully to profit by their stares. *"Den Sorte"*[2] dropped freely, audibly, from many lips.

The time came when she grew used to the stares of the population. And the time came when the population of Copenhagen grew used to her outlandish presence and ceased to stare. But at the end

---

1. Kowtowing.
2. "Black" or "Negro" in Danish.

of that first day it was with thankfulness that she returned to the sheltering walls of the house on Maria Kirkplads.

They were followed by numerous packages, whose contents all had been selected or suggested by Olsen and paid for by Aunt Katrina. Helga had only to wear them. When they were opened and the things spread out upon the sedate furnishings of her chamber, they made a rather startling array. It was almost in a mood of rebellion that Helga faced the fantastic collection of garments incongruously laid out in the quaint, stiff, pale old room. There were batik dresses in which mingled indigo, orange, green, vermilion, and black; dresses of velvet and chiffon in screaming colors, blood-red, sulphur-yellow, sea-green; and one black and white thing in striking combination. There was a black Manila shawl strewn with great scarlet and lemon flowers, a leopard-skin coat, a glittering opera-cape. There were turban-like hats of metallic silks, feathers and furs, strange jewelry, enameled or set with odd semi-precious stones, a nauseous Eastern perfume, shoes with dangerously high heels. Gradually Helga's perturbation subsided in the unusual pleasure of having so many new and expensive clothes at one time. She began to feel a little excited, incited.

Incited. That was it, the guiding principle of her life in Copenhagen. She was incited to make an impression, a voluptuous impression. She was incited to inflame attention and admiration. She was dressed for it, subtly schooled for it. And after a little while she gave herself up wholly to the fascinating business of being seen, gaped at, desired. Against the solid background of Herr Dahl's wealth and generosity she submitted to her aunt's arrangement of her life to one end, the amusing one of being noticed and flattered. Intentionally she kept to the slow, faltering Danish. It was, she decided, more attractive than a nearer perfection. She grew used to the extravagant things with which Aunt Katrina chose to dress her. She managed, too, to retain that air of remoteness which had been in America so disastrous to her friendships. Here in Copenhagen it was merely a little mysterious and added another clinging wisp of charm.

Helga Crane's new existence was intensely pleasant to her; it gratified her augmented sense of self-importance. And it suited her. She had to admit that the Danes had the right idea. To each his own milieu. Enhance what was already in one's possession. In America Negroes sometimes talked loudly of this, but in their hearts they repudiated it. In their lives too. They didn't want to be like themselves. What they wanted, asked for, begged for, was to be like their white overlords.[3] They were ashamed to be Negroes, but not ashamed to beg to be something else. Something inferior. Not quite genuine. Too bad!

---

3. *white overlords*: This appears as "white overloads" in Davis's edition.

Helga Crane didn't, however, think often of America, excepting in unfavorable contrast to Denmark. For she had resolved never to return to the existence of ignominy which the New World of opportunity and promise forced upon Negroes. How stupid she had been ever to have thought that she could marry and perhaps have children in a land where every dark child was handicapped at the start by the shroud of color! She saw, suddenly, the giving birth to little, helpless, unprotesting Negro children as a sin, an unforgivable outrage. More black folk to suffer indignities. More dark bodies for mobs to lynch. No, Helga Crane didn't think often of America. It was too humiliating, too disturbing. And she wanted to be left to the peace which had come to her. Her mental difficulties and questionings had become simplified. She now believed sincerely that there was a law of compensation, and that sometimes it worked. For all those early desolate years she now felt recompensed. She recalled a line that had impressed her in her lonely school-days, "The far-off interest of tears."

To her, Helga Crane, it had come at last, and she meant to cling to it. So she turned her back on painful America, resolutely shutting out the griefs, the humiliations, the frustrations, which she had endured there.

Her mind was occupied with other and nearer things.

The charm of the old city itself, with its odd architectural mixture of medievalism and modernity, and the general air of well-being which pervaded it, impressed her. Even in the so-called poor sections there was none of that untidiness and squalor which she remembered as the accompaniment of poverty in Chicago, New York, and the Southern cities of America. Here the door-steps were always white from constant scrubbings, the women neat, and the children washed and provided with whole clothing. Here were no tatters and rags, no beggars. But, then, begging, she learned, was an offense punishable by law. Indeed, it was unnecessary in a country where everyone considered it a duty somehow to support himself and his family by honest work; or, if misfortune and illness came upon one, everyone else, including the State, felt bound to give assistance, a lift on the road to the regaining of independence.

After the initial shyness and consternation at the sensation caused by her strange presence had worn off, Helga spent hours driving or walking about the city, at first in the protecting company of Uncle Poul or Aunt Katrina or both, or sometimes Axel Olsen. But later, when she had become a little familiar with the city, and its inhabitants a little used to her, and when she had learned to cross the streets in safety, dodging successfully the innumerable bicycles like a true Copenhagener, she went often alone, loitering on the long bridge which spanned the placid lakes, or watching the pageant of the

blue-clad, sprucely tailored soldiers in the daily parade at Amielen-
borg Palace, or in the historic vicinity of the long, low-lying Exchange,
a picturesque structure in picturesque surroundings, skirting as it
did the great canal, which always was alive with many small boats,
flying broad white sails and pressing close on the huge ruined pile
of the Palace of Christiansborg.[4] There was also the Gammelstrand,[5]
the congregating-place of the venders of fish, where daily was enacted
a spirited and interesting scene between sellers and buyers, and
where Helga's appearance always roused lively and audible, but
friendly, interest, long after she became in other parts of the city an
accepted curiosity. Here it was that one day an old countrywoman
asked her to what manner of mankind she belonged and at Helga's
replying: "I'm a Negro," had become indignant, retorting angrily
that, just because she was old and a countrywoman she could not
be so easily fooled, for she knew as well as everyone else that Negroes
were black and had woolly hair.

Against all this walking the Dahls had at first uttered mild protest. "But, Aunt dear, I have to walk, or I'll get fat," Helga asserted.
"I've never, never in all my life, eaten so much." For the accepted
style of entertainment in Copenhagen seemed to be a round of
dinner-parties, at which it was customary for the hostess to tax the
full capacity not only of her dining-room, but of her guests as well.
Helga enjoyed these dinner-parties, as they were usually spirited
affairs, the conversation brilliant and witty, often in several languages. And always she came in for a goodly measure of flattering
attention and admiration.

There were, too, those popular afternoon gatherings for the
express purpose of drinking coffee together, where between much
talk, interesting talk, one sipped the strong and steaming beverage
from exquisite cups fashioned of Royal Danish porcelain and par-
took of an infinite variety of rich cakes and *smørrebrød*. This *smørrebrød*, dainty sandwiches of an endless and tempting array, was
distinctly a Danish institution. Often Helga wondered just how many
of these delicious sandwiches she had consumed since setting foot
on Denmark's soil. Always, wherever food was served, appeared the
inevitable *smørrebrød*, in the home of the Dahls, in every other home
that she visited, in hotels, in restaurants.

At first she had missed, a little, dancing, for, though excellent
dancers, the Danes seemed not to care a great deal for that pastime,
which so delightfully combines exercise and pleasure. But in the

---

4. Former royal residence, later rebuilt for government offices. *Low-lying Exchange*:
    Børsen, the stock exchange, built along the water. *Amielenborg Palace*: Copenhagen's
    royal residence and offices.
5. Copenhagen's fish market.

winter there was skating, solitary, or in gay groups. Helga liked this
sport, though she was not very good at it. There were, however,
always plenty of efficient and willing men to instruct and to guide
her over the glittering ice. One could, too, wear such attractive
skating-things.

But mostly it was with Axel Olsen that her thoughts were occupied. Brilliant, bored, elegant, urbane, cynical, worldly, he was a
type entirely new to Helga Crane, familiar only, and that but little,
with the restricted society of American Negroes. She was aware, too,
that this amusing, if conceited, man was interested in her. They
were, because he was painting her, much together. Helga spent long
mornings in the eccentric studio opposite the Folkemuseum,[6] and
Olsen came often to the Dahl home, where, as Helga and the man
himself knew, he was something more than welcome. But in spite
of his expressed interest and even delight in her exotic appearance,
in spite of his constant attendance upon her, he gave no sign of the
more personal kind of concern which—encouraged by Aunt Katrina's
mild insinuations and Uncle Poul's subtle questionings—she had
tried to secure. Was it, she wondered, race that kept him silent, held
him back. Helga Crane frowned on this thought, putting it furiously
from her, because it disturbed her sense of security and permanence
in her new life, pricked her self-assurance.

Nevertheless she was startled when on a pleasant afternoon while
drinking coffee in the Hotel Vivili, Aunt Katrina mentioned, almost
casually, the desirability of Helga's making a good marriage.

"Marriage, Aunt dear!"

"Marriage," firmly repeated her aunt, helping herself to another
anchovy and olive sandwich. "You are," she pointed out, "twenty-five."

"Oh, Aunt, I couldn't! I mean, there's nobody here for me to
marry." In spite of herself and her desire not to be, Helga was
shocked.

"Nobody?" There was, Fru Dahl asserted, Captain Frederick
Skaargaard—and very handsome he was too—and he would have
money. And there was Herr Hans Tietgen, not so handsome, of
course, but clever and a good business man; he too would be rich,
very rich, some day. And there was Herr Karl Pedersen, who had a
good berth with the Landmands-bank and considerable shares in a
prosperous cement-factory at Aalborg. There was, too, Christian
Lende, the young owner of the new Odin Theater. Any of these
Helga might marry, was Aunt Katrina's opinion. "And," she added,
"others." Or maybe Helga herself had some ideas.

6. A cultural museum displaying life-size dioramas of different Danish ways of life.

Helga had. She didn't, she responded, believe in mixed marriages, "between races, you know." They brought only trouble—to the children—as she herself knew but too well from bitter experience.

Fru Dahl thoughtfully lit a cigarette. Eventually, after a satisfactory glow had manifested itself, she announced: "Because your mother was a fool. Yes, she was! If she'd come home after she married, or after you were born, or even after your father—er—went off like that, it would have been different. If even she'd left you when she was here. But why in the world she should have married again, and a person like that, I can't see. She wanted to keep you, she insisted on it, even over his protest, I think. She loved you so much, she said.—And so she made you unhappy. Mothers, I suppose, are like that. Selfish. And Karen was always stupid. If you've got any brains at all they came from your father."

Into this Helga would not enter. Because of its obvious partial truths she felt the need for disguising caution. With a detachment that amazed herself she asked if Aunt Katrina didn't think, really, that miscegenation was wrong, in fact as well as principle.

"Don't," was her aunt's reply, "be a fool too, Helga. We don't think of those things here. Not in connection with individuals, at least." And almost immediately she inquired: "Did you give Herr Olsen my message about dinner tonight?"

"Yes, Aunt." Helga was cross, and trying not to show it.

"He's coming?"

"Yes, Aunt," with precise politeness.

"What about him?"

"I don't know. *What* about him?"

"He likes you?"

"I don't know. How can I tell that?" Helga asked with irritating reserve, her concentrated attention on the selection of a sandwich. She had a feeling of nakedness. Outrage.

Now Fru Dahl was annoyed and showed it. "What nonsense! Of course you know. Any girl does," and her satin-covered foot tapped, a little impatiently, the old tiled floor.

"Really, I don't know, Aunt," Helga responded in a strange voice, a strange manner, coldly formal, levelly courteous. Then suddenly contrite, she added: "Honestly, I don't. I can't tell a thing about him," and fell into a little silence. "Not a thing," she repeated. But the phrase, though audible, was addressed to no one. To herself.

She looked out into the amazing orderliness of the street. Instinctively she wanted to combat this searching into the one thing which, here, surrounded by all other things which for so long she had so positively wanted, made her a little afraid. Started vague premonitions.

Fru Dahl regarded her intently. It would be, she remarked with a return of her outward casualness, by far the best of all possibilities.

Particularly desirable. She touched Helga's hand with her fingers in a little affectionate gesture. Very lightly.

Helga Crane didn't immediately reply. There was, she knew, so much reason—from one viewpoint—in her aunt's statement. She could only acknowledge it. "I know that," she told her finally. Inwardly she was admiring the cool, easy way in which Aunt Katrina had brushed aside the momentary acid note of the conversation and resumed her customary pitch. It took, Helga thought, a great deal of security. Balance.

"Yes," she was saying, while leisurely lighting another of those long, thin, brown cigarettes which Helga knew from distressing experience to be incredibly nasty tasting, "it would be the ideal thing for you, Helga." She gazed penetratingly into the masked face of her niece and nodded, as though satisfied with what she saw there. "And you of course realize that you are a very charming and beautiful girl. Intelligent too. If you put your mind to it, there's no reason in the world why you shouldn't—" Abruptly she stopped, leaving her implication at once suspended and clear. Behind her there were footsteps. A small gloved hand appeared on her shoulder. In the short moment before turning to greet Fru Fischer she said quietly, meaningly: "Or else stop wasting your time, Helga."

Helga Crane said: "Ah, Fru Fischer. It's good to see you." She meant it. Her whole body was tense with suppressed indignation. Burning inside like the confined fire of a hot furnace. She was so harassed that she smiled in self-protection. And suddenly she was oddly cold. An intimation of things distant,[7] but none the less disturbing, oppressed her with a faintly sick feeling. Like a heavy weight, a stone weight, just where, she knew, was her stomach.

Fru Fischer was late. As usual. She apologized profusely. Also as usual. And, yes, she would have some coffee. And some *smørrebrød*. Though she must say that the coffee here at the Vivili was atrocious. Simply atrocious. "I don't see how you stand it." And the place was getting so common, always so many Bolsheviks and Japs and things. And she didn't—"begging your pardon, Helga"—like that hideous American music they were forever playing, even if it was considered very smart. "Give me," she said, "the good old-fashioned Danish melodies of Gade and Heise. Which reminds me, Herr Olsen says that Nielsen's[8] "Helios" is being performed with great success just now in England. But I suppose you know all about it, Helga. He's already told you. What?" This last was accompanied with an arch and insinuating smile.

---

7. *An intimation of things distant*: This appears as "an intimidation of things distant" in McDowell's edition.
8. Carl Nielsen (1865–1931), Niels Gade (1817–1890), and Peter Heise (1830–1879), Danish composers prominent in the nineteenth and early twentieth centuries.

A shrug moved Helga Crane's shoulders. Strange she'd never before noticed what a positively disagreeable woman Fru Fischer was. Stupid, too.

FIFTEEN

WELL into Helga's second year in Denmark, came an indefinite discontent. Not clear, but vague, like a storm gathering far on the horizon. It was long before she would admit that she was less happy than she had been during her first year in Copenhagen, but she knew that it was so. And this subconscious knowledge added to her growing restlessness and little mental insecurity. She desired ardently to combat this wearing down of her satisfaction with her life, with herself. But she didn't know how.

Frankly the question came to this: what was the matter with her? Was there, without her knowing it, some peculiar lack in her? Absurd. But she began to have a feeling of discouragement and hopelessness. Why couldn't she be happy, content, somewhere? Other people managed, somehow, to be. To put it plainly, didn't she know how? Was she incapable of it?

And then on a warm spring day came Anne's letter telling of her coming marriage to Anderson, who retained still his shadowy place in Helga Crane's memory. It added, somehow, to her discontent, and to her growing dissatisfaction with her peacock's life. This, too, annoyed her.

What, she asked herself, was there about that man which had the power always to upset her? She began to think back to her first encounter with him. Perhaps if she hadn't come away— She laughed. Derisively. "Yes, if I hadn't come away, I'd be stuck in Harlem. Working every day of my life. Chattering about the race problem."

Anne, it seemed, wanted her to come back for the wedding. This, Helga had no intention of doing. True, she had liked and admired Anne better than anyone she had ever known, but even for her she wouldn't cross the ocean.

Go back to America, where they hated Negroes! To America, where Negroes were not people. To America, where Negroes were allowed to be beggars only, of life, of happiness, of security. To America, where everything had been taken from those dark ones, liberty, respect, even the labor of their hands. To America, where if one had Negro blood, one mustn't expect money, education, or, sometimes, even work whereby one might earn bread. Perhaps she was wrong to bother about it now that she was so far away. Helga couldn't, however, help it. Never could she recall the shames and often the absolute horrors of the black man's existence in America without the quickening of her heart's beating and a sensation of disturbing nausea. It was too awful. The sense of dread of it was almost a tangible thing in her throat.

And certainly she wouldn't go back for any such idiotic reason as Anne's getting married to that offensive Robert Anderson. Anne was really too amusing. Just why, she wondered, and how had it come about that he was being married to Anne. And why did Anne, who had so much more than so many others—more than enough—want Anderson too? Why couldn't she— "I think," she told herself, "I'd better stop. It's none of my business. I don't care in the least. Besides," she added irrelevantly, "I hate such nonsensical soul-searching."

One night not long after the arrival of Anne's letter with its curious news, Helga went with Olsen and some other young folk to the great Circus,[1] a vaudeville house, in search of amusement on a rare off night. After sitting through several numbers they reluctantly arrived at the conclusion that the whole entertainment was dull, unutterably dull, and apparently without alleviation, and so not to be borne. They were reaching for their wraps when out upon the stage pranced two black men, American Negroes undoubtedly, for as they danced and cavorted, they sang in the English of America an old rag-time song that Helga remembered hearing as a child, "Everybody Gives Me Good Advice."[2] At its conclusion the audience applauded with delight. Only Helga Crane was silent, motionless.

More songs, old, all of them old, but new and strange to that audience. And how the singers danced, pounding their thighs, slapping their hands together, twisting their legs, waving their abnormally long arms, throwing their bodies about with a loose ease! And how the enchanted spectators clapped and howled and shouted for more!

Helga Crane was not amused. Instead she was filled with a fierce hatred for the cavorting Negroes on the stage. She felt shamed, betrayed, as if these pale pink and white people among whom she lived had suddenly been invited to look upon something in her which she had hidden away and wanted to forget. And she was shocked at the avidity at which Olsen beside her drank it in.

But later, when she was alone, it became quite clear to her that all along they had divined its presence, had known that in her was something, some characteristic, different from any that they themselves possessed. Else why had they decked her out as they had? Why subtly indicated that she was different? And they hadn't despised it. No, they had admired it, rated it as a precious thing, a thing to be enhanced, preserved. Why? She, Helga Crane, didn't admire it. She suspected that no Negroes, no Americans, did. Else why their

1. A permanent entertainment venue across from the train station.
2. Vaudeville tune popular in the 1920s.

constant slavish imitation of traits not their own? Why their constant begging to be considered as exact copies of other people?
Even the enlightened, the intelligent ones demanded nothing more.
They were all beggars like the motley crowd in the old nursery
rhyme:

> Hark! Hark!
> The dogs do bark.
> The beggars are coming to town.
> Some in rags,
> Some in tags,
> And some in velvet gowns.

The incident left her profoundly disquieted. Her old unhappy
questioning mood came again upon her, insidiously stealing away
more of the contentment from her transformed existence.

But she returned again and again to the Circus, always alone, gazing intently and solemnly at the gesticulating black figures, an ironical and silently speculative spectator. For she knew that into her
plan for her life had thrust itself a suspensive conflict in which were
fused doubts, rebellion, expediency, and urgent longings.

It was at this time that Axel Olsen asked her to marry him. And
now Helga Crane was surprised. It was a thing that at one time she
had much wanted, had tried to bring about, and had at last relin-
quished as impossible of achievement. Not so much because of its
apparent hopelessness as because of a feeling, intangible almost,
that, excited and pleased as he was with her, her origin a little
repelled him, and that, prompted by some impulse of racial antagonism, he had retreated into the fastness of a protecting habit of self-
ridicule. A mordantly personal pride and sensitiveness deterred
Helga from further efforts at incitation.

True, he had made, one morning, while holding his brush poised
for a last, a very last stroke on the portrait, one admirably draped
suggestion, speaking seemingly to the pictured face. Had he insin-
uated marriage, or something less—and easier? Or had he paid her
only a rather florid compliment, in somewhat dubious taste? Helga,
who had not at the time been quite sure, had remained silent, striving to appear unhearing.

Later, having thought it over, she flayed herself for a fool. It wasn't,
she should have known, in the manner of Axel Olsen to pay florid
compliments in questionable taste. And had it been marriage that
he had meant, he would, of course, have done the proper thing. He
wouldn't have stopped—or, rather, have begun—by making his
wishes known to her when there was Uncle Poul to be formally consulted. She had been, she told herself, insulted. And a goodly measure of contempt and wariness was added to her interest in the man.

She was able, however, to feel a gratifying sense of elation in the remembrance that she had been silent, ostensibly unaware of his utterance, and therefore, as far as he knew, not affronted.

This simplified things. It did away with the quandary in which the confession to the Dahls of such a happening would have involved her, for she couldn't be sure that they, too, might not put it down to the difference of her ancestry. And she could still go attended by him, and envied by others, to openings in Konigen's Nytorv,[3] to showings at the Royal Academy or Charlottenborg's Palace.[4] He could still call for her and Aunt Katrina of an afternoon or go with her to Magasin du Nord[5] to select a scarf or a length of silk, of which Uncle Poul could say casually in the presence of interested acquaintances: "Um, pretty scarf"—or "frock"—"you're wearing, Helga. Is that the new one Olsen helped you with?"

Her outward manner toward him changed not at all, save that gradually she became, perhaps, a little more detached and indifferent. But definitely Helga Crane had ceased, even remotely, to consider him other than as someone amusing, desirable, and convenient to have about—if one was careful. She intended, presently, to turn her attention to one of the others. The decorative Captain of the Hussars,[6] perhaps. But in the ache of her growing nostalgia, which, try as she might, she could not curb, she no longer thought with any seriousness on either Olsen or Captain Skaargaard. She must, she felt, see America again first. When she returned—

Therefore, where before she would have been pleased and proud at Olsen's proposal, she was now truly surprised. Strangely, she was aware also of a curious feeling of repugnance, as her eyes slid over his face, as smiling, assured, with just the right note of fervor, he made his declaration and request. She was astonished. Was it possible? Was it really this man that she had thought, even wished, she could marry?

He was, it was plain, certain of being accepted, as he was always certain of acceptance, of adulation, in any and every place that he deigned to honor with his presence. Well, Helga was thinking, that wasn't as much his fault as her own, her aunt's, everyone's. He was spoiled, childish almost.

To his words, once she had caught their content and recovered from her surprise, Helga paid not much attention. They would, she knew, be absolutely appropriate ones, and they didn't at all matter. They meant nothing to her—now. She was too amazed to discover suddenly how intensely she disliked him, disliked the shape of his

3. Copenhagen's old town center.
4. Locations used for fine art exhibitions in Kongen's Nytorv.
5. Department store.
6. The Royal Regiment of Danish Guards, protectors of the Royal Family.

head, the mop of his hair, the line of his nose, the tones of his voice, the nervous grace of his long fingers; disliked even the very look of his irreproachable clothes. And for some inexplicable reason, she was a little frightened and embarrassed, so that when he had finished speaking, for a short space there was only stillness in the small room, into which Aunt Katrina had tactfully had him shown. Even Thor, the enormous Persian, curled on the window ledge in the feeble late afternoon sun, had rested for the moment from his incessant purring under Helga's idly stroking fingers.

Helga, her slight agitation vanished, told him that she was surprised. His offer was, she said, unexpected. Quite.

A little sardonically, Olsen interrupted her. He smiled too. "But of course I expected surprise. It is, is it not, the proper thing? And always you are proper, Frøkken[7] Helga, always."

Helga, who had a stripped, naked feeling under his direct glance, drew herself up stiffly. Herr Olsen needn't, she told him, be sarcastic. She *was* surprised. He must understand that she was being quite sincere, quite truthful about that. Really, she hadn't expected him to do her so great an honor.

He made a little impatient gesture. Why, then, had she refused, ignored, his other, earlier suggestion?

At that Helga Crane took a deep indignant breath and was again, this time for an almost imperceptible second, silent. She had, then, been correct in her deduction. Her sensuous, petulant mouth hardened. That he should so frankly—so insolently, it seemed to her—admit his outrageous meaning was too much. She said, coldly: "Because, Herr Olsen, in my country the men, of my race, at least, don't make such suggestions to decent girls. And thinking that you were a gentleman, introduced to me by my aunt, I chose to think myself mistaken, to give you the benefit of the doubt."

"Very commendable, my Helga—and wise. Now you have your reward. Now I offer you marriage."

"Thanks," she answered, "thanks, awfully."

"Yes," and he reached for her slim cream hand, now lying quiet on Thor's broad orange and black back. Helga let it lie in his large pink one, noting their contrast. "Yes, because I, poor artist that I am, cannot hold out against the deliberate lure of you. You disturb me. The longing for you does harm to my work. You creep into my brain and madden me," and he kissed the small ivory hand. Quite decorously, Helga thought, for one so maddened that he was driven, against his inclination, to offer her marriage. But immediately, in extenuation, her mind leapt to the admirable casualness of Aunt Katrina's expressed desire for this very thing, and recalled the

7. Danish for "Miss"; now considered archaic; typically spelled with only one "k."

unruffled calm of Uncle Poul under any and all circumstances. It was, as she had long ago decided, security. Balance.

"But," the man before her was saying, "for me it will be an experience. It may be that with you, Helga, for wife, I will become great. Immortal. Who knows? I didn't want to love you, but I had to. That is the truth. I make of myself a present to you. For love." His voice held a theatrical note. At the same time he moved forward putting out his arms. His hands touched air. For Helga had moved back. Instantly he dropped his arms and took a step away, repelled by something suddenly wild in her face and manner. Sitting down, he passed a hand over his face with a quick, graceful gesture.

Tameness returned to Helga Crane. Her ironic gaze rested on the face of Axel Olsen, his leonine head, his broad nose—"broader than my own"—his bushy eyebrows, surmounting thick, drooping lids, which hid, she knew, sullen blue eyes. He stirred sharply, shaking off his momentary disconcertion.

In his assured, despotic way he went on: "You know, Helga, you are a contradiction. You have been, I suspect, corrupted by the good Fru Dahl, which is perhaps as well. Who knows? You have the warm impulsive nature of the women of Africa, but, my lovely, you have, I fear, the soul of a prostitute. You sell yourself to the highest buyer. I should of course be happy that it is I. And I am." He stopped, contemplating her, lost apparently, for the second, in pleasant thoughts of the future.

To Helga he seemed to be the most distant, the most unreal figure in the world. She suppressed a ridiculous impulse to laugh. The effort sobered her. Abruptly she was aware that in the end, in some way, she would pay for this hour. A quick brief fear ran through her, leaving in its wake a sense of impending calamity. She wondered if for this she would pay all that she'd had.

And, suddenly, she didn't at all care. She said, lightly, but firmly: "But you see, Herr Olsen, I'm not for sale. Not to you. Not to any white man. I don't at all care to be owned. Even by you."

The drooping lids lifted. The look in the blue eyes was, Helga thought, like the surprised stare of a puzzled baby. He hadn't at all grasped her meaning.

She proceeded, deliberately: "I think you don't understand me. What I'm trying to say is this, I don't want you. I wouldn't under any circumstances marry you," and since she was, as she put it, being brutally frank, she added: "*Now.*"

He turned a little away from her, his face white but composed, and looked down into the gathering shadows in the little park before the house. At last he spoke, in a queer frozen voice: "You refuse me?"

"Yes," Helga repeated with intentional carelessness. "I refuse you."

The man's full upper lip trembled. He wiped his forehead, where the gold hair was now lying flat and pale and lusterless. His eyes still avoided the girl in the high-backed chair before him. Helga felt a shiver of compunction. For an instant she regretted that she had not been a little kinder. But wasn't it after all the greatest kindness to be cruel? But more gently, less indifferently, she said: "You see, I couldn't marry a white man. I simply couldn't. It isn't just you, not just personal, you understand. It's deeper, broader than that. It's racial. Some day maybe you'll be glad. We can't tell, you know; if we were married, you might come to be ashamed of me, to hate me, to hate all dark people. My mother did that."

"I have offered you marriage, Helga Crane, and you answer me with some strange talk of race and shame. What nonsense is this?"

Helga let that pass because she couldn't, she felt, explain. It would be too difficult, too mortifying. She had no words which could adequately, and without laceration to her pride, convey to him the pitfalls into which very easily they might step. "I might," she said, "have considered it once—when I first came. But you, hoping for a more informal arrangement, waited too long. You missed the moment. I had time to think. Now I couldn't. Nothing is worth the risk. We might come to hate each other. I've been through it, or something like it. I know. I couldn't do it. And I'm glad."

Rising, she held out her hand, relieved that he was still silent. "Good afternoon," she said formally. "It has been a great honor—"

"A tragedy," he corrected, barely touching her hand with his moist finger-tips.

"Why?" Helga countered, and for an instant felt as if something sinister and internecine flew back and forth between them like poison.

"I mean," he said, and quite solemnly, "that though I don't entirely understand you, yet in a way I do too. And—" He hesitated. Went on. "I think that my picture of you is, after all, the true Helga Crane. Therefore—a tragedy. For someone. For me? Perhaps."

"Oh, the picture!" Helga lifted her shoulders in a little impatient motion.

Ceremoniously Axel Olsen bowed himself out, leaving her grateful for the urbanity which permitted them to part without too much awkwardness. No other man, she thought, of her acquaintance could have managed it so well—except, perhaps, Robert Anderson.

"I'm glad," she declared to herself in another moment, "that I refused him. And," she added honestly, "I'm glad that I had the chance. He took it awfully well, though—for a tragedy." And she made a tiny frown.

The picture—she had never quite, in spite of her deep interest in him, and her desire for his admiration and approval, forgiven Olsen for that portrait. It wasn't, she contended, herself at all, but some disgusting sensual creature with her features. Herr and Fru Dahl had not exactly liked it either, although collectors, artists, and critics had been unanimous in their praise and it had been hung on the line at an annual exhibition, where it had attracted much flattering attention and many tempting offers.

Now Helga went in and stood for a long time before it, with its creator's parting words in mind: ". . . a tragedy . . . my picture is, after all, the true Helga Crane." Vehemently she shook her head. "It isn't, it isn't at all," she said aloud. Bosh! Pure artistic bosh and conceit. Nothing else. Anyone with half an eye could see that it wasn't, at all, like her.

"Marie," she called to the maid passing in the hall, "do you think this is a good picture of me?"

Marie blushed. Hesitated. "Of course, Frøkken, I know Herr Olsen is a great artist, but no, I don't like that picture. It looks bad, wicked. Begging your pardon, Frøkken."

"Thanks, Marie, I don't like it either."

Yes, anyone with half an eye could see that it wasn't she.

SIXTEEN

Glad though the Dahls may have been that their niece had had the chance of refusing the hand of Axel Olsen, they were anything but glad that she had taken that chance. Very plainly they said so, and quite firmly they pointed out to her the advisability of retrieving the opportunity, if, indeed, such a thing were possible. But it wasn't, even had Helga been so inclined, for, they were to learn from the columns of *Politikken,* Axel Olsen had gone off suddenly to some queer place in the Balkans. To rest, the newspapers said. To get Frøkken Crane out of his mind, the gossips said.

Life in the Dahl ménage went on, smoothly as before, but not so pleasantly. The combined disappointment and sense of guilt of the Dahls and Helga colored everything. Though she had resolved not to think that they felt that she had, as it were, "let them down," Helga knew that they did. They had not so much expected as hoped that she would bring down Olsen, and so secure the link between the merely fashionable set to which they belonged and the artistic one after which they hankered. It was of course true that there were others, plenty of them. But there was only one Olsen. And Helga, for some idiotic reason connected with race, had refused him. Certainly there was no use in thinking, even, of the others. If she had refused him, she would refuse any and all for the same reason. It was, it seemed, all-embracing.

"It isn't," Uncle Poul had tried to point out to her, "as if there were hundreds of mulattoes here. That, I can understand, might make it a little different. But there's only you. You're unique here, don't you see? Besides, Olsen has money and enviable position. Nobody'd dare to say, or even to think anything odd or unkind of you or him. Come now, Helga, it isn't this foolishness about race. Not here in Denmark. You've never spoken of it before. It can't be just that. You're too sensible. It must be something else. I wish you'd try to explain. You don't perhaps like Olsen?"

Helga had been silent, thinking what a severe wrench to Herr Dahl's ideas of decency was this conversation. For he had an almost fanatic regard for reticence, and a peculiar shrinking from what he looked upon as indecent exposure of the emotions.

"Just what is it, Helga?" he asked again, because the pause had grown awkward, for him.

"I can't explain any better than I have," she had begun tremulously, "it's just something—something deep down inside of me," and had turned away to hide a face convulsed by threatening tears.

But that, Uncle Poul had remarked with a reasonableness that was wasted on the miserable girl before him, was nonsense, pure nonsense.

With a shaking sigh and a frantic dab at her eyes, in which had come a despairing look, she had agreed that perhaps it was foolish, but she couldn't help it. "Can't you, won't you understand, Uncle Poul?" she begged, with a pleading look at the kindly worldly man who at that moment had been thinking that this strange exotic niece of his wife's was indeed charming. He didn't blame Olsen for taking it rather hard.

The thought passed. She was weeping. With no effort at restraint. Charming, yes. But insufficiently civilized. Impulsive. Imprudent. Selfish.

"Try, Helga, to control yourself," he had urged gently. He detested tears. "If it distresses you so, we won't talk of it again. You, of course, must do as you yourself wish. Both your aunt and I want only that you should be happy." He had wanted to make an end of this fruitless wet conversation.

Helga had made another little dab at her face with the scrap of lace and raised shining eyes to his face. She had said, with sincere regret: "You've been marvelous to me, you and Aunt Katrina. Angelic. I don't want to seem ungrateful. I'd do anything for you, anything in the world but this."

Herr Dahl had shrugged. A little sardonically he had smiled. He had refrained from pointing out that this was the only thing she could do for them, the only thing that they had asked of her. He had been too glad to be through with the uncomfortable discussion.

So life went on. Dinners, coffees, theaters, pictures, music, clothes. More dinners, coffees, theaters, clothes, music. And that nagging aching for America increased. Augmented by the uncomfortableness of Aunt Katrina's and Uncle Poul's disappointment with her, that tormenting nostalgia grew to an unbearable weight. As spring came on with many gracious tokens of following summer, she found her thoughts straying with increasing frequency to Anne's letter and to Harlem, its dirty streets, swollen now, in the warmer weather, with dark, gay humanity.

Until recently she had had no faintest wish ever to see America again. Now she began to welcome the thought of a return. Only a visit, of course. Just to see, to prove to herself that there was nothing there for her. To demonstrate the absurdity of even thinking that there could be. And to relieve the slight tension here. Maybe when she came back—

Her definite decision to go was arrived at with almost bewildering suddenness. It was after a concert at which Dvořák's "New World Symphony"[1] had been wonderfully rendered. Those wailing undertones of "Swing Low, Sweet Chariot" were too poignantly familiar. They struck into her longing heart and cut away her weakening defenses. She knew at least what it was that had lurked formless and undesignated these many weeks in the back of her troubled mind. Incompleteness.

"I'm homesick, not for America, but for Negroes. That's the trouble."

For the first time Helga Crane felt sympathy rather than contempt and hatred for that father, who so often and so angrily she had blamed for his desertion of her mother. She understood, now, his rejection, his repudiation, of the formal calm her mother had represented. She understood his yearning, his intolerable need for the inexhaustible humor and the incessant hope of his own kind, his need for those things, not material, indigenous to all Negro environments. She understood and could sympathize with his facile surrender to the irresistible ties of race, now that they dragged at her own heart. And as she attended parties, the theater, the opera, and mingled with people on the streets, meeting only pale serious faces when she longed for brown laughing ones, she was able to forgive him. Also, it was as if in this understanding and forgiving she had come upon knowledge of almost sacred importance.

---

1. Antonin Dvořák (1841–1904), Czech composer whose "New World" symphony, also known as Symphony no. 9, composed in 1893, was based on African American spirituals including "Going Home" and "Swing Low, Sweet Chariot" and composed in collaboration with African American musician Harry Burleigh. The narrator of James Weldon Johnson's *Autobiography of an Ex-Colored Man* (1912) imagines himself undertaking a grand project, very like an extensive version of Dvořák's popular symphony.

Without demur, opposition, or recrimination Herr and Fru Dahl accepted Helga's decision to go back to America. She had expected that they would be glad and relieved. It was agreeable to discover that she had done them less than justice. They were, in spite of their extreme worldliness, very fond of her, and would, as they declared, miss her greatly. And they did want her to come back to them, as they repeatedly insisted. Secretly they felt as she did, that perhaps when she returned— So it was agreed upon that it was only for a brief visit, "for your friend's wedding," and that she was to return in the early fall.

The last day came. The last good-byes were said. Helga began to regret that she was leaving. Why couldn't she have two lives, or why couldn't she be satisfied in one place? Now that she was actually off, she felt heavy at heart. Already she looked back with infinite regret at the two years in the country which had given her so much, of pride, of happiness, of wealth, and of beauty.

Bells rang. The gangplank was hoisted. The dark strip of water widened. The running figures of friends suddenly grown very dear grew smaller, blurred into a whole, and vanished. Tears rose in Helga Crane's eyes, fear in her heart.

Good-bye Denmark! Good-bye. Good-bye!

SEVENTEEN

A SUMMER had ripened and fall begun. Anne and Dr. Anderson had returned from their short Canadian wedding journey. Helga Crane, lingering still in America, had tactfully removed herself from the house in One Hundred and Thirty-ninth Street to a hotel. It was, as she could point out to curious acquaintants, much better for the newly-married Andersons not to be bothered with a guest, not even with such a close friend as she, Helga, had been to Anne.

Actually, though she herself had truly wanted to get out of the house when they came back, she had been a little surprised and a great deal hurt that Anne had consented so readily to her going. She might at least, thought Helga indignantly, have acted a little bit as if she had wanted her to stay. After writing for her to come, too.

Pleasantly unaware was Helga that Anne, more silently wise than herself, more determined, more selfish, and less inclined to leave anything to chance, understood perfectly that in a large measure it was the voice of Robert Anderson's inexorable conscience that had been the chief factor in bringing about her second marriage— his ascetic protest against the sensuous, the physical. Anne had perceived that the decorous surface of her new husband's mind regarded Helga Crane with that intellectual and æsthetic appreciation which attractive and intelligent women would always draw from him, but that underneath that well-managed section, in a more lawless place where she herself never hoped or desired to enter, was another, a vagrant primitive groping toward something shocking and frightening to the cold asceticism of his reason. Anne knew also that though she herself was lovely—more beautiful than Helga—and interesting, with her he had not to struggle against that nameless and to him shameful impulse, that sheer delight, which ran through his nerves at mere proximity to Helga. And Anne intended that her marriage should be a success. She intended that her husband should be happy. She was sure that it could be managed by tact and a little cleverness on her own part. She was truly fond of Helga, but seeing how she had grown more charming, more aware of her power, Anne wasn't so sure that her sincere and urgent request to come over for her wedding hadn't been a mistake. She was, however, certain of herself. She could look out for her husband. She could carry out what she considered her obligation to him, keep him undisturbed, unhumiliated. It was impossible that she could fail. Unthinkable.

Helga, on her part, had been glad to get back to New York. How glad, or why, she did not truly realize. And though she sincerely meant to keep her promise to Aunt Katrina and Uncle Poul and return to Copenhagen, summer, September, October, slid by and she made no move to go. Her uttermost intention had been a six or eight weeks' visit, but the feverish rush of New York, the comic tragedy of Harlem, still held her. As time went on, she became a little bored, a little restless, but she stayed on. Something of that wild surge of gladness that had swept her on the day when with Anne and Anderson she had again found herself surrounded by hundreds, thousands, of dark-eyed brown folk remained with her. *These* were her people. Nothing, she had come to understand now, could ever change that. Strange that she had never truly valued this kinship until distance had shown her its worth. How absurd she had been to think that another country, other people, could liberate her from the ties which bound her forever to these mysterious, these terrible, these fascinating, these lovable, dark hordes. Ties that were of the spirit. Ties not only superficially entangled with mere outline of features or color of skin. Deeper. Much deeper than either of these.

Thankful for the appeasement of that loneliness which had again tormented her like a fury, she gave herself up to the miraculous joyousness of Harlem. The easement which its heedless abandon brought to her was a real, a very definite thing. She liked the sharp contrast to her pretentious stately life in Copenhagen. It was as if she had passed from the heavy solemnity of a church service to a gorgeous care-free revel.

Not that she intended to remain. No. Helga Crane couldn't, she told herself and others, live in America. In spite of its glamour, existence in America, even in Harlem, was for Negroes too cramped, too uncertain, too cruel; something not to be endured for a lifetime if one could escape; something demanding a courage greater than was in her. No. She couldn't stay. Nor, she saw now, could she remain away. Leaving, she would have to come back.

This knowledge, this certainty of the division of her life into two parts in two lands, into physical freedom in Europe and spiritual freedom in America, was unfortunate, inconvenient, expensive. It was, too, as she was uncomfortably aware, even a trifle ridiculous, and mentally she caricatured herself moving shuttle-like from continent to continent. From the prejudiced restrictions of the New World to the easy formality of the Old, from the pale calm of Copenhagen to the colorful lure of Harlem.

Nevertheless she felt a slightly pitying superiority over those Negroes who were apparently so satisfied. And she had a fine contempt for the blatantly patriotic black Americans. Always when she encountered one of those picturesque parades in the Harlem streets, the Stars and Stripes streaming ironically, insolently, at the head of the procession tempered for her, a little, her amusement at the childish seriousness of the spectacle. It was too pathetic.

But when mental doors were deliberately shut on those skeletons that stalked lively and in full health through the consciousness of every person of Negro ancestry in America—conspicuous black, obvious brown, or indistinguishable white—life was intensely amusing, interesting, absorbing, and enjoyable; singularly lacking in that tone of anxiety which the insecurities of existence seemed to ferment in other peoples.

Yet Helga herself had an acute feeling of insecurity, for which she could not account. Sometimes it amounted to fright almost. "I must," she would say then, "get back to Copenhagen." But the resolution gave her not much pleasure. And for this she now blamed Axel Olsen. It was, she insisted, he who had driven her back, made her unhappy in Denmark. Though she knew well that it wasn't. Misgivings, too, rose in her. Why hadn't she married him? Anne was married—she would not say Anderson— Why not she? It would serve Anne right if she married a white man. But she knew in her soul that she wouldn't. "Because I'm a fool," she said bitterly.

EIGHTEEN

ONE November evening, impregnated still with the kindly warmth of the dead Indian summer, Helga Crane was leisurely dressing in pleasant anticipation of the party to which she had been asked for that night. It was always amusing at the Tavenors'. Their house was large and comfortable, the food and music always of the best, and the type of entertainment always unexpected and brilliant. The drinks, too, were sure to be safe.

And Helga, since her return, was more than ever popular at parties. Her courageous clothes attracted attention, and her deliberate lure—as Olsen had called it—held it. Her life in Copenhagen had taught her to expect and accept admiration as her due. This attitude, she found, was as effective in New York as across the sea. It was, in fact, even more so. And it was more amusing too. Perhaps because it was somehow a bit more dangerous.

In the midst of curious speculation as to the possible identity of the other guests, with an indefinite sense of annoyance she wondered if Anne would be there. There was of late something about Anne that was to Helga distinctly disagreeable, a peculiar half-patronizing attitude, mixed faintly with distrust. Helga couldn't define it, couldn't account for it. She had tried. In the end she had decided to dismiss it, to ignore it.

"I suppose," she said aloud, "it's because she's married again. As if anybody couldn't get married. Anybody. That is, if mere marriage is all one wants."

Smoothing away the tiny frown from between the broad black brows, she got herself into a little shining, rose-colored slip of a frock knotted with a silver cord. The gratifying result soothed her ruffled feelings. It didn't really matter, this new manner of Anne's. Nor did the fact that Helga knew that Anne disapproved of her. Without words Anne had managed to make that evident. In her opinion, Helga had lived too long among the enemy, the detestable pale faces. She understood them too well, was too tolerant of their ignorant stupidities. If they had been Latins, Anne might conceivably have forgiven the disloyalty. But Nordics! Lynchers! It was too traitorous. Helga smiled a little, understanding Anne's bitterness and hate, and a little of its cause. It was of a piece with that of those she so virulently hated. Fear. And then she sighed a little, for she regretted the waning of Anne's friendship. But, in view of diverging courses of their lives, she felt that even its complete extinction would leave her undevastated. Not that she wasn't still grateful to Anne for many things. It was only that she had other things now. And there would, forever, be Robert Anderson between them. A nuisance. Shutting them off from their previous confident companionship and understanding. "And anyway," she said again, aloud, "he's nobody much to have married. Anybody could have married him. Anybody. If a person wanted only to be married— If it had been somebody like Olsen— That would be different—something to crow over, perhaps."

The party was even more interesting than Helga had expected. Helen, Mrs. Tavenor, had given vent to a malicious glee, and had invited representatives of several opposing Harlem political and social factions, including the West Indian, and abandoned them helplessly to each other. Helga's observing eyes picked out several great and near-great sulking or obviously trying hard not to sulk in widely separated places in the big rooms. There were present, also, a few white people, to the open disapproval or discomfort of Anne and several others. There too, poised, serene, certain, surrounded by masculine black and white, was Audrey Denney.

"Do you know, Helen," Helga confided, "I've never met Miss Denney. I wish you'd introduce me. Not this minute. Later, when you can manage it. Not so—er—apparently by request, you know."

Helen Tavenor laughed. "No, you wouldn't have met her, living as you did with Anne Grey. Anderson, I mean. She's Anne's particular pet aversion. The mere sight of Audrey is enough to send her into a frenzy for a week. It's too bad, too, because Audrey's an awfully interesting person and Anne's said some pretty awful things about her. *You'll* like her, Helga."

Helga nodded. "Yes, I expect to. And I know about Anne. One night—" She stopped, for across the room she saw, with a stab of surprise, James Vayle. "Where, Helen, did you get him?"

"Oh, that? That's something the cat brought in. Don't ask which one. He came with somebody, I don't remember who. I think he's shocked to death. Isn't he lovely? The dear baby. I was going to introduce him to Audrey and tell her to do a good job of vamping on him as soon as I could remember the darling's name, or when it got noisy enough so he wouldn't hear what I called him. But you'll do just as well. Don't tell me you know him!" Helga made a little nod. "Well! And I suppose you met him at some shockingly wicked place in Europe. That's always the way with those innocent-looking men."

"Not quite. I met him ages ago in Naxos. We were engaged to be married. Nice, isn't he? His name's Vayle. James Vayle."

"Nice," said Helen throwing out her hands in a characteristic dramatic gesture—she had beautiful hands and arms—"is exactly the word. Mind if I run off? I've got somebody here who's going to sing. *Not* spirituals. And I haven't the faintest notion where he's got to. The cellar, I'll bet."

James Vayle hadn't, Helga decided, changed at all. Someone claimed her for a dance and it was some time before she caught his eyes, half questioning, upon her. When she did, she smiled in a friendly way over her partner's shoulder and was rewarded by a dignified little bow. Inwardly she grinned, flattered. He hadn't forgotten. He was still hurt. The dance over, she deserted her partner and deliberately made her way across the room to James Vayle. He was for the moment embarrassed and uncertain. Helga Crane, however, took care of that, thinking meanwhile that Helen was right. Here he did seem frightfully young and delightfully unsophisticated. He must be, though, every bit of thirty-two or more.

"They say," was her bantering greeting, "that if one stands on the corner of One Hundred and Thirty-fifth Street and Seventh Avenue[1] long enough, one will eventually see all the people one has ever known or met. It's pretty true, I guess. Not literally of course." He was, she saw, getting himself together. "It's only another way of saying that everybody, almost, some time sooner or later comes to Harlem, even you."

He laughed. "Yes, I guess that is true enough. I didn't come to stay, though." And then he was grave, his earnest eyes searchingly upon her.

"Well, anyway, you're here now, so let's find a quiet corner if that's possible, where we can talk. I want to hear all about you."

For a moment he hung back and a glint of mischief shone in Helga's eyes. "I see," she said, "you're just the same. However, you needn't be anxious. This isn't Naxos, you know. Nobody's watching us, or if they are, they don't care a bit what we do."

At that he flushed a little, protested a little, and followed her. And when at last they had found seats in another room, not so crowded, he said: "I didn't expect to see you here. I thought you were still abroad."

"Oh, I've been back some time, ever since Dr. Anderson's marriage. Anne, you know, is a great friend of mine. I used to live with her. I came for the wedding. But, of course, I'm not staying. I didn't think I'd be here this long."

"You don't mean that you're going to live over there? Do you really like it so much better?"

"Yes and no, to both questions. I was awfully glad to get back, but I wouldn't live here always. I couldn't. I don't think that any of us who've lived abroad for any length of time would ever live here altogether again if they could help it."

"Lot of them do, though," James Vayle pointed out.

"Oh, I don't mean tourists who rush over to Europe and rush all over the continent and rush back to America thinking they know Europe. I mean people who've actually lived there, actually lived among the people."

"I still maintain that they nearly all come back here eventually to live."

"That's because they can't help it," Helga Crane said firmly. "Money, you know."

---

1. The intersection of Harlem's two main thoroughfares; the center of Harlem.

"Perhaps, I'm not so sure. I was in the war. Of course, that's not really living over there, but I saw the country and the difference in treatment. But, I can tell you, I was pretty darn glad to get back. All the fellows were." He shook his head solemnly. "I don't think anything, money or lack of money, keeps us here. If it was only that, if we really wanted to leave, we'd go all right. No, it's something else, something deeper than that."

"And just what do you think it is?"

"I'm afraid it's hard to explain, but I suppose it's just that we like to be together. I simply can't imagine living forever away from colored people."

A suspicion of a frown drew Helga's brows. She threw out rather tartly: "I'm a Negro too, you know."

"Well, Helga, you were always a little different, a little dissatisfied, though I don't pretend to understand you at all. I never did," he said a little wistfully.

And Helga, who was beginning to feel that the conversation had taken an impersonal and disappointing tone, was reassured and gave him her most sympathetic smile and said almost gently: "And now let's talk about you. You're still at Naxos?"

"Yes I'm still there. I'm assistant principal now."

Plainly it was a cause for enthusiastic congratulation, but Helga could only manage a tepid "How nice!" Naxos was to her too remote, too unimportant. She did not even hate it now.

How long, she asked, would James be in New York?

He couldn't say. Business, important business for the school, had brought him. It was, he said, another tone creeping into his voice, another look stealing over his face, awfully good to see her. She was looking tremendously well. He hoped he would have the opportunity of seeing her again.

But of course. He must come to see her. Any time, she was always in, or would be for him. And how did he like New York, Harlem?

He didn't, it seemed, like it. It was nice to visit, but not to live in. Oh, there were so many things he didn't like about it, the rush, the lack of home life, the crowds, the noisy meaninglessness of it all.

On Helga's face there had come that pityingly sneering look peculiar to imported New Yorkers when the city of their adoption is attacked by alien Americans. With polite contempt she inquired: "And is that all you don't like?"

At her tone the man's bronze face went purple. He answered coldly, slowly, with a faint gesture in the direction of Helen Tavenor, who stood conversing gayly with one of her white guests: "And I don't like that sort of thing. In fact I detest it."

"Why?" Helga was striving hard to be casual in her manner.

James Vayle, it was evident, was beginning to be angry. It was also evident that Helga Crane's question had embarrassed him. But he seized the bull by the horns and said: "You know as well as I do, Helga, that it's the colored girls these men come up here to see. They wouldn't think of bringing their wives." And he blushed furiously at his own implication. The blush restored Helga's good temper. James was really too funny.

"That," she said softly, "is Hugh Wentworth,[2] the novelist, you know." And she indicated a tall olive-skinned girl[3] being whirled about to the streaming music in the arms of a towering black man. "And that is his wife. She isn't colored, as you've probably been thinking. And now let's change the subject again."

"All right! And this time let's talk about you. You say you don't intend to live here. Don't you ever intend to marry, Helga?"

"Some day, perhaps. I don't know. Marriage—that means children, to me. And why add more suffering to the world? Why add any more unwanted, tortured Negroes to America? Why *do* Negroes have children? Surely it must be sinful. Think of the awfulness of being responsible for the giving of life to creatures doomed to endure such wounds to the flesh, such wounds to the spirit, as Negroes have to endure."

James was aghast. He forgot to be embarrassed. "But Helga! Good heavens! Don't you see that if we—I mean people like us—don't have children, the others will still have. That's one of the things that's the matter with us. The race is sterile at the top. Few, very few Negroes of the better class have children, and each generation has to wrestle again with the obstacles of the preceding ones, lack of money, education, and background. I feel very strongly about this. We're the ones who must have the children if the race is to get anywhere."

"Well, I for one don't intend to contribute any to the cause. But how serious we are! And I'm afraid that I've really got to leave you. I've already cut two dances for your sake. Do come to see me."

"Oh, I'll come to see you all right. I've got several things that I want to talk to you about and one thing especially."

"Don't," Helga mocked, "tell me you're going to ask me again to marry you."

"That," he said, "is just what I intend to do."

Helga Crane was suddenly deeply ashamed and very sorry for James Vayle, so she told him laughingly that it was shameful of him to joke with her like that, and before he could answer, she had gone

<hr />

2. Wentworth is modeled on Carl Van Vechten and also makes an appearance in *Passing*.
3. Van Vechten's wife, Fania Marinoff. Jews, like Marinoff, who was originally Fanny Marinoff, were often referred to as "olive-skinned."

tripping off with a handsome coffee-colored youth whom she had beckoned from across the room with a little smile.

Later she had to go upstairs to pin up a place in the hem of her dress which had caught on a sharp chair corner. She finished the temporary repair and stepped out into the hall, and somehow, she never quite knew exactly just how, into the arms of Robert Anderson. She drew back and looked up smiling to offer an apology.

And then it happened. He stooped and kissed her, a long kiss, holding her close. She fought against him with all her might. Then, strangely, all power seemed to ebb away, and a long-hidden, half-understood desire welled up in her with the suddenness of a dream. Helga Crane's own arms went up about the man's neck. When she drew away, consciously confused and embarrassed, everything seemed to have changed in a space of time which she knew to have been only seconds. Sudden anger seized her. She pushed him indignantly aside and with a little pat for her hair and dress went slowly down to the others.

NINETEEN

THAT night riotous and colorful dreams invaded Helga Crane's prim hotel bed. She woke in the morning weary and a bit shocked at the uncontrolled fancies which had visited her. Catching up a filmy scarf, she paced back and forth across the narrow room and tried to think. She recalled her flirtations and her mild engagement with James Vayle. She was used to kisses. But none had been like that of last night. She lived over those brief seconds, thinking not so much of the man whose arms had held her as of the ecstasy which had flooded her. Even recollection brought a little onrush of emotion that made her sway a little. She pulled herself together and began to fasten on the solid fact of Anne and experienced a pleasant sense of shock in the realization that Anne was to her exactly what she had been before the incomprehensible experience of last night. She still liked her in the same degree and in the same manner. She still felt slightly annoyed with her. She still did not envy her marriage with Anderson. By some mysterious process the emotional upheaval which had racked her had left all the rocks of her existence unmoved. Outwardly nothing had changed.

Days, weeks, passed; outwardly serene; inwardly tumultous. Helga met Dr. Anderson at the social affairs to which often they were both asked. Sometimes she danced with him, always in perfect silence. She couldn't, she absolutely couldn't, speak a word to him when they were thus alone together, for at such times lassitude encompassed her; the emotion which had gripped her retreated, leaving a strange tranquillity, troubled only by a soft stir of desire. And shamed by his silence, his apparent forgetting, always after these dances she tried desperately to persuade herself to believe what she wanted to believe: that it had not happened, that she had never had that irrepressible longing. It was of no use.

As the weeks multiplied, she became aware that she must get herself out of the mental quagmire into which that kiss had thrown her. And she should be getting herself back to Copenhagen, but she had now no desire to go.

Abruptly one Sunday in a crowded room, in the midst of teacups and chatter, she knew that she couldn't go, that she hadn't since that kiss intended to go without exploring to the end that unfamiliar path into which she had strayed. Well, it was of no use lagging behind or pulling back. It was of no use trying to persuade herself that she didn't want to go on. A species of fatalism fastened on her. She felt that, ever since that last day in Naxos long ago, somehow she had known that this thing would happen. With this conviction came an odd sense of elation. While making a pleasant assent to some remark of a fellow guest she put down her cup and walked without haste, smiling and nodding to friends and acquaintances on her way to that part of the room where he stood looking at some examples of African carving. Helga Crane faced him squarely. As he took the hand which she held out with elaborate casualness, she noted that his trembled slightly. She was secretly congratulating herself on her own calm when it failed her. Physical weariness descended on her. Her knees wobbled. Gratefully she slid into the chair which he hastily placed for her. Timidity came over her. She was silent. He talked. She did not listen. He came at last to the end of his long dissertation on African sculpture, and Helga Crane felt the intentness of his gaze upon her.

"Well?" she questioned.

"I want very much to see you, Helga. Alone."

She held herself tensely on the edge of her chair, and suggested: "Tomorrow?"

He hesitated a second and then said quickly: "Why, yes, that's all right."

"Eight o'clock?"

"Eight o'clock," he agreed.

Eight o'clock tomorrow came. Helga Crane never forgot it. She had carried away from yesterday's meeting a feeling of increasing elation. It had seemed to her that she hadn't been so happy, so exalted, in years, if ever. All night, all day, she had mentally prepared herself for the coming consummation; physically too, spending hours before the mirror.

Eight o'clock had come at last and with it Dr. Anderson. Only then had uneasiness come upon her and a feeling of fear for possible exposure. For Helga Crane wasn't, after all, a rebel from society, Negro society. It did mean something to her. She had no wish to stand alone. But these late fears were overwhelmed by the hardiness of insistent desire; and she had got herself down to the hotel's small reception room.

It was, he had said, awfully good of her to see him. She instantly protested. No, she had wanted to see him. He looked at her surprised. "You know, Helga," he had begun with an air of desperation, "I can't forgive myself for acting such a swine at the Tavenors' party. I don't at all blame you for being angry and not speaking to me except when you had to."

But that, she exclaimed, was simply too ridiculous. "I wasn't angry a bit." And it had seemed to her that things were not exactly going forward as they should. It seemed that he had been very sincere, and very formal. Deliberately. She had looked down at her hands and inspected her bracelets, for she had felt that to look at him would be, under the circumstances, too exposing.

"I was afraid," he went on, "that you might have misunderstood; might have been unhappy about it. I could kick myself. It was, it must have been, Tavenor's rotten cocktails."

Helga Crane's sense of elation had abruptly left her. At the same time she had felt the need to answer carefully. No, she replied, she hadn't thought of it at all. It had meant nothing to her. She had been kissed before. It was really too silly of him to have been at all bothered about it. "For what," she had asked, "is one kiss more or less, these days, between friends?" She had even laughed a little.

Dr. Anderson was relieved. He had been, he told her, no end upset. Rising, he said: "I see you're going out. I won't keep you."

Helga Crane too had risen. Quickly. A sort of madness had swept over her. She felt that he had belittled and ridiculed her. And thinking this, she had suddenly savagely slapped Robert Anderson with all her might, in the face.

For a short moment they had both stood stunned, in the deep silence which had followed that resounding slap. Then, without a word of contrition or apology, Helga Crane had gone out of the room and upstairs.

She had, she told herself, been perfectly justified in slapping Dr. Anderson, but she was not convinced. So she had tried hard to make herself very drunk in order that sleep might come to her, but had managed only to make herself very sick.

Not even the memory of how all living had left his face, which had gone a taupe gray hue, or the despairing way in which he had lifted his head and let it drop, or the trembling hands which he had pressed into his pockets, brought her any scrap of comfort. She had ruined everything. Ruined it because she had been so silly as to close her eyes to all indications that pointed to the fact that no matter what the intensity of his feelings or desires might be, he was not the sort of man who would for any reason give up one particle of his own good opinion of himself. Not even for her. Not even though he knew that she had wanted so terribly something special from him.

Something special. And now she had forfeited it forever. Forever. Helga had an instantaneous shocking perception of what forever meant. And then, like a flash, it was gone, leaving an endless stretch of dreary years before her appalled vision.

TWENTY

THE day was a rainy one. Helga Crane, stretched out on her bed, felt herself so broken physically, mentally, that she had given up thinking. But back and forth in her staggered brain wavering, incoherent thoughts shot shuttle-like. Her pride would have shut out these humiliating thoughts and painful visions of herself. The effort was too great. She felt alone, isolated from all other human beings, separated even from her own anterior existence by the disaster of yesterday. Over and over, she repeated: "There's nothing left but to go now." Her anguish seemed unbearable.

For days, for weeks, voluptuous visions had haunted her. Desire had burned in her flesh with uncontrollable violence. The wish to give herself had been so intense that Dr. Anderson's surprising, trivial apology loomed as a direct refusal of the offering. Whatever outcome she had expected, it had been something else than this, this mortification, this feeling of ridicule and self-loathing, this knowledge that she had deluded herself. It was all, she told herself, as unpleasant as possible.

Almost she wished she could die. Not quite. It wasn't that she was afraid of death, which had, she thought, its picturesque aspects. It was rather that she knew she would not die. And death, after the debacle, would but intensify its absurdity. Also, it would reduce her, Helga Crane, to unimportance, to nothingness. Even in her unhappy present state, that did not appeal to her. Gradually, reluctantly, she began to know that the blow to her self-esteem, the certainty of having proved herself a silly fool, was perhaps the severest hurt which she had suffered. It was her self-assurance that had gone down in the crash. After all, what Dr. Anderson thought didn't matter. She could escape from the discomfort of his knowing gray eyes. But she couldn't escape from sure knowledge that she had made a fool of herself. This angered her further and she struck the wall with her hands and jumped up and began hastily to dress herself. She couldn't go on with the analysis. It was too hard. Why bother, when she could add nothing to the obvious fact that she had been a fool?

"I can't stay in this room any longer. I must get out or I'll choke." Her self-knowledge had increased her anguish. Distracted, agitated, incapable of containing herself, she tore open drawers and closets trying desperately to take some interest in the selection of her apparel.

It was evening and still raining. In the streets, unusually deserted, the electric lights cast dull glows. Helga Crane, walking rapidly, aimlessly, could decide on no definite destination. She had not thought to take umbrella or even rubbers. Rain and wind whipped cruelly about her, drenching her garments and chilling her body. Soon the foolish little satin shoes which she wore were sopping wet. Unheeding these physical discomforts, she went on, but at the open corner of One Hundred and Thirty-eighth Street a sudden more ruthless gust of wind ripped the small hat from her head. In the next minute the black clouds opened wider and spilled their water with unusual fury. The streets became swirling rivers. Helga Crane, forgetting her mental torment, looked about anxiously for a sheltering taxi. A few taxis sped by, but inhabited, so she began desperately to struggle through wind and rain toward one of the buildings, where she could take shelter in a store or a doorway. But another whirl of wind lashed her and, scornful of her slight strength, tossed her into the swollen gutter.

Now she knew beyond all doubt that she had no desire to die, and certainly not there nor then. Not in such a messy wet manner. Death had lost all of its picturesque aspects to the girl lying soaked and soiled in the flooded gutter. So, though she was very tired and very weak, she dragged herself up and succeeded finally in making her way to the store whose blurred light she had marked for her destination.

She had opened the door and had entered before she was aware that, inside, people were singing a song which she was conscious of having heard years ago—hundreds of years it seemed. Repeated over and over, she made out the words:

> . . . *Showers of blessings,*
> *Showers of blessings . . .*[1]

---

1. Hymn, taken from Ezekiel 34:26 and set to music. "Helga" comes from "helgel," meaning "blessing" in Danish.

She was conscious too of a hundred pairs of eyes upon her as she stood there, drenched and disheveled, at the door of this improvised meeting-house.

. . . *Showers of blessings* . . .

The appropriateness of the song, with its constant reference to showers, the ridiculousness of herself in such surroundings, was too much for Helga Crane's frayed nerves. She sat down on the floor, a dripping heap, and laughed and laughed and laughed.

It was into a shocked silence that she laughed. For at the first hysterical peal the words of the song had died in the singers' throats, and the wheezy organ had lapsed into stillness. But in a moment there were hushed solicitous voices; she was assisted to her feet and led haltingly to a chair near the low platform at the far end of the room. On one side of her a tall angular black woman under a queer hat sat down, on the other a fattish yellow man with huge outstanding ears and long, nervous hands.

The singing began again, this time a low wailing thing:

> *Oh, the bitter shame and sorrow*
> *That a time could ever be,*
> *When I let the Savior's pity*
> *Plead in vain, and proudly answered:*
> *"All of self and none of Thee,*
> *All of self and none of Thee."*
>
> *Yet He found me, I beheld Him,*
> *Bleeding on the cursed tree;*
> *Heard Him pray: "Forgive them, Father."*
> *And my wistful heart said faintly,*
> *"Some of self and some of Thee,*
> *Some of self and some of Thee."*

There were, it appeared, endless moaning verses. Behind Helga a woman had begun to cry audibly, and soon, somewhere else, another. Outside, the wind still bellowed. The wailing singing went on:

> . . . *Less of self and more of Thee,*
> *Less of self and more of Thee.*

Helga too began to weep, at first silently, softly; then with great racking sobs. Her nerves were so torn, so aching, her body so wet, so cold! It was a relief to cry unrestrainedly, and she gave herself freely to soothing tears, not noticing that the groaning and sobbing of those about her had increased, unaware that the grotesque ebony figure at her side had begun gently to pat her arm to the rhythm of the singing

and to croon softly: "Yes, chile, yes, chile." Nor did she notice the
furtive glances that the man on her other side cast at her between his
fervent shouts of "Amen!" and "Praise God for a sinner!"

She did notice, though, that the tempo, the atmosphere of the
place, had changed, and gradually she ceased to weep and gave
her attention to what was happening about her. Now they were
singing:

> . . . *Jesus knows all about my troubles* . . .

Men and women were swaying and clapping their hands, shouting and stamping their feet to the frankly irreverent melody of the
song. Without warning the woman at her side threw off her hat,
leaped to her feet, waved her long arms, and shouted shrilly: "Glory!
Hallelujah!" and then, in wild, ecstatic fury jumped up and down
before Helga clutching at the girl's soaked coat, and screamed:
"Come to Jesus, you pore los' sinner!" Alarmed for the fraction of a
second, involuntarily Helga had shrunk from her grasp, wriggling out
of the wet coat when she could not loosen the crazed creature's hold.
At the sight of the bare arms and neck growing out of the clinging red
dress, a shudder shook the swaying man at her right. On the face of
the dancing woman before her a disapproving frown gathered. She
shrieked: "A scarlet 'oman. Come to Jesus, you pore los' Jezebel!"

At this the short brown man on the platform raised a placating
hand and sanctimoniously delivered himself of the words: "Remembah de words of our Mastah: 'Let him that is without sin cast de
first stone.' Let us pray for our errin' sistah."

Helga Crane was amused, angry, disdainful, as she sat there, listening to the preacher praying for her soul. But though she was contemptuous, she was being too well entertained to leave. And it was,
at least, warm and dry. So she stayed, listening to the fervent exhor-
tation to God to save her and to the zealous shoutings and groanings
of the congregation. Particularly she was interested in the writhings
and weepings of the feminine portion, which seemed to predomi-
nate. Little by little the performance took on an almost Bacchic
vehemence. Behind her, before her, beside her, frenzied women ges-
ticulated, screamed, wept, and tottered to the praying of the
preacher, which had gradually become a cadenced chant. When at
last he ended, another took up the plea in the same moaning chant,
and then another. It went on and on without pause with the persistence of some unconquerable faith exalted beyond time and reality.

Fascinated, Helga Crane watched until there crept upon her an
indistinct horror of an unknown world. She felt herself in the presence of a nameless people, observing rites of a remote obscure origin. The faces of the men and women took on the aspect of a dim
vision. "This," she whispered to herself, "is terrible. I must get out

of here." But the horror held her. She remained motionless, watching, as if she lacked the strength to leave the place—foul, vile, and terrible, with its mixture of breaths, its contact of bodies, its concerted convulsions, all in wild appeal for a single soul. Her soul.

And as Helga watched and listened, gradually a curious influence penetrated her; she felt an echo of the weird orgy resound in her own heart; she felt herself possessed by the same madness; she too felt a brutal desire to shout and to sling herself about. Frightened at the strength of the obsession, she gathered herself for one last effort to escape, but vainly. In rising, weakness and nausea from last night's unsuccessful attempt to make herself drunk overcame her. She had eaten nothing since yesterday. She fell forward against the crude railing which enclosed the little platform. For a single moment she remained there in silent stillness, because she was afraid she was going to be sick. And in that moment she was lost—or saved. The yelling figures about her pressed forward, closing her in on all sides. Maddened, she grasped at the railing, and with no previous intention began to yell like one insane, drowning every other clamor, while torrents of tears streamed down her face. She was unconscious of the words she uttered, or their meaning: "Oh God, mercy, mercy. Have mercy on me!" but she repeated them over and over.

From those about her came a thunder-clap of joy. Arms were stretched toward her with savage frenzy. The women dragged themselves upon their knees or crawled over the floor like reptiles, sobbing and pulling their hair and tearing off their clothing. Those who succeeded in getting near to her leaned forward to encourage the unfortunate sister, dropping hot tears and beads of sweat upon her bare arms and neck.

The thing became real. A miraculous calm came upon her. Life seemed to expand, and to become very easy. Helga Crane felt within her a supreme aspiration toward the regaining of simple happiness, a happiness unburdened by the complexities of the lives she had known. About her the tumult and the shouting continued, but in a lesser degree. Some of the more exuberant worshipers had fainted into inert masses, the voices of others were almost spent. Gradually the room grew quiet and almost solemn, and to the kneeling girl time seemed to sink back into the mysterious grandeur and holiness of far-off simpler centuries.

TWENTY-ONE

On leaving the mission Helga Crane had started straight back to her room at the hotel. With her had gone the fattish yellow man who had sat beside her. He had introduced himself as the Reverend

Mr. Pleasant Green[1] in proffering his escort for which Helga had been grateful because she had still felt a little dizzy and much exhausted. So great had been this physical weariness that as she had walked beside him, without attention to his verbose information about his own "field," as he called it, she had been seized with a hateful feeling of vertigo and obliged to lay firm hold on his arm to keep herself from falling. The weakness had passed as suddenly as it had come. Silently they had walked on. And gradually Helga had recalled that the man beside her had himself swayed slightly at their close encounter, and that frantically for a fleeting moment he had gripped at a protruding fence railing. That man! Was it possible? As easy as that?

Instantly across her still half-hypnotized consciousness little burning darts of fancy had shot themselves. No. She couldn't. It would be too awful. Just the same, what or who was there to hold her back? Nothing. Simply nothing. Nobody. Nobody at all.

Her searching mind had become in a moment quite clear. She cast at the man a speculative glance, aware that for a tiny space she had looked into his mind, a mind striving to be calm. A mind that was certain that it was secure because it was concerned only with things of the soul, spiritual things, which to him meant religious things. But actually a mind by habit at home amongst the mere material aspect of things, and at that moment consumed by some longing for the ecstasy that might lurk behind the gleam of her cheek, the flying wave of her hair, the pressure of her slim fingers on his heavy arm. An instant's flashing vision it had been and it was gone at once. Escaped in the aching of her own senses and the sudden disturbing fear that she herself had perhaps missed the supreme secret of life.

After all, there was nothing to hold her back. Nobody to care. She stopped sharply, shocked at what she was on the verge of considering. Appalled at where it might lead her.

The man—what was his name?—thinking that she was almost about to fall again, had reached out his arms to her. Helga Crane had deliberately stopped thinking. She had only smiled, a faint provocative smile, and pressed her fingers deep into his arms until a wild look had come into his slightly bloodshot eyes.

The next morning she lay for a long while, scarcely breathing, while she reviewed the happenings of the night before. Curious. She couldn't be sure that it wasn't religion that had made her feel so utterly different from dreadful yesterday. And gradually she became a little sad, because she realized that with every hour she would get

---

1. Thadious Davis notes that there was a Pleasant Green Missionary Baptist Church in Nashville, Tennessee, near where Larsen attended Fisk.

a little farther away from this soothing haziness, this rest from her long trouble of body and of spirit; back into the clear bareness of her own small life and being, from which happiness and serenity always faded just as they had shaped themselves. And slowly bitterness crept into her soul. Because, she thought, all I've ever had in life has been things—except just this one time. At that she closed her eyes, for even remembrance caused her to shiver a little.

Things, she realized, hadn't been, weren't, enough for her. She'd have to have something else besides. It all came back to that old question of happiness. Surely this was it. Just for a fleeting moment Helga Crane, her eyes watching the wind scattering the gray-white clouds and so clearing a speck of blue sky, questioned her ability to retain, to bear, this happiness at such cost as she must pay for it. There was, she knew, no getting round that. The man's agitation and sincere conviction of sin had been too evident, too illuminating. The question returned in a slightly new form. Was it worth the risk? Could she take it? Was she able? Though what did it matter—now?

And all the while she knew in one small corner of her mind that such thinking was useless. She had made her decision. Her resolution. It was a chance at stability, at permanent happiness, that she meant to take. She had let so many other things, other chances, escape her.[2] And anyway there was God, He would perhaps make it come out all right. Still confused and not so sure that it wasn't the fact that she was "saved" that had contributed to this after feeling of well-being, she clutched the hope, the desire to believe that now at last she had found some One, some Power, who was interested in her. Would help her.

She meant, however, for once in her life to be practical. So she would make sure of both things, God and man.

Her glance caught the calendar over the little white desk. The tenth of November. The steamer *Oscar II* sailed today. Yesterday she had half thought of sailing with it. Yesterday. How far away!

With the thought of yesterday came the thought of Robert Anderson and a feeling of elation, revenge. She had put herself beyond the need of help from him. She had made it impossible for herself ever again to appeal to him. Instinctively she had the knowledge that he would be shocked. Grieved. Horribly hurt even. Well, let him!

The need to hurry suddenly obsessed her. She must. The morning was almost gone. And she meant, if she could manage it, to be married today. Rising, she was seized with a fear so acute that she had to lie down again. For the thought came to her that she might

---

2. *other chances, escape her*: This appears as "other changes" in Adelaide Cromwell Hill's edition.

fail. Might not be able to confront the situation. That would be too
dreadful. But she became calm again. How could he, a naïve creature like that, hold out against her? If she pretended to distress? To
fear? To remorse? He couldn't. It would be useless for him even to
try. She screwed up her face into a little grin, remembering that even
if protestations were to fail, there were other ways.

And, too, there was God.

TWENTY-TWO

AND so in the confusion of seductive repentance Helga Crane was
married to the grandiloquent Reverend Mr. Pleasant Green, that rattish yellow man, who had so kindly, so unctuously, proffered his
escort to her hotel on the memorable night of her conversion. With
him she willingly, even eagerly, left the sins and temptations of New
York behind her to, as he put it, "labor in the vineyard of the Lord"
in the tiny Alabama town where he was pastor to a scattered and
primitive flock. And where, as the wife of the preacher, she was a
person of relative importance. Only relative.

Helga did not hate him, the town, or the people. No. Not for a
long time.

As always, at first the novelty of the thing, the change, fascinated
her. There was a recurrence of the feeling that now, at last, she had
found a place for herself, that she was really living. And she had her
religion, which in her new status as a preacher's wife had of necessity become real to her. She believed in it. Because in its coming it
had brought this other thing, this anæsthetic satisfaction for her
senses. Hers was, she declared to herself, a truly spiritual union.
This one time in her life, she was convinced, she had not clutched a
shadow and missed the actuality. She felt compensated for all previous
humiliations and disappointments and was glad. If she remembered
that she had had something like this feeling before, she put the
unwelcome memory from her with the thought: "This time I know
I'm right. This time it will last."

Eagerly she accepted everything, even that bleak air of poverty
which, in some curious way, regards itself as virtuous, for no other
reason than that it is poor. And in her first hectic enthusiasm she
intended and planned to do much good to her husband's parishioners.
Her young joy and zest for the uplifting of her fellow men came back
to her. She meant to subdue the cleanly scrubbed ugliness of her
own surroundings to soft inoffensive beauty, and to help the other
women to do likewise. Too, she would help them with their clothes,
tactfully point out that sunbonnets, no matter how gay, and aprons,
no matter how frilly, were not quite the proper things for Sunday

church wear. There would be a sewing circle. She visualized herself instructing the children, who seemed most of the time to run wild, in ways of gentler deportment. She was anxious to be a true help-mate, for in her heart was a feeling of obligation, of humble gratitude.

In her ardor and sincerity Helga even made some small begin-nings. True, she was not very successful in this matter of innova-tions. When she went about to try to interest the women in what she considered more appropriate clothing and in inexpensive ways of improving their homes according to her ideas of beauty, she was met, always, with smiling agreement and good-natured promises. "Yuh all is right, Mis' Green," and "Ah suttinly will, Mis' Green," fell courteously on her ear at each visit.

She was unaware that afterwards they would shake their heads sullenly over their wash-tubs and ironing-boards. And that among themselves they talked with amusement, or with anger, of "dat uppity, meddlin' No'the'nah," and "pore Reve'end," who in their opin-ion "would 'a done bettah to a ma'ied Clementine Richards." Know-ing, as she did, nothing of this, Helga was unperturbed. But even had she known, she would not have been disheartened. The fact that it was difficult but increased her eagerness, and made the doing of it seem only the more worth while. Sometimes she would smile to think how changed she was.

And she was humble too. Even with Clementine Richards, a strap-ping black beauty of magnificent Amazon proportions and bold shining eyes of jet-like hardness. A person of awesome appearance. All chains, strings of beads, jingling bracelets, flying ribbons, feath-ery neck-pieces, and flowery hats. Clementine was inclined to treat Helga with an only partially concealed contemptuousness, consid-ering her a poor thing without style, and without proper understand-ing of the worth and greatness of the man, Clementine's own adored pastor, whom Helga had somehow had the astounding good luck to marry. Clementine's admiration of the Reverend Mr. Pleas-ant Green was open. Helga was at first astonished. Until she learned that there was really no reason why it should be concealed. Every-body was aware of it. Besides, open adoration was the prerogative, the almost religious duty, of the female portion of the flock. If this unhidden and exaggerated approval contributed to his already over-sized pomposity, so much the better. It was what they expected, liked, wanted. The greater his own sense of superiority became, the more flattered they were by his notice and small attentions, the more they cast at him killing glances, the more they hung enraptured on his words.

In the days before her conversion, with its subsequent blurring of her sense of humor, Helga might have amused herself by tracing the relation of this constant ogling and flattering on the proverbially large families of preachers; the often disastrous effect on their wives of this constant stirring of the senses by extraneous women. Now, however, she did not even think of it.

She was too busy. Every minute of the day was full. Necessarily. And to Helga this was a new experience. She was charmed by it. To be mistress in one's own house, to have a garden, and chickens, and a pig; to have a husband—and to be "right with God"—what pleasure did that other world which she had left contain that could surpass these? Here, she had found, she was sure, the intangible thing for which, indefinitely, always she had craved. It had received embodiment.

Everything contributed to her gladness in living. And so for a time she loved everything and everyone. Or thought she did. Even the weather. And it was truly lovely. By day a glittering gold sun was set in an unbelievably bright sky. In the evening silver buds sprouted in a Chinese blue sky, and the warm day was softly soothed by a slight, cool breeze. And night! Night, when a languid moon peeped through the wide-opened windows of her little house, a little mockingly, it may be. Always at night's approach Helga was bewildered by a disturbing medley of feelings. Challenge. Anticipation. And a small fear.

In the morning she was serene again. Peace had returned. And she could go happily, inexpertly, about the humble tasks of her household, cooking, dish-washing, sweeping, dusting, mending, and darning. And there was the garden. When she worked there, she felt that life was utterly filled with the glory and the marvel of God.

Helga did not reason about this feeling, as she did not at that time reason about anything. It was enough that it was there, coloring all her thoughts and acts. It endowed the four rooms of her ugly brown house with a kindly radiance, obliterating the stark bareness of its white plaster walls and the nakedness of its uncovered painted floors. It even softened the choppy lines of the shiny oak furniture and subdued the awesome horribleness of the religious pictures.

And all the other houses and cabins shared in this illumination. And the people. The dark undecorated women unceasingly concerned with the actual business of life, its rounds of births and christenings, of loves and marriages, of deaths and funerals, were to Helga miraculously beautiful. The smallest, dirtiest, brown child, barefooted in the fields or muddy roads, was to her an emblem of the wonder of life, of love, and of God's goodness.

For the preacher, her husband, she had a feeling of gratitude, amounting almost to sin. Beyond that, she thought of him not at all. But she was not conscious that she had shut him out from her mind. Besides, what need to think of him? He was there. She was at peace, and secure. Surely their two lives were one, and the companionship in the Lord's grace so perfect that to think about it would be tempting providence. She had done with soul-searching.

What did it matter that he consumed his food, even the softest varieties, audibly? What did it matter that, though he did no work with his hands, not even in the garden, his fingernails were always rimmed with black? What did it matter that he failed to wash his fat body, or to shift his clothing, as often as Helga herself did? There were things that more than outweighed these. In the certainty of his goodness, his righteousness, his holiness, Helga somehow overcame her first disgust at the odor of sweat and stale garments. She was even able to be unaware of it. Herself, Helga had come to look upon as a finicky, showy thing of unnecessary prejudices and fripperies. And when she sat in the dreary structure, which had once been a stable belonging to the estate of a wealthy horse-racing man and about which the odor of manure still clung, now the church and social center of the Negroes of the town, and heard him expound with verbal extravagance the gospel of blood and love, of hell and heaven, of fire and gold streets, pounding with clenched fists the frail table before him or shaking those fists in the faces of the congregation like direct personal threats, or pacing wildly back and forth and even sometimes shedding great tears as he besought them to repent, she was, she told herself, proud and gratified that he belonged to her. In some strange way she was able to ignore the atmosphere of self-satisfaction which poured from him like gas from a leaking pipe.

And night came at the end of every day. Emotional, palpitating, amorous, all that was living in her sprang like rank weeds at the tingling thought of night, with a vitality so strong that it devoured all shoots of reason.

TWENTY-THREE

AFTER the first exciting months Helga was too driven, too occupied, and too sick to carry out any of the things for which she had made such enthusiastic plans, or even to care that she had made only slight progress toward their accomplishment. For she, who had never thought of her body save as something on which to hang lovely fabrics, had now constantly to think of it. It had persistently to be pampered to secure from it even a little service. Always she felt extraordinarily and annoyingly ill, having forever to be sinking into chairs. Or, if she was out, to be pausing by the roadside, clinging desperately to some convenient fence or tree, waiting for the horrible nausea and hateful faintness to pass. The light, care-free days of the past, when she had not felt heavy and reluctant or weak and spent, receded more and more and with increasing vagueness, like a dream passing from a faulty memory.

The children used her up. There were already three of them, all born within the short space of twenty months. Two great healthy twin boys, whose lovely bodies were to Helga like rare figures carved out of amber, and in whose sleepy and mysterious black eyes all that was puzzling, evasive, and aloof in life seemed to find expression. No matter how often or how long she looked at these two small sons of hers, never did she lose a certain delicious feeling in which were mingled pride, tenderness, and exaltation. And there was a girl, sweet, delicate, and flower-like. Not so healthy or so loved as the boys, but still miraculously her own proud and cherished possession.

So there was no time for the pursuit of beauty, or for the uplifting of other harassed and teeming women, or for the instruction of their neglected children.

Her husband was still, as he had always been, deferentially kind and incredulously proud of her—and verbally encouraging. Helga tried not to see that he had rather lost any personal interest in her, except for the short spaces between the times when she was preparing for or recovering from childbirth. She shut her eyes to the fact that his encouragement had become a little platitudinous, limited mostly to "The Lord will look out for you," "We must accept what God sends," or "My mother had nine children and was thankful for every one." If she was inclined to wonder a little just how they were to manage with another child on the way, he would point out to her that her doubt and uncertainty were a stupendous ingratitude. Had not the good God saved her soul from hell-fire and eternal damnation? Had He not in His great kindness given her three small lives to raise up for His glory? Had He not showered her with numerous other mercies (evidently too numerous to be named separately)?

"You must," the Reverend Mr. Pleasant Green would say unctuously, "trust the Lord more fully, Helga."

This pabulum did not irritate her. Perhaps it was the fact that the preacher was, now, not so much at home that even lent to it a measure of real comfort. For the adoring women of his flock, noting how with increasing frequency their pastor's house went unswept and undusted, his children unwashed, and his wife untidy, took pleasant pity on him and invited him often to tasty orderly meals, specially prepared for him, in their own clean houses.

Helga, looking about in helpless dismay and sick disgust at the disorder around her, the permanent assembly of partly emptied medicine bottles on the clock-shelf, the perpetual array of drying baby-clothes on the chair-backs, the constant debris of broken toys on the floor, the unceasing litter of half-dead flowers on the table, dragged in by the toddling twins from the forlorn garden, failed to blame him for the thoughtless selfishness of these absences. And, she was thankful, whenever possible, to be relieved from the ordeal of cooking. There were times when, having had to retreat from the kitchen in lumbering haste with her sensitive nose gripped between tightly squeezing fingers, she had been sure that the greatest kindness that God could ever show to her would be to free her forever from the sight and smell of food.

How, she wondered, did other women, other mothers, manage? Could it be possible that, while presenting such smiling and contented faces, they were all always on the edge of health? All always worn out and apprehensive? Or was it only she, a poor weak city-bred thing, who felt that the strain of what the Reverend Mr. Pleasant Green had so often gently and patiently reminded her was a natural thing, an act of God, was almost unendurable?

One day on her round of visiting—a church duty, to be done no matter how miserable one was—she summoned up sufficient boldness to ask several women how they felt, how they managed. The answers were a resigned shrug, or an amused snort, or an upward rolling of eyeballs with a mention of "de Lawd" looking after us all.

"'Tain't nothin', nothin' at all, chile," said one, Sary Jones, who, as Helga knew, had had six children in about as many years. "Yuh all takes it too ha'd. Jes' remembah et's natu'al fo' a 'oman to hab chilluns an' don' fret so."

"But," protested Helga, "I'm always so tired and half sick. That can't be natural."

"Laws, chile, we's all ti'ed. An' Ah reckons we's all gwine a be ti'ed till kingdom come. Jes' make de bes' of et, honey. Jes' make de bes' yuh can."

Helga sighed, turning her nose away from the steaming coffee which her hostess had placed for her and against which her squeamish stomach was about to revolt. At the moment the compensations of immortality seemed very shadowy and very far away.

"Jes' remembah," Sary went on, staring sternly into Helga's thin face, "we all gits ouah res' by an' by. In de nex' worl' we's all recompense'. Jes' put yo' trus' in de Sabioah."

Looking at the confident face of the little bronze figure on the opposite side of the immaculately spread table, Helga had a sensation of shame that she should be less than content. Why couldn't she be as trusting and as certain that her troubles would not overwhelm her as Sary Jones was? Sary, who in all likelihood had toiled every day of her life since early childhood except on those days, totalling perhaps sixty, following the birth of her six children. And who by dint of superhuman saving had somehow succeeded in feeding and clothing them and sending them all to school. Before her Helga felt humbled and oppressed by the sense of her own unworthiness and lack of sufficient faith.

"Thanks, Sary," she said, rising in retreat from the coffee, "you've done me a world of good. I'm really going to try to be more patient."

So, though with growing yearning she longed for the great ordinary things of life, hunger, sleep, freedom from pain, she resigned herself to the doing without them. The possibility of alleviating her burdens by a greater faith became lodged in her mind. She gave herself up to it. It *did* help. And the beauty of leaning on the wisdom of God, of trusting, gave to her a queer sort of satisfaction. Faith was really quite easy. One had only to yield. To ask no questions. The more weary, the more weak, she became, the easier it was. Her religion was to her a kind of protective coloring, shielding her from the cruel light of an unbearable reality.

This utter yielding in faith to what had been sent her found her favor, too, in the eyes of her neighbors. Her husband's flock began to approve and commend this submission and humility to a superior wisdom. The womenfolk spoke more kindly and more affectionately of the preacher's Northern wife. "Pore Mis' Green, wid all dem small chilluns at once. She suah do hab it ha'd. An' she don' nebah complains an' frets no mo'e. Jes' trus' in de Lawd lak de Good Book say. Mighty sweet lil' 'oman too."

Helga didn't bother much about the preparations for the coming child. Actually and metaphorically she bowed her head before God, trusting in Him to see her through. Secretly she was glad that she had not to worry about herself or anything. It was a relief to be able to put the entire responsibility on someone else.

TWENTY-FOUR

IT began, this next child-bearing, during the morning services of a breathless hot Sunday while the fervent choir soloist was singing: "Ah am freed of mah sorrow," and lasted far into the small hours of Tuesday morning. It seemed, for some reason, not to go off just right. And when, after that long frightfulness, the fourth little dab of amber humanity which Helga had contributed to a despised race was held before her for maternal approval, she failed entirely to respond properly to this sop of consolation for the suffering and horror through which she had passed. There was from her no pleased, proud smile, no loving, possessive gesture, no manifestation of interest in the important matters of sex and weight. Instead she deliberately closed her eyes, mutely shutting out the sickly infant, its smiling father, the soiled midwife, the curious neighbors, and the tousled room.

A week she lay so. Silent and listless. Ignoring food, the clamoring children, the comings and goings of solicitous, kind-hearted women, her hovering husband, and all of life about her. The neighbors were puzzled. The Reverend Mr. Pleasant Green was worried. The midwife was frightened.

On the floor, in and out among the furniture and under her bed, the twins played. Eager to help, the church-women crowded in and, meeting there others on the same laudable errand, stayed to gossip and to wonder. Anxiously the preacher sat, Bible in hand, beside his wife's bed, or in a nervous half-guilty manner invited the congregated parishioners to join him in prayer for the healing of their sister. Then, kneeling, they would beseech God to stretch out His allpowerful hand on behalf of the afflicted one, softly at first, but with rising vehemence, accompanied by moans and tears, until it seemed that the God to whom they prayed must in mercy to the sufferer grant relief. If only so that she might rise up and escape from the tumult, the heat, and the smell.

Helga, however, was unconcerned, undisturbed by the commotion about her. It was all part of the general unreality.[1] Nothing reached her. Nothing penetrated the kind darkness into which her bruised spirit had retreated. Even that red-letter event, the coming to see her of the old white physician from downtown, who had for a long time stayed talking gravely to her husband, drew from her no interest. Nor for days was she aware that a stranger, a nurse from Mobile, had been added to her household, a brusquely efficient woman who produced order out of chaos and quiet out of bedlam. Neither did the absence of the children, removed by good neighbors at Miss Hartley's insistence, impress her. While she had gone down into that appalling blackness of pain, the ballast of her brain had got loose and she hovered for a long time somewhere in that delightful borderland on the edge of unconsciousness, an enchanted and blissful place where peace and incredible quiet encompassed her.

After weeks she grew better, returned to earth, set her reluctant feet to the hard path of life again.

"Well, here you are!" announced Miss Hartley in her slightly harsh voice one afternoon just before the fall of evening. She had for some time been standing at the bedside gazing down at Helga with an intent speculative look.

"Yes," Helga agreed in a thin little voice, "I'm back." The truth was that she had been back for some hours. Purposely she had lain silent and still, wanting to linger forever in that serene haven, that effortless calm where nothing was expected of her. There she could watch the figures of the past drift by. There was her mother, whom

---

1. *It was all part of the general unreality*: This sentence is missing in McDowell's edition.

she had loved from a distance and finally so scornfully blamed, who appeared as she had always remembered her, unbelievably beautiful, young, and remote. Robert Anderson, questioning, purposely detached, affecting, as she realized now, her life in a remarkably cruel degree; for at last she understood clearly how deeply, how passionately, she must have loved him. Anne, lovely, secure, wise, selfish. Axel Olsen, conceited, worldly, spoiled. Audrey Denney, placid, taking quietly and without fuss the things which she wanted. James Vayle, snobbish, smug, servile. Mrs. Hayes-Rore, important, kind, determined. The Dahls, rich, correct, climbing. Flashingly, fragmentarily, other long-forgotten figures, women in gay fashionable frocks and men in formal black and white, glided by in bright rooms to distant, vaguely familiar music.

It was refreshingly delicious, this immersion in the past. But it was finished now. It was over. The words of her husband, the Reverend Mr. Pleasant Green, who had been standing at the window looking mournfully out at the scorched melon-patch, ruined because Helga had been ill so long and unable to tend it, were confirmation of that.

"The Lord be praised," he said, and came forward. It was distinctly disagreeable. It was even more disagreeable to feel his moist hand on hers. A cold shiver brushed over her. She closed her eyes. Obstinately and with all her small strength she drew her hand away from him. Hid it far down under the bed-covering, and turned her face away to hide a grimace of unconquerable aversion. She cared nothing, at that moment, for his hurt surprise. She knew only that, in the hideous agony that for interminable hours—no, centuries—she had borne, the luster of religion had vanished; that revulsion had come upon her; that she hated this man. Between them the vastness of the universe had come.

Miss Hartley, all-seeing and instantly aware of a situation, as she had been quite aware that her patient had been conscious for some time before she herself had announced the fact, intervened, saying firmly: "I think it might be better if you didn't try to talk to her now. She's terribly sick and weak yet. She's still got some fever and we mustn't excite her or she's liable to slip back. And we don't want that, do we?"

No, the man, her husband, responded, they didn't want that. Reluctantly he went from the room with a last look at Helga, who was lying on her back with one frail, pale hand under her small head, her curly black hair scattered loose on the pillow. She regarded him from behind dropped lids. The day was hot, her breasts were covered only by a nightgown of filmy *crêpe*, a relic of prematrimonial days, which had slipped from one carved shoulder. He flinched. Helga's petulant lip curled, for she well knew that this fresh reminder of her desirability was like the flick of a whip.

Miss Hartley carefully closed the door after the retreating hus-band. "It's time," she said, "for your evening treatment, and then you've got to try to sleep for a while. No more visitors tonight."

Helga nodded and tried unsuccessfully to make a little smile. She was glad of Miss Hartley's presence. It would, she felt, protect her from so much. She mustn't, she thought to herself, get well too fast. Since it seemed she was going to get well. In bed she could think, could have a certain amount of quiet. Of aloneness.

In that period of racking pain and calamitous fright Helga had learned what passion and credulity could do to one. In her was born angry bitterness and an enormous disgust. The cruel, unrelieved suffering had beaten down her protective wall of artificial faith in the infinite wisdom, in the mercy, of God. For had she not called in her agony on Him? And He had not heard. Why? Because, she knew now, He wasn't there. Didn't exist. Into that yawning gap of unspeak-able brutality had gone, too, her belief in the miracle and wonder of life. Only scorn, resentment, and hate remained—and ridicule. Life wasn't a miracle, a wonder. It was, for Negroes at least, only a great disappointment. Something to be got through with as best one could. No one was interested in them or helped them. God! Bah! And they were only a nuisance to other people.

Everything in her mind was hot and cold, beating and swirling about. Within her emaciated body raged disillusion. Chaotic tur-moil. With the obscuring curtain of religion rent, she was able to look about her and see with shocked eyes this thing that she had done to herself. She couldn't, she thought ironically, even blame God for it, now that she knew that He didn't exist. No. No more than she could pray to Him for the death of her husband, the Reverend Mr. Pleasant Green. The white man's God. And His great love for all people regardless of race! What idiotic nonsense she had allowed herself to believe. How could she, how could anyone, have been so deluded? How could ten million black folk credit it when daily before their eyes was enacted its contradiction? Not that she at all cared about the ten million. But herself. Her sons. Her daughter. These would grow to manhood, to womanhood, in this vicious, this hypo-critical land. The dark eyes filled with tears.

"I wouldn't," the nurse advised, "do that. You've been dreadfully sick, you know. I can't have you worrying. Time enough for that when you're well. Now you must sleep all you possibly can."

Helga did sleep. She found it surprisingly easy to sleep. Aided by Miss Hartley's rather masterful discernment, she took advan-tage of the ease with which this blessed enchantment stole over her. From her husband's praisings, prayers, and caresses she sought refuge in sleep, and from the neighbors' gifts, advice, and sympathy.

There was that day on which they told her that the last sickly infant, born of such futile torture and lingering torment, had died after a short week of slight living. Just closed his eyes and died. No vitality. On hearing it Helga too had just closed her eyes. Not to die. She was convinced that before her there were years of living. Perhaps of happiness even. For a new idea had come to her. She had closed her eyes to shut in any telltale gleam of the relief which she felt. One less. And she had gone off into sleep.

And there was that Sunday morning on which the Reverend Mr. Pleasant Green had informed her that they were that day to hold a special thanksgiving service for her recovery. There would, he said, be prayers, special testimonies, and songs. Was there anything particular she would like to have said, to have prayed for, to have sung? Helga had smiled from sheer amusement as she replied that there was nothing. Nothing at all. She only hoped that they would enjoy themselves. And, closing her eyes that he might be discouraged from longer tarrying, she had gone off into sleep.

Waking later to the sound of joyous religious abandon floating in through the opened windows, she had asked a little diffidently that she be allowed to read. Miss Hartley's sketchy brows contracted into a dubious frown. After a judicious pause she had answered: "No, I don't think so." Then, seeing the rebellious tears which had sprung into her patient's eyes, she added kindly: "But I'll read to you a little if you like."

That, Helga replied, would be nice. In the next room on a high-up shelf was a book. She'd forgotten the name, but its author was Anatole France. There was a story, "The Procurator of Judea."[2] Would Miss Hartley read that? "Thanks. Thanks awfully."

"'Lælius Lamia, born in Italy of illustrious parents,'" began the nurse in her slightly harsh voice.

Helga drank it in.

"'. . . For to this day the women bring down doves to the altar as their victims. . . .'"

Helga closed her eyes.

"'. . . Africa and Asia have already enriched us with a considerable number of gods. . . .'"

Miss Hartley looked up. Helga had slipped into slumber while the superbly ironic ending which she had so desired to hear was yet a

---

2. France was a French critic and novelist (1844–1924) who won the Nobel Prize in Literature, 1921. "The Procurator of Judea," published in 1902, contains conversations between Pontius Pilate and his friend Laelius Lamia, at the end of Pilate's life, including strong expressions of anti-Semitism and fear of interracial reproduction and sexuality, as well as fears of others who are different. It was considered blasphemous in its day. Helga falls asleep before the story's ending, which depicts Pilate not knowing whether or not Jesus was a Jew he executed for being different.

long way off. A dull tale, was Miss Hartley's opinion, as she curiously turned the pages to see how it turned out.

"'Jesus? . . . Jesus—of Nazareth? I cannot call him to mind.'"

"Huh! she muttered, puzzled. "Silly." And closed the book.

TWENTY-FIVE

DURING the long process of getting well, between the dreamy intervals when she was beset by the insistent craving for sleep, Helga had had too much time to think. At first she had felt only an astonished anger at the quagmire in which she had engulfed herself. She had ruined her life. Made it impossible ever again to do the things that she wanted, have the things that she loved, mingle with the people she liked. She had, to put it as brutally as anyone could, been a fool. The damnedest kind of a fool. And she had paid for it. Enough. More than enough.

Her mind, swaying back to the protection that religion had afforded her, almost she wished that it had not failed her. An illusion. Yes. But better, far better, than this terrible reality. Religion had, after all, its uses. It blunted the perceptions. Robbed life of its crudest truths. Especially it had its uses for the poor—and the blacks.

For the blacks. The Negroes.

And this, Helga decided, was what ailed the whole Negro race in America, this fatuous belief in the white man's God, this childlike trust in full compensation for all woes and privations in "kingdom come." Sary Jones's absolute conviction, "In de nex' worl' we's all recompense'," came back to her. And ten million souls were as sure of it as was Sary. How the white man's God must laugh at the great joke he had played on them! Bound them to slavery, then to poverty and insult, and made them bear it unresistingly, uncomplainingly almost, by sweet promises of mansions in the sky by and by.

"Pie in the sky," Helga said aloud derisively, forgetting for the moment Miss Hartley's brisk presence, and so was a little startled at hearing her voice from the adjoining room saying severely: "My goodness! No! I should say you can't have pie. It's too indigestible. Maybe when you're better—"

"That," assented Helga, "is what I said. Pie—by and by. That's the trouble."

The nurse looked concerned. Was this an approaching relapse? Coming to the bedside, she felt at her patient's pulse while giving her a searching look. No. "You'd better," she admonished, a slight edge to her tone, "try to get a little nap. You haven't had any sleep today, and you can't get too much of it. You've got to get strong, you know."

With this Helga was in full agreement. It seemed hundreds of years since she had been strong. And she would need strength. For in some way she was determined to get herself out of this bog into which she had strayed. Or—she would have to die. She couldn't endure it. Her suffocation and shrinking loathing were too great. Not to be borne. Again. For she had to admit that it wasn't new, this feeling of dissatisfaction, of asphyxiation. Something like it she had experienced before. In Naxos. In New York. In Copenhagen. This differed only in degree. And it was of the present and therefore seemingly more reasonable. The other revulsions were of the past, and now less explainable.

The thought of her husband roused in her a deep and contemptuous hatred. At his every approach she had forcibly to subdue a furious inclination to scream out in protest. Shame, too, swept over her at every thought of her marriage. Marriage. This sacred thing of which parsons and other Christian folk ranted so sanctimoniously, how immoral—according to their own standards—it could be! But Helga felt also a modicum of pity for him, as for one already abandoned. She meant to leave him. And it was, she had to concede, all of her own doing, this marriage. Nevertheless, she hated him.

The neighbors and churchfolk came in for their share of her all-embracing hatred. She hated their raucous laughter, their stupid acceptance of all things, and their unfailing trust in "de Lawd." And more than all the rest she hated the jangling Clementine Richards, with her provocative smirkings, because she had not succeeded in marrying the preacher and thus saving her, Helga, from that crowning idiocy.

Of the children Helga tried not to think. She wanted not to leave them—if that were possible. The recollection of her own childhood, lonely, unloved, rose too poignantly before her for her to consider calmly such a solution. Though she forced herself to believe that this was different. There was not the element of race, of white and black. They were all black together. And they would have their father. But to leave them would be a tearing agony, a rending of deepest fibers. She felt that through all the rest of her lifetime she would be hearing their cry of "Mummy, Mummy, Mummy," through sleepless nights. No. She couldn't desert them.

How, then, was she to escape from the oppression, the degradation, that her life had become? It was so difficult. It was terribly difficult. It was almost hopeless. So for a while—for the immediate present, she told herself—she put aside the making of any plan for her going. "I'm still," she reasoned, "too weak, too sick. By and by, when I'm really strong—"

It was so easy and so pleasant to think about freedom and cities, about clothes and books, about the sweet mingled smell of Houbigant[1] and cigarettes in softly lighted rooms filled with inconsequential chatter and laughter and sophisticated tuneless music. It was so hard to think out a feasible way of retrieving all these agreeable, desired things. Just then. Later. When she got up. By and by. She must rest. Get strong. Sleep. Then, afterwards, she could work out some arrangement. So she dozed and dreamed in snatches of sleeping and waking, letting time run on. Away.

And hardly had she left her bed and become able to walk again without pain, hardly had the children returned from the homes of the neighbors, when she began to have her fifth child.

1. Very expensive French perfume. The House of Houbigant was the official perfumer to the royal courts of Europe, and for a long time only royalty could afford, or purchase, most Houbigant perfumes. In the eighteenth century Houbigant also sold skin-whitening products.

BACKGROUNDS AND CONTEXTS

Contemporary Reviews

GWENDOLYN B. BENNETT

The Ebony Flute[†]

By far the most important thing that has happened in the literary world during the last month is the marriage of Countee Cullen to Yolande Du Bois. Mr. Cullen is the editor of *The Dark Tower* as well as the author of several volumes of verse. Miss Du Bois is by her own right something of a literateur. And of course there is *Home to Harlem* by Claude Mc Kay, author of *Harlem Shadows*, a book of poetry. Well now here is something! Heralded by loud hurrahs on the lips of all the critics, it has within a month's period achieved a place on the New York *World*'s list of best sellers. Mr. Mc Kay [*sic*] has approached his novel with the same sensitiveness that he showed in his poetry. However, it is interesting to note how Negroes, themselves, receive what he has written. I am a bit afraid that they are going to resent the subject-matter of his book and in so doing they will miss the surety of his handling the material he has chosen and the beauty of his touch albeit the tale he tells is not a pretty one. Mr. Mc Kay is at present in Marseille where he has been for some time. This is indeed a gala year for Negro literature. Dr. W. E. B. Du Bois' novel *Dark Princess* ought to be in the book stalls any day now. Nella Larsen's *Quicksand* has just arrived. And let me say that many folks will be interested to hear that this book does not set as its tempo that of the Harlem cabaret—this is the story of the struggle of an interesting cultured Negro woman against her environment. Negroes who are squeamish about writers exposing our worst side will be relieved that Harlem night-life is more or less submerged by this author in the psychological struggle of the heroine—and in the fall Walter White will have returned from southern France where he is now at work. Which reminds me of an interesting tale that James Weldon Johnson tells of how Walter White had thought that he would reside in a villa of romantic French nomenclature only to

† From *Opportunity* (May 30, 1928): 153. Reprinted by permission of the National Urban League.

find that the home in which he at present finds himself goes under the name, *Villa Sweet Home*. But to go back to books—*Black Majesty* by John W. Vandercook, author of *Tom-Tom*, is now on sale in the book shops. Having set his beautiful pace in the writing of *Tom-Tom*, he was hard put to maintain it in this story of Henry Christophe, King of Haiti. One is agreeably surprised to find that *Black Majesty* ably keeps pace with *Tom-Tom*—here is historical fact woven into a sequence that reads like a fairy-tale. Dr. Odum of the University of North Carolina has given the public *Rainbow Round My Shoulder* which has received glowing tribute by the critics. Dr. Odum, it will be remembered, wrote two books on Negro spirituals as co-author with Guy B. Johnson.

Up From Slavery by Booker T. Washington is to be translated into Turkish and used in the schools of Turkey.

This seems to have been a month for art exhibits. Allan R. Freelon of Philadelphia showed thirty paintings in an exhibit given under the sponsorship of the Alpha Kappa Alpha Sorority . . . Albert Smith, formerly of Paris and Madrid, also held an exhibit in New York City . . . Mr. Smith's etchings have received much favorable comment.

Keep Shufflin', another Miller and Lyle production, is holding forth with enviable success at *Dalys 63rd Street Theatre* . . . *Porgy*, after a brilliant run in New York City has gone on tour . . . at this writing Washington audiences are experiencing this thing of beauty . . . Alexander Woolcott in the *N. Y. World* for Sunday, March the eighteenth, picks this play for the *Pulitzer Prize* with this word of praise:

The performance, in which the tolling from a distant steeple, the boom of fog-horns in the harbor, the rackety laughter of the pickaninies, the humming of the spirituals, the clink of hammer on stone, the rattle of dice in the courtyard, the snores of the drunken and the sorrowing of the heavy-laden have, by a miracle of imaginative direction, been orchestrated into a rhapsody in brown, remains alive and true. Six months of playing have not staled nor dulled it, nor robbed it of the throb of life. And the climax of the first act, when the monstrous nightmare shadows cast by the tossing arms of the mourners, dance a weird and frightening rigadoon on the bare, scrofulous wall of a once gracious room—that climax seems now, as it seemed when it was new, one of the high memorable moments in the history of the American theatre.

This gives us an opportunity to rejoice in the fact that Paul Robeson played Crown in the caste of *Porgy* for a spell . . . this is as it had originally been planned. However, Paul Robeson has now gone to London where he is to appear in the English edition of *Show Boat*. Speaking of Paul Robeson and his singing reminds us that Maude Cuney Hare, the folk-lorist, has just finished giving a group of four lectures on *Negro and Creole Music* at the *Allied Arts Studio* in Boston. William Richardson, baritone, gave the song illusrations that went with these lectures. But to return to the theatre . . . *Meek Mose* has gone by the board . . . the home edition of *Show Boat* continues with Jules Bledsoe singing very beautifully . . . *Coquette* in which Abbie Mitchell plays a minor part goes along evenly. By the by, Abbie Mitchell has given several successful concerts in the last month. Alexander Woolcott goes so far as to predict that there will eventually be a Negro Theatre of which *In Abraham's Bosom* and *Porgy* are the harbingers. The Negro in drama again comes in for another bit of publicity in the *New York Herald Tribune* for Sunday March eighteenth . . . *Color Notes*, a full-length column by William M. Houghton, appears in the dramatic section of that paper. The entire article is devoted to a discussion of the Negro in the American theatre.

On Thursday evening, March twenty-second, *Opportunity Magazine* held forth in a broadcasting hour over Station WABC at *Steinway Hall* . . . Aaron Douglas read a paper on the Negro artist; Countee Cullen, Jessie Fauset and Arna Bontemps read some of their poems; Dr. Albert C. Barnes gave a lecture on African Art; Miss Ernestine Covington played *Nocturne, E. Sharp Major* by Chopin and *Humoresque* by Rachmaninoff; Mrs. Lyndon Caldwell sang *Die Lotus Blume* and *Widmung* by Schumann and *Were You There* and *Go Down Moses* by Burleigh[.] Charles S. Johnson, editor of *Opportunity Magazine*, was the master of Ceremonies . . . he appropriately ended the evening with the quotation of an old African proverb which seems to have a vast prophetic quality. . . . *If you would tell anything to Heaven, tell it to the wind.*

And as we go to press the cherry blossoms are blooming . . . Just the other day I passed the miracle of a magnolia tree alight with blossoming candles.

ANONYMOUS

Bids for Literary Laurels[†]

MISS NELLA LARSEN

BIDS FOR LITERARY LAURELS—Hitherto unknown, whose new novel, "Quicksands" (Alfred A. Knopf & Co., New York), has been highly rated by critics. Miss Larsen, who deals with the subject of racial crossings, does one of the most interesting bits to be published since Miss Jessie Fauset wrote "There Is Confusion."

† From *Chicago Defender*, May 12, 1928: A1. Reprinted by permission of *Chicago Defender*.

"Quicksands" is written somewhat on the same style as Miss Fauset's book, but lacks much of the interest of the latter. Unusual interest centers around this book because of the fact that so little has been and is known of the author. Many persons are of the opinion that much of her life is reflected in "Quicksands," her first novel.

ANONYMOUS

Book a Week[†]

In some respects this book is an autobiography. The author is a New York woman. Her real name, Mrs. Elmer Imes.

Her mother is Danish and her father was colored, but her stepfather is white.

The heroine of "Quicksand" is such a person, whose white blood will not let her be satisfied amid the military discipline of a southern school where she is a teacher, nor yet in Harlem, where jim crow is absent, but where the color question is always of bobbing up.

In Copenhagen, Denmark, where the heroine goes to live with white relatives, it's the colored blood which rebels and causes her to refuse marriage offers of aristocratic Danes, who are lacking in color complexes of the Dixie type.

Helga Crane, this heroine, makes a botch of life, ending up as a wife of a southern preacher, whom she hates, but to whom she bears five children, one after the other.

In real life, Mrs. Imes has lived in Denmark as well as in the U. S. She has taught at Tuskegee. She did not wed a preacher and have children faster than she ought to.

After the super-sex stories like "Rainbow Round My Shoulder" and "Home to Harlem," "Quicksand" is a refreshing story, built on the proposition there is something else in Negro life besides jazz and cabarets.

ROARK BRADFORD

Mixed Blood[‡]

Here again is the old theme of mixed blood, Negro and Scandinavian this time, with the North, South, Chicago, Harlem and even Denmark for the backgrounds. The result is interesting.

[†] From *Baltimore Afro-American*, May 5, 1928: 6. Reprinted by permission of Afro-American Newspapers, Inc.
[‡] From *New York Herald Tribune*, May 13, 1928: 522. Reprinted by permission of the Estate of Roark Bradford.

Sharper pens than Miss Larsen's have dipped into this muddy brown ink and have come out blunted or inarticulate. Duller pens too have tried it and have written verbosely.

The story has to do with Helga Crane, daughter of a Danish woman and a nameless Negro man. She suffers the discriminations dealt to Negroes in Chicago and her education and the instincts inherited from her mother make her feel these abuses more acutely. At the age of twenty-two—she is a school teacher then—she revolts and flees. Ineffectually, of course. Always ineffectually. Throughout the book she revolts. Even in the last paragraph, after having borne four children as rapidly as the exigencies of nature permits, she revolts at the idea of bringing children into the world to suffer—and goes about preparing to give birth to the fifth.

The real charm of this book lies in Miss Larsen's delicate achievement in maintaining for a long time an indefinable, wistful feeling— that feeling of longing and at the same time a conscious realization of the impossibility of obtaining—that is contained in the idea of Helga Crane. (Helga is an idea more than she is a human being; drawing character does not seem to be one of Miss Larsen's major accomplishments.)

Whether it is possible to hold that feeling throughout the entire length of the book is a matter for speculation. It runs beautifully and artistically through the maze of realities and artificialities; the prim correctness of the school at Naxos; the mad rush of Chicago; the intellectual absurdities of Harlem; the cold gentleness of Copenhagen. Now it is languidly encased in the comforts of civilized culture; now it trembles uncertainly to the straining rumble of old Africa. But always it is there—a wistful note of longing, of anxiety, of futile searching, of an unconscious desire to balance black and white blood into something that is more tangible than a thing that merely is neither black nor white, of a nervous, fretful search for that will o' the wisp called happiness.

It leads directly to a splendid emotional climax. The brief scene is at a party in Harlem. Helga is alone for a moment with the man who first understood that strange emotions swelled within her bosom. (That was years before at Naxos. Now he is the husband of her best friend.) Her nerves are tuned to a high pitch; her soul is stirred; savagery tears at her heart; the black blood chokes the white, and Africa rumbles through her veins. And the man—suddenly the veneers of civilization crackle about him and—well, the reader is as tense as the two actors in the drama.

But alas! Without knowing just where it comes from, the reader suddenly catches a faint odor of talcum powder. And from that point on the book—in this reviewer's opinion—suffers from odors. Burnt cork, mostly . . .

In spite of its failure to hold up to the end, the book is good. No doubt it will be widely read and discussed. The reader, to get the maximum enjoyment, should begin with a mind as free as possible of racial prejudices and preconceived notions and conclusions. Miss Larsen seems to know much about the problems that confront the upper stratum of Negroes, and, happily, she does not get oratorical about what she knows. She is quite sensitive to Negro life, but she isn't hysterical about it. There is a saneness about her writing that, in these hysterical literary times, more than compensates for her faults.

W. E. B. DU BOIS

Two Novels[†]

I have just read the last two novels of Negro America. The one I liked; the other I distinctly did not. I think that Mrs. Imes, writing under the pen name of Nella Larsen, has done a fine, thoughtful and courageous piece of work in her novel. It is, on the whole, the best piece of fiction that Negro America has produced since the heyday of Chesnutt,[1] and stands easily with Jessie Fauset's "There is Confusion", in its subtle comprehension of the curious cross currents that swirl about the black American.

Claude McKay's "Home to Harlem", on the other hand, for the most part nauseates me, and after the dirtier parts of its filth I feel distinctly like taking a bath. This does not mean that the book is wholly bad. McKay is too great a poet to make any complete failure in writing. There are bits of "Home to Harlem", beautiful and fascinating: the continued changes upon the theme of the beauty of colored skins; the portrayal of the fascination of their new yearnings for each other which Negroes are developing. The chief character, Jake, has something appealing, and the glimpses of the Haitian, Ray, have all the materials of a great piece of fiction.

But it looks as though, despite this, McKay has set out to cater for that prurient demand on the part of white folk for a portrayal in Negroes of that utter licentiousness which conventional civilization holds white folk back from enjoying—if enjoyment it can be called. That which a certain decadent section of the white American world, centered particularly in New York, longs for with fierce and

† From *The Crisis* (June 1928): 202, 211. The publisher wishes to thank The National Association for the Advancement of Colored People, for authorizing the use of this material by W. E. B. Du Bois.
1. Charles Waddell Chesnutt (1858–1932) was a lawyer, NAACP activist, and writer, some of whose well-regarded works about complex, often mixed-race characters, were made into early silent films.

unrestrained passions, it wants to see written out in black and white, and saddled on black Harlem. This demand, as voiced by a number of New York publishers, McKay has certainly satisfied, and added much for good measure. He has used every art and emphasis to paint drunkenness, fighting, lascivious sexual promiscuity and utter absence of restraint in as bold and as bright colors as he can.

If this had been done in the course of a well-conceived plot or with any artistic unity, it might have been understood if not excused. But "Home to Harlem" is padded. Whole chapters here and there are inserted with no connection to the main plot, except that they are on the same dirty subject. As a picture of Harlem life or of Negro life anywhere, it is, of course, nonsense. Untrue, not so much as on account of its facts, but on account of its emphasis and glaring colors. I am sorry that the author of "Harlem Shadows" stooped to this. I sincerely hope that he will some day rise above it and give us in fiction the strong, well-knit as well as beautiful theme, that it seems to me he might do.

Nella Larsen on the other hand has seized an interesting character and fitted her into a close yet delicately woven plot. There is no "happy ending" and yet the theme is not defeatist like the work of Peterkin and Green. [2] Helga Crane sinks at last still master of her whimsical, unsatisfied soul. In the end she will be beaten down even to death but she never will utterly surrender to hypocricy and convention. Helga is typical of the new, honest, young fighting Negro woman—the one on whom "race" sits negligibly and Life is always first and its wandering path is but darkened, not obliterated by the shadow of the Veil. White folk will not like this book. It is not near nasty enough for New York columnists. It is too sincere for the South and middle West. Therefore, buy it and make Mrs. Imes write many more novels.

* * *

Social science in America has so long been the foot ball of "nigger"-hating propaganda that we Negroes fail to get excited when a new scientist comes into the field. We have had our fill of Bean, Smith, Brigham and McDougal, so that when a young student turns to the Negro problem, we assume he is going to come out exactly where he went in. When Melville Herskovits[3] started anthropological measurements in Harlem, the only hope we had was that he was a pupil of Franz Boaz.[4] But he proved to be more than this. Herskovits is a

---

2. Julia Peterkin (1880–1961); Paul Green (1894–1981)—both white.
3. Melville Herskovits (1895–1963) studied under Franz Boas and helped to found African studies.
4. Franz Boas (1858–1942), often called the father of American anthropology, was especially well known for opposing biological ideas of race and advancing cultural differences.

real scientist. That is: a man who is more interested in arriving at truth than proving a thesis of race superiority.

His book, "The American Negro", (Knopf) built up from a number of papers and studies is, in a real sense, epoch-making. First of all, he proves by a series of careful measurements and compilations that the American Negro is a new definite group. All of that nonsense fostered by the United States Census as to mulattos is swept away. I myself told the Census authorities of 1910 when I collaborated with them, that their figures on mulattos made a serious underestimate and was laughed at for my pains. Now comes Herskovits and proves by a wide study that less than one-fourth of the Negroes of the United States are of unmixed Negro blood and that forty per cent of them have as much or more white blood as Negro. This in itself is neither advantage nor disadvantage; but it shows on the one hand the idiocy of talking about the Negro as an "unassimilable" and distinct race in the United States, and of arguing about American Negroes from the same premises as we argue about the Bantu.

Indeed the interesting thing about Mr. Herskovits' conclusions is that we have in the American Negro, by actual physical measurements, a group which resembles in many important respects, a pure race. That is: the intermixture has gone on for so long and the "racial" inbreeding and inter-thinking have become so strong, that a singular group stability has been attained. Moreover, one feels that this group stability has been even more largely a matter of social and rational accomplishment than of mere physical descent.

The implications of Herskovits' studies are really tremendous, not simply for the race problem in the United States, but also for the whole question of human contact, intermingling of blood and social heredity. It is a little book of 92 pages and costs a trifle. It ought to be in every Negro's library.

We may end this review with one interesting quotation.

"The American Negroes are, after all, a homogeneous population. They are also a greatly mixed group. How may one reconcile these two statements? It is not so difficult when one really considers the proposition from all angles. For is it not true that all human groups represent large amounts of mixture? This brings us back to the theory of race. Students have wondered at the number of varieties of human types, and have been unable to account for them. They have also been at a loss to account for the degree to which all the so-called 'races' of man seem to shade from one type into another; with never the sharp lines of demarcation that are found when we divide one biological species from another."

W. E. B. D.

ARTHUR HUFF FAUSET

Quicksand[†]

Whatever else may be said about the comparative merits of Nella Larsen's novel, Quicksand, this much ought to be admitted by every reader: Quicksand is a step forward in the literature produced by American Negroes. For the first time, perhaps, a Negro author has succeeded in writing a novel about colored characters in which the propaganda motive is decidedly absent.

Not that the propaganda novel is without its purposes. We cannot see the point of insisting upon "art for art's sake," because of which many New Negroes frown down upon every use that art may be made of in order to further the cause of the Negro. If the "pure" artist desires to create pure art, then of course let him create pure art; but whoever set up any group of Negroes to demand that all art by Negroes must conform to such a standard?

And now to return to Quicksand. Nella Larsen has written a very interesting story, almost, we might say, a thrilling story. Her style is as acceptable for the type of novel as that of any other Negro writer we know of. What is more to her credit, Miss Larsen is as clear as she is swift and concise, which cannot be said of all of our writers. Her one great lack is a throbbing, penetrating depth. One gets the impression that Miss Larsen does not feel what she writes so much as she feels the need of writing. Perhaps this is the result of the objective attitude which the author has adopted. It is much easier to wax hot from within than to essay the role of impersonal observer, and thereafter lend warmth and color to the observed facts. Despite this rather glaring deficiency, Miss Larsen shows flashes of a capacity to be much more feelingful than she is in Quicksand, and this is very reassuring.

Unfortunately for the story, it fails to be convincing at the end. It is hard to reconcile Helga, the wife of a most ordinary third rate Baptist preacher who rarely takes a bath, with the demure young creature who is nothing if not most solicitous about those dainty touches which are absolutely essential to the happiness of the modern young woman.

This is of little importance, however. Nella Larsen has caught a stride. If she can maintain it in a story which does not falter at the end, she is likely to make us forget the rather timid attempts of earlier writers of the novel. There is a suggestion of her

† From Black Opals (June 1928): 19–20.

consummate artistry in the last sentence of the story—a whole story in itself—it is a hint of her essential fitness to essay the role of true novelist.

BAREFIELD GORDON

The Quest of Life[†]

Here above all other considerations is excellence in the artistry of the novel. The forte of the novel is in gradual development of character over lengthy periods of time and under varied circumstances. Helga Crane in "Quicksand" begins a hectic search for something which is indefinable even to herself. In the search Helga's character is kneaded over and over in an attempt to clarify a rather twisted personality. Finaly [sic] Helga's muddled emotions are made articulate, and with the same illogical rashness and propensity for trying anything, she ventures into quicksand. Here in quicksand, Helga meets a fate which the author has prepared us to expect and accept from the psychological weaknesses shown by various changes and indecision in the character's actions.

Naxos, the scene of Helga's first escape from boredom, is an institution of Tuskegeean characteristics. The rigid army discipline of institution irritated her because she thinks it forces the spontaneity out of the youths and tries to educate as the American forces attempt education in Haiti. Half cultured teachers trying to dictate the social dress and tastes of youths—monastery separation and discipline—stifled Helga's joy of living. She leaves.

In New York working for an insurance company, Helga becomes bored with Harlem society, with interracial propaganda, and escapes to Denmark. Helga passes through a season or more of Copenhagen social whirl before she is again wearied and returns to New York. Then in a fit of passion she marries a minister from Alabama. Helga marries into quicksand.

The hectic and varied career of Helga, bordering on melodrama, is sustained in reality by the style of writing. A lucid simplicity of expression and a fine sensitiveness of emotional heights imply more than the context. An excellent atmosphere is created externally for her inner broodings, but through various stages of discontent for which we are willing to concede sympathy, we desire to know an inkling of the goal of her desires—so much we know of her undesires and dissatisfactions. At the end of the book, Helga longs

† From *Chicago Defender*, 25 August, 1928: A1. Reprinted by permission of *Chicago Defender*.

to be back under soft lights, smoking cigarets [*sic*] and listening to exquisite toneless music. Helga has not shown any previous desires to enjoy such ecstacy [*sic*], and we have to account this to her vacillating mind.

This is, nevertheless, a fine written novel, and artistically sound from a technical view. The use of the Negro as a theme is neither for exhibition or propaganda, but for the author's idea of telling a good story.

EUGENE GORDON

Negro Fictionist[s] in America[†]

* * *

Nella Larsen in "Quicksand" writes beautifully at first; later, she apparently loses all sense of beauty of style, and her work reveals her as being rather wearied with her task. Somewhat beyond the middle of her book, Miss Larsen apparently made no effort to maintain the attractive style of the beginning. Thenceforward the tale limps like a tired freshman's English composition. Helga Crane, the central character of "Quicksand," is quite real at times. Until she perversely does a most unhuman thing, she is consistently the kind of human being most of us know,—ordinary, given to petty spites and silly contradictions. Such inconsistencies as she evinces in the earlier portion of the book are promptly forgiven, for they are consistently feminine.

My criticism must not imply a denial of Helga Crane's authenticity nor even a refusal to accept her as an excellent character of fiction; my criticism is for Helga's creator, who forgot to indicate in some way that Helga Crane's temperament was such as to impel her into committing unhuman acts. Helga, incidentally, is the only flesh and blood in the book; yet, being thus wracked with major inconsistencies, she may cause one to have reasonable doubt whether one has ever met or will ever meet her kind. If she were supposed to be a psychopath I should accept her as at least authentic. But she is not. No, I cannot accept her, despite her flesh and blood and some genuinely human impulses.

* * *

† From *Saturday Evening Quill* 2 (April 1928): 18–19.

G. W. K.

New Novels†

* * *

The American Negro has in the past few years come decisively into fiction, and since the very recent creation of the large and flourishing coloured city of Harlem, on the upper east side of New York (first celebrated in *Nigger Heaven*), the stories dealing with Negroes are wholly different from those that have come from the world of Uncle Remus. They are full of Society, of cocktail parties and modern talk, and you may sometimes read many pages before learning that you are in Afro-America. Miss Larsen breaks new ground. Her heroine has a coloured father and a Danish mother. From Negro Harlem she escapes to Denmark, where she is made much of, but she returns to New York in the full conviction that the coloured folk are her own people. The end is a wild surrender and a tragedy which to many readers will seem not only heartbreaking but unreal. Miss Larsen throws in an occasional piece of social criticism such as: "The race is sterile at the top. Few, very few, Negroes of the better class have children." She writes with directness and brevity; why then should she indulge repeatedly in mannered sentences that have no proper place except in the pages of Henry James?

G. W. K.

KATHARINE SHEPARD HAYDEN

[Review of *Quicksand*]‡

"Quicksand" is the story of a few central years of a girl's life. It is essentially the story of her inner life; the outer events are for the most part of secondary importance, merely the result of her inner conflicts, tangles, inexplicable moods and impulses. It is distinctly a subjective novel, and a thoroughly modern, sophisticated one, with very little characterization, very few characters, and no particular plot.

Helga Crane is an orphan, the daughter of a Danish girl and an American Negro. The conflicts that star her course arise chiefly out of the strange blend in her blood. Living with Negroes, she is still

† From *New Statesman* (June 2, 1928): 259–60. Reprinted by permission of New Statesman, Ltd.
‡ From *Annals of the American Academy of Political and Social Science* (November 8, 1928): 344–45. Reprinted by permission of Sage Publishing.

involuntarily a person apart—just remote enough to never fit in. Living with her white kindred in Denmark, she is still so dominated by her Negro blood that she refuses marriage to the Danish artist who could have given her multitudes of the things she desires but could not stir her emotions. She goes back to America and after a few intense emotional experiences, she is "converted" by a series of accidents, and, blinded by her senses, rushes into marriage with an Alabama preacher. We leave her, exhausted and disillusioned on nearly every score, bearing children in the Negro quarter of an Alabama town.

The book is well written, though the style has that choppy, involved, self-conscious quality that marks the majority of the sophisticated novels coming off the press now. The pictures of Harlem are tremendously interesting, full of color and delightful detail. The portrait of Helga Crane is rich and vivid; and yet it struck us as being elusively incomplete. It is too subjective, too fragmentary, too much of a psychological study; it is a chain of sudden and keen insights into the girl's nature and experience, but not quite the portrait of a fused and living creature, moving independently across the stage. This may not be fair criticism, however, for it is not such persons that the average modern novels endeavor to portray. Their aim is not to tell a story or create a heroine and her cohorts, but to make an informal study, profound, but necessarily fragmentary. Judged on this score, the novel is indeed a good one, artistically and compellingly done.

H. W. R.

Quicksand:
A Story of the Revolt of a Negro School Teacher[†]

The first half of the novel deals with the revolt of a negro schoolteacher from the altruistic and rather stupid task of educating backward members of her race. This revolt, beginning with a flight to Chicago and continuing with the agony of fruitless job-hunting in a big, impervious city, reaches a happy and unexpected conclusion. Helga Crane is adopted as the secretary to an influential woman lecturer through whose agency she is received as a more or less permanent guest into the home of Anne Grey, a lady of refinement, ease and social distinction in the upper level of Harlem society. The sunlit boudoirs, the fine fluffy clothes, the flowers, the elegant furnishings which Helga's vehemently feminine mind had so often dreamed

† From *Boston Evening Transcript* (June 20, 1928): 2.

of—all these, as if by a stroke of magic, have now become the usual and accepted stuff of her surroundings. She should have been happy. But here the central theme of the story becomes forcibly apparent, for under the impulse of a strange, insatiable craving, just at the time when fortune seemed to have smiled her broadest, the lady becomes dissatisfied and leaves for Denmark to visit relatives.

Thus, in the second portion of the novel, we get a new and interesting account of the negro in Europe; for there, as Helga soon discovers, her color actually seems to enhance her charm, and from the triumph she had previously achieved in the realm of bettering her wardrobe and her manner of life, she proceeds to a dazzling victory as a person of charm, actually desired and frankly accepted as a woman of social distinction. But her momentary elation falls away with the same rapidity that restlessness had overtaken her at Naxos and in Harlem. Back in America once more, the whole tone of her existence becomes increasingly darker until we leave her troubled as never before, reduced to the prosaic tale of marriage, and harassed by the commonplace occupation of bearing the fifth of her children.

Miss Larsen's novel deals with a universal story—the sad and mysterious one of the woman who seems destined never to comprehend the dangers of seeking an unattainable Heaven upon earth. For Helga Crane is a vivid and pathetically drawn portrait of a woman grasping at the flowers of life for her nutriment and overlooking its fruit. Hers is a tragedy of mistaken values, a tragedy that is independent of social rank and racial distinction. "Quicksand" proves quite definitely that a colored author can blend successfully the ever-moving history of the American negro with the broad, universal problems that cling to humanity as a whole.

H. W. R.

MARGERY LATIMER

Nella Larsen's "Quicksand"†

This book makes you want to read everything that Nella Larsen will ever write. It is neither distinguished nor excellent and it is not "a modern masterpiece" but it wakes you up, it makes you aware that there are other races besides the white race. You see the great space between black and white, the elaborate mental barrier, and in the same moment you are conscious of the reason for it and the inhumanity of it. The book is objective enough to keep you from

† From *Book World* (July 22, 1928): 7M. Reprinted by permission of the Estate of Margery Latimer.

speculating about its author and wondering if she is like Helga Crane, Danish and colored, but you feel the deepest part of her in the character and you give to it your deepest.

The jacket states that the heroine is not confronted by the problems of a class or a race but that she is so confronted by race, in her dividedness, in her swinging between the Negro and the white that her one problem is to transcend race. Helga has no real home on this earth, the struggle in her between the Danish and the Negro blood is never ending.

In every background there are the elements of her conflict, every person she meets has his effect, every contact is unsatisfactory.

When she longs for people who really appreciate the Negro and enters an educated group in Harlem she finds them bitterly prejudiced in favor of their race but copying white characteristics, scorning the black, kinky hair, hating the distinctions made between black and white, scorning all the primitive, rich aspects of their race. So she goes to Denmark to her mother's people and there she is appreciated, loved and respected, but she longs for Harlem and for black people. Now that she is with white people she misses something in them just as she had missed something in the black.

The style, in its elegance and some of its mannerisms, suggests Mr. Hergesheimer [1] and that elegance is retained even when Helga marries the Negro revivalist and begins to live her life as a colored woman, bearing children in a dream, living in poverty. Then one day she plans to escape, her eyes are open, she is horrified at what she has done, at her black children, her tired, sleepy body, her rags. But by the time she is strong enough to go away she is about to have her fifth child.

MARGERY LATIMER

ALAIN LOCKE

1928: A Retrospective Review[†]

The year 1928 represents probably the floodtide of the present Negrophile movement. More books have been published about Negro life by both white and Negro authors than was the normal output of more than a decade in the past. More aspects of Negro life have been treated than were ever even dreamed of. The

---

1. Joseph Hergesheimer (1880–1954), known for naturalistic novels about the rich.
† From *Opportunity* (January 1929): 8–11. Reprinted by permission of the National Urban League.

proportions show the typical curve of a major American fad, and to
a certain extent, this indeed it is. We shall not fully realize it until
the inevitable reaction comes; when as the popular interests flags,
the movement will lose thousands of supporters who are now under
its spell, but who tomorrow would be equally hypnotized by the next
craze.

A retrospective view ought to give us some clue as to what to
expect and how to interpret it. Criticism should at least forewarn us
of what is likely to happen. In this, as with many another boom, the
water will need to be squeezed out of much inflated stock and many
bubbles must burst. However, those who are interested in the real
Negro movement which can be discerned behind the fad, will be
glad to see the fad subside. Only then will the truest critical appraisal
be possible, as the opportunity comes to discriminate between
shoddy and wool, fair-weather friends and true supporters, the stock-
brokers and the real productive talents. The real significance and
potential power of the Negro renaissance may not reveal itself until
after this reaction, and the entire top-soil of contemporary Negro
expression may need to be ploughed completely under for a second
hardier and richer crop.

To my mind the movement for the vital expression of Negro life
can only truly begin as the fad breaks off. There is inevitable distor-
tion under the hectic interest and forcing of the present vogue for
Negro idioms. An introspective calm, a spiritually poised approach,
a deeply matured understanding are finally necessary. These may
not, need not come entirely from the Negro artist; but no true and
lasting expression of Negro life can come except from these more
firmly established points of view. To get above ground, much forcing has had to be endured; to win a hearing, much exploitation has
had to be tolerated. There is as much spiritual bondage in these
things as there ever was material bondage in slavery. Certainly the
Negro artist must point the way when this significant moment
comes, and establish the values by which Negro literature and art
are to be permanently gauged after the fluctuating experimentalism
of the last few years. Much more could be said on this subject,—but
I was requested to write a retrospective review of the outstanding
literary and artistic events of 1928 in the field of Negro life.

The year has been notable particularly in the field of fiction,—a
shift from the prevailing emphasis in Negro expression upon poetry.
In this field there were three really important events,—Claude
McKay's *Home to Harlem*, Rudolph Fisher's *Walls of Jericho* and Julia
Peterkin's *Scarlet Sister Mary*. An appraisal of the outstanding creative achievement in fiction a year ago would not have given us a
majority on the Negro side. That in itself reflects a solid gain, gauged

by the standard I have set,—for no movement can be a fad from the inside. Negro fiction may even temporarily lose ground in general interest, but under cover of the present vogue there has been nurtured an important new articulateness in Negro life more significant than mere creativeness in poetry. For creative fiction involves one additional factor of cultural maturity,—the art of social analysis and criticism. * * *

* * *

Of course, it is the problem novel which is the acid test for propaganda. *Dark Princess*, marking the reappearance in fiction of the versatile Dr. DuBois, for all its valuable and competent social portraiture, does not successfully meet this test, but falls an artistic victim to its own propagandist ambushes. This novel by the veteran must on this account cede position in this field to the quite successful thrust of the novice,—Nella Larsen's *Quicksand*. This study of the cultural conflict of mixed ancestry is truly a social document of importance, and as well, a living, moving picture of a type not often in the foreground of Negro fiction, and here treated perhaps for the first time with adequacy. Indeed this whole side of the problem which was once handled exclusively as a grim tragedy of blood and fateful heredity now shows a tendency to shift to another plane of discussion, as the problem of divided social loyalties and the issues of the conflict of culture. * * *

* * *

T. S. MATTHEWS

What Gods! What Gongs!†

Ol' Man Adam an' His Chillun, by Roark Bradford. New York: Harper and Brothers. $2.50.
Quicksand, by Nella Larsen. New York: Alfred A. Knopf. $2.50.
Home to Harlem, by Claude McKay. New York: Harper and Brothers. $2.50.
Black Majesty, by John W. Vandercook. New York: Harper and Brothers. 207 pages. $2.50.

We are all apt to be defensive about the Negro, even if we like him. Mr. Bradford, the author of "Ol' Man Adam an' His Chillun," exemplifies this attitude by confessing that it is the nigger, as opposed to

† From *The New Republic* (May 30, 1928): 50–51. © 1928 The New Republic. All rights reserved. Used under license.

the Negro, that interests him. We still like to consider the Negro a child, if we think of him as a human being at all. And unself-conscious children, if they are of a happy disposition—and Mr. Bradford's invariably are—are much more attractive than children who have copied some airs and graces from their elders. The stories in "Ol' Man Adam an' His Chillun"—all Biblical but mighty free—are in the line of Uncle Remus, and remind us more than once of that limber-tongued old story-teller. "De Lawd," who figures genially in them all, is a kind of good-natured Southern Colonel, dignified in his leisurely way, but easygoing enough to be popular. He arouses not so much amusement as delight. Here he is at the Creation, the heavenly fish-fry having run out of firmament.

> So de Lawd r'ared back and passed a miracle and say, "Let hit be some firmament. And when I say let hit be some firmament, I mean let hit be a whole heap of firmament. I'm sick and tired of lettin' hit be jest a little bitty dab of firmament when I pass a miracle."

There are no airs and graces about Mr. Bradford's niggers, but they are, after all, old-fashioned. Harlem has changed all that. With "Quicksand," the story of an educated mulatto girl, we are brought up to date with a jerk. Helga Crane, teacher at a Southern Negro institution, becomes bored with its cramped life and goes North, first to Chicago and then to New York. This, ladies and gentlemen of Park Avenue, is what she finds in Harlem: "Their sophisticated cynical talk, their elaborate parties, the unobtrusive correctness of their clothes and homes, all appealed to her craving for smartness, for enjoyment." If your knowledge of New York Negro life has been bounded by Florence Mills and Carl Van Vechten, this social mirror may surprise you. Are you, through no fault of your own, a member of the D. A. R., or descended from the one true Mayflower? Listen and tremble. ". . . Miss MacGooden, humorless, prim, ugly, with a face like dried leather, prided herself on being a 'lady' from one of the best families—an uncle had been a Congressman in the period of the Reconstruction." In case you should think irony has been intended, it might be added that the heroine, when she is being very bitter and thoughtful, talks to herself like this: "'A beggar,' she thought ruefully, 'cannot expect to choose.'" Helga Crane eventually tires of the high life of Harlem, and, after an extended visit to Copenhagen, where she makes a distinct social hit, returns to New York, is accidentally converted, seduces her evangelist, marries him, and subsides hopelessly into a little Negro community in the South. The book is compact of "fine writing," but it is not funny: it makes you uncomfortable. You have met the Negro.

In "Home to Harlem" you meet the nigger again, but this time he has the breath of life in him: he is neither the black-faced minstrel of a white man's plantation nor the stilted creature of a white man's culture, but the haphazard and lively spawning of a city street. Jake, when he works, is sometimes a stoker, sometimes a longshoreman, sometimes a dining-car waiter, but we see him mostly pursuing enjoyment. And, as Jake himself might say, he catches plenty. Jake is a "good nigger." He is a Negro unaware of our world. It is a Negro world he inhabits, a world of "gals" and liquor, a world where work is only the price of play. It is a world of pure sensation; Jake never bothers about ideas, ideas never bother him; he is a creature of impulse and appetite, his progress a free and animal rhythm. And though the rhythm is too perfect to be quite convincing, it is impressive. There is only one character in the book who is bothered by ideas, and he is an educated Negro—morose, ineffectual and priggish. And he makes us uncomfortable: he reminds us of the Problem. Jake does not make us uncomfortable: though quite savage by our standards, he is a human being, and a Mystery. We can live comfortably with mysteries, but not with problems.

"Black Majesty" is the epic, *in parvo,* of King Christophe of Haiti, successor of Toussaint l'Ouverture and Dessalines. It is an historical record, with a bibliography appended, but written with the freedom of a novel. * * * As our author shows him to us, Christophe was one of that rare breed of despot occasionally visited on a people to plague them into greatness. But Christophe's people were niggers. As he told a British visitor, "We have no pride because we have nothing to remember." And in order to build something that should endure, he drove his subjects relentlessly, in a kind of hurried frenzy. * * * That agonizing failure was the failure of Haiti.

Of these four books, only one leaves a pleasant taste in the mouth, and that one, naturally, is Mr. Bradford's collection of fairy tales. "Quicksand" deals with reality, but as falsely as its characters ape the envied and hated whites. "Home to Harlem" has the most documentary interest, for it is a simple picture of the crude and violent life of the jungle nigger in the jungle city. All these books tell us facts—interesting, humorous, sordid, pathetic—about the Negro; but "Black Majesty" captures our imagination, for it shows us the Negro, not as we know him, but as he might have been, perhaps might be—it is the tale of a black man who tried to be, not a white man, but a giant.

ANONYMOUS

Miscegenation? Bah![†]

It was rumored recently that a Harlem lady was about to publish a novel on the theme of miscegenation. It was expected with eager curiosity; people wondered whether it would be pro or con. They need not have been excited, for the subject of miscegenation is not worth colored people's worry. Let white people do the worrying; they are the ones who bring it about. We might as well worry because water does not flow uphill.

The expected book has arrived and miscegenation is in it. The book is neither pro nor con. It is not loaded down with lengthy arguments on the good or evil of race mixtures; it is neither a plea to be taken into the white race nor a long scream of hate for everything Caucasian; it is a story, and mostly a well-told one.

In her determination to keep to her story the author pares it down more than is necessary. There are places in the book where an author might be forgiven for spreading out into description or philosophizing, but this author yields not to temptation. She cleaves to the line of a personal narrative.

Helga Crane, the heroine, is the child of an American Negro and a beautiful Danish woman. This is original and enlightening. It is original because in a mulatto's parentage the father is generally white and the mother colored. It is enlightening because an American publisher has dared to issue a book in which a Nordic white woman voluntarily has a child by a Negro. And the unhappy result of the union is due not to the miscegenation but to the personal character of the man. If Helga's mother had married a decent colored man she would have been happy. But then this story would not have been written.

Helga is one of those unfortunates who are born and die dissatisfied. The story begins with her teaching English at Naxos, a Negro school in the South. She stands it for a while, but at length her gorge rises at the narrow life, with its smugness and cant. She quits the place in mid-term and goes back to Chicago, where she was born. Her white uncle's white wife is aghast at the idea of a Negro niece, so Helga leaves Chicago and comes to New York under favorable conditions. The favorable conditions are—but this is a book review, not a book.

† From *New York Amsterdam News* (May 16, 1928): 16. Reprinted by permission of *New York Amsterdam News*.

Soon Helga begins to hate New York. The reader, who has sympathized with her so far, wonders if there is any place this side of heaven, or in heaven, where she will be contented. By a romantic turn of fate, which all girls dream of and few experience, she goes to Copenhagen, Denmark, the home of her mother.

There she finds that not only on the question of race, but in everything else, Denmark is different from America. The very things that make her a social outcast in America make her a social triumph in Denmark. For a while she lives in a maiden's Paradise. But soon her general dissatisfaction with life asserts itself, she grows homesick for black faces and an annoying experience brings matters to a head, and she seizes on an excuse for returning to America.

In the meantime, the man she has always secretly loved has married her best friend. But Helga is still in his blood, and at a party, stimulated by forbidden spirits, he loses his head for a moment. So does Helga. They make an assignation, and Helga blissfully contemplates adultery. They meet and—believe it or not—the man gets cold feet. In a rage she slaps him in the face. Who wouldn't?

Helga concludes that the thing she has always missed, in Naxos, Chicago, Copenhagen and New York, is biological fulfillment. She has certainly traveled a long way to find out such a simple thing. Then comes the incredible part of the story, which has thus far held the reader by its fidelity to life. Helga's intelligence deserts her; she snatches what she wants, not, indeed, in the worst way, but one of the worst ways for a girl of her training, aspirations and tendencies. Thus she finds herself in a bog, a quicksand, from which there is no escape. For the rest of her days she will beat her life out against the walls of a prison.

The last part of the story, though interesting, is a disappointment. The reader has not been artistically prepared for it. Given such a character as Helga, he finds it hard to fit her into such a picture. He would find it more logical if she had become a courtesan, or at least something by which she might have satisfied her aesthetic tastes. Some girls might have gone down into drab ugliness, but not Helga, unless she was forced. And she was not forced.

One of the best things about this story is the author's style, especially in the first chapters. It is fresh, clear and limpid; in its easy, natural, crystal grace there is no striving for effect. If the plot were as good as the style it would raise the story considerably. One feles [sic] that a much stronger story could have been written around Helga's Danish mother and the Negro gambler who was Helga's father.

RAYMOND MORTIMER

New Novels†

Home to Harlem. By Claude McKay. (Harpers. 7s. 6d.)
Quicksand. By Nella Larsen. (Knopf. 7s. 6d.)
The Magic Mountain. By Thomas Mann. (Secker. 7s. 6d.)

*   *   *

"Home to Harlem" is perhaps the novel I have enjoyed most of the new ones I have read this year; but even the professional reviewer has a weak spot for certain subjects. Some readers like blue lagoons, others the Yukon, some always fall for a circus, others for picturesque peasants. I happen to have a passion for negroes, and I recommend "Home to Harlem" chiefly to my fellow-enthusiasts. As literature it is inferior to "Sorrow and Sunlight," but that was a fantasy, and this is written by a negro: the picture it presents of negro life in New York is presumably realistic and authentic. Mr. Claude McKay writes of the less educated members of his race affectionately, but without illusion; he does not draw a moral, he is not superior. All the charm of the negro character is here, the unworldliness, vitality, directness, and divine spontaneity. These coloured people drink too much and make love too easily. But their hearts are open, they take no thought for the morrow, they are those to whom was promised the Kingdom of Heaven. Mr. McKay's book is always amusing and sometimes moving.

Miss Nella Larsen is, I believe, herself a Mulatto. She writes gravely and sometimes bitterly of the colour problem. Her heroine is at home with neither white nor coloured people. But at the end she succumbs, against all her conscious wishes, to the negro blood in her, with disastrous effects. This may be probable; Miss Larsen does not succeed in making it appear so. Her heroine is a prig, entirely lacking in just those qualities which one admires in Mr. McKay's characters; a person who makes the worst of both worlds, exciting pity but not sympathy; and the book supports, unintentionally no doubt, the repulsive and, I suspect, quite untrue theory that education takes away from the negro everything that makes him admirable and delightful.

*   *   *

With great enterprise Mr. Secker has republished Thomas Mann's "The Magic Mountain" in one volume costing only 7s. 6d. It is a most remarkable novel, unnecessarily long, I think, and full of

---

† From *The Nation and Athenaeum* (June 23, 1928): 397. Reprinted by permission of New Statesman, Ltd.

philosophical arguments which are neither very new nor very profound. But the author has exploited the possibilities of illness as a subject to an extraordinary extent. Many readers would complain that the book is morbid. This is true, and the chief cause, I think, of its excellence.

ANONYMOUS

[The New Books]†

Put together to a large extent from autobiographical materials, Miss Larsen's story of the life and struggles of a mulatto woman, the daughter of a negro man and a Scandinavian woman, is no more than mildly interesting. It has a distinctly cosmopolitan touch, as its principal character moves from Tuskeegee, called Naxos in the book, to the upper circles of Copenhagen society, from Copenhagen to New York, and from New York back to a little Alabama town as the wife of a typical negro minister of the revivalistic type.

Miss Larsen is herself the daughter of a negro by a Danish woman, and most of the important incidents of the book follow her own life closely. She herself is married to a Doctor of Philosophy from the University of Michigan, however, and it is in her one direct departure from her own life story as the framework of her book that she becomes wholly unconvincing. She would have us believe that her young and attractive mulatto woman, after life has failed to please her, could fall in love with and marry a man far beneath her in every respect and be willing to bear his children—one a year—and to endure the unutterable stupidity of an Alabama village.

A great love even between two people so different as her Helga Crane and the Reverend Mr. Pleasant Green might account for such strange behavior, but there is nothing to indicate that any such feeling exists.

The silly assertion on the jacket of the book that "it is almost the only Negro novel of recent years which is wholly free from the curse of propaganda" indicates, it appears to this reviewer, that the jacketeer has not read much of the new fiction dealing with the negro. Most of it is altogether free from propaganda, freer indeed, than Miss Larsen's book.

The style of the book is well-mannered and touched here and there with beauty. But its chief interest lies in the fact that its principal character is a person of a quite unusual mixture of blood rather than in what she does or says or what happens to her.

† From *Saturday Review of Literature* (May 19, 1928): 895–96. Reprinted by permission of JTE Multimedia.

ANONYMOUS

[New Books and Reprints][†]

The rather old-fashioned and occasionally stilted manner in which this novel is written does not obscure its genuine feeling, although it makes now and again for dull reading. Helga Crane, a young mulatto girl teaching in a negro school in one of the Southern States of America, throws up her job and goes to live in New York. Harlem provides her with a good deal that she had previously lacked, but still disappoints her. After an abortive love affair she decides to go to Copenhagen, in which town her mother was born, and where the colour problem does not exist. Here, too, she finds new things to interest her for a time, but eventually becomes restless and home-sick and decides to return to America. Religion sways her as she grows more disillusioned, and she marries the Rev. Mr. Pleasant Green, a "rattish" negro preacher, unctuous and self-satisfied. The story ends on a note of hopelessness, with Helga condemned to a life of domestic cares and incessant child-bearing. It is a rather drab, mournful narrative, but informed by intense earnestness.

MARY WHITE OVINGTON

Book Chat[‡]

Immediate Release   August 3, 1928

Book Chat

By

MARY WHITE OVINGTON,

Chairman, Board of Directors of the N.A.A.C.P.

The critics are agreed that this book of Nella Larsen's (we in New York know her as Mrs. Imes, librarian) is free from propaganda. "It is a human not a sociological tragedy", [*sic*] we read on the jacket. And this is to some extent true. Nevertheless, few books dealing with

---

† From *Times Literary Supplement* (July 26, 1928): 553. Reprinted by permission of News UK & Ireland Limited.
‡ From NAACP (New York: NAACP, 1928). The publisher wishes to thank The National Association for the Advancement of Colored People, for authorizing the use of this material by Mary White Ovington.

the Negro have such a keen insight into the race problem. Has anyone better expressed the Negro's revolt against the race consciousness that hedges him in than this: "Even the two rough days found her on deck (Helga, the heroine, is on her way to her white relatives in Denmark) reveling like a released bird in her returned feeling of happiness and freedom, that blessed sense of belonging to herself alone and not to a race." And yet, the theme of the book is, that something within her makes her incapable of keeping that freedom.

Helga Crane is a mulatto whose early years were spent among whites more than among colored. The story opens when as a teacher in a Negro school she finds herself in revolt against the whole atmosphere of the place, "its shame, lies, hypocrisy, cruelty, servility and snobbishness." She has gone there impelled by a desire for service. A year and a half has dulled this feeling and her love of beauty, her independence, has made her hate her environment. She lies in bed, thinking over it all, determined to leave it that very day. Which she does. For one of the notable things about Helga is her way of picking up and leaving a situation when it becomes hateful to her.

The author, we understand, is a Dane herself, and her picture of Helga in Copenhagen has added interest when we realize the likelihood of its veracity. Helga there learns to accentuate her race, to bring out the darkness of her skin, the brilliancy of her eyes. Her social success depends on the emphasis she puts on her African descent. And she attains social success, the chance for a brilliant marriage, but something keeps her from tying up with these alien people, and she returns to her native land.

But I am telling too much of the story. It is not an exciting one but it holds one's interest. Whether the end is possible I am not capable of deciding. To me it is the least real part of the book. But it has the merit of being unusual.

Nella Larsen may have published much or little, this is the first volume of hers that I have been fortunate enough to see, but she has a finished style, beautiful in its choice of words and * * * imagery. She has not been attracted by the jerkiness of the modern school. Her secondary figures are a little indistinct, but Helga is clear, unforgettable. As she sits on the bedside idly dangling a mule across her bare toes, telling the astonished friend who comes in to see if she is ill, "I am not going to be late to my class, I'm not going to be there at all", we like her and applaud her reckless courage. We want greatly to learn what she will do next. She is a real person one who will be long remembered by those who are interested in the literature of the colored race; and, we hope, by many others who are interested in literature with whatever race it may deal.

ALICE BEAL PARSONS

Three Novels[†]

Debonair. By G. B. Stern. Alfred A. Knopf. $2.50.
Bad Girl. By Vina Delmar. Harcourt, Brace and Company. $2.
Quicksand. By Nella Larsen. Alfred A. Knopf. $2.50.

Each of these novels possesses the qualities that make a literary curiosity; each explores a country still new to the majority of readers. In "Debonair" G. B. Stern presents the newest and swankiest flapper. * * *

* * *

After the disappointing facility of this book, "Bad Girl" seems as fresh as a dill pickle on a hot summer day. * * *
"Quicksand" is the story of a mulatto who is dragged one way by her Negro blood and another by her white. Although it lacks the professional polish of Miss Stern's work, and the very real flair for literary craftsmanship of Mrs. Delmar's, although its style and manner are still imitative and often too conscientiously correct, and although there is a certain naivete in the presentation of the culture, wealth, and sophistication of the Harlem intellectuals, the book is an attempt to portray a real person in all her complexities, instead of being a complimentary or a spiteful version of some individual never really revealed. The motivation of this character is not always convincingly explained; the intention of the book is not even always clear; but it is a mine of information about one human being. Its writer shows a passion for understanding. This is perhaps a quality even more rare than Mrs. Delmar's gift for seizing the seemingly trivial details that make us see a person. Whether it promises more for the future remains to be seen.

R. H. A.

[*Quicksand*, by Nella Larsen][‡]

This sets out to be the tale of a mulatto girl caught in the conflict of two races; it becomes a tragedy of the commonplace that actually has nothing to do with race troubles; and it remains a good, and in

† From *The Nation* (May 9 1928): 540. © 1928 The Nation Company. All rights reserved. Used by permission.
‡ From *Canadian Forum* (1928): 730. Reprinted by permission of the publisher.

many ways an unusual, story. That it is a first novel possibly explains the inadequacy of its style. 'An observer would have thought her well fitted to that framing of light and shade.' Oh, yes, Helga was a girl with well turned arms and legs, delicately chiselled [*sic*] ears and an air of radiant, careless health. Her room was comfortable and furnished with rare and intensely personal taste. But such inanities are forgiven by the odd flash: 'The husband of Mrs. Hayes-Rore had at one time been a dark thread in the soiled fabric of Chicago's South Side politics.' And more serious than hackneyed phrases and meaningless adjectives is the author's shirking from action. She prefers to relate an incident, reflectively, after it has happened and overworks the auxiliary 'had.' Perhaps she was afraid that if she became dramatic she would be theatric. There is this to be said for her restraint: it saves her from being flamboyant and from making capital out of the 'picturesqueness' of Harlem. There is more life in the book when, toward the climax, she joins the heroine in letting go. In the woman who is neither white nor black and who longs to be both. Helga's fear of marrying a white and bringing more trouble into the world is quite casual, and her yearning for the negro is, after all, no more than a symbol of her physical dissatisfaction. There is ironic humour in this book, although the last stroke is too deliberately labeled 'Irony, after Anatole France'. What a pity Miss Larsen was afraid of her comic spirit! Let's hope that in her next novel she will give it a show and that she will allow herself to be more vivid. —R.H.A.

E. MERRILL ROOT

Ebony Hour-Hand, Pointing to Midnight†

The fine poet Robert Frost wrote, in one of his infrequent lapses,

> "How are we to write
> The Russian novel in America
> As long as life goes so unterribly?"

"Quicksand" is a mordant footnote to such facile comment upon that America which is, without doubt, the saddest of the continents. A new indictment against that spiritual Labrador upon whose grey rocks and under whose blood-red sunsets we live, the book is a significant document of the contemporary Negro consciousness and a poignant document of the contemporary human tragedy. It is an

† From *Christian Century* 18 (October 1928): 1261–62. Copyright © 1928 by the Christian Century. Reprinted by permission of the Christian Century.

ebony hour-hand, pointing, simply and terribly, to the hour which
the Negro soul (and indeed the modern soul) has reached in America. All who are interested in the psychography of the modern Negro,
all who are interested in the sickness which has become the soul of
articulate America, should read "Quicksand."

As a work of art, it is good but not great. Its style has not the rolling echoes and the dying fall of great writing; rather it is too remi-
niscent of the staccato but broken click of typewriters in a newspaper
office. Nor is the story in its architecture flawless or great. While it
has everywhere an impetus of interest, it does not everywhere lay
broad philosophical and psychological bases for eternity beneath the
narrative.

The story is the pathody (rather than the tragedy) of Helga Crane,
whose father was a Negro gambler in Chicago, whose mother was a
Danish emigrant. In Helga ice and fire forever war, denying her
peace or power or even a sure purpose. As in the tragedy immortally
sung by Housman, the "truceless armies" of the hostile races, "tram-
ple rolled in blood and sweat." Helga, like Housman, could well say:

> "None will part us, none undo
> The knot that makes one flesh of two . . .
> When shall I be dead and rid
> Of the wrong my father did?
> How long, how long, till spade and hearse
> Put to sleep my mother's curse?"

A race-divided soul, she does not know what she wants—but she
knows that she wants it. Starting as an idealist devoting her life to
uplift in a southern Negro college, she suddenly realizes the boredom, poverty, hypocrisy, and weary clockwork cruelty of it—and
leaves to seek a new life (carrying the old life in her veins). From
starvation in Chicago to opulence in Harlem she goes, until the glit-
ter and gayety of Negro urbanity (which at first she loved) weary
and sicken her fickle and divided soul. Especially (and here is the
typical note of the book) does she hate the platitudes of the "race
problem"—the eternal attempt of caricatures of Prometheus to uplift
everything but themselves. And so again she goes, chasing like a true
naive modern the rainbow's end—supposing again like a typical
modern that happiness exists in space and not in spirit. She goes to
Copenhagen—and finds herself waiting for her there. "Coelum, non
animam." Feted, feasted, free from race discrimination; the fad and
sensation of society; proposed to by fashion's darling, the man-of-
the-world turned artist . . . yet, to her, all this is but ashes for beauty.
The ice can no more satisfy her than the fire. These Danes who accept
her are (at last she realizes) cold, decorous, white; they lack the
African color of copper suns. And Helga Crane returns to Harlem.

In Harlem she falls again in love, with a Dr. Anderson whom she always would have loved had she let herself. He too loves her, but fears her; married to another, he kisses Helga in a moment of passion—and then apologizes . . . whereupon she slaps his face. Sick with the suppressed desire which her unsuppressed knowledge tells her he will never satisfy now, she blunders into a Negro revival, takes the crude evangelism for religion, marries the greasy shepherd of the flock, and in a fervor of suppressed "religion" follows him gladly to some Gopher Prairie in Alabama where (between amorousness and religious epilepsy) she lives happily until child-bearing wears her out.

The death and all her woe of this ending hardly convince. Helga has been no fool; that she—traveled, sophisticate, selfish, hypercivilized, beauty-loving—should, even in the stress of inner tempest, turn to negroid Billy Sundayism and the arms of the Rev. Pleasant Green is (fortunately) too bad to be true. It seems invented to point a moral and adorn a tale.

As a document of Negro disillusion—as a picture of a decade that has hitched its Cadillac to Mr. Mencken's Mercury—the book is significant. It is unillusioned, candid, civilized (in its bad as well as its good sense). As representation it is good; as interpretation it is bad.

*   *   *

The publishers claim that it is art because it is "free from the curse of propaganda"—which is like saying that the cry of the suicide, "I will drown, I will drown, no one shall save me!" is not an attitude toward life. It is propaganda for the folded hands—which is never recognized as propaganda. It is an indictment against life: an assertion that human beings are creatures of "a certain gallant and a pitiful inadequacy"; that the follies into which our blind fever and fret of appetite lead us prove that there is no God; that we are all (but especially Negroes) sick rats in the sinking ship of the world.

The book furnishes the best reply to its own philosophy and to the whole modern ignorance and naivete that calls itself disillusion. Helga is supposed to be "civilized." She goes into a Negro mission and hears the poor people howling the name of God and, utterly ignorant and naive about the greatest experience of life (which is religion), she supposes that this crude return to jungle emotion is religion! Shades of Blake, of Bunyan, of Augustine, of Tolstoi! It is as if a very ignorant rustic, his senses esthetically untrained, his mind vacant of Dante and Romeo and Abelard, should visit a city and stray into the house of a harlot and suppose that such orgies were—love. And such ignorance is supposed today to be sophistication!

But the book, in so far as it is Miss Larsen herself, is excellent. She has, in so far as she has simply bared a modern Negro soul, race-divided and disillusioned by our current misosophy, done us a service, and done it interestingly, powerfully. The book is a noteworthy hour-hand of ebony, pointing to midnight in the Negro soul, in the modern soul. But it is for us to realize that midnight is the beginning of morning.

ANONYMOUS

Selections from the New Spring Fiction[†]

A story of an incomplete life. Helga Crane, whose mother was a Dane and whose father was a Negro, is torn with the conflicting impulses of two races. A phase of life in Harlem, working, talking of the race problem, and she is satiated with black faces and longing for white ones. A phase with her mother's fashionable relatives in Copenhagen, and she is restless, dissatisfied, longing for Harlem.

"This knowledge, this certainty of the division of her life into two parts in two lands, into physical freedom in Europe and spiritual freedom in America, was unfortunate, inconvenient, expensive. It was, too, as she was uncomfortably aware, even a trifle ridiculous, and mentally she caricatured herself moving shuttle-like from continent to continent."

Helga's problems are presented with sympathy and understanding; but it is difficult to escape an impression of unreality in the nightmarish ending. She emulates her Negro father's "facile surrender to the irresistible ties of race." Helga's surrender is not only facile, it is sordid: the accidental conversion at an hysterical revival meeting, the wretched marriage with the Reverend Mr. Pleasant Green. An outcome incompatible, somehow, with her fine high arrogance, her courage.

The sense of impending tragedy has been subtly conveyed—this marriage and this minister constituting tragedy—and the story, except for some irritating mannerisms of style and some lapses into poor writing, is fairly well done. "Quicksand" is a first novel.

[†] From *Manitoba Free Press* (June 4, 1928): 12.

GEORGE S. SCHUYLER

Views and Reviews[†]

QUICKSAND, the novel of Negro life and character by the Negro woman, Nella Larsen, and published by Alfred A. Knopf, Inc., of New York City, has the virtue of being sufficiently interesting to keep one reading until the book is finished. Here is no story of bull-dikers, faggots, slums, cabarets, prostitution, gin parties, and whiskey socials, such as we have received from the pens (or typewriters) of too many writers of late years. Instead we meet Negroes in the pages of this novel who very closely resemble people we know: the professional type, the gay metropolitan crowd, the Negro who hates all white people, the Negro who is civilized enough to be tolerant and thus superior, the Negro overburdened with an inferiority complex, Negroes of culture and refinement who wear good clothes, eat well, live in fine houses. In short, we meet Negroes who are just human, like all other people. One may disagree with the author in some of her insinuations and assumptions, and to many—as to me—the heroine, Helga Crane, will appear unreal and incredible, and yet the story smacks of biography and is very well done. Few Negroes have written with the objectivity that characterizes this first novel. And few of them have etched character as successfully as Nella Larsen.

WALLACE THURMAN

High, Low, Past and Present[‡]

* * *

The author of *Quicksand* no doubt pleases Dr. Du Bois for she stays in her own sphere and writes about the sort of people one can invite to one's home without losing one's social prestige. She doesn't give white people the impression that all Negroes are gin drinkers, cabaret hounds and of the half world. Her Negroes are all of the upper class. And how!

Nevertheless, one has to admit that the performance here is a little less impressive than Mr. Fisher's.[1] Not because of her people or because of the milieu in which they move, but purely because the

---

† From *Pittsburgh Courier* (April 14, 1928): 2.8. Reprinted by permission of *New Pittsburgh Courier*.
‡ From *Harlem* (November 1928): 32.
1. Rudolph Fisher (1897–1934); *The Walls of Jericho*.

author seems to be wandering around lost, as lost as her leading character who ends up by doing such an unexpected and inexplainable thing that I was forced to reread the book, wondering, if in my eagerness to reach the end, I had perhaps skipped a hundred pages or so. But no, such had not been the case. Helga does get blown into the gutter and Helga does let herself be carried away by a religious frenzy to the point where she marries a Southern minister and spends the rest of her life having babies. This would have been all right for anyone except the Helga to whom Miss Larsen had introduced us, and even then it would have been all right had the author even as much as hinted that some day her character might do either the expected or the unexpected. But for the most part all Helga ever does is run away from certain situations and straddle the fence; so consistently, in fact, that when she does fall on the dark side the reader has lost all interest and sympathy, nor can he believe that such a thing has really happened.

＊　＊　＊

EDA LOU WALTON

Quicksand, by Nella Larsen[†]

To tell the story of a cultivated and sensitive woman's defeat through her own sex-desire is a difficult task. When the woman is a mulatto and beset by hereditary, social and racial forces over which she has little control and into which she cannot fit, her character is so complex that any analysis of it takes a mature imagination. This, I believe, Miss Larsen is too young to have[.] [T]he book, *Quicksand*, is a first novel. The attempt is to present Helga Crane not as a young colored woman, but as a young woman with problems unique to her temperament, and her background one largely of her own choice. Supposedly, save for a deep-rooted weakness, she has the vitality to manipulate the machinery of her days. But of this we are never quite convinced. As portrayed, the character is not quite of one pattern. Now it is Helga, the aesthete, the impulsively intelligent girl whom we feel; now it is Helga, the mulatto, suffering from an inferiority complex about her mixed ancestry, her lack of social status. Since she is supposedly complex, her character should be turned to us as a jewel of many facets. Instead we get it as a piece of bright red glass or as smoke-colored.

---

† From *Opportunity*, (July 1928): 212–13. Reprinted by permission of the National Urban League.

Besides the difficulty of incomplete characterization there is the fault of fine-writing in the worst sense of that word. The opening paragraph is a good example of that elaborateness of uninteresting detail into which Miss Larsen plunges in order to assure us that her Helga is cultured and modern.

"Helga Crane sat alone in her room, which at that hour, eight in the evening, was in soft gloom. Only a single reading lamp dimmed by a great black and red shade, made a pool of light on the blue Chinese carpet, on the bright covers of the books which she had taken down from their long shelves, on the white pages of the opened one selected, on the shining brass bowl crowded with many-colored nasturtiums beside her on the low table, and on the oriental silk which covered the stool at her slim feet. It was a comfortable room, furnished with rare and intensely personal taste, flooded with Southern sun in the day, but shadowy just then with the drawn curtains and single shaded light. Large, too. So large that the spot where Helga sat was a small oasis in a desert of darkness. And eerily quiet."

Born of a Danish mother and a colored father, an outcast from the American branch of her mother's family and a curiosity to the Danish branch, educated carefully by a pitying uncle, Helga has decided to devote her life to the betterment of her father's race. For this purpose she has become a teacher in Naxos, the most advanced of the Negro schools. For this reason, likewise, she has engaged herself to James Vayle, a young man of acknowledged social position in the settlement there. She wants a place in life, and social position, and work. But her mind is too keen to accept the patronizing attitude of the leaders in education, and her adjustment to the environment impossible; therefore she breaks with it.

In Chicago she suffers only a brief time from poverty and rejection and then becomes the companion of a lecturer on race problems. This older woman befriends her, finds her a congenial position in a New York insurance company for colored people and leaves her in a delightful social background and living with her own niece, Anne Grey.

In New York the problems are few. She moves among Harlem's most intellectual people. Her aesthetic sensibilities have full play in Anne's charming home. "Bonneted old highboys, tables that might be by Duncan Phyfe, rare spindle-legged chairs, and others whose ladder backs gracefully climbed the delicate wall-panels" and "Anne, herself, pretty maybe, brownly beautiful—with the face of a golden Madonna grave and calm and sweet, with shining black hair and eyes." These facts of daily life gave Helga freedom. She seems about to decide upon a suitable marriage to a properly wealthy man when restlessness again grips her and luck flies into her hands. She receives five thousand dollars from a penitent uncle and decides to leave

Harlem. Reveling in the thought, she chooses a dress to announce her plan:

"What should she wear? White? No, everybody would, because it was hot. Green? She shook her head, Anne would be sure to. The blue thing. Reluctantly she decided against it; she loved it but she had worn it so often. There was that cobwebby black net touched with orange, which she had bought last spring in a fit of extravagance and never worn because on getting it home both she and Anne considered it too decollete, too outre. She was going "because there were moments when it was as if she were shut up, boxed with hundreds of her race, closed up with that something in the racial character which had always been, to her, inexplicable, alien."

In Copenhagen, Frau Dahl (her aunt[)] treats her like an exotic doll, dresses her and parades her and puts her in the marriage market. When an excellent offer comes from a Danish artist, Helga refuses it. Another flight and she is back at Anne's wedding to Dr. Anderson. Dr. Anderson, first met as Helga's principal in Naxos, has moved shadow-like through the pages. Helga has always shown some slight interest in him. But nothing has prepared us for the sudden shift in her that comes now. There is a silly incident. Dr. Anderson, in his cups, embraces her. When he formally apologizes, she, realizing that she wants him, slaps him for his conventionality. Suddenly all the forces of passion are loose in her. Finding no outlet, she turns to revivalistic religion of a stupid sort, then, more illogically, to a flabby, dull minister who happens to take her home from the church meeting. Having given herself to him, she marries him with a certain exultation in her own power.

She is, of course, lost. As a minister's wife she can for a time be pleased with her "status" (a bit pitiful, but certain). For a time she has drugged peace in the flesh. Then come children, weariness, serious illness. She is brought back to living to discover her mistake and her hatred of her husband. She makes many resolutions for freeing herself only to discover her body laden with a fifth child. The end is, I suppose, a sordid death.

But in none of the latter Helga have we found any particular meaning. If she was at all the young woman of the first of the book, she cannot be the older woman of the latter half. There is no continuity of development, no wholeness here.

Miss Larsen writes a little too carefully of the objective evidences of culture and too carelessly of the refinement within the woman herself. We are told again and again that Helga is restless, unhappy, passionate, but we don't believe it until, arbitrarily, Miss Larsen introduces proofs of action.

Quicksand is, for all this comment, a good tale, and a good first novel. Miss Larsen's prettiness of style may, with more writing,

become power. She will undoubtedly learn a more effectual working out of laws of cause and event within characters. She has already
the ability to interest us in her people and their problems.

But she has not in this first book anything of the usual richness
and fullness of character presentation, or the zestful interest in life
in Harlem that other novelists of Negro life have given us.

RUTH L. YATES

[Review of *Quicksand*][†]

"Quicksand," by Nella Larsen, is the latest addition to the now long
list of books dealing with the so-called Negro problem. The story is
that of a mulatto girl, Helga Crane, who is born of a Danish mother
and Negro father. Helga is well educated and teaches school in a
small Southern town. She finds the lives of the people with whom
she comes in contact dull and aimless and the people themselves
willing to go along as so much clay in the hands of the Southern
whites, to be moulded [*sic*] or shaped after their desires. Realizing
that she does not fit in with this group, she goes to New York, where
she mingles with a group of Negroes somewhat of the "Bohemian"
class. She believes she is satisfied with their style of living until an
indefinable longing comes over her. Helga finally decides to go to
her mother's sister, who is in Denmark. Her dark skin and hair make
her a novelty—a curiosity to those white people of Denmark; and
while she is shown every courtesy and consideration, she realizes
there is an invisible barrier shutting her off from this group. In conclusion, Helga returns to America, marries a Negro minister and
goes to live in the Southland, where she begins raising a large family.
Her immediate associates are of the illiterate element and life in general seems to lose all of its glamour.

In "Quicksand" Miss Larsen portrays the inner struggles of a
mulatto. However, Miss Larsen seems to have been able to master
the emotions which made Helga Crane restless, unsatisfied, and
misfit in the various social groups.

As for the Negro characters portrayed, three distinct groups are
illustrated, the Southern hypocrites, the Bohemian set of Harlem
and the uneducated. Perhaps if Helga Crane had been placed with
other groups of Negroes she would have been able to find happiness.
Too much stress has been placed upon the illiterate Negro, the jazz-
crazed Negro and the Negro who thinks that the white man is next

† From *Pittsburgh Courier* (May 26 1928): 20. Reprinted by permission of *New Pittsburgh Courier.*

to almighty. There are other classes of Negroes. Why not use them as examples once in a while? We have schools and teachers comparing favorably with white schools and teachers; we have intellectual Negroes, and we have Negroes who are not suffering from inferiority complex. Literary works woven around the types of Negroes just mentioned would be an incentive to the race in general and would go far toward acquainting the white race with the much overlooked fact that the uncultured Negro no more represents the entire Negro group than the crude and uncultured white man represents the entire white race.

"Quicksand" is worth reading; it is different and, above all things, it permits one to elevate his mind above the mire of lasciviousness that has been the general theme of late books dealing with the Negro. This is Miss Larsen's first attempt at writing a novel and she is to be commended on bringing us something different.

About Nella Larsen:
Contemporary Articles

NAHUM DANIEL BRASCHER
Random Thoughts[†]

"Novelist Here."—Nella Larsen of New York, native of Chicago though, spent several days in Chicago. Author of "Quicksand" and "Passing." In private life Mrs. Williams [*sic*] S. Imes. Traveled and studied abroad. Delightful to chat with. Dewey R. Jones of The Chicago Defender editorial staff and Mrs. Jones called in a few friends to informally greet Miss Larsen. It was a most delightful evening. A number of intellectuals, musicians, writers, teachers and social workers, both races. No program, no bridge, no dancing. Informal conversation between people who have traveled in many parts of the world, read late books, know what life is all about—oh, at least think so—and enjoy exchange of opinion. Such occasions help one to grow.

ANONYMOUS
Honor Author of 'Quicksand' at Tea[‡]

In line with the educational policy of the women's committee of the N.A.A.C.P., a group of distinguished people interested in literary and artistic development was invited to meet Mrs. Nella Larsen Imes, author of "Quicksand," at an honor tea at the Walker studio Sunday. Mrs. Inez Richardson Wilson, chairman of the committee, presided and introduced first Miss Roberta Bosley, who sang two spirituals, accompanied by Miss Consuela Papi, after which J. Rosamond Johnson and Taylor Gordon were persuaded to contribute two numbers in their inimitable style.

---

† From *Chicago Defender* (September 30, 1933): 11. Reprinted by permission of *Chicago Defender*.
‡ From *Chicago Defender* (May 26, 1928): 11. Reprinted by permission of *Chicago Defender*.

151

Mrs. Florence Henderson, the committee's delegate to the conference at Los Angeles, expressed the belief that she would have much to bring back from the conference. Mrs. Sari Price Patton, Miss Iris Hall and Miss Claudia Scott, entrants in the popularity contest, were introduced. James Weldon Johnson presented Mrs. Imes, who gave an interesting summary of her reasons for writing "Quicksand." Refreshments were served by a committee under the direction of Mrs. Florence DeLoatch Richardson: Mrs. Helen Press, Mrs. Estelle Anderson, Mrs. Corinne Wright, Mrs. Irene Jordan, Miss Wilhelmina Adams and Mrs. Sarah Butler. Mrs. Rose Riley had charge of members' identifications [sic] cards.

The studio was beautifully decorated with cut flowers, the gifts of Mrs. A. C. Deming and Mrs. Bertha Lee. The punch table, decorated by Miss Lucille V. Miller, attracted the following list of guests furnished by Mrs. Abbot [a long list of names follows, including Mrs. Du Bois, Harold Jackman, Alain Locke, Dr. and Mrs. Rudolph Fisher, Carl Van Vechten, Donald Angus, and many other central figures of the Harlem Renaissance]. * * *

Nella Larsen's Writings

NELLA LARSEN

[Review of *Black Sadie*]†

BLACK SADIE. By T. Bowyer Campbell. Houghton Mifflin, Boston, $2.50.

Black Sadie—what a title! Great, isn't it? Unfortunately the book, which is the story of a Negro dancing girl's rise to popularity, isn't.

The tale opens in the south with a rape and closes in New York with a murder. Every strangeness, every crudity, every laxity, which by ancient superstition has been ascribed to the black man, Mr. Campbell has incorporated into this story—and some others. In this way he has managed to produce an effect of difference with traits and habits which every intelligent person knows to be utterly usual, by throwing into exaggerated relief characteristics found in some degree in all human beings, and in themselves commonplace. The result is clever but inaccurate.

It must, however, be admitted that the white characters are not more kindly handled than the black. But, they are not set down as thieving, sexually immoral, and brutal. The method which the author uses for their outlining is ridicule and heavy-handed sarcasm. What he does is not so much grin as to grimace.

Black Sadie is an awkwardly written and disorderly book. Mr. Campbell seems not to have learned the art of selection and arrangement. And there are certain peculiarities of style that after a while become tedious, the too frequent repetition of the same phrases and words. Though this is a deliberate mannerism, it is none the less tiresome.

Nevertheless, in spite of its twaddle concerning the inherent qualities of the Negro, in spite of its affectations of style, the book is worth reading. Sadie, a handsome black wench, is an interesting and forceful character, which no one interested in modern Negro fiction can afford to ignore. She is absolutely without subtlety and her

† From "Our Book Shelf," *Opportunity* (January 1929): 24. Reprinted by permission of the National Urban League.

ways of obtaining the things she wants are rude and often terribly direct. But she *is* successful. And her personality leaves its impression not only on all the other people in the book, but on the reader as well.

In some of its episodes Black Sadie is brutal, stark, gruesome almost. Some of the drama is pitiful. But Sadie herself is a delightfully sunny person. And often its very inaccuracies make much of the book very amusing—especially to the Negro reader.

Don't miss it.

NELLA LARSEN

Sanctuary[†]

I

On the Southern coast, between Merton and Shawboro, there is a strip of desolation some half a mile wide and nearly ten miles long between the sea and old fields of ruined plantations. Skirting the edge of this narrow jungle is a partly grown-over road which still shows traces of furrows made by the wheels of wagons that have long since rotted away or been cut into firewood. This road is little used, now that the state has built its new highway a bit to the west and wagons are less numerous than automobiles.

In the forsaken road a man was walking swiftly. But in spite of his hurry, at every step he set down his feet with infinite care for the night was windless and the heavy silence intensified each sound; even the breaking of a twig could be plainly heard. And the man had need of caution as well as haste.

Before a lonely cottage that shrank timidly back from the road the man hesitated a moment, then struck out across the patch of green in front of it. Stepping behind a clump of bushes close to the house, he looked in through the lighted window at Annie Poole, standing at her kitchen table mixing the supper biscuits.

He was a big, black man with pale brown eyes in which there was an odd mixture of fear and amazement. The light showed streaks of gray soil on his heavy, sweating face and great hands, and on his torn clothes. In his woolly hair clung bits of dried leaves and dead grass.

He made a gesture as if to tap on the window, but turned away to the door instead. Without knocking he opened it and went in.

† From *Forum* 83 (January 1930): 15–18.

II

The woman's brown gaze was immediately on him, though she did not move. She said, "You ain't in no hurry, is you, Jim Hammer?" It wasn't, however, entirely a question.

"Ah's in trubble, Mis' Poole," the man explained, his voice shaking, his fingers twitching.

"W'at you done done now?"

"Shot a man, Mis' Poole."

"Trufe?" The woman seemed calm. But the word was spat out.

"Yas'm. Shot 'im." In the man's tone was something of wonder, as if he himself could not quite believe that he had really done this thing which he affirmed.

"Daid?"

"Dunno, Mis' Poole. Dunno."

"White man o' niggah?"

"Cain't say, Mis' Poole. White man, Ah reckons."

Annie Poole looked at him with cold contempt. She was a tiny, withered woman—fifty perhaps—with a wrinkled face the color of old copper, framed by a crinkly mass of white hair. But about her small figure was some quality of hardness that belied her appearance of frailty. At last she spoke, boring her sharp little eyes into those of the anxious creature before her.

"An' w'at am you lookin' foh me to do 'bout et?"

"Jes' lemme stop till dey's gone by. Hide me till dey passes. Reckon dey ain't fur off now." His begging voice changed to a frightened whimper. "Foh de Lawd's sake, Mis' Poole, lemme stop."

And why, the woman inquired caustically, should she run the dangerous risk of hiding him?

"Obadiah, he'd lemme stop ef he was to home," the man whined.

Annie Poole sighed. "Yas," she admitted, slowly, reluctantly, "Ah spec' he would. Obadiah, he's too good to youall no 'count trash." Her slight shoulders lifted in a hopeless shrug. "Yas, Ah reckon he'd do et. Emspecial' seein how he allus set such a heap o' store by you. Cain't see w'at foh, mahse'f. Ah shuah don' see nuffin' in you but a heap o' dirt."

But a look of irony, of cunning, of complicity passed over her face. She went on, "Still, 'siderin' all an' all, how Obadiah's right fon' o' you, an' how white folks is white folks, Ah'm a-gwine hide you dis one time."

Crossing the kitchen, she opened a door leading into a small bedroom, saying, "Git yo'se'f in dat dere feather baid an' Ah'm a-gwine put de clo's on de top. Don' reckon dey'll fin' you ef dey does look foh you in mah house. An Ah don' spec' dey'll go foh to do dat. Not lessen you been keerless an' let 'em smell you out gittin' hyah." She turned on him a withering look. "But you allus been triflin'. Cain't do nuffin propah. An' Ah'm a-tellin' you ef dey warn't white folks an' you a po' niggah, Ah shuah wouldn't be lettin' you mess up mah feather baid dis ebenin', 'cose Ah jes' plain don' want you hyah. Ah done kep' mahse'f outen trubble all mah life. So's Obadiah."

"Ah's powahful 'bliged to you, Mis' Poole. You shuah am one good 'oman. De Lawd'll mos' suttinly—"

Annie Poole cut him off. "Dis ain't no time foh all dat kin' o' fiddle-de-roll. Ah does mah duty as Ah sees et 'thout no thanks from you. Ef de Lawd had gib you a white face 'stead o' dat dere black one, Ah shuah would turn you out. Now hush yo' mouf an' git yo'se'f in. An' don' git movin' and scrunchin' undah dose covahs and git yo'se'f kotched in mah house."

Without further comment the man did as he was told. After he had laid his soiled body and grimy garments between her snowy sheets, Annie Poole carefully rearranged the covering and placed piles of freshly laundered linen on top. Then she gave a pat here and there, eyed the result, and finding it satisfactory, went back to her cooking.

III

Jim Hammer settled down to the racking business of waiting until the approaching danger should have passed him by. Soon savory odors seeped in to him and he realized that he was hungry. He wished that Annie Poole would bring him something to eat. Just one biscuit. But she wouldn't, he knew. Not she. She was a hard one, Obadiah's mother.

By and by he fell into a sleep from which he was dragged back by the rumbling sound of wheels in the road outside. For a second fear clutched so tightly at him that he almost leaped from the suffocating shelter of the bed in order to make some active attempt to escape the horror that his capture meant. There was a spasm at his heart, a pain so sharp, so slashing that he had to suppress an impulse to cry out. He felt himself falling. Down, down, down. . . . Everything grew dim and very distant in his memory. . . . Vanished. . . . Came rushing back.

Outside there was silence. He strained his ears. Nothing. No footsteps. No voices. They had gone on then. Gone without even stopping to ask Annie Poole if she had seen him pass that way. A sigh of relief slipped from him. His thick lips curled in an ugly, cunning smile. It had been smart of him to think of coming to Obadiah's mother's to hide. She was an old demon, but he was safe in her house.

He lay a short while longer listening intently, and, hearing nothing, started to get up. But immediately he stopped, his yellow eyes glowing like pale flames. He had heard the unmistakable sound of men coming toward the house. Swiftly he slid back into the heavy, hot stuffiness of the bed and lay listening fearfully.

The terrifying sounds drew nearer. Slowly. Heavily. Just for a moment he thought they were not coming in—they took so long. But there was a light knock and the noise of a door being opened. His whole body went taut. His feet felt frozen, his hands clammy, his tongue like a weighted, dying thing. His pounding heart made it hard for his straining ears to hear what they were saying out there.

"Ebenin', Mistah Lowndes." Annie Poole's voice sounded as it always did, sharp and dry.

There was no answer. Or had he missed it? With slow care he shifted his position, bringing his head nearer the edge of the bed. Still he heard nothing. What were they waiting for? Why didn't they ask about him?

Annie Poole, it seemed, was of the same mind. "Ah don' reckon youall done traipsed 'way out hyah jes' foh yo' healf," she hinted.

"There's bad news for you, Annie, I'm 'fraid." The sheriff's voice was low and queer.

Jim Hammer visualized him standing out there—a tall, stooped man, his white tobacco-stained mustache drooping limply at the ends, his nose hooked and sharp, his eyes blue and cold. Bill Lowndes was a hard one too. And white.

"W'atall bad news, Mistah Lowndes?" The woman put the question quietly, directly.

"Obadiah—" the sheriff began—hesitated—began again. "Obadiah—ah—er he's outside, Annie. I'm 'fraid—"

"Shucks! You done missed. Obadiah, he ain't done nuffin', Mistah Lowndes. Obadiah!" she called stridently, "Obadiah! git hyah an' splain yo'se'f."

But Obadiah didn't answer, didn't come in. Other men came in. Came in with steps that dragged and halted. No one spoke. Not even Annie Poole. Something was laid carefully upon the floor.

"Obadiah, chile," his mother said softly, "Obadiah, chile." Then, with sudden alarm, "He ain't daid, is he? Mistah Lowndes! Obadiah, he ain't daid?"

Jim Hammer didn't catch the answer to that pleading question. A new fear was stealing over him.

"There was a to-do, Annie," Bill Lowndes explained gently, "at the garage back o' the factory. Fellow tryin' to steal tires. Obadiah heerd a noise an' run out with two or three others. Scared the rascal all right. Fired off his gun an' run. We allow et to be Jim Hammer. Picked up his cap back there. Never was no 'count. Thievin' an' sly. But we'll git 'im, Annie. We'll git 'im."

The man huddled in the feather bed prayed silently. "Oh, Lawd! Ah didn't go to do et. Not Obadiah, Lawd. You knows dat. You knows et." And into his frenzied brain came the thought that it would be better for him to get up and go out to them before Annie Poole gave him away. For he was lost now. With all his great strength he tried to get himself out of the bed. But he couldn't.

"Oh Lawd!" he moaned, "Oh Lawd!" His thoughts were bitter and they ran through his mind like panic. He knew that it had come to pass as it said somewhere in the Bible about the wicked. The Lord had stretched out his hand and smitten him. He was paralyzed. He couldn't move hand or foot. He moaned again. It was all there was left for him to do. For in the terror of this new calamity that had come upon him he had forgotten the waiting danger which was so near out there in the kitchen.

His hunters, however, didn't hear him. Bill Lowndes was saying, "We been a-lookin' for Jim out along the old road. Figured he'd make tracks for Shawboro. You ain't noticed anybody pass this evenin', Annie?"

The reply came promptly, unwaveringly. "No, Ah ain't sees nobody pass. Not yet."

IV

Jim Hammer caught his breath.

"Well," the sheriff concluded, "we'll be gittin' along. Obadiah was a mighty fine boy. Ef they was all like him—. I'm sorry, Annie. Anything I c'n do let me know."

"Thank you, Mistah Lowndes."

With the sound of the door closing on the departing men, power to move came back to the man in the bedroom. He pushed his dirt-caked feet out from the covers and rose up, but crouched down again. He wasn't cold now, but hot all over and burning. Almost he wished that Bill Lowndes and his men had taken him with them.

Annie Poole had come into the room.

It seemed a long time before Obadiah's mother spoke. When she did there were no tears, no reproaches; but there was a raging fury in her voice as she lashed out, "Git outen mah feather baid, Jim Hammer, an' outen mah house, an' don' nevah stop thankin' yo' Jesus he done gib you dat black face."

Correspondence

NELLA LARSEN

To Carl Van Vechten[†]

[Postmarked September 18, 1925]
Mr. Carl Van Vechten
150 W. 55th Street
New York City
U.S.A.

1284 Rue St. Denis
Montreal,
Canada

My dear Carl:
  I wonder if you are responsible for two books and a letter which I had from Mr. Alfred Knopf just before setting out for this wonderful wet Dominion. If you are, please take thanks.
  We find Montreal very interesting; have been stopping in the old French section. Among the many interesting sights are the Americans with nice edges on. You will know, of course, that we are not included among these.
  Tomorrow we start for the city of Quebec.
  Please give our best love to Miss Marinoff.

                                          Nella Larsen Imes.

† The following letters in this section are from the James Weldon Johnson Collection, Beinecke Library, Yale University. Letters have been transcribed by the editor of this Norton Critical Edition.

To Carl Van Vechten

[July 1, 1926]
Wednesday.

Dear Carl:

Thanks for your kind note. I have been intending to write or 'phone you, to say thank you for a pleasant evening. It's three o'clock now, isn't it?

How do these things get about?

It is the awful truth. But, who knows if I'll ever get through with the damned thing. Certainly not I.

I had thought of entering it in the A. & C. Boni contest. I understand, though, that they are a bit disgusted with what is being submitted. It is being whispered about that anything literate is sure to be awarded the honor. That's discouraging. Of course, it would be nice to get a thousand dollars, just so, and, - the publicity. Not so nice, however, to be merely the best of a bad lot. What do you think?

I like Knopf. He does things so well, sends them out looking attractive, - nice type, bindings, title pages, and everything, - but, he seems very hard to please, (see Mr. Llewlyn Powys and hear Miss Jessie Fauset). True, good makeups deserve good books.

Forget you? D'you know any more jokes? But, I must say, you're a trusting soul. The thing might turn out to be utter rot, you know. When I first started, I honestly thought it was really good; now, something more than half way, I'm afraid it's frightfully bad. Too, I'm getting rather bored with it. I wonder how many half finished novels there are knocking about the world. Perhaps, it may be good enough for Knopf. Certainly you would know, if anybody.

Mrs. Valentine was with us for two days last week. She spoke, with evident pleasure, of your visit on Commencement day, and she was charmed with Fania. So was Mrs. Penelope, (her mother, Mrs. Booth)

Again, gramercy!

Nella Imes

To Carl Van Vechten

Wednesday 21st
[July 1926]

Dear Carl:—

Thanks awfully, for an interesting evening. We did enjoy it. Did Mr. Stevens (?) recover from his bewilderment?

The advertisement in the Mercury is very attractive. Quite unusual too; as is the descriptive book note. Every one is on tip-toe. As Elmer remarked to me "'Your people' don't buy books, but that's one they are all going to buy."

I have definitely decided against the Bonis, even if Knopf won't have me. In that case, I think I'll try the Viking Press.

Please say to Fania that we were both devastated, not to have seen her.

Thanks.
Nella Imes.

To Carl Van Vechten

Wednesday 29th
[September 1926]

My dear Carl:—

In the confusion Sunday I am afraid I didn't thank you properly for the Goldoni book. I was particularly glad for it as I mean eventually to acquire most of the Blue Jade series. This makes seven. I am curious about the period too, although I know little of it except through Casanova's memoirs which I read some four years ago when I was learning French in order that I might pass the Library School entrance exams—and of course Elinor Wylie.

I've been unable to sleep since Sunday,—so excited about the book shop. Yesterday, I spent in town talking to people about it. To everyone except Walter I merely said that a friend of mine was thinking of opening a book shop in Harlem.

You will be interested to learn that Walter has been bitten by the same idea almost. He had thought of consulting Doubleday about it and then to talk to me—that [sic] why I told him about it being your plan. We had a very good talk together, in the midst of which we became so excited that we were seized with the desire to rush up to Harlem and evict a poor music shop keeper on Seventh Avenue and

135th Street, so that we could fix up the shop at once, but the phone rang and saved the music shop keeper.

Mr. Johnson (James Weldon) was also favorably impressed. He said that he had on occasion talked with various publishers about the distributing of books (certain books I think he said) in Harlem, and that they all deplored the absence of a shop up there and would be very glad t[o] cooperate with any reliable and competent agency or person.

Secretaries at the YMCA and YWCA would both welcome and help to advertise the shop and order the few books which they buy through it. They also said that the visiting summer school students purchase a great many books. The branch library too would help with the advertising and place a few orders. (Every branch in the city does this except the 135th [and] 145th street branches) and to buy from the shop the few books which now and then they must have P.D.Q and can't wait for them to go through the regular channels. [An author is coming to tea or to lecture, and the branch hasn't a copy of his latest book, or it's out; so they must buy one at once, or some such thing.

Next time I go up, I will visit the churches and the schools. There must be some teachers who buy a few books sometimes. I'm sure the ministers will be glad to help. Elmer's brother, I know recommends books to his congregation and they have a small imprint/ incipient[?] library in the church to which they add now and then. And Bibles!—Mrs. Booth whos [sic] father is the minister of St. Phillips Episcopal church says that some ten dozen prayerbooks are bought by individual membe[rs] of the church at times like Easter and Christmas and confirmation. They too have a church library.

Several doctors promised to order through the shop, and Dr. Booth said he would help whoop it up and also advice all his patients to buy certain books on care of the teeth. And we may place a poster in his office—(he has a huge practice) and I am sure there are others.

Several friends of mine who buy from twenty to forty books a year promised patronage, and one who buys a book every week— and is proud of it.

Several people spoke enthusiastically about Nigger Heaven, and said they would have bought several copies at various times for friends if a shop had been near.

Nella Imes

My love to Fania

To Carl Van Vechten

[November 12, 1926]
51 Aububon Avenue,
Jersey City, N. J.

My dear Carl:

It was nice to have your letter yesterday when I got back from a tiresome visit in Philadelphia among the ultra-religious.

Thanks awfully for the clippings. They are pathetically amusing. Have you noticed that when Nordics talk against the admission of Negroes to their homes, etc., it is rank predjudice [*sic*], but when we take the same attitude about white folks it is race loyalty? I met Floyd Calvin some five years ago just once. He is a fool, a boor and a snob.

Rudolph and Jane Fisher were over here Sunday. "Bud" told us that he blew in on you unexpectedly one day last week and thought that he had gotten into a house in the wrong neighborhood because "the place was full of niggers". Incidently [*sic*], we were all cross because we didn't know that the WEAF Players were to read The School for Scandal. We tuned in accidently just in time to here [*sic*] the announcer say "Ladies and gentlemen you <u>have just heard</u>"—etc. It was horrid of Fania not to tell us.

Yes, we did have a good time at your house last Thursday. I enjoyed every minute of the whole SEVEN hours. We almost spent the night, didn't we? Isn't Mr. Heyward interesting to meet? —and natural? You know, theoretically, I hate all Southereners [*sic*] as "a matter of principle", but actually, I have never yet met one that I didn't like. I'm terribly anxious about his play. I mean I hope that he is able to get the people he wants to do it.

I've read all three of the books you gave me. Pablo de Segovia is marvelous. A tale of a Negro ruffian told in this naive manner would be interesting. (I think somebody, Mencken perhaps, has made this suggestion somewhere.)

I enjoyed interpreters and interpretations although a great deal of it was beyond me. The sardonic manner, however was enough to hold me, if my curiosity hadn't. But it did. I've picked more information from the constant reading of your books than from any other source though, certainly I don't read you merely as a text book. The Merry-go-round is delightful. I read every one of the papers even the ones that I have read recently in other things. I specially like "In Defense of Bad Taste" and De Senectute Cantorum. And the catalog!

My love to Fania,

Yours for crime and punishment,
Nella Imes

November twelfth   over

1. Why doesn't someone write a paper for, say, Opportunity or the Crisis, on Carl Van Vechten tracing in earlier works his interest in your people?
2. You must have known Bert Williams[1] very well, or have seen him very often. Which?
3. Where is theman [sic] from whom you got "the wife of his youth."

Miss Benson in Vanity Fair is amusing—and not so bad. She has the discrimination to know who is important.

To Carl Van Vechten

New York City
236 West 135 Street
[June 29, 1927]

My dear Carl:—

Yesterday Dorothy came to tea—about which more later—She told me that you'd had to go back to Chicago. I am sorry. Elmer too—he's back. Colin called this morning.

Well, Ethel Waters never came to the tea that I was having for her. I had asked Dorothy P. and Mary Skinner, a rather interesting girl from Chicago, who was sailing that night. We sat about and waited and waited, got hungrier and hungrier. In the meanwhile Gussie phoned up to find out if I was home, so I told her to come up. Finally, at seven o'clock we ate the cakes and sandwiches. I was very disappointed because I felt sure it was going to be a success. Everything was just right. Mary Skinner who is good-looking, rich and intelligent knows the secret of being friendly without being patronizing. Dorothy really wanted to meet her, and had intended, if things fell out that way, to ask her to go over to Brooklyn with me and Elmer on Friday night. Gussie knows nothing about her—and doesn't care, so she would have been perfectly natural.

When you return maybe you can find out what happened. Did she get stage fright at the last minute? Was she disconcerted because she had been asked to come alone, without friend [or] husband? Why didn't she phone if she was tied up?

Probably I should have phoned when she didn't arrive by five thirty. Still that seems a little unusual. Not done. We parted quite pleasantly after leaving your house last week. Our last words were "Monday then, about five." It's all very mysterious.

1. Bert Williams (1874–1922), entertainer, comedian, actor, and recording star.

Gladys called up to inquire why I hadn't called to gaze upon the son and heir(?) I congratulated her effusively on its being a boy. "Yes", she said triumphantly. "Walter wanted a boy to <u>carry on this name</u>." There are only five pages of Whites in the New York telephone directory alone. And two in the Brooklyn one. Now if it had been Van Vechten, or Imes. I <u>have</u> been working. Finished a kind of a short story about 6000 wds which I think of sending to Harpers though I'm not at all sure it's quite the type. Now that it's done I'm inclined to believe that I've squandered an idea that would have made a novel.

Eddie gave me Twilight Sleep. It's a beautiful satire on all these pseudo religions. If I were courageous enough I would send it to Dorothy Harris when she sails next Wednesday.

Please give our love to Duane. Keep a big share for yourself.

Nella

Tuesday

P.S. Elmer had a comfortable and successful trip. Not the slightest suspicion of unpleasantness. Even his presence at the dance tripping it with Nordic ladies seemed not to cause any remark.

N

To Gertrude Stein

2588 Seventh Avenue
New York City

Miss Gertrude Stein
27 Rue de Fleurus
Paris
France

Dear Miss Stein

I have often talked with our friend Carl Van Vechten about you. Particularly about you and Melanctha, which I have read many times. And always I get from it some new thing. A truly great story. I never cease to wonder how you came to write it and just why you and not some one of us should so accurately have caught the spirit of this race of mine.

Carl asked me to send you my poor first book and I am doing so. Please don't think me too presumptuous.

I hope some day to have the great good fortune of seeing and talking with you.

Very Sincerely yours,

Nella Larsen Imes

February first 1928

To Gertrude Stein

February twenty-sixth

My dear Miss Stein:

Thanks for your kind letter. It is a disappointment that I am not to see you in the spring. But life is like that. I've just had a note from Carl berating me for not having seen you.

Yes, I shall be in Paris again in the fall. I should go back there, anyway, to see you, because I don't know when I'll get over again.

A good summer for you!

Until the fall

Very Sincerely

Nella Larsen Imes

Cultural Contexts

MARITA O. BONNER

Feminist writer, playwright, and musician Marita O. Bonner (1898–1971) published essays, stories, and plays in many of the significant magazines of the Harlem Renaissance, including both *The Crisis* and *Opportunity*. Her first published essay, "On Being Young—a Woman—and Colored," which appeared in *The Crisis*, won the yearly essay contest. In the 1920s she also published numerous short stories, plays, and literary reviews, occasionally under the pseudonym Joseph Maree Andrew. Bonner was born in Boston, and attended Brookline High School and Radcliffe College, though she was denied the opportunity to live on campus. She taught school in West Virginia, Washington, D.C., and Chicago, where she moved with her husband, William Almy Occomy, whom she married in 1930.

On Being Young—a Woman—and Colored[†]

Marita O. Bonner, winner of the first prize essay in our contest, was born and educated in Brookline, Massachusetts. In her junior year at Radcliffe she was admitted to the famous course in writing given by Professor Charles Townsend Copeland, a rare distinction since this course is limited to the sixteen best writers, graduates and undergraduates in each college year. One of her sketches, "Dandelion Season," was selected to be read annually to Radcliffe classes. She holds the degree of A.B. and is a teacher of English in the Armstrong High School of Washington, D.C.

You start out after you have gone from kindergarten to sheepskin covered with sundry Latin phrases.

At least you know what you want life to give you. A career as fixed and as calmly brilliant as the North Star. The one real thing that money buys. Time. Time to do things. A house that can be as delectably out of order and as easily put in order as the doll-house of

---

† From *The Crisis* 31.2 (December 1925): 63–65, Rpt. in *The Crisis*, Authorized Reprint Edition (New York: Arno Press, 1969), pp. 63–65. Reprinted by permission of the Estate of Marita O. Bonner.

"playing-house" days. And of course, a husband you can look up to without looking down on yourself.

Somehow you feel like a kitten in a sunny catnip field that sees sleek, plump brown field mice and yellow baby chicks sitting coyly, side by side, under each leaf. A desire to dash three or four ways seizes you.

That's Youth.

But you know that things learned need testing—acid testing—to see if they are really after all, an interwoven part of you. All your life you have heard of the debt you owe "Your People" because you have managed to have the things they have not largely had.

So you find a spot where there are hordes of them—of course below the Line—to be your catnip field while you close your eyes to mice and chickens alike.

If you have never lived among your own, you feel prodigal. Some warm untouched current flows through them—through you—and drags you out into the deep waters of a new sea of human foibles and mannerisms; of a peculiar psychology and prejudices. And one day you find yourself entangled—enmeshed—pinioned in the sea-weed of a Black Ghetto.

Not a Ghetto, placid like the Strasse that flows, outwardly unperturbed and calm in a stream of religious belief, but a peculiar group. Cut off, flung together, shoved aside in a bundle because of color and with no more in common.

Unless color is, after all, the real bond.

Milling around like live fish in a basket. Those at the bottom crushed into a sort of stupid apathy by the weight of those on top. Those on top leaping, leaping; leaping to scale the sides; to get out.

There are two "colored" movies, innumerable parties—and cards. Cards played so intensely that it fascinates and repulses at once.

Movies.

Movies worthy and worthless—but not even a low-caste spoken stage.

Parties, plentiful. Music and dancing and much that is wit and color and gaiety. But they are like the richest chocolate; stuffed costly chocolates that make the taste go stale if you have too many of them. That make plain whole bread taste like ashes.

There are all the earmarks of a group within a group. Cut off all around from ingress from or egress to other groups. A sameness of type. The smug self-satisfaction of an inner measurement; a mea-surement by standards known within a limited group and not those of an unlimited, seeing, world. . . . Like the blind, blind mice. Mice whose eyes have been blinded.

Strange longing seizes hold of you. You wish yourself back where you can lay your dollar down and sit in a dollar seat to hear voices,

strings, reeds that have lifted the World out, up, beyond things that
have bodies and walls. Where you can marvel at new marbles and
bronzes and flat colors that will make men forget that things exist
in a flesh more often than in spirit. Where you can sink your body
in a cushioned seat and sink your soul at the same time into a section of life set before you on the boards for a few hours.

You hear that up at New York this is to be seen; that, to be heard.
You decide the next train will take you there.

You decide the next second that that train will not take you, nor
the next—nor the next for some time to come.

For you know that—being a woman—you cannot twice a month
or twice a year, for that matter, break away to see or hear anything
in a city that is supposed to see and hear too much.

That's being a woman. A woman of any color.

You decide that something is wrong with a world that stifles and
chokes; that cuts off and stunts; hedging in, pressing down on eyes,
ears and throat. Somehow all wrong.

You wonder how it happens there that—say five hundred miles
from the Bay State—Anglo Saxon intelligence is so warped and
stunted.

How judgment and discernment are bred out of the race. And
what has become of discrimination? Discrimination of the right sort.
Discrimination that the best minds have told you weighs shadows
and nuances and spiritual differences before it catalogues. The kind
they have taught you all of your life was best: that looks clearly past
generalization and past appearance to dissect, to dig down to the
real heart of matters. That casts aside rapid summary conclusions,
drawn from primary inference, as Daniel did the spiced meats.

Why can't they then perceive that there is a difference in the
glance from a pair of eyes that look, mildly docile, at "white ladies" and
those that, impersonally and perceptively—aware of distinctions—
see only women who happen to be white?

Why do they see a colored woman only as a gross collection of
desires, all uncontrolled, reaching out for their Apollos and the Qua-
simodos with avid indiscrimination?

Why unless you talk in staccato squawks—brittle as sea-shells—
unless you "champ" gum—unless you cover two yards square when
you laugh—unless your taste runs to violent colors—impossible perfumes and more impossible clothes—are you a feminine Caliban
craving to pass for Ariel?

An empty imitation of an empty invitation. A mime; a sham; a
copy-cat. A hollow re-echo. A froth, a foam. A fleck of the ashes of
superficiality?

Everything you touch or taste now is like the flesh of an unripe
persimmon.

. . . Do you need to be told what that is being . . . ?

Old ideas, old fundamentals seem worm-eaten, out-grown, worthless, bitter; fit for the scrap-heap of Wisdom.

What you had thought tangible and practical has turned out to be a collection of "blue-flower" theories.

If they have not discovered how to use their accumulation of facts, they are useless to you in Their world.

Every part of you becomes bitter.

But—"In Heaven's name, do not grow bitter. Be bigger than they are",—exhort white friends who have never had to draw breath in a Jim-Crow train. Who have never had petty putrid insult dragged over them—drawing blood—like pebbled sand on your body where the skin is tenderest. On your body where the skin is thinnest and tenderest.

You long to explode and hurt everything white; friendly; unfriendly. But you know that you cannot live with a chip on your shoulder even if you can manage a smile around your eyes—without getting steely and brittle and losing the softness that makes you a woman.

For chips make you bend your body to balance them. And once you bend, you lose your poise, your balance, and the chip gets into you. The real you. You get hard.

. . . And many things in you can ossify . . .

And you know, being a woman, you have to go about it gently and quietly, to find out and to discover just what is wrong. Just what can be done.

You see clearly that they have acquired things.

Money; money. Money to build with, money to destroy. Money to swim in. Money to drown in. Money.

An ascendancy of wisdom. An incalculable hoard of wisdom in all fields, in all things collected from all quarters of humanity.

A stupendous mass of things.

Things.

So, too, the Greeks . . . Things.

And the Romans. . . .

And you wonder and wonder why they have not discovered how to handle deftly and skillfully, Wisdom, stored up for them—like the honey for the Gods on Olympus—since time unknown.

You wonder and you wonder until you wander out into Infinity, where—if it is to be found anywhere—Truth really exists.

The Greeks had possessions, culture. They were lost because they did not understand.

The Romans owned more than anyone else. Trampled under the heel of Vandals and Civilization, because they would not understand.

Greeks. Did not understand.

Romans. Would not understand.

"They." Will not understand.

So you find, they have shut Wisdom up and have forgotten to find the key that will let her out. They have trapped, trammeled, lashed her to themselves with thews and thongs and theories. They have ransacked sea and earth and air to bring every treasure to her. But she sulks and will not work for a world with a whitish hue because it has snubbed her twin sister, Understanding.

You see clearly—off there is Infinity—Understanding. Standing alone, waiting for someone to really want her.

But she is so far out there is no way to snatch at her and drag her in.

So—being a woman—you can wait.

You must sit quietly without a chip. Not sodden—and weighted as if your feet were cast in the iron of your soul. Not wasting strength in enervating gestures as if two hundred years of bonds and whips had really tricked you into nervous uncertainty.

But quiet; quiet. Like Buddha—who brown like I am—sat entirely at ease, entirely sure of himself; motionless and knowing, a thousand years before the white man knew there was so very much difference between feet and hands.

Motionless on the outside. But inside?

Silent.

Still . . . "Perhaps Buddha is a woman."

So you too. Still; quiet; with a smile, ever so slight, at the eyes so that Life will flow into and not by you. And you can gather, as it passes, the essences, the overtones, the tints, the shadows; draw understanding to your self.

And then you can, when Time is ripe, swoop to your feet—at your full height—at a single gesture.

Ready to go where?

Why . . . Wherever God motions.

BOOKER T. WASHINGTON

Booker T. Washington (1856–1915) was a prominent leader in the African American community, advocating self-help and industrial education in the pursuit of racial "uplift" and economic equality. Founded on the model of Hampton, Tuskegee Institute was established by Washington in 1881, and he continued to work there until his death. Tuskegee primarily functioned to train teachers and instill industrial skills in African Americans, furthering Washington's belief in the importance of schooling and entrepreneurship for black progress. Other black leaders sometimes criticized Washington for what was perceived as his accommodating stance toward whites, as he often spoke for white audiences and courted white philanthropists. His efforts were successful, though, in funneling money toward black causes in the South and, for that, many saw him as a hero. Washington also published several books, perhaps most notably his autobiography, *Up From Slavery* (1901).

The Standard Printed Version of the Atlanta Exposition Address[†]

"The Atlanta Exposition Address," commonly referred to as the "Atlanta Compromise," was delivered in Atlanta, Georgia, on September 18, 1895, at the Cotton States Exposition. Washington published a version of this speech in *Up From Slavery* (1901)

Mr. President and Gentlemen of the Board of Directors and Citizens: One-third of the population of the South is of the Negro race. No enterprise seeking the material, civil, or moral welfare of this section can disregard this element of our population and reach the highest success. I but convey to you, Mr. President and Directors, the sentiment of the masses of my race when I say that in no way have the value and manhood of the American Negro been more fittingly and generously recognized than by the managers of this magnificent Exposition at every stage of its progress. It is a recognition that will do more to cement the friendship of the two races than any occurrence since the dawn of our freedom.

Not only this, but the opportunity here afforded will awaken among us a new era of industrial progress. Ignorant and inexperienced, it is not strange that in the first years of our new life we began at the top instead of at the bottom; that a seat in Congress or the state legislature was more sought than real estate or industrial skill; that the political convention or stump speaking had more attractions than starting a dairy farm or truck garden.

A ship lost at sea for many days suddenly sighted a friendly vessel. From the mast of the unfortunate vessel was seen a signal, "Water, water; we die of thirst!" The answer from the friendly vessel at once came back, "Cast down your bucket where you are." A second time the signal, "Water, water; send us water!" ran up from the distressed vessel, and was answered, "Cast down your bucket where you are." And a third and fourth signal for water was answered,

---

† From *The Souls of Black Folks: A Norton Critical Edition*, ed. Henry Louis Gates Jr. and Terri Oliver Hume (New York: W. W. Norton and Company, 1999), pp. 167–70. Copyright © 1999 by Henry Louis Gates Jr. and Terri Hume Oliver. Used by permission of W. W. Norton & Company, Inc.

"Cast down your bucket where you are." The captain of the distressed vessel, at last heeding the injunction, cast down his bucket, and it came up full of fresh, sparkling water from the mouth of the Amazon River. To those of my race who depend on bettering their condition in a foreign land or who underestimate the importance of cultivating friendly relations with the Southern white man, who is their next-door neighbour, I would say: "Cast down your bucket where you are"—cast it down in making friends in every manly way of the people of all races by whom we are surrounded.

Cast it down in agriculture, mechanics, in commerce, in domestic service, and in the professions. And in this connection it is well to bear in mind that whatever other sins the South may be called to bear, when it comes to business, pure and simple, it is in the South that the Negro is given a man's chance in the commercial world, and in nothing is this Exposition more eloquent than in emphasizing this chance. Our greatest danger is that in the great leap from slavery to freedom we may overlook the fact that the masses of us are to live by the productions of our hands, and fail to keep in mind that we shall prosper in proportion as we learn to dignify and glorify common labour, and put brains and skill into the common occupations of life; shall prosper in proportion as we learn to draw the line between the superficial and the substantial, the ornamental gewgaws of life and the useful. No race can prosper till it learns that there is as much dignity in tilling a field as in writing a poem. It is at the bottom of life we must begin, and not at the top. Nor should we permit our grievances to overshadow our opportunities.

* * *

The wisest among my race understand that the agitation of questions of social equality is the extremest folly, and that progress in the enjoyment of all the privileges that will come to us must be the result of severe and constant struggle rather than of artificial forcing. No race that has anything to contribute to the markets of the world is long in any degree ostracized. It is important and right that all privileges of the law be ours, but it is vastly more important that we be prepared for the exercise of these privileges. The opportunity to earn a dollar in a factory just now is worth infinitely more than the opportunity to spend a dollar in an opera-house.

In conclusion, may I repeat that nothing in thirty years has given us more hope and encouragement, and drawn us so near to you of the white race, as this opportunity offered by the Exposition; and here bending, as it were, over the altar that represents the results of the struggles of your race and mine, both starting practically empty-handed three decades ago, I pledge that in your

effort to work out the great and intricate problem which God has
laid at the doors of the South, you shall have at all times the
patient, sympathetic help of my race; only let this be constantly in
mind, that, while from representations in these buildings of the
product of field, of forest, of mine, of factory, letters, and art, much
good will come, yet far above and beyond material benefits will be
that higher good, that, let us pray God, will come, in a blotting out
of sectional differences and racial animosities and suspicions, in a
determination to administer absolute justice, in a willing obedi-
ence among all classes to the mandates of law. This, coupled with
our material prosperity, will bring into our beloved South a new
heaven and a new earth.

W. E. B. DU BOIS

Sociologist, scholar, pacifist, activist, anti-imperialist, historian, editor,
and writer, W. E. B. Du Bois (1868–1963) was one of the leading intellectuals of the twentieth century and one of the most influential
senior figures of the Harlem Renaissance. Considered a "gatekeeper"
of black culture, his opinions wielded enormous influence.

* * *

From The Damnation of Women†

I remember four women of my boyhood: my mother, cousin Inez,
Emma, and Ide Fuller. They represented the problem of the widow,
the wife, the maiden, and the outcast. They were, in color, brown
and light-brown, yellow with brown freckles, and white. They existed
not for themselves, but for men; they were named after the men to
whom they were related and not after the fashion of their own souls.

They were not beings, they were relations and these relations were
enfilmed with mystery and secrecy. We did not know the truth or
believe it when we heard it. Motherhood! What was it? We did not
know or greatly care. My mother and I were good chums. I liked her.
After she was dead I loved her with a fierce sense of personal loss.

Inez was a pretty, brown cousin who married. What was marriage?
We did not know, neither did she, poor thing! It came to mean for
her a litter of children, poverty, a drunken, cruel companion, sickness, and death. Why?

† From *Darkwater: Voices from Within the Veil* (New York: Harcourt, 1920), pp. 95–96.

There was no sweeter sight than Emma,—slim, straight, and dainty, darkly flushed with the passion of youth; but her life was a wild, awful struggle to crush her natural, fierce joy of love. She crushed it and became a cold, calculating mockery.

Last there was that awful outcast of the town, the white woman, Ide Fuller. What she was, we did not know. She stood to us as embodied filth and wrong,—but whose filth, whose wrong?

Grown up I see the problem of these women transfused; I hear all about me the unanswered call of youthful love, none the less glorious because of its clean, honest, physical passion. Why unanswered? Because the youth are too poor to marry or if they marry, too poor to have children. They turn aside, then, in three directions: to marry for support, to what men call shame, or to that which is more evil than nothing. It is an unendurable paradox; it must be changed or the bases of culture will totter and fall.

The world wants healthy babies and intelligent workers. Today we refuse to allow the combination and force thousands of intelligent workers to go childless at a horrible expenditure of moral force, or we damn them if they break our idiotic conventions. Only at the sacrifice of intelligence and the chance to do their best work can the majority of modern women bear children. This is the damnation of women.

All womanhood is hampered today because the world on which it is emerging is a world that tries to worship both virgins and mothers and in the end despises motherhood and despoils virgins.

The future woman must have a life work and economic independence. She must have knowledge. She must have the right of motherhood at her own discretion. The present mincing horror at free womanhood must pass if we are ever to be rid of the bestiality of free manhood; not by guarding the weak in weakness do we gain strength, but by making weakness free and strong.

*   *   *

W. E. B. DU BOIS

Of Mr. Booker T. Washington and Others[†]

From birth till death enslaved; in word, in deed, unmanned!

. . .

Hereditary bondsmen! Know ye not
Who would be free themselves must strike the blow?

BYRON.

Easily the most striking thing in the history of the American Negro since 1876 is the ascendancy of Mr. Booker T. Washington. It began at the time when war memories and ideals were rapidly passing; a day of astonishing commercial development was dawning; a sense of doubt and hesitation overtook the freedmen's sons,—then it was that his leading began. Mr. Washington came, with a simple definite programme, at the psychological moment when the nation was a little ashamed of having bestowed so much sentiment on Negroes, and was concentrating its energies on Dollars. His programme of industrial education, conciliation of the South, and submission and silence as to civil and political rights, was not wholly original; the Free Negroes from 1830 up to wartime had striven to build industrial schools, and the American Missionary Association had from the first taught various trades; and Price[1] and others had sought a way of honorable alliance with the best of the Southerners. But Mr. Washington first indissolubly linked these things; he put enthusiasm, unlimited energy, and perfect faith into this programme, and changed it from a by-path into a veritable Way of Life.[2] And the tale of the methods by which he did this is a fascinating study of human life.

It startled the nation to hear a Negro advocating such a programme after many decades of bitter complaint; it startled and won the applause of the South, it interested and won the admiration of the North; and after a confused murmur of protest, it silenced if it did not convert the Negroes themselves.

[†] From *The Souls of Black Folk: A Norton Critical Edition*, ed. Henry Louis Gates Jr. and Terri Hume Oliver (New York: W. W. Norton and Company, 1999), pp. 34–35, 40, 43, 45. Copyright © 1999 by Henry Louis Gates Jr. and Terri Hume Oliver. Used by permission of W. W. Norton & Company, Inc. Revised from "The Evolution of Negro Leadership," *The Dial* (July 16, 1901): 53–55. The three lines of verse are from Canto 2 of Lord Byron's *Childe Harold's Pilgrimage* (1812).

1. Joseph C. Price (1854–1893), A. M. E. Zion minister, orator, and liberal arts advocate, founded Zion Wesley College in 1882 and Livingstone College in 1885.

2. Booker Taliaferro Washington (1856–1915) published his autobiography, *Up From Slavery*, in 1901. It has been called the autobiography of an institution because much of its content concerns Washington's founding of Tuskegee Institute.

To gain the sympathy and coöperation of the various elements comprising the white South was Mr. Washington's first task; and this, at the time Tuskegee[3] was founded, seemed, for a black man, well-nigh impossible. And yet ten years later it was done in the word spoken at Atlanta: "In all things purely social we can be as separate as the five fingers, and yet one as the hand in all things essential to mutual progress." This "Atlanta Compromise"[4] is by all odds the most notable thing in Mr. Washington's career. The South interpreted it in different ways: the radicals received it as a complete surrender of the demand for civil and political equality; the conservatives, as a generously conceived working basis for mutual understanding. So both approved it, and to-day its author is certainly the most distinguished Southerner since Jefferson Davis,[5] and the one with the largest personal following.

* * *

Mr. Washington represents in Negro thought the old attitude of adjustment and submission; but adjustment at such a peculiar time as to make his programme unique. This is an age of unusual economic development, and Mr. Washington's programme naturally takes an economic cast, becoming a gospel of Work and Money to such an extent as apparently almost completely to overshadow the higher aims of life. Moreover, this is an age when the more advanced races are coming in closer contact with the less developed races, and the race-feeling is therefore intensified; and Mr. Washington's programme practically accepts the alleged inferiority of the Negro races. Again, in our own land, the reaction from the sentiment of war time has given impetus to race-prejudice against Negroes, and Mr. Washington withdraws many of the high demands of Negroes as men and American citizens. In other periods of intensified prejudice all the Negro's tendency to self-assertion has been called forth; at this period a policy of submission is advocated. In the history of nearly all other races and peoples the doctrine preached at such crises has been that manly self-respect is worth more than lands and houses,

3. Washington founded Tuskegee Institute in 1881 as a normal, or secondary, school in Tuskegee, Alabama. He served as president until his death, turning the Institute from two unequipped buildings into a complex of over one hundred buildings. Washington also expanded Tuskegee into a college dedicated to industrial education and the training of black schoolteachers.
4. Speech delivered in Atlanta on September 18, 1895, at the Cotton States Exposition. In this famous and controversial speech, Washington not only emphasizes economic self-development for blacks but he also accepts social segregation between the races (see p. 173).
5. President of the Confederate States of America during the Civil War. Davis (1808–1889) was also the topic for Du Bois's commencement address, delivered when he graduated from Harvard in 1890.

and that a people who voluntarily surrender such respect, or cease striving for it, are not worth civilizing.

*   *   *

* * * [T]he way for a people to gain their reasonable rights is not by voluntarily throwing them away and insisting that they do not want them; that the way for a people to gain respect is not by continually belittling and ridiculing themselves; that, on the contrary, Negroes must insist continually, in season and out of season, that voting is necessary to modern manhood, that color discrimination is barbarism, and that black boys need education as well as white boys.

*   *   *

* * * His doctrine has tended to make the whites, North and South, shift the burden of the Negro problem to the Negro's shoulders and stand aside as critical and rather pessimistic spectators; when in fact the burden belongs to the nation, and the hands of none of us are clean if we bend not our energies to righting these great wrongs.

*   *   *

The black men of America have a duty to perform, a duty stern and delicate,—a forward movement to oppose a part of the work of their greatest leader. So far as Mr. Washington preaches Thrift, Patience, and Industrial Training for the masses, we must hold up his hands and strive with him, rejoicing in his honors and glorying in the strength of this Joshua[6] called of God and of man to lead the headless host. But so far as Mr. Washington apologizes for injustice, North or South, does not rightly value the privilege and duty of voting, belittles the emasculating effects of caste distinctions, and opposes the higher training and ambition of our brighter minds,— so far as he, the South, or the Nation, does this,—we must unceasingly and firmly oppose them. By every civilized and peaceful method we must strive for the rights which the world accords to men, clinging unwaveringly to those great words which the sons of the Fathers would fain[7] forget: "We hold these truths to be self-evident: That all men are created equal; that they are endowed by their Creator with certain unalienable rights; that among these are life, liberty, and the pursuit of happiness."[8]

---

6. After the death of Moses, Joshua, his deputy, was called by God to lead the Israelites into the Promised Land.
7. Happily; gladly.
8. The preamble of the Declaration of Independence, 1776.

W. E. B. DU BOIS

Race Pride[†]

Our friends are hard—very hard—to please. Only yesterday they were preaching "Race Pride."

"Go to!" they said, "and be PROUD of your race."

If we hesitated or sought to explain—"Away," they yelled; "Ashamed-of-Yourself and Want-to-be-White!"

Of course, the Amazing Major is still at it, but do you notice that others say less—because they see that bull-headed worship of any "race," as such, may lead and does lead to curious complications?

For instance: Today Negroes, Indians, Chinese, and other groups, are gaining new faith in themselves; they are beginning to "like" themselves; they are discovering that the current theories and stories of "backward" peoples are largely lies and assumptions; that human genius and possibility are not limited by color, race, or blood. What is this new self-consciousness leading to? Inevitably and directly to distrust and hatred of whites; to demands for self-government, separation, driving out of foreigners: "Asia for the Asiatics," "Africa for the Africans," and "Negro officers for Negro troops!"

No sooner do whites see this unawaited development than they point out in dismay the inevitable consequences: "You lose our tutelage," "You spurn our knowledge," "You need our wealth and technique." They point out how fine is the world rôle of Elder Brother.

Very well. Some of the darker brethren are convinced. They draw near in friendship; they seek to enter schools and churches; they would mingle in industry—when lo! "Get out," yells the White World—"You're not our brothers and never will be"—"Go away, herd by yourselves"—"Eternal Segregation in the Lord!"

Can you wonder, Sirs, that we are a bit puzzled by all this and that we are asking gently, but more and more insistently, Choose one or the other horn of the dilemma:

1. Leave the black and yellow world alone. Get out of Asia, Africa, and the Isles. Give us our states and towns and sections and let us rule them undisturbed. Absolutely segregate the races and sections of the world

Or—

2. Let the world meet as men with men. Give utter Justice to all. Extend Democracy to all and treat all men according to their individual desert. Let it be possible for whites to rise to the highest

† From *The Crisis* 19.3 (January 1920): 107.

positions in China and Uganda and blacks to the highest honors in England and Texas.

Here is the choice. Which will you have, my masters?

LANGSTON HUGHES

Langston Hughes (1902–1967) was one of the most recognized and brilliant writers of the Harlem Renaissance, the author of such works as *The Weary Blues* (1926), where "Cross" originally appeared, *Fine Clothes to the Jew* (1927), *Not Without Laughter* (1930), *Dear Lovely Death* (1931), *The Ways of White Folks* (1934), *The Big Sea* (1940), and many others. In addition to poetry, Hughes wrote fiction, autobiography, essays, plays, and reviews.

Cross†

My old man's a white old man
And my old mother's black.
If ever I cursed my white old man
I take my curses back.
If ever I cursed my black old mother   5
And wished she were in hell,
I'm sorry for that evil wish
And now I wish her well.
My old man died in a fine big house.
My ma died in a shack.   10
I wonder where I'm gonna die,
Being neither white nor black?

CHARLES S. JOHNSON

Sociologist Charles S. Johnson (1893–1956) was a teacher, writer, and social activist. Born in Virginia to a preacher and teacher, he received a PhD from the University of Chicago. As Director of Research for the National Urban League from 1921 to 1928, Johnson played a central role in Harlem's social and cultural politics. He founded and edited *Opportunity*, which was one of the two most important black journals of the movement (*The Crisis* was the other). In 1928 he returned to Fisk to teach and was appointed its first black president in 1946. His most important books include *The Negro in Chicago* (1922),

---

† From *The Crisis* 31.2 (December 1925): 66. Rpt. in *The Crisis*, Authorized Reprint Edition (New York: Arno Press, 1969), pp. 66. Copyright © 1994 by the Estate of Langston Hughes. Used by permission of Alfred A. Knopf, an imprint of the Knopf Doubleday Publishing Group, a division of Penguin Random House LLC. All rights reserved.

The Negro in American Civilization (1930), *Shadow of the Plantation* (1934), and *Growing Up in the Black Belt* (1941).

An Opportunity for Negro Writers[†]

A new period in creative expression among Negroes is foreshadowed in the notable, even if fugitive and disconnected successes of certain of the generation of Negro writers now emerging. The body of experience and public opinion seem ripe for the development of some new and perhaps distinctive contribution to art, literature, and life. But these contributions demand incentives. The random and obviously inadequate methods of casual inquiry have already disclosed an unexpected amount and degree of writing ability among Negroes which gives promise of further development on a large scale. The ability of these scattered writers has become known largely by the accident of locality. There are undoubtedly others to be discovered. The question of markets has been an agent of inertia in this regard. Even for those of acknowledged competence an almost insuperable discouragement has been the unpopularity of those themes with which Negro writers have been most familiar. This is changing now. The judgment of some of the foremost students of American literature offers encouragement for the future of imaginative writing by Negroes.

There is an extreme usefulness for the cause of inter-racial good-will as well as racial culture and American literature in interpreting the life and longings and emotional experiences of the Negro people to their shrinking and spiritually alien neighbors; of flushing old festers of hate and disgruntlement by becoming triumphantly articulate; of forcing the interest and kindred feeling of the rest of the world by sheer force of the humanness and beauty of one's own story. The old romantic Negro characters of fiction are admittedly *passe*. Negroes have been swept along, even if at the rear of the procession, with the forward movement of the rest of the world. There is an opportunity now for Negroes themselves to replace their out-worn representations in fiction faithfully and incidentally to make themselves better understood.

* * *

JAMES WELDON JOHNSON

When diplomat, editor, and writer James Weldon Johnson (1871–1938) first published his classic passing tale *The Autobiography of an*

† From *Opportunity* 2 (September 1924): 258. Reprinted with permission of the National Urban League.

Ex-Colored Man in 1912, he did so anonymously, leading many readers to believe that the novel was a true account. In the short excerpt that follows, the main character suddenly longs for the race he has left, after hearing the spirituals or "sorrow songs," just as Helga does in *Quicksand*. *The Autobiography of an Ex-Colored Man* was reissued in the 1920s, under Johnson's own name, and was one of the most successful novels of the Harlem Renaissance.

From The Dilemma of the Negro Author[†]

The Negro author—the creative author—has arrived. He is here. He appears in the lists of the best publishers. He even breaks into the lists of the best-sellers. To the general American public he is a novelty, a strange phenomenon, a miracle straight out of the skies. Well, he *is* a novelty, but he is by no means a new thing.

The line of American Negro authors runs back for a hundred and fifty years, back to Phillis Wheatley, the poet.[1] Since Phillis Wheatley there have been several hundred Negro authors who have written books of many kinds. But in all these generations down to within the past six years only seven or eight of the hundreds have ever been heard of by the general American public or even by the specialists in American literature. As many Negro writers have gained recognition by both in the past six years as in all the generations gone before. What has happened is that efforts which have been going on for more than a century are being noticed and appreciated at last, and that this appreciation has served as a stimulus to greater effort and output. America is aware today that there are such things as Negro authors. Several converging forces have been at work to produce this state of mind. Had these forces been at work three decades ago, it is possible that we then should have had a condition similar to the one which now exists.

Now that the Negro author has come into the range of vision of the American public eye, it seems to me only fair to point out some of the difficulties he finds in his way. But I wish to state emphatically that I have no intention of making an apology or asking any special allowances for him; such a plea would at once disqualify him

† From *American Mercury* (December 1928): 477–81. Rpt. in *The Autobiography of an Ex-Colored Man: A Norton Critical Edition*, ed. Jacqueline Goldsby (New York: W. W. Norton and Company, 2015), pp. 258–59. Reprinted with permission of the James Weldon Johnson Estate. Footnotes for this excerpt are Goldsby's.
1. In both her first book, *Poems on Various Subjects, Religious and Moral* (1773) and her person, Wheatley (1753–1784) embodied the dilemma Johnson's essay identifies. Her neoclassical verse style defied white stereotypes about the illiteracy of enslaved blacks; her literary techniques sometimes turned black readers away from her work—a distance Johnson kept himself, judging by his commentary about Wheatley in his preface to the 1922 *Book of American Negro Poetry*.

and void the very recognition he has gained. But the Negro writer does face peculiar difficulties that ought to be taken into account when passing judgment upon him.

It is unnecessary to say that he faces every one of the difficulties common to all that crowd of demon-driven individuals who feel that they must write. But the Aframerican[2] author faces a special problem which the plain American author knows nothing about—the problem of the double audience. It is more than a double audience; it is a divided audience, an audience made up of two elements with differing and often opposite and antagonistic points of view. His audience is always both white America and black America. The moment a Negro writer takes up his pen or sits down to his typewriter he is immediately called upon to solve, consciously or unconsciously, this problem of the double audience. To whom shall he address himself, to his own black group or to white America? Many a Negro writer has fallen down, as it were, between these two stools.

It may be asked why he doesn't just go ahead and write and not bother himself about audiences. That is easier said than done. It is doubtful if anything with meaning can be written unless the writer has some definite audience in mind. His audience may be as far away as the angelic host or the rulers of darkness, but an audience he must have in mind. As soon as he selects his audience he immediately falls, whether he wills it or not, under the laws which govern the influence of the audience upon the artist, laws that operate in every branch of art.

✳   ✳   ✳

SHEILA KAYE-SMITH

Sheila Kaye-Smith (1887–1956) was a popular English writer whose novels included rural topics, religious themes, and women's choices. Her story "Mrs. Adis," which Larsen was accused—then cleared—of plagiarizing, was published in *The Century*, in 1922. Ironically, this story may be more familiar to American readers than any of Kaye-Smith's other works because of the plagiarism scandal involving Larsen.

---

2. This fused term, joining "Afro" to "American," first appeared in black denominational periodicals of the 1890s, such as the *African Methodist Episcopal Church Review*. It became widespread in the black secular media by the early twentieth century. Johnson used it in print as early as his 1922 preface to the *Book of American Negro Poetry*. My thanks to Joan Bryant, P. Gabrielle Foreman, and Richard Yarborough for sharing information about this term's etymology.

Mrs. Adis[†]

In northeastern Sussex a great tongue of land runs into Kent by Scotney Castle. It is a land of woods, the old hammer-woods of the Sussex iron industry, and among the woods gleam the hammer-ponds, holding in their mirrors the sunsets and sunrises. Owing to the thickness of the woods, great masses of oak and beech in a dense undergrowth of hazel and chestnut and frail sallow, the road that passes Mrs. Adis's cottage is dark before the twilight has crept away from the fields beyond. That night there was no twilight moon, only a few pricks of fire in the black sky above the trees. But what the darkness hid, the silence revealed. In the absolute stillness of the night, windless and clear with the first frost of October, every sound was distinct, intensified. The distant bark of a dog at Delmonden sounded close at hand, and the man who walked on the road could hear the echo of his own footsteps following him like a knell.

Every now and then he made a futile effort to go quietly, but the roadside was a mass of brambles, and their cracking and rustling sounded nearly as loud as the thud of his feet on the marl. Besides, they made him go slowly, and he had no time for that.

When he came to Mrs. Adis's cottage he paused a moment. Only a small patch of grass lay between it and the road. He went stealthily across it, and looked in at the lighted, uncurtained window. He could see Mrs. Adis stooping over the fire, taking off some pot or kettle. He hesitated and seemed to ponder. He was a big, hulking man, with reddish hair and freckled face, evidently of the laboring class, though not successful, judging by the vague grime and poverty of his appearance. For a moment he made as if he would open the window; then he changed his mind and went to the door instead.

He did not knock, but walked straight in. The woman at the fire turned quickly.

"What, you, Peter Crouch?" she said. "I didn't hear you knock."

"I didn't knock, ma'am. I didn't want anybody to hear."

"How's that?"

"I'm in trouble." His hands were shaking a little.

"What you done?"

"I shot a man, Mrs. Adis."

"You?"

"Yes, I shot him."

"You killed him?"

"I dunno."

† From *The Century Magazine* 103.3 (January 1922): 321–26.

For a moment there was silence in the small stuffy kitchen; then the kettle boiled over, and Mrs. Adis sprang for it, mechanically putting it at the side of the fire.

She was a small, frail-looking woman, with a brown, hard face on which the skin had dried in innumerable small hair-like wrinkles. She was probably not more than forty-two, but life treats some women hard in the agricultural districts of Sussex, and Mrs. Adis's life had been harder than most.

"What do you want me to do for you, Peter Crouch?" she said a little sourly.

"Let me stay here a bit. Is there nowhere you can put me till they've gone?"

"Who's they?"

"The keepers."

"Oh, you've had a shine with the keepers, have you?"

"Yes, I was down by Cinder Wood seeing if I could pick up anything, and the keepers found me. There was four to one, so I used my gun. Then I ran for it. They're after me; reckon they aren't far off now."

Mrs. Adis did not speak for a moment.

Crouch looked at her searchingly, beseechingly.

"You might do it for Tom's sake," he said.

"You haven't been an over-good friend to Tom," snapped Mrs. Adis.

"But Tom's been an unaccountable good friend to me; reckon he would want you to stand by me to-night."

"Well, I won't say he wouldn't, seeing as Tom always thought better of you than you deserved, and maybe you can stay till he comes home tonight; then we can hear what he says about it."

"That'll serve my turn, I reckon. He'll be up at Ironlatch for an hour yet, and the coast will be clear by then, and I can get away out of the county."

"Where'll you go?"

"I dunno. There's time to think of that."

"Well, you can think of it in here," she said dryly, opening a door which led from the kitchen into the small lean-to of the cottage. "They'll never guess you're there, specially if I tell them I ain't seen you to-night."

"You're a good woman, Mrs. Adis."

She did not speak, but shut the door, and he was in darkness save for a small ray of light that filtered through one of the cracks. By this light he could see her moving to and fro, preparing Tom's supper. In another hour Tom would be home from Ironlatch Farm, where he worked every day. Peter Crouch trusted Tom not to revoke his mother's kindness, for they had been friends since they went together to the national school at Lamberhurst, and since then the friendship had not been broken by their very different characters and careers.

Peter Crouch huddled down upon the sacks that filled one corner of the lean-to and gave himself up to the dreary and anxious business of waiting. A delicious smell of cooking began to filter through from the kitchen, and he hoped Mrs. Adis would not deny him a share of the supper when Tom came home, for he was very hungry and he had a long way to go.

He had fallen into a kind of helpless doze, haunted by the memories of the last two hours, recast in the form of dreams, when he was roused by the sound of footsteps on the road. For a moment his poor heart nearly choked him with its beating. They were the keepers. They had guessed for a certainty where he was—with Mrs. Adis, his old pal's mother. He had been a fool to come to the cottage. Nearly losing his self-control, he shrank into the corner, shivering, half sobbing. But the footsteps went by. They did not even hesitate at the door. He heard them ring away into the frosty stillness. The next minute Mrs. Adis stuck her head into the lean-to.

"That was them," she said shortly—"a party from the castle. I saw them go by. They had lanterns, and I saw old Crotch and the two Boormans. Maybe it 'u'd be better if you slipped out now and went toward Cansiron. You'd miss them that way and get over into Kent. There's a London train comes from Tunbridge Wells at ten to-night."

"That 'u'd be a fine thing for me, ma'am, but I haven't the price of a ticket on me."

She went to one of the kitchen drawers.

"Here's seven shillun'. It's all I've got, but it'll be your fare to London and a bit over."

For a moment he did not speak; then he said:

"I don't know how to thank you, ma'am."

"Oh, you needn't thank me. I am doing it for Tom. I know how unaccountable set he is on you and always was."

"I hope you won't get into any trouble because of me."

"There ain't much fear. No one's ever likely to know you've been in this cottage. That's why I'd sooner you went before Tom came back, for maybe he'd bring a pal with him, and that 'u'd make trouble. I won't say I sha'n't have it on my conscience for having helped you to escape the law, but shooting a keeper ain't the same as shooting an ordinary sort of man, as we all know, and maybe he ain't so much the worse; so I won't think no more about it."

She opened the door for him, but on the threshold they stood still, for again footsteps could be heard approaching, this time from the far south.

"Maybe it's Tom," said Mrs. Adis.

"There's more than one man there, and I can hear voices."

"You'd better go back," she said shortly. "Wait till they've passed, anyway."

With an unwilling shrug he went back into the little lean-to, which he had come to hate, and she shut the door upon him.

The footsteps drew nearer. They came more slowly and heavily this time. For a moment he thought they also would pass, but their momentary dulling was only the crossing of the strip of grass outside the door. The next minute there was a knock. It was not Tom, then.

Trembling with anxiety and curiosity, Peter Crouch put his eye to one of the numerous cracks in the door of the lean-to and looked through into the kitchen. He saw Mrs. Adis go to the cottage door, but before she could open it, a man came quickly in and shut it behind him.

Crouch recognised Vidler, one of the keepers of Scotney Castle, and he felt his hands and feet grow leaden cold. They knew where he was, then; they had followed him. They had guessed that he had taken refuge with Mrs. Adis. It was all up. He was not really hidden; there was no place for him to hide. Directly they opened the inner door they would see him. Why couldn't he think of things better? Why wasn't he cleverer at looking after himself, like other men? His legs suddenly refused to support him, and he sat down on the pile of sacks.

The man in the kitchen seemed to have some difficulty in saying what he wanted to Mrs. Adis. He stood before her silently, twisting his cap.

"Well, what is it?" she asked.

"I want to speak to you, ma'am."

Peter Crouch listened, straining his ears, for his thudding heart nearly drowned the voices in the next room. Oh, no, he was sure she would not give him away, if only for Tom's sake. She was a game sort, Mrs. Adis.

"Well," she said sharply, as the man remained tongue-tied.

"I have brought you bad news, Mrs. Adis."

Her expression changed.

"What? It ain't Tom, is it?"

"He's outside," said the keeper.

"What do you mean?" said Mrs. Adis, and she moved toward the door.

"Don't, ma'am, not till I've told you."

"Told me what? Oh, be quick, man, for mercy's sake!" and she tried to push past him to the door.

"There's been a row," he said, "down by Cinder Wood. There was a chap there snaring rabbits, and Tom was walking with the Boormans and me and old Crotch down from the castle. We heard a noise in the spinney, and there—it was too dark to see who it was, and directly he saw us he made off. But we'd scared him, and he let fly with his gun."

He stopped speaking and looked at her, as if beseeching her to fill in the gaps of his story. In his corner of the lean-to Peter Crouch was as a man of wood and sawdust.

"Tom—" said Mrs. Adis.

The keeper had forgotten his guard, and before he could prevent her she had flung open the door.

The men outside had evidently been waiting for the signal, and they came in, carrying something on a hurdle, which they put down in the middle of the kitchen floor.

"Is he dead?" asked Mrs. Adis, without tears.

The men nodded. They could not find a dry voice, like hers.

In the lean-to Peter Crouch had ceased to sweat and tremble. Strength had come with despair, for he knew he must despair now. Besides, he no longer wanted to escape from this thing that he had done.

"O Tom! and I thinking it was one of them demmed keepers! Tom! and it was you that got it—got it from me! Reckon I don't want to live."

And yet life was sweet.

Mrs. Adis was sitting in the old basket arm-chair by the fire. One of the men had helped her into it. Another, with rough kindness, had poured her out something from a flask he carried in his pocket.

"Here, ma'am, take a drop of this. It'll give you strength. We'll go around to Ironlatch Farm and ask Mrs. Gain to come down to you. Reckon this is a tur'ble thing to have come to you, but it's the will o' Providence, as some folks say, and as for the man who did it, we've a middling good guess who he is, and he shall swing."

"We didn't see his face," said Vidler, "but we've got his gun. He threw it into an alder when he bolted, and I swear that gun belongs to Peter Crouch, who's been up to no good since the day when Mus' Scales got shut of him for stealing his corn."

"Reckon, though, he didn't know it was Tom when he did it," said the other man, "he and Tom always being better friends than Crouch deserved."

Peter Crouch was standing upright now, looking through the crack of the door. He saw Mrs. Adis struggle to her feet and stand by the table, looking down on the dead man's face. A whole eternity seemed to roll by as she stood there. He saw her put her hand into her pocket, where she had thrust the key of the lean-to.

"The Boormans have gone after Crouch," said Vidler, nervously breaking the silence. "They'd a notion as he'd broken through the woods Iron-latch-way. There's no chance of his having been by here? You haven't seen him to-night, have you, ma'am?"

There was a pause.

"No," said Mrs. Adis, "I haven't seen him. Not since Tuesday." She took her hand out of her pocket.

"Well, we'll be getting around and fetch Mrs. Gain. Reckon you'd be glad to have her."

Mrs. Adis nodded.

"Will you carry him in there first?" she said, and pointed to the bedroom-door.

The men picked up the hurdle and carried it into the next room; then silently each wrung the mother by the hand and went away.

She waited until they had shut the door; then she came toward the lean-to. Crouch once more fell a-shivering. He couldn't bear it. No, he'd rather swing than face Mrs. Adis. He heard the key turn in the lock and he nearly screamed.

But she did not come in. She merely unlocked the door, then crossed the kitchen with a heavy, dragging footstep, and shut herself into the room where Tom was.

Peter Crouch knew what he must do, the only thing she wanted him to do, the only thing he could possibly do: he opened the door and silently went out.

From Negro Womanhood's Greatest Needs: A Symposium Conducted by the Leading Negro Clubwomen of the United States†

The Needs: A larger opportunity opened to her to enter schools of higher education, to be accepted as a student and not as one apart. A broader understanding of other peoples than her own. An economic privilege of filling positions for which she is fitted and capable. The encouragement, confidence and respect of her own race. To exercise her right of Franchise giving careful study and deliberation to legislation. To enter more actively into world activities whenever the opportunity presents itself. To give much thought, deep thought and wise thought to the problems confronting the world in which she is a part. To remember God and have faith in Him. To build strong character by embracing that which is good, noble and pure. To temper her judgments sagely in this great era for the Negro, not to flare up as a meteor

---

† From *The Black Experience in America: Negro Periodicals in the United States, 1840–1960* (New York: Negro UP, 1969), pp. 109, 150, 198–99. Originally published in *The Messenger* 9.4–6 (April, May, and June 1927), pp. 109, 150–53, 198–99.

then fall into oblivion but be cautious and never forget her tender womanly and great motherly heritage. To hold fast to the highest rung in the ladder of perfect womanhood. To cling to the home, great men and women evolve from the environment of the hearthstone.

(Mrs.) Bonnie Bogle,
Portland, Oregon.

Like all other groups, representing other races and peoples, our women have their special needs. Chief among them I would place respect and protection. When this is entertained and practiced by those of our own group it will naturally and logically be forced upon others with whom we come in contact. I am not unmindful of the necessity of earning this estimate after securing it we must be sure to retain it.

Ours is an age of ambition and progress and our women must be encouraged to keep pace with our sisters of other groups.

Capability forms a large part of one's accomplishments but opportunity is always knocking at every door. One of the lessons we need to learn is that all cannot be leaders—some of us must learn to follow. As much or even more can be accomplished from this position as at the head.

Imitation is one of our greatest gifts. We need to be discreet as to our choosing. We cannot and ought not to adopt all that even appeals to us. Let us be wise in our selections. Let us be kindly in our judgments and keep jealousy, envy and prejudice far from us.

I can never think of a woman as being irreligious. As she has been permitted to enter public life and is filling different vocations, she must remember that her example can wield great influence and she must help others to rise to her station of Godliness.

Loyalty to God, race, man and brother and to a principle are requirements of us all. Our women are learning these things as they are becoming wiser and broader.

In our conferences and deliberations we need to be more thoughtful and sustain only those methods to which we will be loyal and true.

We must be dependable. "My word is my bond" should carry its full meaning and is an excellent slogan to adopt. With our limited opportunities our women have made wonderful progress. We still need greater encouragement and more privileges for our fullest development. May God give us wisdom, patience and perseverance. If we practice these, we will surely win respect, protection and advancement.

(Mrs.) Nattie Langston Napier,
Nashville, Tenn.

*   *   *

The greatest needs of Negro womanhood today are *vision*, or the realization of the powers within herself and their possibilities of achievement material and spiritual; *organization*, in order that these possibilities may become realities; and a *deeper appreciation of her value* by those for whom she works whether in the home or in public service based upon a fundamental need of all women—love.

Suppose two million Negro women could be led to see how much they could help to create avenues of employment for themselves by purchasing articles manufactured by Negroes; by at least sharing their trade with Negro grocers, druggists, dry cleaners, dry goods stores, shoe stores, etc.

Suppose these two million women could be led to see the wisdom of insurance of the various types and in addition supported the companies owned and operated by their own people?

Women usually control the purchase of the basic supplies, food, clothing, shelter and hence they could be potent factors in the development of the economic life of their people.

And then—Suppose these two million women should grow tired of seeing themselves and their people crudely caricatured—as buffoons and worse—should quietly ignore these periodicals and books and read the best of the productions of their own writers, and those who picture them as human beings. The results tangible and intangible would be far reaching.

These suppositions can be made realities.

We have many strong organizations denominational, fraternal and social, already at work. It would not be a difficult task for these leaders to agree on one or two definite aims towards which all of our women could be urged to strive.

The National Association of Colored Women is a nucleus for such effort; the establishment of its headquarters at the National Capital offers a channel through which all Negro women may help toward these ends. For more than three hundred years the Negro woman has been a burden bearer, denied much of the tenderness, the protecting love and sympathetic understanding which she so richly deserves. She needs vision to see more clearly her needs and her duties; organization as the most effective means for the accomplishment of her self-imposed tasks; and loving appreciation to sustain her when she falters.

(Mrs.) Augusta Dean Zuber,
West Point, Miss.

(Note: This discussion is continued in the May number by other prominent clubwomen from different sections of the country.)

* * *

Now that the colleges, universities and seminaries are teeming with our young women who are eager to play their part in life's drama, eager to give to her race and to the world the best she has, her greatest need is opportunity for development. However high the ideals of our women, they must have an outlet for expansion or they will become dwarfed and finally wither or decay. That the Negro woman of today needs the opportunity afforded other racial groups is seen by the hundreds of them who have made the necessary preparation for life's race, but are deprived of entrance through the gateway. This fact, however, must not deter our women from equipping themselves. Capability, efficiency and preparation along all lines must be the entering wedge to higher and better opportunities for the Negro womanhood of today.

Wherever our women have served, they have made good. Hundreds of them are filling positions of trust reflecting credit not only on themselves and their race but they are breaking down the bars of discrimination and segregation which have hitherto handicapped them and stunted their growth, impeded their progress in the march of advancement, therefore, my opinion is, that the greatest need of the Negro womanhood of today is opportunity.

(Mrs.) M. C. Lawton,
Brooklyn, N. Y.

* * *

The work of Negro woman is in lifting up that portion of the American people that suffers at least a half-century handicap in the race of civilization. When Abraham Lincoln dipped his pen into the blood of the martyrs of the civil war, still in progress, and attached his immortal signature to that great instrument of liberty—he did not free the Negro woman; slavery had placed a ban upon her as a human soul that nothing but her own virtuous hand could lift. We found her, sinned against far more than she had sinned, but today, given equal opportunity for advancement, intellectually, morally and spiritually, she can stand four square to the winds of destiny unashamed and unafraid before the womanhood of the entire world.

Education is one of the greatest needs of our womanhood today. It will not do for us to sit by and say we are not interested. It must be from our hearts that we make sacrifices. And along with education must be associated character building. We are trying to show to the world that we are American citizens with God-given rights.

The only reason we shall fail is on account of ourselves. Our young women must have unblemished character and untarnished names along with their education. Education without character is as a rose without a scent.

*   *   *

Ethel Minor Gavin,
Chicago, Ill.

*   *   *

Education. If much depends, as is allowed, upon the early education of youth and the first principles which are instilled take deep root, then great benefit must arise from the literary accomplishments in women. Left free to act, woman naturally gravitates to the philanthropies. Today, if we look through literature devoted to, and springing out of the philanthropies, you will find that it emanates largely from the brain and heart of woman. With the achievement of women in the past as incentive are the women of today alert to their advantages which lie within a hand-grasp? They should aspire to greater intelligence. This does not mean that a woman should go to school, have her name enrolled on class books and receive at the end of a course, a degree—a Greek letter—a "Key" for brilliant scholarship; but that she obtain an education which grows out of experience to adjust herself to present day conditions to attain higher intelligence which fits her for clearly understanding her relations to society and her race. Under Education, I would stress the need of our women fitting themselves to enter the business world. As a race we are weak industrially. Attending the Industrial Conferences where hundreds of women of other races are present and a part of the great industries of the world, we are pained to note the absence and lack of interest of our women in the field of industry. True there are serious economic conditions which hinder but we must show by thrift, economy and business acumen that we are competent to master the problems in industrial activities and hammer away until we gain recognition.

*   *   *

Let the Negro woman appropriate the high ideals and become more active in the arena of life. May she not become obsessed with fashion and things of pleasure only, let these be her servant. Neither let the madness and love of money dwarf her soul, rather let it be a tool in the art of living. In summing up the foregoing—May she cleave to those things which enlarge her sphere and tend to uplift, which make for better citizenship; for education in its broadest sense; for child welfare legislation; health and sanitation; to work for higher standards in art and literature; for improvement in moral, social, and industrial conditions and World Peace. In short, may she have an awakening and become interested in all questions pertaining to practical everyday life—sounding the keynote organization, education, work, thus increasing our hope and faith in the race with the Negro Womanhood of today as its prime factor.

Miss Hallie Q. Brown,
Wilberforce, O.

*   *   *

CHANDLER OWEN

Along with A. Phillip Randolph, writer and editor Chandler Owen (1889–1967) co-founded the influential magazine, *The Messenger*, in 1917. *The Messenger* began as a union paper, then served as one of the most radical and progressive outlets for both literary and political writings by African Americans during the Harlem Renaissance, often publishing emerging black authors. A member of the American Socialist Party, Owen eventually became disillusioned with the political climate in New York. He moved to Chicago where he served as the managing editor of the *Chicago Bee*, a weekly newspaper for African Americans.

Black Mammies[†]

One writer has said: *"The existence of monuments is justified on but two grounds—as works of art and that for which they stand."* We do not agree with his first proposition. We do not believe a mere work of art justifies a monument. We think that a monument ought to be erected to some idea or ideal and that that ideal should be portrayed through a work of art. In other words, art should be made the hand-maiden of truth and justice.

To illustrate: At the present time the Ku Klux Klan is planning to erect in Atlanta a monument which will probably be one of the greatest works of art in America. They have secured the services of sculptors of world-wide reputation. Yet the monument they erect will necessarily be condemned by the sober opinion of the present and the future, on account of the vicious principles which the statue will be designed to commemorate.

† From *The Messenger* 5.4 (April 1923): 670–71.

The Daughters of the Confederacy (Jefferson Davis Chapter No. 1650) have asked Congress to grant them permission to erect a statue in Washington in memory of the "Black Mammies." They want to bring back memories of the slave days when *black mammies* toiled in the cotton fields, cleaned the houses, cared for the children, nursed them at their bosoms. They want to bring back what (to them) Bert Williams would call *"those wonderful days"*—days when the pay for Negro Labor was the "cruel lash of arrogant idleness upon the naked back of patient 'toil'." They want a memorial of the Southern white's good times gone. To the Southern bourbons these memories are like the photo of a choice and fond friend who has passed away. Though we cannot bring back the friend, we may often look upon and kiss the picture.

Now we don't want any "mammy" statues anywhere. We want the children of this generation to abhor and forget those days when the white madam had leisure and the black mammy had labor—when the white lady loitered and the black mistress toiled. We want to orient ourselves—turn our faces from the dark and discouraging past, and direct it toward a bright and hopeful future.

In fact, people erect monuments for things of which they are fond, and in order to perpetuate the ideas for the future. And that is just what these Daughters of the Confederacy are doing. The "black mammies" made it *soft* for them and they made it *hard* for the "black mammies." They are justified in wanting the "black mammies" to return, but we Negroes are justified in fighting to say that these "black mammies" will be like Poe's Raven—*"nevermore."* What one person desires to memorialize, another person may want to forget. For instance: you will not find in Alabama, Florida or Georgia, the statues of Grant or Lincoln; nor will you find in Boston the statues of Jeff Davis, Stonewall Jackson or Robert E. Lee. It would be quite impossible to find in Paris a statue of Hindenburg or Ludendorff, nor would you find in Berlin a monument erected to Foch or Sir Douglas Haig. Why? Because in these respective cases the persons referred to had used their power to injure their opponents.

The writer favors having some statues and monuments erected in this country. We favor one erected to the 200,000 Negro soldiers who fought to wipe out slavery and to unfurl the flag of freedom and let it float like a cloud over this land. We favor a statue to these men who helped to save the Union, who indeed were a great factor in crushing out the iniquitous viper—slavery—which vitiated the entire American atmosphere with its venomous and poisonous breath. We favor a monument to the runaway slaves who had the courage to dash for freedom.

We favor erecting a monument to the New Negro, who is carving a new monument in the hearts of our people. We favor the erection of a monument to the Negroes of Washington, Chicago, Longview, Texas, Knoxville, Tenn., Tulsa, Okla., and Philadelphia, who rose in their might and said to the authorities: *If you cannot protect us, we will protect ourselves—if you cannot uphold the law, we will maintain constituted authority."* We favor erecting a monument to the Negro artists and poets, the Negro inventors and discoverers, the Negro scholars and thinkers, who have gone without food, clothing and shelter, in order to lay upon the altar of progress the Negro's meed of achievement. We favor a monument to the Negro women who have risen above insult, assault, debauchery, prostitution and abuse, *to which these unfortunate "black mammies" were subjected.* Yes, we favor erecting a monument to these women, who have almost wiped out this chasm of caste, who have broken the cordon of chains and are now trying to throw them off.

Let this "mammy" statue go. Let it fade away. Let it be buried in that blissful oblivion to which the brave sons of this nation have consigned it; and when it rises again, let its white shaft point like a lofty mountain peak to *a New Negro mother*, no longer a *"white man's woman,"* no longer the sex-enslaved *"black mammy"* of Dixie—but the apotheosis of triumphant Negro womanhood!

ERNESTINE ROSE

Ernestine Rose (1880–1961) was a career librarian whose positions included working for the American Library Association as the director of hospital libraries and serving as head librarian at the 135th Street branch in Harlem. As head librarian, Rose, a white woman, was responsible for racially integrating the staff and hiring African American library assistants, one of whom was Nella Larsen. Rose was also instrumental in acquiring the Arthur Schomburg collection, which later became the Schomburg Center for Research in Black Culture.

From Books and the Color Line[†]

It might reward the interested observer, standing on the corner of 135 Street and Lenox Avenue in New York, to watch the varieties of black folk who stream into the library building which serves the book needs of that colored section of the city—black and yellow, stately Hindoo, proud West Indian, mulatto American, little black pickaninny, turbanned mammy, porter, college professor, nursemaid, student.

† From *The Survey* 48 (April 15, 1922): 75–76.

Then let this observer step inside and ask the librarian who these people are. As he listens every profession and trade and a bewildering variety of occupations pass before his eyes. Incongruities strike his eye. Here is a medical student who takes a waiter's tips in the Pennsylvania Station, a bookseller who supports a precarious business on a Pullman porter's fees, an artist who all night runs an elevator up and down, an art connoisseur of national reputation who passes bills in a bank. The application desk of a public library serves as a doorway into the "other half" of many lives, the half which lives while not working for a living, the half which thinks, aspires and endures.

* * *

Perhaps it is time to draw some conclusions before one is overwhelmed and confused by details and conflicting issues. A librarian who tries to supply the inner needs of a suffering minority race may not permit herself to become so overwhelmed. She needs always to raise herself above the conflicting details of her work and, looking down upon it, observe its main currents and form certain conclusions as to its direction and purpose. Let me define two such conclusions. One of them is the inevitable democratizing tendency of good books. "What do these people read?" one hears. And with the book truck in mind one answers, "Dante, Longfellow, Spencer, Darwin, H. G. Wells." Minds which feed on the same food must develop into a similarity of growth, and some time meet on the same level. Those who serve these minds in their development bear testimony that this is true. The workers in this library—white and black—are serving the same need, doing the same work, and in it they are learning to sink all differences, not to overlook them, but to judge them at their true value, and to appreciate diverse gifts. Nor is this happy condition a result merely of working together, but of working and living together with books, which are the most democratizing things in the world, because they develop rational thought in black and white, African and Anglo-Saxon alike.

* * *

The librarian who wishes to form a common ground on the basis of thought and educated intellect for all these conflicting impulses and ambitions finds a twofold task. On the one hand, race pride and race knowledge must be stimulated and guided. To this end, clubs for the study of race history are established. Books on Africa and the Negro are provided as extensively as possible. Negro folk-lore and stories are told the children. Interest in Negro art and music is stimulated. An annual Negro arts exhibit is held, and a forum is conducted for the discussion of race matters.

But the library aims not only to be an intellectual center for Negroes; its further purpose is to fulfil its function as an American democratic institution and to furnish a common ground where diverse paths may meet and clashing interests find union. To this end colored and white workers stand side by side against segregation in work and thought.

*   *   *

ERNESTINE ROSE

From A Librarian in Harlem[†]

To all eyes except God's we must appear as fixed in our stubborn racial attitude of yesterday as seem the stars in their places. And yet it is well to remember that all social as all natural changes, though they seem cataclysmic, are only the result of long periods of apparent inertia during which the forces of man or of nature have been slowly and imperceptibly gathering themselves together. We are now in such a cataclysm of readjusting nationalities. Any day may see a similar catastrophe, with races as the readjusting units.

*   *   *

Another short step towards racial readjustment in the library was made when the 135th Street Branch and the Woodstock Branch in The Bronx Borough made an exchange in assistants, a Negro worker going to this large library in a thickly populated white neighborhood and one of the white workers coming in exchange to the branch library which serves New York's greatest colored population.

Then the 135th Street Library itself is the most active experiment station for racial readjustment. Two southern girls have been on the staff during the winter, one as a permanent assistant, one for practice work during her student course at Pratt Institute. The first, characterized by a certain thoughtful radicalism, has gained a background and foundation for her opinions. The latter is learning that educated and refined colored girls are of the same stuff as white, and that they may live and work together.

But it is in its effect upon the Northern white girl that the library is performing its most valuable experiments. The average white person in the North does not know the Negro at all. His ideas are preconceived, and colored by sentimentality. He sees colored people

† From *Opportunity* (July 1923): 206–207, 220. This material originally appeared in a paper read before the American Library Association Conference in Hot Springs, Arkansas, 1923.

still as ex-slaves, pitiful objects grateful for his helping hand. When he learns that they are intelligent, struggling, resentful and aggressive participants in the industrial and social battle of life, his sensibilities are shocked and his illusions destroyed.

In our little epitome of life at 135th Street the give-and-take of common effort and work annihilates such sentimental illusions, and breeds instead a real understanding and a proper and genuine relationship. In this direction the last year has taken us a long step forward.

* * *

GEORGE S. SCHUYLER

Controversial journalist, satirist, editor, and novelist George Samuel Schuyler (1895–1977) worked in a number of different genres, from essay to science fiction, but became most famous as a novelist. His biracial marriage to white Texas heiress Josephine Cogdell became famous as a racial "experiment" (their term). *Black No More*, Schuyler's most well-known novel, lampooned racial attitudes on both sides of the color line. He took over the *Illustrated Feature Section*, an insert for the black national press, for five months in 1928. His "Instructions for Contributors" were reprinted in 1929 by black writer Eugene Gordon.

From Instructions for Contributors[†]

The *Illustrated Feature Section* of the Negro press, formerly edited by George S. Schuyler, once managing editor of the *Messenger* and still a frequent contributor to such reviews as the *American Mercury* and the *American Parade*, has sent out the following "Instructions for Contributors":

Every manuscript submitted must be written in each-sentence-a-paragraph style.

Stories must be full of human interest. Short, simple words. No attempt to parade erudition to the bewilderment of the reader. No colloquialisms such as "nigger," "darkey," "coon," etc. Plenty of dialogue, and language that is realistic.

We will not accept any stories that are depressing, saddening, or gloomy. Our people have enough troubles without

† From *Saturday Evening Quill* 2 (April 1929): 20. Reprinted by permission of the Estate of George S. Schuyler.

reading about any. We want them to be interested, cheered, and buoyed up; comforted, gladdened, and made to laugh.

Nothing that casts the least reflection on contemporary moral or sex standards will be allowed. Keep away from the erotic! Contributions must be clean and wholesome.

Everything must be written in that intimate manner that wins the reader's confidence at once and makes him or her feel that what is written is being spoken exclusively to that particular reader.

No attempt should be made to be obviously artistic. Be artistic, of course, but "put it over" on the reader so he or she will be unaware of it.

Stories must be swiftly moving, gripping the interest and sweeping on to a climax. The heroine should always be beautiful and desirable, sincere and virtuous. The hero should be of the he-man type, but not stiff, stereotyped, or vulgar. The villain should obviously be a villain and of the deepest-dyed variety: crafty, unscrupulous, suave, and resourceful. Above all, however, these characters must live and breathe, and be just ordinary folks such as the reader has met. The heroine should be of the brown-skin type.

All matter should deal exclusively with Negro life. Nothing will be permitted that is likely to engender ill feeling between blacks and whites. The color problem is bad enough without adding any fuel to the fire.

✳   ✳   ✳

CRITICISM

LAURA DOYLE

From Queering Freedom's Theft in Nella Larsen[†]

* * *

QUEER RUIN

The chapter that precedes and, arguably, most urgently propels Helga's flight to Copenhagen ends on a very queer note. The moment is embedded, furthermore, in the most racially troubled scene in the novel, set in the Harlem cabaret that Helga "half unwillingly" goes to with Anne and her friends (58) [52]. In her rendering of this scene, Larsen creates the kind of "break" in consciousness that Ralph Ellison's narrator in *Invisible Man* describes in discussing the effects of jazz on the "invisible" black listener,[1] although Larsen allows us a fuller glimpse than he does of the queer predicaments submerged within it. "Invisibility," Ellison's narrator explains, "gives one a slightly different sense of time, you're never quite on the beat. . . . Instead of the swift and imperceptible flowing of time, you are aware of its nodes, those points where time stands still or from which it leaps ahead. And you slip into the breaks and look around."[2]

* * *

[A] constellation of queerness, ruin, and biracial heritage in Ellison's novel retrospectively offers a guide to the cabaret scene in *Quicksand*, where in the midst of a jazz tune, Helga falls into a similar "break." And again here it seems that Larsen negotiates with not only her protagonist's but also her own ambivalent feelings about race in relation to a "ruined," that is, racially mixed and queer, sexuality. In *Quicksand*, the cabaret scene is cast in a provocatively racialized language. Helga "half unwillingly" accompanies Anne and friends to the cabaret, feeling "singularly apart from it all" as they enter the "gay, grotesque" streets of Harlem (58) [52]. Although Helga marvels at, and Larsen takes great care to enumerate, the variety of people around her—"sooty black, shiny black, taupe, mahogany, bronze, copper, gold, orange, yellow, peach, ivory, pinky white, pastry

---

† From *Freedom's Empire: Race and the Rise of the Novel in Atlantic Modernity, 1640–1940* (Durham: Duke UP, 2008), pp. 400–05. Copyright, 2008, Duke University Press. All rights reserved. Republished by permission of the copyright holder. Doyle's notes have been renumbered and edited. Page numbers to this Norton Critical Edition appear in square brackets.
1. See Fred Moten, *In the Break: The Aesthetics of the Black Radical Tradition* (Minneapolis, U of Minnesota P, 2003), for a powerful set of meditations on this aesthetic and ontology of "the break."
2. Ralph Ellison, *Invisible Man* (New York: Vintage Books, 1995), 8.

white . . . yellow hair, black hair, brown hair; straight hair, straightened hair, curly hair, crinkly hair, wooly hair . . . black eyes in white faces, brown eyes in yellow faces, gray eyes in brown faces, blue eyes in tan faces"—the language of savagery also pervades the descriptions. The group is led to their table by "a black giant," served by a waiter "indefinitely carved out of ebony," while people dance "ecstatically to the thumping of unseen tomtoms" and the "savage strains of music" so that Helga later feels on leaving the dance floor that she had "been in the jungle" (59) [52–53].

All of this is cast as Helga's perception, as that of a woman alienated from her race. And yet as the scene develops, its syntax also suggests the presence of an alienated *author*, a writer who was not only like Ellison in being displaced *by* race but was also unlike him in being displaced *within* race.[3] We can glimpse this attitude as Helga fleetingly loses herself in the jazz band's "jungle" music when she joins her friends on the dance floor. In the midst of Helga's dancing—precisely when Helga is least critical and most lost to the joy of it all—the narrator steps away from her, as if she, too, must take care to stand outside this race-immersion. "For a while, Helga was oblivious of the reek of flesh, smoke, and alcohol, oblivious of the oblivion of other gyrating pairs, oblivious of the color, the noise, and the grand distorted childishness of it all" (59) [53]. In noting the reeking smells and the "childishness" that Helga is temporarily overlooking, the narrator provocatively beckons her readers to join her in this condescension. Vacillating, however, like her character-in-flight, the narrator then seems momentarily to merge with Helga's joyful participation, for the prose moves with the rhythms of the music: Helga was "drugged, lifted, sustained, by the extraordinary music, blown out, ripped out, beaten out, by the joyous, wild, murky orchestra" (59) [53]. This may be the only moment in the narrative when Helga *and* her narrator shed their vexed sense of double-consciousness. In this here and now, the narrator tells us, "life seemed bodily motion" (59) [53], and Larsen's prose is all verbs.

3. Linda Dittmar, "When Privilege Is No Protection:" "The Woman Artist in *Quicksand* and *House of Mirth*," in *Writing the Woman Artist: Essays on Poetics, Politics, and Portraiture*, ed. Suzanne W. Jones. Philadelphia: U of Pennsylvania P, 1991; pp. 133–54, likewise notes that Larsen expressed ambivalence about blackness in this scene, wishing both "to affirm and castigate" it (147). But most discussions of this scene attribute ambivalence to Helga, not to Larsen: see Mary Esteve, "Nella Larson's [*sic*] Moving Mosaic: Harlem, Crowds, and Anonymity," *American Literary History* 9.2 (Summer 1997): 278; Kimberly Monda, "Self-Delusion and Self-Sacrifice in Nella Larsen's *Quicksand*," *African American Review* 31.1 (Spring 1997): 27–28; Chip Rhodes, "Writing Up the New Negro: The Construction of Consumer Desire in the Twenties," *Journal of American Studies* 28.2 (August 1994): 192; Deborah B. Silverman, "Nella Larsen's *Quicksand*: Untangling the Web of Exoticism," *African American Review* 27.4 (Winter 1993): 610; Cheryl Wall, *Women of the Harlem Renaissance* (Bloomington: Indiana UP, 1995), 100.

This "motion" appears on the one hand as the "essence" of a race; but this raciality—as its many-colored surround and its "*orchestra*" playing "*jungle*" rhythms suggest—is on the other hand a manifestation of modernity's racial crisscrossings, also expressed in Helga's nomadic life and pale-brown skin. Motion is the essence of life for Helga (and perhaps for jazz) not because she belongs to a race but because she doesn't, quite. Her continual return to race, like the plot's, like William Faulkner's or Gertrude Stein's wandering narration, reveals that there is no there, there; yet all the while the fiction of race feeds the motion of modernity (including Stein's racist portraits).[4] Helga leaves the dance floor, dogged by "a shameful certainty that not only had she been in the jungle, but that she had enjoyed it" and so "[s]he hardened in her determination to get away. She wasn't, she told herself, a jungle creature" (59) [53]. Thus does this scene begin to move Helga closer to her transatlantic passage.

But this impulse to flee is precipitated most urgently by what follows. When the music begins again and someone asks her to dance, "she declined" and "sat looking curiously about her" as "the crowd became a swirling mass" dancing to the "syncopated jangle" (59) [53]. In the midst of this break, in which Helga is not "quite on the beat," as Ellison would put it, she "discover[s] Dr. Anderson sitting at a table on the far side of the room, with a girl in a shivering apricot frock" (60) [53]. This girl, Audrey Denney, rivets Helga's attention. After silently nodding to Anderson, Helga begins to turn her eyes away, "[b]ut they went back immediately to the girl beside him, who sat indifferently sipping a colourless liquid, or puffing a precariously hanging cigarette. Across dozens of tables, littered with corks, with ashes, with shriveled sandwiches, through slits in the swaying mob, Helga Crane studied her" (60) [53].

Across a series of obstacles suggestive of sexuality and its "shriveled" aftermath, Helga peers through a slit to fix her attention on Audrey Denney. Through Helga's eyes, the text caressingly details Denney's appearance, lingering over her "softly curving" yet "sorrowful" mouth, her pitch-black eyes "a little aslant . . . veiled by long,

---

4. For discussions of Gertrude Stein's racism, especially in *Three Lives*, see Sonia Saldivar-Hull, "Wrestling Your Ally: Stein, Racism, and Critical Practice," in *Women's Writing in Exile*, ed. Mary Lynn Broe and Angela Ingram (Chapel Hill: U of North Carolina P, 1989.), 181–98; Milton Cohen, "Black Brutes and Mulatto Saints: The Racial Hierarchy of Stein's 'Melanctha," *Black American Literature Forum* 18.3 (Fall 1984): 119–21; Deborah B. Silverman, "Nella Larsen's *Quicksand*: Untangling the Web of Exoticism," *African American Review* 27.4 (Winter 1993): 599–614"; Carla L. Peterson, "The Remaking of Americans: Gertrude Stein's 'Melanctha' and African American Musical Traditions," in *Criticism and the Color Line*, ed. Henry B. Wonham (New Brunswick, N.J.: Rutgers UP, 1996), 140–57; and Laura Doyle, "The Flat, the Round, and Gertrude Stein: Race and the Shape of Modernist History," *Modernism/Modernity* 7.2 (April 2000): 249–72.

drooping lashes," her "pale" and "peculiar, almost deathlike pallor,"
her "dark hair brushed severely back," and finally the "extreme décolleté of her simple apricot dress show[ing] a skin of unusual color, a
delicate, creamy hue, with golden tones": "'Almost like an alabaster,' thought Helga" (60) [53–54].

Like Helga, Denney herself displays the light-skinned body that
signifies both desire and ruin. Audrey's appearance openly queers
sexual and racial norms, with slanted black eyes and her peculiar,
creamy skin as well as her mannishly brushed-back hair above an
alluring décolleté, a mixture of styles that extends into her choice
of company, here the gray-eyed African American Anderson, and
elsewhere, white people. Helga's dreamy enrapture by this body is
sharply interrupted when, in the next sentence, the music stops and
Helga's friend Anne arrives at the table "with rage in her eyes" (60)
[54]. A long, heated conversation between Anne and Helga follows,
in which Anne recoils from Helga's observation that "[s]he's lovely"
and condemns Audrey Denney as a "disgusting creature" who "ought
to be ostracized" because she "goes about with white people" and
throws racially mixed parties in which "white men dance with the
coloured women"—all of which Anne reports in a voice "trembling
with cold hatred" (61) [54–55]. Helga challenges Anne's racial polic-
ing of sexuality in a series of questions, speaking "with a slowness
almost approaching to insolence," until finally she goes quiet, feeling
"it would be useless to tell them that what she felt for the beautiful,
calm, cool girl who had the assurance, the courage so placidly to
ignore racial barriers and give her attention to people, was not contempt, but envious admiration. So she remained silent, watching the
girl" (62) [55]. It's worth noting here that Helga's attraction to Audrey
parallels Irene's attraction to Clare in *Passing*, both in its sensual
magnetism and in its admiration (more grudging in Irene's case) of
her boldness in racial transgression. The chapter closes with a long
paragraph devoted to Helga's observation of Audrey as she dances
with Anderson "with grace and abandon, gravely, yet with obvious
pleasure, her legs, her hips, her back, all swaying gently, swung by
that wild music from the heart of the jungle" (62) [55]. The pleasure
is obviously Helga's as well.

That is, Audrey Denney is clearly a charged object for Helga Crane
(not to mention Anne or Larsen), a point of cathexis for Helga's
"jungle" ambivalence as well as her bodily desire. Audrey's pairing
with Anderson is also charged insofar as, for Helga, Anderson is
directly associated with those "hidden wounds" of her own biracial
past. In fact in the second half of this closing paragraph, Helga's emotion begins to encompass both Denney and Anderson in way that con-
flates them as objects of her desire. The narrator tells us that she

began to feel "a more primitive emotion" as she watched them dance. Neither the exact emotion nor the exact object of it is specified in the description that follows, but the pressing, syncopated syntax builds a moment of racial and sexual panic:[5]

> She forgot the garish crowded room. She forgot her friends. She saw only two figures, closely clinging. She felt her heart throbbing. She felt the room receding. She went out the door. She climbed endless stairs. At last, panting, confused, but thankful to have escaped, she found herself again out in the dark night alone, a small crumpled thing in a fragile, flying black and gold dress. A taxi drifted toward her, stopped. She stepped into it, feeling cold, unhappy, misunderstood, and forlorn. (62) [55].

Thus this chapter ends, and the next one opens with Helga on an ocean liner headed across the Atlantic, "glad to be alone at last, free of that superfluity of human beings, yellow, brown, and black" (63) [56]. In escaping these bodies, however, Helga is perhaps also escaping her heart's desire, which takes the "lovely" form of the racially and sexually "superfluous" Audrey Denney.

And indeed Helga is drawn back exactly to this superfluity of queer beings who exceed the proper boundaries. Feeling trapped by race again in Copenhagen, she recrosses the Atlantic and immediately attends a polyracial party where she again meets Dr. Anderson, who still carries the shadow-presence of Audrey Denney. In fact Denney is at the party too, and she again momentarily stands, for Helga, at the center of it. As Helga looks around, she sees African Americans, West Indians, a few white people, and "[t]here too, poised, serene, certain, surrounded by masculine black and white, was Audrey Denney" (99) [84]. On this occasion, Helga directly asks to be introduced to this woman so oddly "surrounded by masculine black and white."

But this is the event that never occurs, neither in the chapter nor in the book—not until, in displaced form, it perhaps surfaces in Larsen's next novella, *Passing*, in Irene's "Encounter" and "Re-Encounter" (as the book's first two parts title them) with Clare Kendry. In *Quicksand*, Helga's movement toward Denney is interrupted by two men: first, her old fiancé from Naxos, James Vayle (who, like Anne, condemns the racial mixing at the party), and then, finally, in the last paragraph of the chapter, when some of us might be wondering when Helga will meet Audrey Denney, by Anderson, in a physical collision that leads to Helga's final "ruin," as she calls

5. See Patricia Juliana Smith, *Lesbian Panic: Homoeroticism in Modern British Women's Fiction* (New York: Columbia UP, 1997), for analysis of recurring scenes of sexual panic in twentieth-century British fiction.

it (108) [91]. It is at the Harlem party that this undoing begins, when
Helga steps through a doorway, and

> somehow, she never quite knew exactly just how, into the arms
> of Robert Anderson. She drew back and looked up smiling to
> offer an apology.
>   And then it happened. He stooped and kissed her, a long kiss,
> holding her close. She fought against him with all her might.
> Then, strangely, all power seemed to ebb away, and a long-
> hidden, half-understood desire welled up in her with the sud-
> denness of a dream. Helga Crane's own arms went up about the
> man's neck. (104) [88]

Just when Helga begins to face the fact that her "freeing" transatlantic travel is always in some way a return to race; just as she
comes to "[t]his knowledge, this certainty of the division in her life
into two parts in two lands" (96) [82]; just after she has expressed to
James Vayle her lack of interest in marriage and children; and just
at the moment when she might approach a "lovely" woman she
admires—Robert Anderson kisses her.

She draws away from his forceful embrace as "[s]udden anger
seized her" and she "pushe[s] him indignantly aside" to return to the
party, but meanwhile she has discovered a well of desire within herself. The wording of the text suggests that she discovers desire as a
phenomenon of her own being rather than a desire *for* Anderson in
particular. In an echo of the depersonalized description in which
"Helga Crane's own arms went up about the man's neck," on the following day she finds herself thinking "not so much of the man
whose arms had held her as of the ecstasy which had flooded her"
during the long kiss, which is the first of that kind she has experienced (104–5) [88]. (She explains that she "was used to kisses" during her "mild engagement with James Vayle" but "none had been
like that of last night" [105] [88]).

In modernism, such kisses mark the turning point—the deflated,
debatable, ambiguous, early-twentieth-century version of the swoon—
in the protagonist's voyage out. As Richard Dalloway kisses Rachel
Vinrace in *The Voyage Out*, as Rochester kisses Bertha in *Wide
Sargasso Sea*, as Adele *says* Aziz kisses her in *Passage to India*, Anderson's kiss reignites an old tainted history, the Gothic racial and sexual
core of the liberty plot. At this crisis, one can fairly hear the ghosts
rattling their chains or see what Rachel Vinrace dreams as the mocking goblins munching in their wet, dark corners, and what Helga
calls the "skeletons that stalked lively and in full health through the
consciousness of every person of Negro ancestry in America" (96)
[82]. These kisses seem to initiate the heroine's discovery of her own

desire—but in the end they turn that premonition of "ecstasy" into an experience of violation or ruin. Certainly Anderson's kiss reopens the "wound" of Helga's childhood, that sensation, as she describes it, of being "an obscene sore" in other people's lives, which she repeatedly says Anderson recalls for her (29) [30]. When he arranges a clandestine meeting with her after this evening of the kiss, despite her hopes for an illicit affair with him (he is now married to Anne), he simply apologizes for his drunken "mistake." Overcome by "this mortification, this feeling of ridicule and self-loathing," she concludes that she "had ruined everything" (108–9) [91].

If this kiss interrupts and displaces the pending encounter with Audrey Denney—the queer figure who has aroused Helga's sensual gaze—then the rest of the novel emerges as a reaction not just to the transgressive encounter with Anderson but also as a reaction to the way Anderson comes between Helga Crane and Audrey Denney. Her kiss-gone-astray and the desire it reveals repeat the crime of her mother's out-of-bounds kiss, but, by way of Audrey Denney, Larsen now subtextually hints that the boundaries at issue are as much those of heteronormativity as they are those of race.

* * *

ANN duCILLE

From Blues Notes on Black Sexuality: Sex and the Texts of Jessie Fauset and Nella Larsen†

* * *

The Bourgeois Blues of Jessie Fauset and Nella Larsen

> She came out on the stage in ostrich feathers, beaded satin, and shone that smile on us and sang.
> [Robert Hayden, "Homage to the Empress of the Blues"]

Ostrich feathers, beaded satin, yards of pearls, hats, headdresses, furs. These are among the accoutrements that black women blues singers donned in constructing their performance personas. In the novels of Jessie Fauset and Nella Larsen, such accessories not only construct the woman character herself but also help to tell her story.

---

† From *Journal of the History of Sexuality* 3.3 (1993): 429–32, 442–43. Copyright © 1993. All rights reserved. Used by permission of the publisher. Notes have been renumbered. Page numbers to this Norton Critical Edition appear in square brackets.

Silks and satins, capes and coats, dresses and lounging pajamas are
as central to the bourgeois brand of "somebody done somebody
wrong" songs that these texts sing as paints and powders were to
the classic blues performance. Tremendous attention is paid in these
novels to what women put on their bodies; the characters are acutely
aware of how their bodies look in what they put on them. It is important to understand, however, that all this dressing and draping,
primping and preening is not merely the frivolous fluff of which
novels of manners are made—the affectations and petty preoccu-
pations of bourgeois domesticity, as many critics have suggested.
Rather, clothes function semiotically as sexual and racial signifiers.
As part of the texts' signifying systems, the dressed or, in Harlem
slang, the "draped down" body is the literary equivalent of the
woman-proud blues lyric—one of the not always so subtle instruments through which both Fauset and Larsen sing and sign female
sexuality.

Helga Crane, for example, the heroine of Larsen's first novel,
Quicksand (1928), is a studied and deliberate dresser, whose relationship to her wardrobe is a recurrent theme in the text. Throughout the novel, Helga, the daughter of a white Danish mother and a
black father, struggles to define and declare her sexual self in the
face of iconographies that objectify, exoticize, "ladify," and otherwise
oppress her. Clothes (putting them on the body, rather than taking
them off) are part of the stuff of Helga's bourgeois blues. They signal both her sexuality and her tenuous relationship to the moral and
behavioral codes of the two disparate societies she stands among but
not of. As a teacher at Naxos, a southern school for upwardly mobile
Negroes, Helga is immediately established as a person apart from
the white-worshiping "great [black] community" around her. "A
slight girl of twenty-two" with "skin like yellow satin," Helga, we
learn in the early pages of the novel, is too fond of vivid green and
of gold negligees and glistening brocaded mules to be a proper Naxos
Negro. Rather, her taste in colorful clothes links her to that other
life whose bodacious blues rhythms will not be entirely repressed,
no matter how bourgeois her surroundings. A Naxos Negro's knowledge of place is confirmed by conservatism, "good taste," and mod-
eration in all things, including proper attire. Helga's distinctive dark
purples, deep reds, clinging silks, and luxurious woolens signify the
pride, vanity, and "uppity" otherness that bring her into disfavor at
Naxos. "Clothes," as Larsen writes, "had been one of [Helga's] difficulties at Naxos," with its "intolerant dislike of difference." Larsen
continues: "Helga Crane loved clothes, elaborate ones. Nevertheless
she had tried not to offend. But with small success, for, although
she had affected the deceptively simple variety, the hawk eyes of

dean and matrons had detected the subtle difference from their own irreproachably conventional garments."[1]

Perhaps even more than her yellow skin, Helga Crane's clothes mark her racial and sexual alterity. In a later scene, Helga, draped in a stunning red dress, wanders dazed into a storefront church in Harlem. When her bare arms and neck and her clinging red dress are revealed under her coat, the erotic spectacle causes the man next to her to shudder and a sanctified sister to label her a scarlet woman. Helga need not sing the blues to be claimed as a red-hot mama; even just a glimpse of her bare flesh and red dress are enough to earn her the label of Jezebel.

At the end of the novel, taste in clothes again becomes the great *un*equalizer that distinguishes the now married and perpetually pregnant Helga from the folk—the tiny, rural Alabama community around which she has wrapped her life and to which she is trying desperately to belong. Fatally (as opposed to fatefully) married to a grandiloquent Baptist preacher, Mrs. Reverend Pleasant Green immediately makes herself unpopular with the women of her husband's "primitive flock" by trying to "help them with their clothes," tactfully pointing out that aprons and sunbonnets are not proper Sunday church attire.[2]

The final pages of the novel not only return Helga Crane Green to the South (as a site of psychic and physical violence), but they also place her in the ill-fitting and doubly ironic role of *matron,* helpmate, race woman. Like the dean and matrons at Naxos who judged her wardrobe harshly, Helga sets herself up as the standard-bearer of proper dress, "gentler deportment," and home beautification. In other words, here in the backwoods of Alabama, it is Helga who comes to represent the convention, prescription, and smug self-satisfaction she so despised in her Naxos colleagues. Her sense of style and propriety make her even more a misfit among her husband's poor parishioners than her fondness for the unconventional had made her at Naxos. To the women she tries to instruct, she is an "uppity, meddlin' No'the'nah." Even as she is devoured and diminished by too many children too quickly come, even as the body she once thought of only as "something on which to hang lovely fabrics" becomes constantly swollen with child and racked with pain, the women around her pity not Helga but her husband.

We hear no more talk of satin gowns and brocaded mules. But as the story closes, like a lid on a casket, I cannot help wondering if

1. Larsen, *"Quicksand" and "Passing,"* p. 18 [21].
2. Ibid., pp. 118–19 [98–99].

the next garment that will drape the perhaps terminally pregnant Helga is a shroud. Yet, it is not childbirth or motherhood, or even patriarchy, that overcomes Helga, as much as it is the irreconcilable social, psychosexual, and racial contradictions that become her quicksand. Helga is unable to fashion an individual identity against the competing ideological and iconographical forces that ultimately render her invisible. Unlike her blues-singing contemporaries, she does not have the luxury of donning a woman-proud persona and acting out the days of her life as a performer on a stage. Yet, Helga too has sung the blues. It is just that no one has listened.

*   *   *

In my reading of the 1920s and 1930s, it is only through a disturbing twist of literary fate and intellectual history that Fauset and Larsen have been criticized for not measuring up to the sexual and textual liberation of their blues-singing sisters. At another time, in another context, these two women authors might have been praised for their roles in advancing literary discourse toward a moment where black female desire could be boldly sung on the printed page as well as on the nightclub stage. Perpetually measured against Bessie Smith, on the one hand, and Zora Neale Hurston, on the other, however, Fauset and Larsen have rarely been read in terms of their particular contributions to modernism, to American and African American literature, and to the development of the woman's novel.

Far from silent on the topic of sexuality, these artists are more rightly claimed, I believe, as the first black women novelists to depict openly sensual black female subjects, the first black writers to explore the dialectics of female desire and to address what having children can mean to a woman's physical and mental health, as well as to her independence. They were the first black women artists to depict successful, independent, single black professional and working-class women—not all of whom ultimately surrender their careers to male-dominated, bourgeois marriages, as many critics have claimed. Their heroines are by no means passionless decorations, adorning the pristine pages of immaculately conceived "lace-curtain romances." They are, on the contrary, implicitly sexual beings, finely tuned to both the power and the vulnerability of their own female bodies. At a moment when black female sexuality was either completely unwritten to avoid endorsing sexual stereotypes or sensationally overwritten to both defy and exploit those stereotypes, Fauset and Larsen edged the discourse into another realm: a realm precariously balanced on the cusp of the respectable and the risqué; a realm that is at times *neutral*, perhaps, but never *neuter*; a realm in which they, too, participated in reclaiming the black body and in defining African American expressive culture.

* * *

LORI HARRISON-KAHAN

From "Structure Would *Equal* Meaning": Blues and Jazz Aesthetics in the Fiction of Nella Larsen†

* * *

Since their rediscovery in the 1970s, *Quicksand* and *Passing* have generated a large body of literary criticism and become staples on syllabi in a range of college courses. Spurred on by Deborah McDowell's argument about Larsen's sexual subtexts printed in the 1986 foreword to the Rutgers University Press edition of the two novels, most critics have focused on the intersections of race, class, gender, and sexuality.[1] In a recent reading of Larsen that shifts the tides slightly, Cherene Sherrard-Johnson examines the relationship between Larsen's prose and visual culture to "argue . . . for a painterly rather than writerly reading of Larsen's work."[2] Expanding on this understanding of how Larsen's fiction participates in the

---

† From *Tulsa Studies in Women's Literature* 28.2 (Fall 2009): 269–70, 277–81, 286–89. Reprinted by permission of Tulsa Studies in Women's Literature. Notes have been renumbered and edited. Page numbers in square brackets refer to this Norton Critical Edition.

1. While I agree with Deborah McDowell's identification of sexual and homoerotic subtexts in Larsen's writing, my purpose here is to redirect attention to her use of vernacular culture. It is worth noting, however, that the erotics of Larsen's prose are relevant to her blues form. Readings of the lesbian subtext in *Passing*, for example, are enhanced by placing the work in the context of the blues since many female blues singers had intimate relationships with other women and sang of their same-sex preference; one of the best examples of this is Ma Rainey's "Prove It On Me Blues," which clearly states: "Went out last night with a crowd of my friends / They must've been women, 'cause I don't like no men." In addition to McDowell, "Introduction to *Quicksand and Passing* by Nella Larsen" (New Jersey: Rutgers UP, 1986), see Judith Butler, "Passing, Queering: Nella Larsen's Psychoanalytic Challenge," in *Bodies That Matter* (New York: Routledge, 1993); David L. Blackmore, "'That Unreasonable Restless Feeling': The Homosexual Subtexts of Nella Larsen's *Passing*," *African American Review*, 26.3 (1992): 475–84; Corinne E. Blackmer, "The Veils of the Law: Race and Sexuality in Nella Larsen's *Passing*," in *Race-ing Representation*, ed. Kosta Myrsiades and Linda Myrsiades (New York: Rowman and Littlefield, 1998), pp. 98–116; Helena Michie, *Sororophobia: Differences Among Women in Literature and Culture* (New York: Oxford UP, 1992), pp. 147–54; Catherine Rottenberg, "*Passing*: Race, Identification, Desire," *Criticism: A Quarterly for Literature and the Arts*, 45.4 (2003): 435–52; and my own essay, "Her 'Nig': Returning the Gaze of Nella Larsen's *Passing*," *Modern Language Studies*, 32.2 (2002): 107–36. Jennifer DeVere Brody offers a reading of the novel that prioritizes the intersections of race and class above sexuality. See Brody, "Clare Kendry's 'True' Colors: Race and Class Conflict in Nella Larsen's *Passing*," *Callaloo*, 15.4 (1992): 1053–65.

2. Cherene Sherrard-Johnson, "A Plea for Color," *American Literature*, 76.4 (December 2004): 836.

modernist project of transgressing boundaries between different media, I propose an oral reading of her work, the kind usually reserved for Hurston, originator of the "speakerly" text.[3] Larsen's novels are not "speakerly"; in fact, they share a tendency with high modernism to probe characters' interior consciousnesses—the realm of the unsaid—through free indirect discourse. Yet her novels also employ the expressive forms of a black oral tradition in order to convey the machinations of her characters' minds and thus achieve a voice that is at once singular and plural, private and public.

If critics have overlooked the musical aesthetic of her writing, Larsen has nevertheless been at the forefront of debates surrounding the relationship between black women's writing and music. In her study of the empowered agency of black female blues singers, Hazel Carby uses Larsen as her counterpoint, criticizing the tendency among black feminist theorists to privilege "literate forms of black women's intellectual activity"[4] above popular forms. She argues that, in contrast to Larsen's novels, which reproduce "the denial of desire and the repression of sexuality" (p. 472), black female singers, working in the genre of the classic blues, compose "an alternative form of representation, an oral and musical women's culture that explicitly addresses the contradictions of feminism, sexuality, and power" (p. 472). Responding to Carby, Ann duCille finds that Larsen's writing *is* an important alternative form of representation since the privileging of the folk elides the diversity of the African American experience and treats rural black expression as the only authentic mode. DuCille proposes that Larsen's "bourgeois blues,"[5] as she calls them, challenge Houston Baker's "vernacular theory"[6] of African American literature; according to duCille, the critical investment in oral folk culture—a culture that, in Baker's theory, is dominated by the ideology of the blues—leads to the dismissal and condemnation of black female novelists who take middle-class black women's lives as their subjects (p. 68). What Carby and duCille share is a tendency to read Larsen's writing *against* the female blues singers: either the blues singers present a liberatory alternative to the sexually repressed representations of educated middle-class writers such as Larsen, or Larsen presents a valid

---

3. See Henry Louis Gates Jr., *The Signifying Monkey: A Theory of African-American Literary Criticism* (New York: Oxford UP, 1988), pp. 170–216.
4. Hazel Carby, "It Jus Be's Dat Way Sometime: The Sexual Politics of Women's Blues," in *The Jazz Cadence in American Culture*, ed. Robert G. O'Meally (New York: Columbia UP, 1998), p. 472. Subsequent page references will be cited parenthetically in the text.
5. See Ann duCille, *The Coupling Convention: Sex, Text and Tradition in Black Women's Fiction* (New York: Oxford UP, 1993). Subsequent page references will be cited parenthetically in the text.
6. See Houston Baker, *Blues, Ideology, and Afro-American Literature: A Vernacular Theory* (Chicago: U of Chicago P, 1984).

literary option outside of the romanticized folk roots that obscure intellectual urbanism.

* * * [T]here is much more common ground between Larsen and her musical contemporaries than has been previously thought. * * * [T]he narrative of *Quicksand* responds to the calls of the blues singers while employing jazz as an overall structuring voice. Larsen adapts vernacular culture to her writing, and thus acknowledges its influence upon her. But she also engages in give-and-take with other black cultural producers in a manner that carves out intermediary spaces between literacy and orality. With both texts, then, Larsen contributes to another, related discourse: the debate about the criteria for African American art that took place during the Harlem Renaissance. In an essay closely identified with this debate, "The Negro Artist and the Racial Mountain" (1926), Langston Hughes advocates for a black aesthetic that would find its inspiration in the vernacular and in black music in particular. Taking aim at fellow African American poets such as Claude McKay and Countee Cullen, who relied on traditional poetic forms, Hughes decries "this urge within the race towards whiteness . . . to be as little Negro and as much American as possible,"[7] and famously imagines it as "the mountain standing in the way of any true Negro art in America" (p. 91).[8] Describing instead his own reliance on "the meanings and rhythms" of blues and jazz music, Hughes writes, "jazz to me is one of the inherent expressions of Negro life in America; the eternal tom-tom beating in the Negro soul—the tom-tom of revolt against weariness in a white world, a world of subway trains, and work, work, work; the tom-tom of joy and laughter, and pain swallowed in a smile" (pp. 94–95). According to Hughes, only when black artists adapt "the blare of Negro jazz bands and the bellowing voice of Bessie Smith singing the Blues" will they "stand on top of the mountain, free within" themselves (p. 95). Reflecting back on this debate, the current critical consensus insists that Larsen's work bears little relationship to vernacular culture. By illuminating the jazz and blues aesthetic of her prose, I demonstrate that, on the contrary, Larsen took to heart Hughes's prescription for an African American literature derived from black musical forms and was thus highly invested in the idea that structure could produce racial meaning.

* * *

7. Langston Hughes, "The Negro Artist and the Racial Mountain" (1926), rpt. in *The Portable Harlem Renaissance Reader*, ed. David Levering Lewis (New York: Penguin, 1994), p. 91. Subsequent page references will be cited parenthetically in the text.
8. Lyrics to songs recorded by Gertrude "Ma" Rainey and Bessie Smith that are cited in this essay can be found in Angela Davis, *Blues Legacies and Black Feminism* (New York: Vintage, 1998), pp. 199–358.

The Jazz Form of Quicksand

My old man died in a fine big house.
My ma died in a shack.
I wonder where I'm gonna die,
Being neither white nor black?
　　　　—Langston Hughes, "Cross," epigraph to *Quicksand* (p. xlii) [5]

One three centuries removed
From the scenes his father loved,
Spicy grove, cinnamon tree,
What is Africa to me?
　　　　—Countee Cullen, "Heritage," epigraph to *Passing* (p. 141)

Quicksand relies upon the innovations of jazz music to assert a black aesthetic. With her epigraphs to *Quicksand* and *Passing*, Larsen signals her own participation in the African American tradition of call and response. The four lines from Hughes's "Cross" and Cullen's "Heritage" are both formulated as questions, suggesting that Larsen conceived of her own novels as responses to these black male poets. The content of the epigraphs foregrounds her attempt to address, if not resolve, questions of mixed-race subjectivity (proposed by Hughes) and African diasporic identity (raised by Cullen) through the situations of *Passing*'s white-skinned black characters Irene Redfield and Clare Kendry, and the related plight of *Quicksand*'s semi-autobiographical protagonist Helga Crane, orphaned daughter of a black father and Danish immigrant mother. However, the aesthetic principles associated with these two poets also provide an important key to Larsen's response. The fact that one epigraph is from Hughes and the other from Cullen is of great significance here, since the two writers were often viewed in opposition to one another, and their work formed the core of debates about black aesthetics during the Harlem Renaissance. "The Negro Artist and the Racial Mountain" opens with a veiled attack on Cullen in which Hughes indicts his unnamed contemporary for his desire "to write like a white poet" and thus "to run away spiritually from his race" (p. 91). The contrast between Hughes and Cullen is evident in the poems Larsen selected as epigraphs. Cullen's epic poem "Heritage" follows a fixed poetic structure and employs formal language and syntax, while Hughes's short poem "Cross" displays his characteristic use of simplicity and everyday speech. It is worth noting here that the debate is *not* centered on subject matter—after all, Cullen, too, is addressing racial themes in "Heritage," even as he questions the relevance of racial background to the speaker's identity. Instead, the points of contention focus on aesthetic elements.

While critics such as Hutchinson have aligned Larsen politically with Hughes, few analyses of her work are attentive to the influence of the African American vernacular, and specifically to the jazz and blues aesthetic advocated in "The Negro Artist and the Racial Mountain." In fact, Hutchinson consistently links Larsen's novels with formal motifs characteristic of white literary tradition, finding dramatic structure in *Passing* (a structure notably characteristic of *Western* drama) and an arabesque pattern in *Quicksand* that he claims is derived from the classical myth of the Labyrinth. In one of the few readings devoted to musical rather than literary influences, A. Yemisi Jimoh does analyze some of the references to black music in *Quicksand* to show that Helga Crane is a blues character.[9] But Jimoh focuses largely on content rather than form. I argue here that *Quicksand*'s invocation of spirituals, blues, and jazz supplies more than "a musical background, or decorative references," in Morrison's words. Rather, Larsen's novel itself becomes "a manifestation of the music," employing strategies of repetition and variation in at least two ways: first, by signifying on blues tropes to create an antiphonal relationship with contemporary female musicians; and secondly, by adhering to jazz-like structures and rhythms that achieve effects of improvisation and syncopation both in individual passages and across the narrative's span. Larsen's writing thus employs "the meanings and rhythms" of blues and jazz to become, in Hughes's words, an "expression . . . of Negro life in America" (pp. 94–95).

* * *

The initial chapters of the novel take place in the South, where Helga becomes increasingly dissatisfied with the conservative policies of racial uplift rigidly in place at Naxos, the black school where she is employed as a teacher. In these chapters, Larsen signifies on themes central to women's rural blues: loneliness, resistance against the cage of domesticity, and migration. The first two of these themes are established from the opening line of the novel: "Helga Crane sat alone in her room, which at that hour, eight in the evening, was in soft gloom" (p. 1) [7]. Larsen's opening sentence may set a modernist scene of alienation, but the alienated self was also one of the chief topics of the blues. Moreover, the rhyme between "room" and "gloom" reinforces the aural dimension of Larsen's writing, giving it a prosodic quality typically associated with poetry or music.

9. See A. Yemisi Jimoh, *Spiritual, Blues, and Jazz People in African American Fiction* (Knoxville: U of Tennessee P, 2002).

The opening chapter of *Quicksand* continues to signify on some of the subjects favored by blue singers, such as those exemplified by Bessie Smith's "In the House Blues":

Settin' in the house with everything on my mind (Repeat)
Lookin' at the clock and can't even tell the time

Walkin' to my window, and lookin' out of my door (Repeat)
Wishin' that my man would come home once more.

Can't eat, can't sleep, so weak I can't walk my floor (Repeat)
Feel like hollerin' murder, let the police squad get me once more

They woke me before day with trouble on my mind (Repeat)
Wringing my hands and screamin', walkin' the floor hollerin' and
    cryin'

Like Smith's persona in "In the House Blues," Helga is indeed sitting in her room with "everything on [her] mind," though in this case, Larsen pointedly tells us the time. Carby argues that, in defiance of the content of the lyrics, the music and Smith's signature growl transform songs like "In the House Blues" into parodies of feminine weakness (p. 476). Larsen similarly sets up the theme of female containment only to undermine, at least temporarily, the assumption that women lack power and mobility. By the end of the second chapter of *Quicksand*, Helga has decided to treat her dissatisfaction with one of the modes of resolution (in addition to death or murder) most favored by the blues singers: travel.

With its scenario of a woman angrily awaiting the return of an unfaithful man who has likely deserted her, songs like "In the House Blues" contrast male mobility with female confinement. This contrasting theme is picked up in numerous tunes that use trains as recurring images of migration. The following verse from Bessie Smith's "Freight Train Blues" is a case in point: "When a woman gets the blues she goes [to] her room and hides (Repeat) / When a man gets the blues he catch the freight train and rides." "Freight Train Blues" depicts an historical reality for black women who often did not have the freedom to travel on their own in the same way that their male counterparts did during the Great Migration. Yet Angela Davis discusses how, in contrast to "Freight Train Blues," many songs do depict women on the move, arguing that "blues representations of traveling women constructed" an imaginary "site where masses of black women could associate themselves aesthetically with travel as a mode of freedom" (p. 67). Unlike the woman of "In the House Blues" who wishes her "man would come home once more," Helga sits in her room contemplating her own escape on a train, which will leave behind a man, her fiancé, James Vayle. Resolving not to sit in her room and hide, Helga Crane intends to catch the train and ride, thus protesting the gender and economic constraints on black women's movement.

This departure, occurring in the opening chapters of *Quicksand,* sets into motion a cause-and-effect pattern of dissatisfaction and movement that constantly circles back on itself to create the swirling effect of the novel's title. Like the rambling women of the blues imaginary, Helga remains in motion. She travels from the South to the North, from Chicago to Harlem, from Harlem to Copenhagen and back again; she ends her narrative still unsatisfied, married to a preacher in the South but vowing to return North, only to find herself confined by the birth of her fifth child. In each scenario, Helga changes her location, her livelihood, and her male love interest (her list of beaux include fellow teacher James Vayle, Naxos principal Robert Anderson, Danish artist Axel Olsen, and finally her husband, the Reverend Pleasant Green). The episodes also involve her relationship to female figures, who are ideological opponents and at times rivals for men's affection: the Naxos matron Miss MacGooden; two other mixed-race urbanites, the bourgeois Anne Grey and the bohemian Audrey Denney; and spiritually inclined Clementine Richards. Symbolically rendered through recurring images of death and rebirth, sleeping and awakening, Helga's continual attempts to re-invent new lives for herself are invariably subjected to a kind of "changing same"; the various locations, men, and women operate as riffs on one another, and Helga, despite her attempts to break free, finds herself worrying the line, as the old patterns of her life are repeated in a stultifying cycle.[1] Just as she saw the need to escape Naxos at the beginning, for example, she has the same reaction in Harlem, declaring, "I can't stay in this room any longer. I must get out or I'll choke" (p. 110) [92]. She expresses the same fear of suffocation when she vows once again to leave the South behind at the novel's conclusion. In contrast to *Passing*'s blues structure, which produces meaning by varying and improvising on similarities, the repetitive pattern of *Quicksand* emphasizes sameness in spite of change.

While the larger structures of Larsen's novels reproduce forms of blues and jazz music, the sentence-level structures of her prose are similarly influenced by African American oral traditions in ways that affirm her engagement with the criteria for black art mandated by Hughes. Set in the South, the opening of *Quicksand* uses the motifs of the rural blues to configure Helga's plight. As Helga migrates

---

1. On the notion of the "changing same" in black music, see Amiri Baraka, "The Changing Same (R&B and New Black Music)," in *The LeRoi Jones/Amiri Baraka Reader,* ed. William J. Harris (New York: Thunder's Mouth Press, 1991), pp. 186–209.

North first to Chicago and then to Harlem, the pace of the text shifts from the slower, lowdown sound of the blues to the fast-paced, up-tempo of jazz. In describing the Northern cities to which Helga sojourns, Larsen's language captures movement and sound even more than visuals. The portrayal of these urban locales becomes a manifestation of dance and music, as in the initial description of Chicago, which opens chapter five: "Gray Chicago seethed, surged, and scurried about her" (p. 27) [27]. As she continues to describe Helga's first stop in the North, Larsen varies this triple repetition of verbs so that Chicago is "marked . . . by the noise, the dash, the crowds" and, one line later, becomes "this dirty, mad, hurrying city" (p. 27) [28]. In this descriptive passage, the parts of speech—first verbs, then nouns, then adjectives—are equivalent to different instruments, sounding the reverberating notes that compose the portrait of the city.

* * *

ARNE LUNDE and ANNA WESTERSTAHL STENPORT

From Helga Crane's Copenhagen: Denmark, Colonialism, and Transnational Identity in Nella Larsen's *Quicksand*[†]

In his 1993 book *The Black Atlantic: Modernity and Double Consciousness*, Paul Gilroy posits an as yet open and unanswered question: "What of Nella Larsen's relationship to Denmark?" (18). Although she fell into obscurity relatively soon after the publication of her last novel in 1929, today Larsen ranks with Langston Hughes and Zora Neale Hurston as one of the major writers of the Harlem Renaissance. Indeed, Larsen's two novels, *Quicksand* in 1928 and *Passing* in 1929, are not only complex expressions of African-American racial and gender identity in the twenties but also important modernist experiments. However, although recent scholarship has explored how black Atlantic culture transcends conventional ethnic and national boundaries by studying, among other topics, twentieth-century African Americans (Langston Hughes, Paul Robeson, Josephine Baker, and James Baldwin, for example) who moved to Europe—and especially to France—to escape American

† From *Comparative Literature* 60.3 (2008): 228–32, 236–38, 240, 242–43. Reprinted by permission of the authors. Page numbers to this Norton Critical Edition appear in square brackets.

racism, Gilroy's question has mostly remained under the critical radar. The fact that the entire middle section of Larsen's *Quicksand* is set in Copenhagen has only made this canonical Harlem Renaissance work more enigmatic and problematic for many critics. In a novel whose first and last third explore its protagonist's odyssey through very different parts of black America in the 1920s, what is the significance of Helga Crane's two-year detour (in the dead center of the novel) to a small Scandinavian capital city? In this article, we trace the implications of this critical oversight in order to indicate that there may be much more to Helga Crane's relationship to Denmark than previously noted. In *Quicksand,* Larsen critiques a lingering silence with respect to Denmark's conflicted relationship to its own colonial past. At the same time, Larsen identifies as an artist with several of the major figures of the Scandinavian Modernist Breakthrough movement of the late nineteenth century—most notably Jens Peter Jacobsen and Henrik Ibsen.

Most Larsen scholarship of the past three decades has defined her as, first and foremost, an African-American writer who played an essential role in the aesthetic and literary rethinking of race and class that characterized the Harlem Renaissance. Larsen's Danish origins (Danish-European, Danish-Afro-Caribbean, and Danish-American) and her self-identification with her Danish ethnic background are elements that Larsen scholarship has tended either to dismiss or gloss over. Indeed, several key Larsen scholars (Thadious Davis, Cheryl Wall, and Charles Larson) have either doubted or denied that Larsen ever traveled to Denmark at all, let alone lived there for several years. As a result, her journeys to Denmark have sometimes been read as fantasy projections. Given the challenges of recovering surviving records and Larsen's own tendency towards self-mythologizing, this approach has not been entirely unjustified. But the impulse to suppress Larsen's Danish family ties and her direct experiences in Scandinavia may also have resulted from a desire (whether conscious or not) to secure her status within a feminist, African-American literary canon, a status that Larsen's own identification with her "Nordic" side and Danish roots threatens to destabilize.

Efforts to expand Larsen's canonical Harlem Renaissance identity in transnational directions are now changing the field of Larsen scholarship. George Hutchinson's extensive scholarship on Larsen's Danish connections (most recently in his 2006 work *In Search of Nella Larsen*) have been especially transformative. In the 1990s, Hutchinson discovered ship's records that prove that Larsen's mother Marie took Nella and her white half-sister Anna on an extended trip to Denmark to visit relatives in 1898, when Nella was seven years old ("Nella Larsen and the Veil of Race"). And it is now virtually certain that Larsen did live in Denmark between 1909 and 1912 (see also Hutchinson, "Racial Labyrinth" and "Subject"). Such evidence helps support a transnational, pan-ethnic way of looking at Larsen's authorship, one that acknowledges her Scandinavian heritage as much as the artist did herself. Within Denmark, Nella Larsen has remained almost completely unknown until quite recently, and *Quicksand* has not yet been translated into Danish. But as Martyn Bone has shown, Danish students studying *Quicksand* in today's multiethnic, multicultural Denmark find extensive connections between Larsen's representations of race in Copenhagen and their own experiences. Moreover, the international conference "Denmark and the Black Atlantic" at the University of Copenhagen in May 2006 has already proved pivotal to further investigations of Larsen's relationship to Denmark—from its keynote address by George Hutchinson, to a walking tour of Larsen's Copenhagen and several panels dealing with Denmark and race (in one of which the authors presented an earlier version of this article).

The present study makes two interrelated arguments. In the article's first section, we argue that the novel's Denmark scenes contain within them a structuring absence. Denmark's own vexed attitudes (pride, glorification, shame, and amnesia) toward its colonial heritage in the Danish West Indies (which was sold to the United States in 1917) and the nation's role in the black Atlantic slave trade haunt the text in ways that have not been sufficiently interrogated. Although the novel's main character, Helga Crane, rarely speaks her mind to the white Danes in the novel, the text employs sophisticated narrative focalization strategies to convey suppressed and denied tensions of racism and xenophobia, particularly in the novel's middle chapters set in Copenhagen. The novel's silence (its present "absence" if you will) about the Danish colonial legacy thus parallels the Danish public silence regarding its own colonial heritage in the early twentieth century. Second, we argue that *Quicksand* functions as an early modernist prose text within not only an African-American context but also a Scandinavian-American one. *Quicksand* makes many explicit and implicit references to Scandinavian literary modernism, including the legacy of Jens Peter Jacobsen, Henrik Ibsen, and what Georg Brandes has called the Modern Breakthrough movement. Larsen read widely in Scandinavian literature, and *Quicksand*'s Helga Crane has more than a passing resemblance to Jacobsen's and Ibsen's most self-conflicted protagonists: Niels Lyhne and Hedda Gabler respectively. These elements reveal not only Larsen's familiarity with late nineteenth- and early twentieth-century Scandinavian culture, but also her active engagement with Scandinavian modernism, in order to shape a new kind of transnational, trans-racial modernism. Therefore, Larsen's absence thus far from even a loose definition of a "Scandinavian-American canon"—one that includes works by Ole Rølvaag, Vilhelm Moberg, and even Willa Cather—seems especially glaring.

Nella Larsen's family history indicates the triangulating and transnational relationships we are exploring. Born to a Danish mother, with a father of color from the Danish West Indies, Larsen grew up as the stepdaughter of a white Danish immigrant on the south side of Chicago in neighborhoods that included large Scandinavian and German ethnic populations. After attending high school at the allblack Fisk Normal School in Nashville, she spent the period 1909–1912 in Copenhagen, after which she returned to New York City to study nursing. It is unclear how much subsequent contact she had with her Danish relatives. By the early 1920s, Larsen had begun to move in the upper classes of New York's black society, was married to a prominent African-American physicist, Dr. Elmer S. Imes, and had befriended influential people within the Harlem Renaissance movement. Unlike many of her Harlem Renaissance compatriots, however, Nella Larsen enjoyed only a brief period of literary productiveness and fame. Her second and final novel, *Passing,* appeared in 1929, the year after *Quicksand* was published, and Larsen traveled in southern Europe as the recipient of a Guggenheim fellowship in 1930–31 (she did not visit Denmark). But she returned to the United States without a completed manuscript, and, after a public divorce and gradual withdrawal from friends, she eventually returned to nursing as a profession. As Hutchinson shows, Larsen lived in almost complete anonymity in lower Manhattan from 1938 until her death in 1964 (*In Search* 452–82). Almost no personal papers remain.

Like its author, *Quicksand*'s protagonist Helga Crane has a mixed racial heritage, and the novel, which takes place in six different locations—Naxos College in Georgia, Chicago, Harlem, Copenhagen, Harlem again, and rural Alabama—shares many plot details with Larsen's life. The Copenhagen section (chapters 12–17) occupies the novel's compositional center. The descriptions of Copenhagen (including the Tivoli Gardens, the Christiansborg and Amalienborg palaces, Kongens Nytorv, the Folkemuseum, Gammelstrand, and the Circus vaudeville house) are filled with period details and realistic observations, and the many accurate depictions of street scenes, place names, language use, customs, and institutions clearly corroborate Hutchinson's research on Larsen's first-hand familiarity with Danish culture. Copenhagen is consistently contrasted with Harlem and its noisy crowds: European "toylike streets" (97) [58] and their "amazing orderliness" (109) [68] are juxtaposed to the "feverish rush" (124) [81] of the New York that Helga has just left behind. Helga also remarks on the widespread practice of bicycling in Copenhagen. The young *Frøkken* Crane quickly learns to dodge the velocipeds like a "true Copenhagener" (105) [65].

In the novel's early chapters, Helga's memories of growing up a miserable and often-despised mulatta on the south side of Chicago, as well as her impressions of the stifling racial conventions at the all-black college where she is teaching in Naxos, are countered by impressions of the fairy-tale-like tranquility and charm—seemingly inspired by one of Hans Christian Andersen's stories—of her time in Copenhagen as a child. Indeed, after socializing with a black coterie of intellectuals and artists in Harlem—and before arriving in Copenhagen—Helga indulges in "daydreams of a happy future in Copenhagen, where there were no Negroes, no problems, no prejudice" (87) [50]. Curiously, Helga's phantasmagoria of an all-white, ethnically homogeneous stability far from a conflicted heterogeneous America contradicts not only Denmark's history as a colonial power and involvement in the trans-Atlantic slave trade, but also the documented presence of Afro-Caribbeans in early twentieth-century Copenhagen.

The Danish West Indies was colonized in 1666 and ruled by Denmark for three and a half centuries until it was sold to the United States in 1917 and renamed the Virgin Islands. Although these three islands (especially Saint Thomas) played a vital role in the black Atlantic's Middle Passage and the transfer of slaves, goods, and capital in the eighteenth century and beyond, Denmark's legacy as a slave trader and colonizer continues to be overlooked. Denmark imported 1,000 slaves annually from Africa to the West Indies until the trade was abolished in 1803. At that time, however, 35,000 African slaves remained on the islands, where slavery continued until 1848 under unusually harsh rule. By the end of the nineteenth century, the Danish West Indies had become a significant problem for Denmark's agrarian-based economy. The islands did not produce enough sugar cane and other cash crops to provide their own subsistence, and workers' uprisings and calls for civic justice and freedom of the press indicated a growing unrest. By 1902, their toll on the Danish mainland economy prompted the Danish government to establish a commission to make the islands profitable again.

Very few Danes who were not in military or governmental positions related to the colony would have visited the West Indies or would have had familiarity with the region. In fact, while Danish may have been an official language, it was rarely spoken in the commercial and public life of the West Indies, which mostly used a Creole drawing on English, Dutch, and, to a limited extent, Danish. The colony's presence in Danish newspapers, illustrated journals, and public discourse was also quite limited by the year 1900, perhaps because the Danish West Indies did not figure into *Grundtvigisim*, a construction of Danishness based on a "farmer's class ideology" (Østergard 23) that emphasized small-scale capitalist entrepreneurship, self-reliance, and community and was widely promoted in Danish public discourse at the time. Nevertheless, a parliamentary referendum in 1903 to sell the colony failed because of "strong nationalistic sentiments" ("A Brief History"). The Danish West Indies thus seems to have functioned in the Danish public's awareness as an abstractly remote but symbolically important satellite of Danish national ideology, a status reflected by the coexistence of a general disinterest in the rapidly deteriorating conditions on the islands with efforts to preserve the national value of the enterprise.

Organized at Tivoli Gardens in Copenhagen, the Colonial Exhibition of 1905 was promoted as an explicit attempt to raise the public awareness and support of the colonies. The author Emma Gad, a women's rights activist and close friend of the Brandes family, was instrumental in organizing the exhibition. Former Afro-Caribbean slaves from the West Indies and their descendants were brought to Copenhagen, along with artifacts and items from the islands and from other Danish colonies, mostly in West Africa (Kildegaard 152–64). After the exhibition, it became increasingly common for Copenhagen families to employ African servants and nannies, some from the West Indies, which presumably led to a fairly substantial presence, clearly coded in terms of class, of Danes of color in the city—a situation much like that in Copenhagen during the 1760 monarchy, when "the number of Afro-Caribbeans in service to the Danish aristocracy and the moneyed bourgeoisie numbered in the many hundreds, largely as a consequence of the scale of Danish involvement in Saint Thomas and Saint Croix (Hansen, cited in Pred 63).

At the time of Nella Larsen's second stay in Denmark (from 1909 until 1912), the presence of the Danish West Indies in the public imagination had increased, as had deliberations about the status of the colony and the conditions of its African population. The illustrated journal *Verden og vi,* for example, ran a series of articles on the Danish West Indies in 1912. *Quicksand*'s depiction of Helga as not only an anomaly, but also a prize trophy of her wealthy Aunt Katrina and Uncle Poul indicates an intriguing perspective on Larsen's part. As a surrogate daughter, the twenty-three-year-old Helga becomes the toast of the town's social elite. Larsen reveals, however, an unspoken racialized tension around Helga's presence in Denmark. While Katrina and Poul Dahl love their niece, they also exploit her as a tool to "advance their social fortunes" (98) [60]. The novel stresses Helga's exoticism, and her costuming, make-up, and jewelry are all strategically selected by her aunt to show Helga off to the best possible effect in high society. As Katrina tells her: "you're young. And a foreigner, and different" (98) [59].

Helga is in such passages presented as a cosmopolitan, delocalized foreigner of dark complexion; she is not explicitly coded as

European-American, African-American, or Afro-Caribbean, but, rather, as a generally exoticized and eroticized Other. This strategy is critical to the multi-layered complexity of *Quicksand*'s Copenhagen sections for a number of reasons. As Hutchinson argues, "Larsen's uses of Copenhagen pointedly revise the uses of Europe as an interracial haven in earlier American novels" (*In Search* 235). Taking Hutchinson's observation one step further into a triangulated black Atlantic context, one can also detect an attempt to confront a transnational, transracial Denmark with its colonial bonds to the Danish West Indies. Compared to the Jazz Age Harlem of the novel, Larsen's Copenhagen exists as a kind of pre-First World War utopia (see Hutchinson, *In Search* 69) rather than within the mid-1920's cultural setting of the rest of the novel. *Quicksand*'s Copenhagen is thus temporally dislocated and projected back in time. It clearly hides the presence of the Danish West Indies in Danish cultural discourse during a period of domestic debate that led to its sale to the United States in 1917.

* * *

When Larsen composed *Quicksand* in 1926, at the height of the Harlem Renaissance, she was part of a bohemian coterie. She was a good friend of Carl Van Vechten, the white author of the 1926 Harlem Renaissance novel *Nigger Heaven,* and she also associated with W. E. B. Du Bois and his circle. This coterie promoted an aesthetic avant-garde and was explicitly interested in challenging stereotypical representations of race. Larsen's first published writings appeared in the African-American children's magazine *The Brownies' Book,* an offshoot of the NAACP's flagship journal, *The Crisis,* edited by Du Bois. Significantly, Larsen's contributions to the magazine were two essays on Danish children's games—"Playtime: Three Scandinavian Games" and "Danish Fun"—which she herself had learned first-hand in Denmark as a child. This context is important. Because *Quicksand* was composed within and for this group of Harlem Renaissance intellectuals, it is not surprising that Larsen reconstructed parts of her experiences in Copenhagen to reflect its political and aesthetic inclinations and address its interest in reconceptualizing racial politics. It also helps to explain the novel's explicit challenges to the export of facile, stereotypical images of African-American performers to Europe.

Thus, although Helga is portrayed as an exoticized Other to be exhibited for social and monetary profit (i.e., the wedding game played by her relatives), her sexual innocence, especially in her relations with Olsen, also offers a very explicit counter-example to the export of African-American sensuality that has striking parallels to the expatriate performer Josephine Baker, who had moved to Paris during the same period (see Wall 103–11). In a Harlem scene early in *Quicksand* there is mention of "the advantages of living in Europe, especially in France" and of "a favorite Negro dancer who had just secured a foothold on the stage of a current white musical comedy" (83) [47–48]. These serve as oblique references to the cult status of Josephine Baker in Paris at the time of Larsen's writing. Baker was of course most famous, if not infamous, for her notorious Banana Dance and its evocation of a wildly uninhibited jungle creature (see DeFalco).

What critics who mention the Josephine Baker parallels in *Quicksand* tend to overlook, however, is that Baker's erotic cabaret performances were not only a sensation in Paris, but played to rapt audiences in Copenhagen and Stockholm as well. Scandinavians were clearly fascinated by Baker; a nude, bracelet-clad Baker, for example, was featured on the cover of the Swedish magazine *Våra nöjen* (issue Number 20 from 1927). The cover caption reads: "Josephine Baker, Charlestondrottningen—parisarnas gunstling" or "Queen of the Charleston—the Parisians' Favorite." In fact, Scandinavian fascination with Baker remained strong from her first tours there in the summer of 1928 through subsequent tours well into the 1950s, and, indeed, as Baker biographers have noted, it is difficult to separate fact from fiction in the performer's recollections of her Jazz Age high life. For example, Baker told several versions of a story in which she and the Swedish Crown Prince carried on a passionate love affair during the 1928 tour. In the version related by Baker's adopted son Jean-Claude Baker, she was reportedly taken to the Royal Palace and "led through a secret door into a room with a four-poster bed covered in precious furs. She lay down, naked, and the prince summoned a servant who came in with a silver tray heaped with jewels, and one by one, the prince covered Josephine's body with diamonds, emeralds, rubies. Every time I go to Stockholm, someone tells me this story; it is now part of the country's folklore" (159).

In *Quicksand* Larsen anticipates the kind of cultish sensation and upper-class fascination Baker would attract in Copenhagen, yet Larsen formulates Helga's reactions to such sensationalism very differently. Needless to say, Helga Crane is quite the opposite of Baker. Helga's relatives and suitors, not her own desires, push her to be ever more sensual and primitive. Likewise, because of Helga's bi-racial, transnational identity, Olsen wrongly assumes her to be a sexualized Josephine Baker-figure beneath the surface (see Gilman for a discussion of the threatening aspects of black female sexuality at this time). Between the lines of his proposal, Olsen reveals his sublimated fantasy—playing the role of the slave-owning colonizer—and Helga rebels against her assumed role in this sexualized colonial economic exchange.

Later Helga recognizes another white fantasy of blackness. Along with her family and Olsen, she goes to the great Circus, a vaudeville house in Copenhagen (112) [71]. There a blackface minstrel act delights the crowd, much to Helga's discomfort: "Out upon the stage pranced two black men, American Negroes undoubtedly, for as they danced and cavorted, they sang in the English of America an old ragtime song that Helga remembered hearing as a child" (112) [71]. That "these pink and white people among whom she had lived had suddenly been invited to look upon something she had hidden away and wanted to forget" (112) [71] makes Helga feel ashamed and betrayed. She returns alone to watch the two African-Americans, who have "blacked up" with burnt cork, perform plantation blackness for a white audience, and their performance unexpectedly changes her view of both the Danes and her black biological father: "For the first time, Helga felt sympathy rather than contempt and hatred for that father [. . .]. She understood, now, his rejection, his repudiation, of the formal calm her mother had represented. She understood his yearning, his intolerable need for the inexhaustible humor and the incessant hope of his own kind" (122) [79]. Inwardly and silently, Helga charts a new transnational identity that draws on her subjective reactions to performances of blackness for Scandinavian consumption: female exhibitions of blackness that seem modeled on Josephine Baker and imperialist fantasies, and male performances of blackface that can never be black enough.

The many paradoxes attending Larsen's own life, as well as the experiences of Helga in *Quicksand*, are further illustrated by the contrast between Larsen's activities in Copenhagen and those of her characters. Larsen herself attended lectures at Copenhagen University, kept up with the cultural news of the liberal and intellectually engaged daily paper *Politiken*, and gained a broad acquaintance with the writing of Georg Brandes, J. P. Jacobsen, Henrik Ibsen, and perhaps August Strindberg (Hutchinson, *In Search* 67, 73, and 225–26). These intellectual encounters are excluded from the plot in *Quicksand*, however. As an author, Larsen adopts the position of the social outsider, much like her compatriots of the Modern Breakthrough movement some decades earlier, and she writes like "a Scandinavian modernist [who] foregrounds the snobbishness of the Scandinavian bourgeoisie, their obsession with class status, and the role of the exchange of women through marriage in cementing class ties" (Hutchinson, *In Search* 235). There are several key connections between *Quicksand* and modern Scandinavian literature in the novel's themes, its tight formal construction, and its reliance on a highly sophisticated aesthetic conceptualization, in order to put "problems under debate," as Brandes so famously pronounced in his lecture series at Copenhagen University. * * *

Quicksand is both a canonical work of the Harlem Renaissance and a modernist novel of distinctly European vintage. * * *

*   *   *

Intriguing parallels between the United States and Denmark, between transnational and heterogeneously racialized vectors of influence thus operate on many levels throughout Larsen's novel. Yet even though *Quicksand* clearly charts an unusual, if not unique, triangulating geography of transnational identity, Larsen's narrative devices and Helga's character suggest that such a transnational and transracial identity remains elusive. Paul Gilroy's provocative question, "What of Nella Larsen's relationship to Denmark," is not easily answered if that question is posed only in the singular. The relationships are multiple, and Larsen's representation of Denmark in *Quicksand* is highly unusual in its implicit and explicit references to the country's colonial heritage and racialized conceptions of modernity. It is obvious, in this respect, that *Quicksand* has critical relevance not only for twenty-first-century Scandinavian studies, but also for transnational, postcolonial, feminist, and identity studies. * * *

*   *   *

WORKS CITED

Baker, Jean-Claude, and Chris Chase. *Josephine: The Hungry Heart.* New York: Random House, 1993.

Bone, Martyn. "African American, Danish American, Black Danish: Teaching Nella Larsen's *Quicksand* in Denmark." *European Scholars Teaching African American Texts.* Ed. Karla Simcikova. Ostrava: University of Ostrava Press, 2007. 11–32.

Brandes, Georg. "Inaugural Lecture, 1871." Trans. Evert Sprinchorn. *The Theory of the Modern Stage.* Ed. Eric Bentley. New York: Applause, 1997. 383–402.

"A Brief History of the Danish West Indies, 1666–1917." *Virgin Islands History.* 2002. Danish National Archives. 11 May 2007 <http://www.virgin-islands-history.dk/eng/vi_hist.asp>.

Davis, Thadious M. *Nella Larsen, Novelist of the Harlem Renaissance. A Woman's Life Unveiled.* Baton Rouge: Louisiana State University Press, 1994.

DeFalco, Amelia. "Jungle Creatures and Dancing Apes: Modern Primitivism and Nella Larsen's *Quicksand.*" *Mosaic: A Journal for the Interdisciplinary Study of Literature* 38.2 (2005): 19–35.

Gilman, Sander L. "Black Bodies, White Bodies: Toward an Iconography of Female Sexuality in Late Nineteenth-Century Art, Medicine, and Literature." *"Race," Writing, and Difference.* Ed. Henry

Louis Gates, Jr. Chicago: University of Chicago Press, 1986. 223–61.

Gilroy, Paul. *The Black Atlantic: Modernity and Double Consciousness*. Cambridge: Harvard University Press, 1993.

Hutchinson, George. *In Search of Nella Larsen: A Biography of the Color Line*. Cambridge: Belknap-Harvard University Press, 2006.

———. "Nella Larsen and the Veil of Race." *American Literary History* 9.2 (1997): 329–49. *JSTOR*. 1 November 2004 http://www.jstor.org/stable/490290.

———. "*Quicksand* and the Racial Labyrinth." *Soundings* 80.4 (1997): 543–71.

———. "Subject to Disappearance: Interracial Identity in Nella Larsen's *Quicksand*." *Temples for Tomorrow: Looking Back at the Harlem Renaissance*. Ed. Geneviève Fabre and Michel Feith. Bloomington: Indiana University Press, 2001. 543–71.

Jacobsen, J. P. *Niels Lyhne*. Trans. Tiina Nunally. Seattle: Fjord Press, 1990.

Kildegaard, Bjarne. *Fru Emma Gad*. Copenhagen: Tiderne skifter, 1984.

Larsen, Nella. *The Complete Fiction of Nella Larsen*. Ed. Charles R. Larson. New York: Anchor Books, 2001.

Larson, Charles R. *Invisible Darkness: Jean Toomer and Nella Larsen*. Iowa: University of Iowa Press, 1993.

Østergard, Uffe. "Peasants and Danes: The Danish National Identity and Political Culture." *Comparative Studies in Society and History* 34.1 (1992): 3–27. *JSTOR*. 11 May 2007 http://www.jstor.org/stable/178983.

Pred, Allan. *The Past Is Not Dead: Facts, Fictions, and Enduring Racial Stereotypes*. Minneapolis: University Minnesota Press, 2004.

Wall, Cheryl A. *Women of the Harlem Renaissance*. Bloomington: Indiana University Press, 1995.

DEBORAH E. McDOWELL

From The "Nameless . . . Shameful Impulse": Sexuality in Nella Larsen's *Quicksand* and *Passing*†1

Anne had perceived that the decorous surface of her new husband's mind regarded Helga Crane with . . . intellectual and aesthetic appreciation . . . but that underneath that well-managed section, in a more lawless place . . . was another, a vagrant primitive groping toward something shocking and frightening to the cold asceticism of his reason . . . that *nameless . . . shameful impulse* . . . [emphasis added by author]

—*Quicksand*2

Irene . . . was trying to understand the look on Clare's face as she had said goodbye. Partly mocking, it had seemed, and partly menacing. *Something else for which she could find no name.* [emphasis added by author]

—*Passing*

Based on her treatment of the black middle class and her examination of the dynamics of racial passing, Nella Larsen is usually paired with Jessie Fauset in studies of the Harlem Renaissance,3 though most critics rightly find Larsen a more gifted writer than Fauset.4 Larsen demonstrates a poised facility with writing, a knowledge and mastery of the elements of fiction—especially narrative economy, effective language, focused characterization, unity, point-of-view—not always evident in Fauset's novels. While critics have commended these features of Larsen's writing since the

---

† From *"The Changing Same": Black Women's Literature, Criticism, and Theory* (Bloomington and Indianapolis: Indiana UP, 1995), pp. 78–84, 86–87, 191–94. Reprinted with permission of Indiana University Press. Notes have been renumbered and edited. Page numbers in square brackets are to this Norton Critical Edition.

1. A version of this chapter introduced the edition of *Quicksand and Passing*, published by Rutgers University in 1986 in its American Women Writers series.
2. Nella Larsen, *Quicksand and Passing* (1928; rpt. New Brunswick: Rutgers UP, 1986), pp. 94–95. Subsequent references will be indicated by page numbers in parentheses.
3. See, for example, Hiroko Sato, "Under the Harlem Shadows: A Study of Jessie Fauset and Nella Larsen," in Arna Bontemps, ed., *The Harlem Renaissance Remembered* (New York: Dodd Mead, 1972), pp. 63–89; Robert Bone, *The Negro Novel in America* (1958; rpt. New Haven: Yale UP, 1972); David Littlejohn, *Black on White: A Critical Survey of Writing by American Negroes* (New York: Viking, 1966; Addison Gayle, *The Way of the New World* (New York: Anchor/Doubleday, 1976).
4. In "The Aesthetics of Race and Gender in Nella Larsen's *Quicksand*," in *PMLA* 105 (January 1990), Ann E. Hostetler asserts that "Larsen goes far beyond Fauset in both stylistic experimentation and the daring self-examination of her protagonist" (p. 36). See also Hiroko Sato, "Under the Harlem Shadows: A Study of Jessie Fauset and Nella Larsen," in *The Harlem Renaissance Remembered*, p. 84; and Amritjit Singh, *The Novels of the Harlem Renaissance* (University Park and London: Pennsylvania State UP, 1976).

beginning of her career, they have consistently criticized the endings of *Quicksand* (1928) and *Passing* (1929). Both novels obviously
reveal Larsen's difficulty with rounding off stories convincingly.
* * *

* * * Though both novels feature daring and unconventional heroines, in the end, they sacrifice these heroines to the most conventional fates of narrative history: marriage and death, respectively.
In *Quicksand* the cultured and refined Helga Crane marries a rural
southern preacher and follows him to his backwoods church to
"uplift" his parishioners. At the end of the novel, she is in a state of
emotional and physical collapse from having too many children. In
Passing the defiant and adventurous Clare, who flouts all the social
rules of the black bourgeoisie, falls to her death under melodramatic
and ambiguous circumstances.

It is little wonder that critics of Larsen have been perplexed by
these abrupt and contradictory endings. But if examined through the
prism of black female sexuality, not only are these resolutions more
understandable, they also illuminate the peculiar pressures on
Larsen as a woman writer during the male-dominated Harlem
Renaissance. They show her grappling with the conflicting demands
of her racial and sexual identities and the contradictions of a black
and feminine aesthetic. Although the endings of *Quicksand* and
Passing, like the resolution of *Plum Bun*, seem to be concessions to
the dominant ideology of romance—marriage and motherhood—
viewed from a feminist perspective, they are much more radical
and original efforts to acknowledge a female sexual experience most
often repressed in both literary and social realms.

To be writing about black female sexuality within this conflicted
context, then, posed peculiar dilemmas for Larsen: How could she
write about black female sexuality in a literary era that often sensa-
tionalized it and pandered to the stereotype of the primitive exotic?
How could she give a black female character the right to healthy
sexual expression and pleasure without offending the proprieties
established by the spokespersons of the black middle class? The
answers to these questions for Larsen lay in attempting to hold these
two virtually contradictory impulses in the same novel. We might
say that Larsen wanted to tell the story of a black woman with sexual desires, but was constrained by a competing desire to establish
black women as respectable in black middle-class terms. The latter
desire committed her to exploring black female sexuality obliquely
and, inevitably, to permitting it only within the context of marriage,
despite the strangling effects of that choice both on her characters
and on her narratives.

* * *

Behind the safe and protective covers of traditional narrative subjects and conventions, Jessie Fauset and Nella Larsen could only hint at the idea of black women as sexual subjects. * * *

* * *

* * * [T]he ideological ambivalences of Larsen's novels were rooted in the artistic politics of the Harlem Renaissance regarding the representation of black sexuality, especially black female sexuality. In the power relations of the period, Fauset's allegiances seemed clear-cut and straightforward compared to Larsen's. We might say that, in the battleground over black representation at this historical moment, Larsen was indeed caught between the proverbial rock and hard place. On the one side was her friend, Carl Van Vechten, roundly excoriated, along with his "followers," by many members of the black middle-class intelligentsia. He was responsible for introducing *Quicksand* to Knopf, and perhaps Larsen showed her gratitude by dedicating *Passing* to him and his wife, Fania Marinoff. On the other side, Larsen was herself a member of the black intelligentsia whom Van Vechten had criticized for failing to exploit the fresh, untapped material in Harlem, a criticism he inserted in *Nigger Heaven*, using the character Russett Durwood as his mouthpiece. Durwood advises Byron Kasson, the black would-be writer, to abandon the old clichés and formulas and write about what he knows— black life in the raw. Harlem is "overrun with fresh, unused material," he tells Kasson. "Nobody has yet written a good gambling story; nobody has touched the outskirts of cabaret life; nobody has gone into the curious subject of the *diverse tribes of the region*" [emphasis added by author]. He ends by predicting that if the "young Negro intellectuals don't get busy, a new crop of Nordics is going to spring up . . . and . . . exploit this material before the Negro gets around to it."[5] Van Vechten was one such Nordic whose sounds are echoed in a review of *Quicksand* that described the novel as "a harmonious blending of the barbaric splendor of the savage with the sophistication of the European." In depicting such black bourgeois intellectuals as Robert Anderson and James Vayle in *Quicksand*, Larsen would seem to share some of Van Vechten's opinions of that class. But as much as she could poke fun at their devotion to "racial uplift," she belonged, blood and breath, to that class, and must have found it extremely difficult to cut her ties with it.

The contradictory impulses of Larsen's novels are clear in the psychic divisions of her characters, divisions especially apparent in

---

5. Carl Van Vechten, *Nigger Heaven* (New York: Knopf, 1926), pp. 222–23.

Helga Crane of *Quicksand*.[6] Most critics locate the origins of that dualism in Helga's mixed racial heritage.[7] Classifying her as the classic "tragic mulatta," alienated from both races, critics see Helga defeated by her struggle to resolve the psychic confusion created by this mixed heritage. The argument that Helga's is a story of the "tragic mulatta" is clearly supported by the novel's epigraph from Langston Hughes's poem "Cross," which treats the problem of racial dualism as seen in the last two lines: "I wonder where I'm gonna die, / Being neither white nor black?" But the epigraph suits *Quicksand* only partially, for it touches only indirectly the issue of sexuality that dominates the novel. In other words, in focusing on the problems of the "tragic mulatto," readers miss the more urgent problem that Larsen tried to explore: the pleasure and danger of female sexual experience.

Helga is divided psychically between a desire for sexual fulfillment and a longing for social respectability. The pressures of the divisions intensify to the point that she wonders "Why [she] couldn't . . . have two lives?" (p. 93)[80]. The novel works out this tension between sexual expression and repression in both thematic impulse and narrative strategy. Helga's psychic struggle seems the same war fought by Nella Larsen between narrative expression and repression of female sexuality as literary subject. The novel, like its protagonist, would seem to want two lives as well: as female sexual confession and novel of racial uplift.

* * *

* * * Helga goes, appropriately, to Harlem, which, at least in Harlem Renaissance mythology, is the site of sexual freedom and abandon; even here, however, her dress is conspicuous and outlandish. At a dinner party, for example, Helga decides to wear a "cobwebby black net [dress] touched with orange," even though she is aware that it is too "décolleté" (p. 56)[51]. The cut and color of the dress suggest warmth and passion, but, significantly, the lure of sexuality is trapped in a net. Here, unlike at Naxos, Helga's conflicts are not with a repressive environment, but rather with herself.

* * *

6. For a discussion of the psychic duality in Larsen's heroines, see Addison Gayle, *The Way of the New World* (New York: Anchor/Doubleday), p. 139.
7. See for example, Hugh Gloster, *Negro Voices in American Fiction* (New York: Russell and Russell, 1948) and Saunders Redding, *To Make a Poet Black* (Chapel Hill: U of North Carolina P, 1945).

Like so many novels by women, *Quicksand* likens marriage to death for women.[8] Larsen attacks the myth that marriage elevates women in the social scale, suggesting that, for them, the way up is, ironically and paradoxically, the way down. Helga's marriage and the children that issue from it "use her up" (p. 123) [102] and freeze her development, not even leaving time for laboring "in the vineyard of the Lord" (p. 118) [98]. The aftermath of the birth of her fourth child is likened to a death and burial (she "go[es] down into that appalling blackness of pain") followed by a symbolic resurrection when she "return[s] to earth" (p. 128) [105]. But Helga's is a mock resurrection, for she rises from the dead only to be reentombed.[9] At the novel's end, she is in labor with her fifth child.

The ending completes the structural opposites on which the novel has turned. Whereas it opens on Helga in an elegantly furnished room, dressed in a "vivid green and gold negligee," the picture of "radiant, careless health" (p. 2) [7] and sexual energy, it closes on her trapped in the "four rooms of her ugly brown house" with "white plaster walls" and naked "uncovered painted floors" (p. 121) [100]. Though near the novel's end she is pictured in a "filmy crepe" negligee, "a relic of her prematrimonial days" (p. 129) [106], it is clear that Larsen wants to stress the reality that "legitimate" sex, for women, is harnessed to its reproductive consequences, for Helga wears this negligee while she is in labor with her fourth child. Though she initially accepts the social script that marriage makes sex moral in the eyes of the law and the church, Helga comes to regard it as "immoral" (p. 134) [110]. Appropriately, she requests that the nurse read Anatole France's "The Procurator of Judea" to her as she recovers from the birth of this child, for its blasphemous, anti-Christian views parallel Helga's own belated insight into the role of Christianity in her oppression.

Larsen's sympathies seem to lie with Helga, who is powerless to resist these binding and suffocating institutions that deny her the right to define the terms of her own sexuality. But in the end she undercuts her own critique through her images of Helga's desire. However much Larsen criticizes the repressive standards of sexual

8. While many novels show marriage as a dead end, especially for women, two strong examples from the 1920s come to mind: Ellen Glasgow's *Barren Ground* (1925) and Emma Summer Kelley's *Weeds*. For a discussion of novels of marriage by women, see Annis Pratt, *Archetypal Patterns in Women's Fiction* (Bloomington: Indiana UP, 1981), pp. 41–58.

9. Likening motherhood to annihilation of the self, to a form of death for women, is a common pattern in women's writing. Alice Walker's *Meridian* (New York: Harcourt, 1976), is one of a host of possible examples, mentioned here again because of its many parallels to *Quicksand*. Walker's character, Meridian, haunted by the thought that she has "shatter[ed] her mother's emergent self," likens motherhood to being "buried alive, walled away from . . . life, brick by brick" (p. 51).

morality upheld by the black middle class, she is finally unable to escape them. Significantly suggesting moral degradation, sexuality is linked throughout the novel to imagery of descent and animalism.[1]

The structure of the novel is a vertical line downward, a movement reinforced by several echoing scenes. In the Harlem cabaret, for example, Helga and her party "[descend] through a furtive, narrow passage into a vast subterranean room . . . characterized by the righteous as hell." The church into which Helga stumbles near the end is a former stable. There the "frenzied women" crawl over the floor "like reptiles," "tearing off their clothing."[2]

Just before her "religious conversion" Helga is literally thrown, "soaked and soiled," "into the gutter." Finally, as if to atone for these "transgressions," Helga goes to the deep South where she is buried alive.[3]

Perhaps this resolution was as unsatisfying for Larsen as it has remained for her readers, and may well explain her decision to return in her next novel to the complex issue of black female sexuality in order to pose a different resolution. In other words, in *Quicksand*, Larsen stakes her exploration of female sexuality in the narrative zone that women writers have traditionally used: within the genre of the romance in which sex for women is enacted and legitimated within marriage and harnessed to motherhood.

✳   ✳   ✳

1. Robert Bone also makes this suggestion. He sees an "underlying moralism" in Larsen's tone. He adds, "Helga's tragedy in Larsen's eyes is that she allows herself to be declassed by her own sexuality. The tone of reproach is unmistakable." *The Negro Novel in America* (New Haven, CT: Yale UP, 1958. Rpt. New Haven, CT: Yale UP, 1992), p. 105.
2. It has long been a stereotype that the church has provided black women a "safe" and controlled release of unexpressed sexual desires. In her essay "A Cultural Legacy Denied and Discovered: Black Lesbians in Fiction by Women," Jewelle Gomez describes "Black women who have hidden from their sexuality behind a church pew." The black church, she continues, has been "a place for Black women to redirect their energy from physical passions to pungent spirituality and socializing." See *Home Girls: A Black Feminist Anthology*, ed. Barbara Smith (New York: Kitchen Table: Women of Color Press, 1983), pp. 120–21.
3. Larsen's use of the trope of descent in *Quicksand* departs significantly from its popular use in other Afro-American fiction. Used by such writers as James Weldon Johnson (*The Autobiography of an Ex-Colored Man*), Jean Toomer (*Cane*), Zora Neale Hurston (*Their Eyes Were Watching God*), Ralph Ellison (*Invisible Man*), Alice Walker (*Meridian*), among many others, the descent to the South is essential, whether psychically or spiritually, to their protagonists' health and survival. With Larsen, it is associated with a form of death.

HANNA MUSIOL

From Cosmopolitan Intimacies in Nella Larsen's *Quicksand*†

'Cosmopolitanism is not just an idea. Cosmopolitanism is infinite ways of being.'
—Sheldon Pollock et al.[1]

'Refocusing on the intimate opens up to what haunts [. . .] social relations, to the untoward, to the strangely familiar that proximities and inequalities may produce.'
—Ann Laura Stoler[2]

Contradictory local and global forces, with their legacies in slavery and colonization, made the America of the first half of the twentieth century into a complex social space, where the physical and symbolic proximity of bodies marked by racial, national, or sexual difference was at once common and feared, policed and punished, and celebrated. On the one hand, the increased intra- and transnational migration, developments in print and visual culture and transportation technologies, and the consumer boom, as well as rapid urbanization, literally and figuratively brought different human bodies into much closer contact with each other. On the other hand, local, state, and federal laws regulating many aspects of social activities, from how businesses could operate, to who could own property and where, to who could marry whom, to, literally, how human bodies were distributed in physical spaces, placed firm restrictions on practices and representations of cross-racial, cross-class, same-sex, or transnational intimacies.[3] Thus, as Ann Laura Stoler reminds

---

† From *Creoles, Diasporas, Cosmopolitanism: Creolization of Nations, Cultural Migrations, Global Languages and Literatures*, ed. David Gallagher (Dublin and Palo Alto: Academica Press, 2011), pp. 1–9, 17–20. Reprinted with permission of the publisher. Notes have been renumbered and edited. Page numbers to this Norton Critical Edition appear in square brackets.
1. Sheldon Pollock, Homi K. Bhabha, Carol Appadurai Breckenridge, and Dipesh Chakrabarty, "Cosmopolitanisms", *Public Culture*, 12.3 (2000), 577–89.
2. Ann Laura Stoler, *Haunted by Empire: Geographies of Intimacy in North American History* (Durham: Duke UP, 2006), p. 14.
3. For example, Jim Crow laws enforced physical segregation of whites and African Americans; interracial marriages between whites and African Americans, as well as whites and Asian Americans, were illegal in many states, and even in places where they were legal, it was nearly impossible to find ministers or state officials who would officiate such marriages (George Hutchinson, *In Search of Nella Larsen: A Biography of the Color Line* (Cambridge, MA: The Belknap Press of Harvard UP, 2006), p. 20. Also, strict covenant laws excluded people of certain ethnic or racial backgrounds (African Americans, Jews, immigrants of East or central Europe, or certain parts of Asia) from acquiring real estate in certain areas, while censorship of the arts, such as the Production Code (1934–60), made it illegal to represent, or affirm, miscegenation, or nonnormative sexuality on-screen.

us, it is important to remember that human intimacies are never simply a matter of personal choices restricted to romantic and sexual relations within the domestic sphere;[4] instead, intimacies of human bodies are deeply 'implicated in the exercise of power'[5] and thus are deeply, and intimately, political.

Early-twentieth-century national, institutionalized racism in the US—thriving on anxieties about interracial mixing and proximity—was met with several distinctly cosmopolitan reimaginings of human closeness and connectivity, and the nature of cosmopolitanism, then and now, is a most debated subject. Sheldon Pollock and others warn us against narrow, Eurocentric understanding of cosmopolitanism as simply a world citizenship.[6] They urge us to recognize that people 'are and have always been cosmopolitan',[7] but that human subjects also always redefine what cosmopolitanism is and what it should do for them. In other words, while human bodies are always connected, regulated, and influenced by national and transnational forces, frameworks, and grammars of meaning, people always engage in practices that redraw geographies of human belonging. In the US of the first half of the twentieth century, national legal frameworks failed to address and remedy localized racial discrimination and endemic patterns of social exclusion of certain human bodies in public spaces, and in response, phenomena such as primitivism, religiosity, and even consumerism provided hopes for new modes of cosmopolitan belonging, of rearranging humans and connecting them, physically or symbolically, across national boundaries.

Nella Larsen * * * perhaps better than most female writers of the period, recognized the power of historically situated intimacies and cosmopolitanisms to shape the social identity of politically and economically marginalized social groups, and to actually define the contours of one's lived experience in early-twentieth-century American culture. She also understood well the paradoxes of being a worldly biracial, bilingual African-American, and a Danish-American.[8] She was a cosmopolitan by the simple virtue of her complex background, but she was also a member of various collectivities that reinvented

---

4. See her "Intimidations of Empire: Predicament of the Tactile and Unseen" and "Tense and Tender Ties: The Politics of Comparison in North American History and (Post)Colonial Studies" in *Haunted By Empire*, p. 15.
5. Ibid., p. 15.
6. Sheldon Pollock et al., "Cosmopolitanisms," p. 7.
7. Ibid., p. 588.
8. For a brilliant essay about *Quicksand* as a novel that addresses legacies of American and Danish colonialism and that examines Larsen and Helga Crane's transnational as well as biracial identity, see Arne Lunde and Anna Westerstahl Stenport, "Helga Crane's Copenhagen: Denmark, Colonialism, and Transnational Identity," *Comparative Literature*, 60 (2008), 228–43. [This essay is excerpted in this volume—Editor's note.]

cosmopolitanism anew, stressing some globally-shared racial, class, gender, or religious similarities, and deemphasizing others.

Born close to 'the Western Hemisphere's most infamous red-light district' in Chicago—a crowded city 'bursting with families recently arrived'[9]—to a white Danish mother and a black father from the Danish West Indies, Larsen was haunted throughout her life by her parents' mysterious, possibly illicit relationship, and by her multiracial, multicultural, and multinational background. After Larsen's father's disappearance,[1] Larsen's mother married a white man and moved to a more respectable part of the city. However, as Chicago's racial segregation intensified mixed-race households were accepted in respectable areas only as long as their non-white members were servants, not family members.[2] Again, larger structures of oppression that relegated non-white bodies to subhuman status, and that regulated the conditions of interracial proximity at the time, entered into the intimate relations of the Larsens' family. In that period, Nella Larsen's multicultural heritage, but specifically her visibly raced body, 'continually threatened to compromise the safety and the livelihood of her family even within the bounds of the domestic space.'[3] Eventually, the family was forced to move back to Levee, the ill-reputed gambling and prostitution district of Chicago.[4] Larsen's biographer, George Hutchinson, emphasizes the psychological trauma these events must have caused young Nella Larsen, who, by her sixteenth birthday, simply 'could no longer live with her family' in the same house.[5] As an adult, Larsen actively participated in Harlem's distinctly international culture, and later, as a Harlem Renaissance literary celebrity of sorts, travelled in Europe on a Guggenheim fellowship.[6]

Larsen's 1928 novel, *Quicksand*, while not simply biographical, does tell the story of a woman whose life bears much similarity to Larsen's own. The novel's protagonist, Helga Crane, is a biracial woman who speaks Dutch and English but cannot revel in her multicultural and biracial background; she simply cannot 'have two lives' (Q 95) [80]. Helga endures a series of life complications caused by

---

9. Hutchinson, *In Search of Nella Larsen: A Biography of the Color Line*, pp. 14–15.
1. Not enough documents survived to clarify whether he had died or abandoned his family when Nella Larsen was little. See Hutchinson, *In Search of Nella Larsen*, p. 19.
2. Hutchinson, *In Search of Nella Larsen*, p. 37.
3. Laura E. Tanner, "Intimate Geography: The Body, Race, and Space in Larsen's *Quicksand*," *Texas Studies in Literature and Language* 51 (2009): 183.
4. Hutchinson, *In Search of Nella Larsen*, p. 36.
5. Ibid. p. 36.
6. She travelled to Spain and France in 1930: Nella Larsen, *Quicksand*, ed. by Thadious M. Davis (New York: Penguin Books, 2002), p. xxxiii. All further references will be given in parentheses in the text marked by the abbreviation Q and Arabic numerals for page numbers. She also travelled to Denmark as a child, and Hutchinson in *In Search of Nella Larsen* (pp. 64–65) confirms accounts of her second excursion to Denmark, where she stayed for three years as a young adult.

larger social forces that defined the social meaning of gender as well as race, and provided patterns for acceptable human intimacies at that time. As a result, she is never 'satisfied in one place' and never experiences fulfilling human intimacy with her relatives, sexual partners, or friends, whites and blacks, Americans and Europeans alike (Q 95) [80].

*   *   *

Quicksand is often seen as an intimate examination of Helga's subjectivity, of her personal journey toward self-fulfillment, and it certainly explores Helga's unsuccessful quest for pleasure, happiness, stability, and freedom. What is fascinating about the novel is that by interrogating the very intimate episodes in Helga's life—the crumbling of her career as a teacher; her family troubles; the ostracism she suffers from her white family in the US; the exoticization bestowed on her by her Scandinavian relatives in Europe; her misfortunes with men; the fiancé she abandons in Naxos; Dr. Anderson, whom she unsuccessfully desires; Axel Olson, who wants to marry her because she will not become his lover; and the unappealing Reverend Pleasant Green, whom she eventually marries and grows to hate; her fears, desires, confusions, pregnancies, and illness—Larsen returns us to the large-scale politics and ideologies of the era, to the very 'structures of dominance'[7] that Helga struggles to evade throughout her life. In other words, Nella Larsen narrates different stages of Helga's life journey as personal but always already political. Larsen brings attention to the different laws and customs that regulate Helga's mobility and closeness to people of different races, classes, religions, social and national backgrounds, and that limit the spaces she can inhabit and even define the clothes she can wear. However, Larsen simultaneously tackles key modernist cosmopolitanisms of the era, popular primitivism, consumerism, Pan-Africanism, and antisecularism/religiosity.

In her novel, Larsen argues that these movements and their conflicting ideologies shaped cultural, social, and economic life in early-twentieth-century America. They all re-conceptualized notions of human intimacy, as well as provided models of collective practices aimed at reversing existing patterns of social exclusion. Pan-Africanism, primitivism, religion, and women's culture all offered new possibilities for public participation, and articulated their affiliations and solidarities, intentionally or not, in distinctly transnational terms. As such, Larsen demonstrates, they had a direct impact on the process of individual and social formation of her novel's protagonist. Larsen stresses the promise and the seductive power that

---

7. Stoler, *Haunted By Empire: Geographies of Intimacy in North American History*, p. 13.

each of these trends initially wields for Helga Crane and that make her disillusionment so painful, so visceral in the end.[8]

In their work on cosmopolitanism, Sheldon Pollock and others argue that cosmopolitanism is 'not some known entity existing in the world, with a clear genealogy from the Stoics to Immanuel Kant'.[9] It is instead a myriad of theories and actual practices, or 'embodiments',[1] that are 'not pregiven or foreclosed by the definition of any particular society or discourse'.[2] Such an understanding of cosmopolitanism(s), as a practice concretely situated in history, can reveal to us how people manage to, or imagine that they can, 'live tenaciously in terrains of historic and cultural transition'.[3] In this context, Larsen's attention to early-twentieth-century cosmopolitanisms is not accidental. Their diverse, overlapping and contradictory, articulations of transnational thought and human connections played a crucial role in providing models for how 'to live tenaciously' to those whose equal rights were not supported by national economic-legal frameworks at the time. In fact, diverse American instantiations of cosmopolitanism sealed the collective identities of some social groups—women, ethnic minorities, the poor, for example—and allowed them to demand or claim most basic human rights, which were consistently and explicitly denied by nationalist ideologies and institutions at the time.

What is surprising however is that Larsen critiques all key cosmopolitanisms of the era, regardless of their political ambitions, methods, or even historical record of political effectiveness. In order to understand why Larsen finds them ineffective, if not downright dangerous, for her female protagonist who attempts and fails at projects of 'tenacious living' in several different social and geopolitical environments, it is important to examine the kind of social work such trends performed and how, in American and European culture.

As an expression of perceived cultural crisis in the West, primitivism depended on transnational exchanges of art, epistemologies, and experiences. While it was sometimes viewed as a trend in

---

8. It is important to note here that Helga Crane is always initially seduced by a new space associated with a new type of cosmopolitanism. For example, she initially is very happy in New York and feels that "Harlem, teeming black Harlem, had welcomed her and lulled her into something that was, she was certain, peace and contentment" (Q 46) [40]. Later, she feels just this hopeful after moving to Copenhagen, enjoying 'this new life' with all its "luxury [. . .] admiration and attention" (Q 69) [59]. After witnessing the scene of religious frenzy in a New York church, "the weird orgy resound[s] in her heart" (Q 114) [95], and she wants to prolong the "soothing haziness" that offered her 'rest from her long trouble of body and of spirit' (Q 117) [97]. But in each episode, in each space and community, Helga's happiness doesn't last (Q 50, Q 83, and Q 122).

9. Sheldon Pollock, et al., p. 577.
1. Ibid., p. 578.
2. Ibid., pp. 577–78.
3. Ibid., p. 580.

European and American visual arts, in the first half of the twentieth century primitivism was as common in popular films,[4] in the
human exhibits at the numerous and widely popular World's Fairs
and Expositions,[5] and in social sciences, as it was in iconic paintings by Pablo Picasso or Paul Gauguin. In literature, the sciences,
and the visual arts, in high and low culture, primitivists trespassed
national boundaries, made references to foreign, exotic, mostly
transhistorical 'them,' in order to remake the familiar 'us,' to revital-
ize 'our' arts, and 'our' society—or, as the Danish painter in *Quicksand*, Axel Olsen, says proposing to Helga, to make him 'great.
Immortal' (Q 88)[75].

Not less (if differently) cosmopolitanism was early-twentieth-
century consumerism, blending the cult of new consumer products
with the rhetoric of transnational (although not transracial) suf-
frage. In popular articulations of consumerist ideology, modern(ist)
commodities, the '[n]ice things' the protagonist of Larsen's novel,
Helga Crane, loves so much in the novel (Q 10, 134, 136)[12],
were of particular importance to American women, who in the
1920s, despite the passage of the 19th Amendment, still enjoyed
limited civil rights. Consumerism and modern advertising offered
female consumers [6] the promise of social visibility and public participation; and their rhetoric and consumption practices hinted at
the possibility of consumption-based female citizenship of the
world.

Various racial uplift movements, from the Booker T. Washington
kind to Marcus Garvey's racial nationalism to W. E. B. Du Bois' New
Negro Pan-Africanism, emphasized ways in which racial heritage
could override geopolitical boundaries and restrictions. Finally, the
'pie in the sky' religions Larsen describes in her novel, in references
to Christian churches in Naxos, Alabama, and New York or in the
texts Helga reads—Marmaduke Pickthall's *Saïd the Fisherman*, Anatole France's 'The Procurator of Judea'—emphasized the unity of

---

4. See, for example, the notorious talkie, *The Jazz Singer* (1927); one of the first 'race'
movies produced by an American studio, *Hallelujah* (1929); or any of the internation-
ally popular films with Josephine Baker, *Siren of the Tropics* (1927), *Zou Zou* (1934), or
Princess Tam Tam (1935).

5. For a great overview of American World's Fairs, consult Robert W. Rydell, *All the
World's a Fair: Visions of Empire at the American International Institutions, 1876–1916*
(Chicago: U of Chicago P, 1984). For a study of popular primitivism, see Elazar Barkan
and Ronald Bush, eds., *Prehistories of the Future: The Primitivist Project and the Culture of Modernism* (Stanford, CA: Stanford UP, 1995), and Jack Flam and Miriam
Deutch, eds., *Primitivism and Twentieth Century Art: A Documentary History* (Berkeley, CA, and London: U of California P, 2003).

6. It's important to note here that ethnic and racial minorities, female and male alike,
were rarely portrayed as consumers of new goods in the American national press; one
would not find images of an African American or Native American female sipping
Coke, driving a Chrysler, or using Listerine in mass magazines of the era such as *Cosmopolitan, Ladies Home Journal*, or *Collier's*. In other words, consumption of modern
products was also articulated as a white privilege.

all believers across man-produced boundaries, even as they had to accept deferred access to human rights on earth. In the case of religious movements, solidarity of all mankind was to be found not only in transnational, but also in otherworldly, spaces. As Richard Wright poignantly put it in his visual documentary, '[w]e, who had had our personalities blasted with two hundred years of slavery'[7] and 'who needed the ritual and guidance of institutions,'[8] 'never belonged to any organizations except the church and burial societies.'[9] Wright's comments emphasize that in the segregated America, only these two social institutions 'welcomed' African American bodies, dead or alive.

These and earlier mentioned historic articulations of 'cosmopolitan coexistence,'[1] as well as their institutions, their publics, and social rituals, offered a much-needed critique of the state-imposed architecture of exclusion of entire social groups from the public sphere. Thus, it is significant Nella Larsen, herself victimized by institutionalized racial and gender discrimination in the United States, chooses to examine only the crippling impact of such cosmopolitan ideologies and their 'intimate publics.'[2]

* * *

In the end, we learn from *Quicksand* that Helga's body, marked by national, sexual, and racial difference in multiple ways, cannot be emancipated with transnational fictions that obscure global and local 'designs' of inequality. Not surprisingly, Helga experiences the 'feeling of happiness and freedom, that blessed sense of belonging to herself alone and not to a race,' mainly when alone or in the extraterritorial space of the sea (Q 66) [56]. The ideology of cosmopolitan solidarity and the structures that normalize her experiences of difference, either in the conservative Naxos or among the liberal New Negro Harlem activists and European primitivists, or in the South, work to sustain—not overcome—the racial, gender, and class inequalities national frameworks code her body with. Moreover, the struggle for new, cosmopolitan, human intimacies is still fought over Helga's body. She is either asked to give it up for the sexual and social pleasure of others, or asked to offer it to the Lord, or to her race to reproduce her 'good stock' (Q 24; 104) [24], or it is simply taken as art material, and so on. The recognition of Helga's cosmopolitan

7. Richard Wright, *12 Million Black Voices: A Folk History of the Negro in the United States* (New York: Thunder's Mouth Press, 1969), p. 97.
8. Ibid. p. 95.
9. Ibid. p. 96.
1. Sheldon Pollock, Homi K. Bhabha, Carol A. Breckenridge, and Dipesh Chakrabarty, 'Cosmopolitanisms,' p. 581.
2. Lauren Berlant, *The Female Complaint: The Unfinished Business of Sentimentality in American Culture* (Durham and London: Duke UP, 2008), p. viii

identity always depends on 'others' views'[3] of her body, and it is the publics that infuse it with meaning and then police her body's *stylistic* coherence. Intimate publics centered on fantasies of global citizenship, Helga finds out, exclude non-discriminatory reciprocity and mutuality, and make her intimacy with other people and material objects a reflection of larger structures of oppression, foreclosing the promise of transnational emancipation.

SUSAN M. REVERBY

[Hallowed Ground][†]

"Hallowed ground." That's how Tuskegee Institute is often referred to, although no one seems to remember exactly who spoke these words or when.

* * *

Tuskegee Institute was built in a small Southern town in a county parceled out of the huge Southern lands of the Creek (Muskogee), Tallassee and other Native American peoples.[1] By the end of the French and Indian Wars in 1763, what would become Alabama was ceded by France to England and a fort at Tuskegee handed over to the English as traders moved in.[2] In 1819 Alabama was admitted to the Union as a frontier state where fear of death by bear attack or childbirth or through the cruelties of slavery in the fields, mills and mines defined daily realities.[3] It took until 1832 for Macon County's borders to be set with Tuskegee as its county seat. When the Indian wars ended with treaties that were broken over and over, Creek and other Native American peoples were driven out as their land was given out to whites, tribal laws unrecognized, hunting prohibited, plantations formed, forests cut down, swamps drained and farmed. In the 1840s, the trail of tears left dispersed those Native Americans not killed in the wars, leaving their legacy behind in Macon County in the bloodlines of both blacks and whites and in the names of the towns that were originally called Taskigi and Tallasi.[4]

---

3. I am alluding here again to Franz Fanon's discussion in *Black Skin White Masks*, p. 109.
† This previously unpublished essay is reprinted by permission of the author.
1. Sarah Lawless, "Tuskegee," *Encyclopedia of Alabama*, http://www.encyclopediaofalabama.org/article/h-2051, accessed 10/24/2018.
2. *The Tuskegee News*, 100th Anniversary Edition, v. 100, no. 3, November 11, 1965.
3. Leah Rawls Atkins, "From Early Times to the End of the Civil War," in William Rogers et al., eds., *Alabama: The History of a Deep South State* (Tuscaloosa, Alabama: U of Alabama P, 1994), pp. 58, 60, 72.
4. The word "Taskigi" meant "warrior" in the language spoken by the Muskogee people.

By 1860, those identified as black Americans (both free and slave) outnumbered whites in Macon County by over two to one (18,177 to 8,624).[5] Plantation homes, with their doric columns and imposing porches, were outnumbered, too, by small log or shotgun cabins in the red clay back ways as barely 12 percent of Macon County's white population identified themselves as slaveowners.[6] Cotton, as in other counties of what became known as the Black Belt, covered the fields made fertile by slave labor.[7] Other enslaved African Americans found themselves sent to work in sawmills and the county's one textile mill. Intense farming exhausted much of the soil of the county and small land-owning white farmers had a hard time meeting even the minimal taxes to keep hold of their property.[8] Except for the large plantation owners, a Southern way of hardscrabble making-do dominated most of Macon County's black and white population's working lives.

The Civil War's battlefields never got as far as Tuskegee, only to what would become the Chehaw railhead several miles out of the town. An offshoot of Sherman's Army defeated the Tuskegee Home Guard at Chehaw in July of 1864. Union soldiers made it to nearby Loachapoka, Auburn, Opelika and Notasulga while destroying track and burning the rail line and achieving Sherman's goal of making the re-supply of Atlanta difficult. But it was supposedly, as the story goes, the college friendship between a Northern officer and planter Edward Varner (whose Tuskegee mansion Grey Gables now houses the Tuskegee University president and whose gate and chandelier are rumored to have been used as props for *Gone with the Wind*) that kept the Union men of General James Wilson's "raiders" from burning down the town.[9] As with much of the history of both the town and the Institute, the vagaries of location, the link to the North, and the political skills and connections of the populace made things happen.

Reconstruction in Alabama dashed many of the hopes that the end of the Civil War had raised in Tuskegee. Much too soon it became clear that for many African Americans slavery would be exchanged for serfdom. General Wager Swayne, the Freedman's Bureau's Alabama chief, declared to the state's newly freed men and women that

5. "Macon County, Alabama, Largest Slaveholders from 1860 Slave Census Schedule," http://freepages.rootsweb.com/~ajac/genealogy/almacon.htm., accessed 10/24/2018.
6. According to the 1860 census, there were 1020 slaveholders in Macon County out of white population of 8,624, see, Historical Census of the United States, accessed 7/15/1999 http://fisher.lib.edu/census.
7. The term "black belt" has been given geological, political and metaphoric readings by a variety of authors, see Houston Baker, Jr., *Blues, Ideology, and Afro-American Literature* (Chicago, IL.: U of Chicago P, 1984), pp. 94–95.
8. Robert J. Norrell, *Reaping the Whirlwind: The Civil Rights Struggle in Tuskegee* (New York: Knopf, 1986), p. 11.
9. Ibid.; Atkins, "From Early Times," pp. 216–17.

they should "hope for nothing, but go to work and behave yourselves."[1] Work in this case meant the instituting of a contract labor that left most former slaves deep inside a crop lien system and outside a cash nexus.[2] Migration in search of better land and more political power was on the minds of many Macon County African Americans as ". . . a local Democratic paper . . . reported in 1876 that one party of forty blacks had just left the county, having been preceded by another group only days before, and that an emigration agent was working secretly in Tuskegee."[3] Between 1860 and 1870 the black population of the county did drop by over 5,000.[4] But the fears on the part of white landowners that they would lose their entire black workforce did not come to fruition.[5] Macon County's black population remained at about 13,000 in the 1870s and 1880s.

* * *

As the story is repeatedly told, it was an ex-Confederate colonel and lawyer in Macon County and an ex-slave who made a political deal that led to the Institute. While seeking election in 1880 to the state senate, Wilbur F. Foster traded voter support in the African American male community through black Republican powerbroker Lewis Adams for the promise of legislative support for black education.[6] Thus, after Foster won his seat, the Alabama legislature made $2000 available for "the Normal School for colored teachers in Tuskegee." The funds, however, couldn't even cover the site of what Booker T. Washington would refer to as "'the Farm' . . . 100 acres of spent farmland on which stood 'a cabin, formally used as a dining room, an old kitchen, a stable and an old hen-house' where the 'big house' had burned down during the war."[7] With almost nothing, Washington began with what may be his own ironic signifying, or an apocryphal image, when he recalled that the first animal given to the school by a local white patron was "an old blind horse."[8]

1. Quoted in John B. Myers, "The Freedman and the Law in Post-Bellum Alabama, 1865–1867," *Alabama Review* 23 (January 1970): 60.
2. William Warren Rogers and Robert David Ward, "From 1865 through 1920," in Rogers et al, *Alabama*, p. 237.
3. Norrell, *Reaping the Whirlwind*, p. 9.
4. Ibid., p. 9. Historian Robert J. Norrell's argument is that there was stability in the post–Civil War years, but he only gives the 1870 and 1880 statistics. The drop of nearly a third of the black population suggests he underestimated the out-migration figures between 1860 and 1870, even if this population change cannot be explained entirely by out-migration.
5. On the importance of the debate over free labor in the post-Civil War years, see Eric Foner, "Reconstruction and the Crisis of Free Labor," *Politics and Ideology in the Age of the Civil War* (New York: Oxford UP, 1980), pp. 97–127.
6. Addie Butler, *The Distinctive Black College* (Metuchen, NJ: Scarecrow Press, 1977), p. 56.
7. Booker T. Washington, *Up from Slavery* (Garden City: Doubleday, 1901), p. 130, quoted in K. Ian Grandison, "From Planation to Campus: Progress, Community, and the Lay of the Land in Shaping the Early Tuskegee," *Landscape Journal* 15 (1996): p. 6.
8. William L. Andrews, ed. *Booker T. Washington Up from Slavery* (New York: Oxford UP, 1996), p. 65.

On this failed and blighted plantation land, Tuskegee Institute
began in Booker T. Washington's imagination and what he believed
were the reflected hopes of both whites and blacks.[9] Recommended
for the leadership of Tuskegee by General Samuel C. Armstrong at
Hampton Institute, over the next three decades Washington created
a critically important educational institution in the rural South. As
he told the story in his carefully crafted and popular 1901 autobiography, *Up from Slavery*, it was his ability to define and realize the
needs of the black rural masses while translating them *publicly* in
the least threatening way possible to the local white population and
to the *noblesse oblige beliefs* of Northern and Midwestern philanthropists that made Tuskegee Institute possible.[1]

*   *   *

On the surface, Washington cooperated with the tightening hold
of Jim Crow segregation that denied black Americans political and
voting rights, underfunded a separate educational system, sustained
economic peonage, and kept power through frequent eruptions of
state-sanctioned violence.[2] Fear of his inability to carefully gauge
how to calculate the appropriate balance of the needs of blacks and
whites and meet the financing of the Institute haunted Washington's
continual efforts. The public mask of accommodation he wore
allowed him to build up a black educational institution with black
faculty and an increasing local middle class of teachers, profession-
als and small landowners. He created a hierarchy of power within
the institution, one based often on skin tone, class, and closeness
to his power.[3] To make all of this work, those at Tuskegee acceded to
"elaborate rituals of segregation" when whites came to visit. They
kept the Institute visibly away from those blacks who directly chal-
lenged the system, and presented white philanthropists with an institution for African American education they could fund without
compromising the sensibilities of the majority of Southern whites.[4]

*   *   *

9. For a sense of Washington's publicly declared intentions for Tuskegee Institute, see *Up
from Slavery*.
1. There is an enormous amount of literature on Booker T. Washington. The most iconic
is Louis Harlan's *Booker T. Washington* (New York: Oxford UP, 2 volumes, 1975) and
the most recent critique of Harlan is Kenneth M. Hamilton, *Booker T. Washington in
American Memory* (Champaign, IL.: U of Illinois P, 2017.)
2. See Leon Litwack, *Trouble in Mind: Black Southerners in the Age of Jim Crow* (New
York: Knopf, 1998) and Louis R. Harlan, "Booker T. Washington in Biographical Perspective," in Andrews, *Booker T. Washington*, pp. 204–19.
3. For insight into the politics of Tuskegee, see Harlan, *Booker T. Washington* and Adele
Logan Alexander, *Homelands and Waterways: The American Journey of the Bond
Family 1846–1926* (New York: Pantheon, 1999).
4. Harlan, *Booker T. Washington*, Volume 2, pp. 165–78.

"The Wizard," as Washington was called, built up the "Tuskegee machine" to become the most well known and powerful black man in early 20th century America. Many of course, most notably W. E. B. Du Bois and William Monroe Trotter, thought Washington's mask too deeply imbedded, too easily read as the real, too simply used to place blame on black Americans for the system that kept them from voting, sanctioned lynching as form of state power, and perpetuated economic serfdom.[5] However cleverly Washington wore the mask, in the end critic Eric Sundquist has noted, his "protest is buried so deep as to be virtually indistinguishable from accommodationism."[6]

※　※　※

CHERENE SHERRARD-JOHNSON

From "A Plea for Color": Nella Larsen's Iconography of the Mulatta[†]

※　※　※

Larsen's Orientalism: "A Fantastic Motley of Ugliness and Beauty"

Quicksand, for several African American feminist critics, is a "portrait of the failed artist as a woman of color."[1] While the exact nature of her potential is never made plain, Helga Crane does possess a visual artist's perception and appreciation of decor, color, and style. Her contemplation of the idea that someone should write a treaty entitled "A Plea for Color?" suggests that writing might have been a productive outlet for her aesthetic views had that option been open to her.[2] Whether Helga is potentially an artist or a writer, her

---

5. The most famous critique is W. E. B. Du Bois, "Of Mr. Booker T. Washington and Others," in Du Bois, *The Souls of Black Folk* (Chicago: A.C. McClurg & Co., 1903), pp. 36–48. [This essay is excerpted in this volume.]
6. Eric Sundquist, *To Wake the Nations: Race in the Making of American Literature* (Cambridge, MA.: Belknap Press, 1993), p. 252.
† From *American Literature* 76.4 (2004): 837–38, 840–42, 844–49, 862–63, 856–69. Copyright, 2004, Duke University Press. All rights reserved. Republished by permission of the copyright holder, Duke University Press. Notes have been renumbered and edited. All notes are the author's unless indicated. Page numbers in square brackets are to this Norton Critical Edition.
1. Thadious M. Davis, *Nella Larsen: Novelist of the Harlem Renaissance, A Woman's Life Unveiled* (Baton Rouge: Louisiana State Univ. Press, 1994), 274.
2. See Nella Larsen, *Quicksand*, in *"Quicksand" and "Passing,"* ed. Deborah E. McDowell (New Brunswick, N.J.: Rutgers Univ. Press, 1996), 18; further references are to this edition and will be cited parenthetically in the text as *Q*. Helga detests the severe color aesthetics that require students at Naxos to wear uniform, unadorned clothing in dismal colors that downplay both their dark skin and their individual style. She secretly loves brilliant colors, and she wants to see African Americans celebrate their complexions with complementary colors that accentuate their difference.

creative and sexual desires are inseparable. Each time she suppresses a sexual desire, she suppresses a creative impulse. A sexualized encounter or quandary precipitates each of her decisions to leave a social or professional environment in what becomes her compulsive search for "a new life" (*Q*, 66) [58].

Helga's struggle for agency and honest self-expression is imperiled by her reluctance to emulate the new race-woman ideal or its ostensible opposite, the Jezebel. Her oscillation between these two prescriptive identities recalls the trope of warring black and white blood responsible for the tragic conclusions of many nineteenth-century mulatta narratives.[3] During her first sojourn in Harlem, Helga is compelled to subscribe to the visual ideal of the New Negro woman depicted in the art and illustrations of periodicals like the *Crisis* and *Opportunity* * * *. A model of service, propriety, and moral character, this figure is, more often than not, light-skinned. Helga's benefactor, Mrs. Hayes-Rore, intensifies Helga's discomfort with the stultifying propriety of the race woman by advising her to perform what she visually represents to others: a light-skinned "colored" woman with, in Dr. Anderson's words, "dignity and breeding"—not the child of an interracial union "born in a Chicago slum" (*Q*, 21) [23]. It is Mrs. Hayes-Rore who introduces Helga to Anne Grey, a widow who takes Helga under her wing and introduces her to Harlem society. Anne "had the face of a golden Madonna, grave and calm and sweet, with shining black hair and eyes. She carried herself as queens are reputed to bear themselves, and probably do not" (*Q*, 45) [42]. In establishing Anne as Helga's model for the ideal race woman, Larsen draws upon popular cultural images, such as the fourteen color portraits of "racial leaders" included in the original edition of Alain Locke's *The New Negro* (1925).[4]

The frontispiece of *The New Negro* is Winold Reiss's *Brown Madonna* (1925), an idealized portrait of an African American mother and infant child emphasizing the race woman's social role. Like Motley, Reiss, who was originally a Bavarian landscape painter, aimed to "portray the soul and spirit of a people."[5] The language Larsen uses to describe the "brownly beautiful" Anne resonates with the tone of Reiss's portraits of Locke's identified "racial leaders," which provide a visual supplement to Locke's occasionally

3. See Werner Sollors, *Neither Black nor White Yet Both* (New York: New York UP, 1997).
4. Alain Locke, *The New Negro: An Interpretation* (New York: Albert and Boni, 1925), 7; further references are to this edition and will be cited parenthetically in the text as *NN*. The first edition contains color portraits of Jean Toomer, Alain Locke, Countee Cullen, Paul Robeson, Charles Johnson, and W. E. B. Du Bois by Winold Reiss in addition to drawings by Miguel Covarrubias and Aaron Douglas. In later editions, Reiss's work is omitted, reducing the incredible interdisciplinary nature of this ground-breaking anthology and eclipsing the efforts of the few white modernist painters who sought to portray African Americans as dignified and sophisticated.
5. Locke, "Notes to the Illustrations," in *The New Negro*, 419.

contradictory characterizations of the "intelligent Negro of to-day" as "inevitably moving forward under the control largely of his own objectives," a figure who welcomes the "new scientific rather than the old sentimental interest" (*NN*, 8). In Reiss's portrait of educator and social organizer Elise McDougald, which accompanies her essay "The Task of Negro Womanhood,"[6] McDougald's golden-brown skin contrasts with her white clothing, which blends into a white background to give the portrait a celestial quality. This quality is mirrored in the other portraits, suggesting the figures' suitability as models to emulate as well as guardians to sift out those who do not fit the mold. Endorsing a womanliness that nurtures others, McDougald's essay draws from sentimental representations of African American women as teachers, homemakers, or nurses engaged in supporting the "uplift" endeavors of New Negro men—the race leaders. Reiss's portrait of McDougald, especially when considered beside his "Type Sketches of Negro Woman," provides a ready reference to better "visualize the New Negro woman at her job" (*NN*, 370). A former teacher and librarian, Larsen was intimately aware of the challenges and constraints of such roles. Her depiction of Anne "as almost too good to be true" and "almost perfect" accentuates the illusory nature of these roles and the difficulty of living up to them (*Q*, 45) [42].

Despite Larsen's equivocating critique, which by turns admires and disdains the New Negro woman, Locke praised *Quicksand* as a "social document of importance, and as well, a loving, moving picture of a type not often in the foreground of Negro fiction, and here treated for the first time with adequacy," demonstrating that he perceived the visual dimensions of Larsen's writing.[7] Through visual tableaux like the textual "golden Madonna," and the Orientalist mulatta that I will discuss presently, Larsen challenges racist and sexist encoding in visual art and interrogates the iconicity of both the race-woman ideal and the mulatta as figures marked by interracial and intraracial desire. The oppositional unity encapsulated by her phrase "a fantastic motley of ugliness and beauty," which she uses to describe the varied hues of "this oppressed race of hers" on display in a Harlem nightclub, deftly captures the conflicting elements of black femininity that surface in *Quicksand* (*Q*, 59) [52]. The New Negro woman, styled as the ideal template for measuring black

---

6. The New Negro woman, writes McDougald, "realizes that the ideals of beauty, built up in the fine arts, have excluded her almost entirely. Instead, the grotesque Aunt Jemimas of the streetcar advertisements proclaim only an ability to serve, without grace of loveliness [*sic*]" ("The Task of Negro Womanhood," *The New Negro*, 369–70). McDougald refers to the advertising industry's popularization of the mammy figure as a promotional icon. (Less than ten years later, of course, the image of the mammy reached epic proportions in John Stahl's film *Imitation of Life* [1934], which features an enormous, neon "Aunt Jemima" flipping pancakes atop a skyscraper.)
7. Alain Locke, "1928: A Retrospective Review," *Opportunity*, January 1929, 9, quoted in Davis, *Nella Larsen, Novelist of the Harlem Renaissance*, 281.

femininity, is a constrained throwback to Victorian womanhood, but she can also be a seductive temptress, or a deceptive, independent modern woman. Helga's quandary, overlaid by the fraught race and class dimensions of the mulatta figure, is analogous to contemporary African American women's struggles to reconcile the template of the race woman with their own self-definitions.

Several tableaux in *Quicksand* establish Helga as exotic and reveal the seemingly contradictory layers of her desire to escape the Jezebel–race woman dilemma and circumvent the objectifying gaze of both black and white spectators. Helga's experiences in Copenhagen and in several visually commodifying moments elsewhere illustrate Larsen's understanding of how racist and sexist projections can penetrate the psyches of both the subject and the observer, preventing Helga from reinventing herself and transcending race. In *Quicksand*'s first tableau, Larsen depicts Helga as a traditional nineteenth-century mulatta figure with fair skin, dark hair, and Caucasian features but situates her within a modern setting saturated with Orientalist motifs. This establishes Helga as a sensualized subject amid the repression and sterility of Naxos, a small, repressive African American college based on Larsen's experiences at Fisk and Tuskegee:

> An observer would have thought her well fitted to that framing of light and shade. A slight girl of twenty-two years, with narrow, sloping shoulders and delicate, but well-turned, arms and legs, she had, none the less, an air of radiant, careless health. In vivid green and gold negligee and glistening brocaded mules, deep sunk in the big high-backed chair, against whose dark tapestry her sharply cut face, with skin like yellow satin, was distinctly outlined, she was—to use a hackneyed word—attractive. Black, very broad brows over soft, yet penetrating, dark eyes, and a pretty mouth, whose sensitive and sensuous lips had a slight questioning petulance and a tiny dissatisfied droop, were the features on which the observer's attention would fasten; though her nose was good, her ears delicately chiseled, and her curly blue-black hair plentiful and always straying in a little wayward, delightful way. (*Q*, 2) [7–8]

*   *   *

* * * Larsen relies on Orientalist representations of African American women to distinguish Helga from the race women at Naxos and in Harlem. Fusing Orientalist imagery with mulatta iconography, Larsen contrasts Helga's personal space with her physical form in a concise passage depicting a decor evocative of Delacroix's exoticism:[8]

8. French painter Eugène Delacroix, who influenced Motley, was especially known for his portrait "Aline, The Mulatress" [*Editor*].

> Only a single reading lamp, dimmed by a great black and red shade, made a pool of light on the blue Chinese carpet, on the bright covers of the books which she had taken down from their long shelves, on the white pages of the opened one selected, on the shining brass bowl crowded with many-colored nasturtiums beside her on the low table, and on the Oriental silk which covered the stool at her slim feet. (Q, 1) [7]

The "blue Chinese carpet," "black and red shade," and "Oriental silk" label the unique, exotic nature of Helga's beauty as Oriental; her clothing, accessories, and furniture are frequently described as "Chinese."

Although Helga's locale changes over the course of the narrative, the Oriental iconography follows her. Larsen deploys this imagery, which relies heavily on stereotypical conceptions of Asian women as sexually submissive, to situate Helga as an exoticized and eroticized figure within the black as well as the white community. At Naxos and in Harlem, Helga's beauty and light skin indicate breeding, but in Denmark, her brown skin has an exotic appeal: "she had enjoyed the interest and admiration which her unfamiliar color and dark curly hair, strange to those pink, white and gold people had evoked" (Q, 55) [50]. The inclusion in Helga's library of Marmaduke Pickthall's Saïd the Fisherman, an English Orientalist novel, indicates Larsen's familiarity with Orientalism as a genre.[9] While Larsen's use of Orientalist imagery to describe Helga is not anti-Orientalist, it does illustrate, whether contentiously or not, the permeation of Western discourse on the other into modern conceptions of the mulatta.[1]

Larsen's iconic representation of black femininity, particularly the exotic construction of Helga's body, raises questions about the place of primitivism in Harlem Renaissance visual art and literature. Larsen's visual tableaux demonstrate her awareness that the intersecting discourses of primitivism, capitalism, sexism, and racism constitute the othering gaze.[2] Primitivist discourse, specifically in the primitive-as-high-art stage, successively popularized by European modern artists like Gauguin and Picasso, governs the other characters' treatment of Helga in Denmark, which is further

---

9. Jean-Auguste-Dominique Ingres's Odalisque with a Slave (1842) epitomizes the proliferation of the mid-nineteenth-century genre of harem paintings in which the white, central figure is served or framed by African or Asiatic figures. It is also no coincidence that this proliferation coincides with the rise of colonialism as a system of economic oppression to replace slavery.
1. See Edward W. Said, Orientalism (New York: Vintage, 1979); and Robert Lee, Orientals: Asian Americans in Popular Culture (Philadelphia: Temple UP, 1999).
2. Primitivism has a long history in the Western psyche as a rationalization for slavery, as does colonialism and the wholesale transport of so-called primitive art from the third to the first world; see Marianna Torgovnick, Gone Primitive: Savage Intellects, Modern Lives (Chicago: U of Chicago P, 1990).

complicated by Helga's complicity in her own commodification. She admits that she "loved color with a passion that perhaps only Negroes and Gypsies know," and amid the delight of receiving so many new clothes, she "gave herself up wholly to the fascinating business of being seen, gaped at, desired" (Q, 74) [64].[3] The tactile pleasure she takes in her own objectification delays her acknowledgement of the consequences that accompany her favored position among the Danes. In Denmark, Helga realizes that whether she is in Europe or the United States, her mixed-raced body renders her an exoticized other. In each setting, her desire to invent herself differently is interrupted as the spectatorial gaze transforms her into a commodity, confirming that internal reinvention, without societal change, leads to alienation. Helga's experiences in Denmark explicitly mark her as subject to rather than an agent of her desire, interrupting the "rapture" and "blissful sensation" of "visualizing herself in different, strange places" (Q, 57) [52].

The painting of Helga that the Danish painter Axel Olsen assures her is the "true Helga Crane" (Q, 88) [76], as well as the costumes he and her aunt select for her, reveal that they see her as an object to be adorned and displayed. Their ideas about primitivism, which they project onto her body, are so entrenched that they emerge in apparently complimentary statements. For instance, her aunt remarks: "You must have bright things to set off the color of your lovely brown skin. Striking things, exotic things," while Olsen observes that Helga has the "warm impulsive nature of the women of Africa" but "the soul of a prostitute" (Q, 68, 87) [59, 75]. Warmth and spontaneity, then, are seen as pure, primitive traits, but Olsen intimates that Helga's "soul" has been tainted by Western notions of commodity exchange. His painting, with its gesture toward Oscar Wilde's *The Picture of Dorian Gray*, portrays a soulless being who can be owned and displayed; it is a purchasable version of Helga as a sexualized, primitive objet d'art. While Olsen's romanticized notions of the primitive woman imply that Helga's sexuality should be free (accessible to him) and natural (she should be willing), the idea that Helga might control her sexuality offends his sensibilities. Walter Benjamin's theorization of the modern prostitute as "commodity and seller in one" doubly applies to Helga, who is defined by her race, sex, and beauty as a commodity shadowed by the history of slavery and illegitimacy.[4] She realizes too late that like her

3. This is the second time that Larsen associates Helga, and African Americans, with gypsies, a significant allusion given the European-Scandinavian context. Gypsies have been Europe's racialized other since their arrival in England at the beginning of the sixteenth century. The migratory connotations of the word *gypsy* identify a lifestyle that reiterates the alienation and dislocation Helga experiences.
4. Rebecca Schneider suggests that "[f]or Walter Benjamin, theorizing modernism, the prostitute presented a prime dialectical image because of the ambivalence inherent in

favorite tea sandwiches, the smørrebrød, which are displayed in an "endless and tempting array" at every social event in Denmark, she is being consumed (*Q*, 77) [68].

Not until Helga attends the minstrel show in Copenhagen does she truly understand the European consumption of black people as spectacle, in spite of assurances she receives that "this foolishness about race" means nothing "here in Denmark" (*Q*, 91) [78]. When Helga attends an American theatrical review, she observes the black performers enacting a masquerade of minstrelsy and American ragtime, playing into Danish perceptions of race and providing the show that Helga is reluctant to perform: "She felt shamed, betrayed, as if these pale pink and white people among whom she lived had suddenly been invited to look upon something in her which she had hidden away and wanted to forget. And she was shocked at the avidity at which Olsen beside her drank it in" (*Q*, 83) [71].

The shock of recognition Helga experiences while watching the performers reminds her that she too has been performing by allowing her aunt and uncle to bedeck her in batik dresses, leopard skins, and Eastern perfume. She feels "like nothing so much as some new and strange species of pet dog being proudly exhibited" (*Q*, 70) [61]. At one of their parties she recognizes that "[n]o other woman in the stately pale-blue room was so greatly exposed" (*Q*, 70) [61]. During this party, she is "effectively posed on a red satin sofa, the center of an admiring group, replying to questions about America and her trip over, in halting, inadequate Danish" (*Q*, 70) [62]. This reclining image of Helga suggests Larsen's familiarity with Paul Colin's feathered drawings of Josephine Baker, who was at the height of her fame as the star of *La Revue Nègre* and the *Folies-Bergère* at the time Larsen was writing.

A dangerous collusion occurs when subjects participate, either inadvertently or willingly, in their exploitation as spectacle. Though Helga is not a singer or dancer, like Baker, she performs her sexuality; and she restricts herself to speaking in broken Danish, just as the newly arrived Baker spoke only in broken French to create, according to Adah "Bricktop" Smith, a "charming" impression and to disguise her working-class St. Louis roots.[5] Although Helga imagines herself as unique, the pervasiveness of the figure of the primitive in European art and imagination indicates that there is nothing new, or flattering, about situating a black woman as an objet d'art; her displayed body evokes Saartje Baartman, the Venus

---

her status as both a 'commodity and seller in one'" (*The Explicit Body in Performance* [New York: Routledge, 1997], 24).

5. Adah "Bricktop" Smith with James Haskins, *Bricktop* (New York: Atheneum, 1983), 108.

Hottentot, who was brought from South Africa to Europe by a Danish entrepreneur and exhibited naked as a specimen and a spectacle.

Visually, Helga's pose on the red satin couch in "practically nothing but a skirt" invokes the reclining nude, (*Q*, 70) [61]. This scene, framed by Olsen's painting of Helga, replaces the white female nude with a light-skinned black subject. Because Helga's beauty and appropriateness as an artistic subject is based on her blackness in the Danish setting rather than her fairness in the Harlem locale, Larsen's replacement of a white with a black subject is not a reinscription but an articulation of the danger of challenging Eurocentric standards of beauty by installing the black female on the objectified pedestal that has been the province of white women. The female nude is not in an enviable position; she is an object of display.[6] This scene in *Quicksand* revises Edouard Manet's *Olympia*, a nude painting of a prostitute and her black maid that caused a scandal in 1863. Manet's painting is the prime representative of the tradition of the reclining nude in which a black woman is used as a marginal figure to intensify the sexual content of the portrait. By situating Helga on Olympia's couch, Larsen engages a modernist tradition of fascination with the contradictory status of the prostitute as Benjamin's "commodity and seller." Though Helga is not a prostitute, her subject position as a black female renders her an accessible commodity, even though she sees herself as being in control of her image and at times enjoys the attention.

By placing Helga on the couch—and black female beauty at the center of the scene—Larsen reverses the black woman's role as the foil for white femininity. Unfortunately, the reversal is undercut by Larsen's replication of Eurocentric standards in Helga's eroticized light-skinned body. However exotic this body may be in Denmark, it is not that different from the body of Manet's Olympia. In a later scene in *Quicksand*, however, Larsen rephrases the relationship between Olympia and her maid by positioning them as viewers rather than subjects of the portrait. In Manet's painting, Olympia gazes directly at the spectator while her black maid's gaze is on Olympia. In *Quicksand*, Larsen's maid, Marie, invalidates Olsen's portrait when Helga, searching for recognition, asks her: "[I]s this a good picture of me?" and Marie replies: "I know Herr Olsen is a great artist, but no, I don't like that picture. It looks bad, wicked" (*Q*, 89) [77]. In condemning this painting, and refusing Olsen's offer, the women interrupt the gaze and insert themselves as spectators viewing

6. John Berger defines the category of the nude as distinct from nakedness: nakedness is natural but nudeness is display (*Ways of Seeing* [London: British Broadcasting Company, 1972]). That is why, with few exceptions, the eyes of the nude subject are averted so that her gaze does not disturb the spectator's pleasure.

Olsen's art, just as Olympia's gaze and the gaze of her maid discon-
cert viewers by preventing easy identification and erotic pleasure.

Olsen refers to his painting of Helga as the "true Helga Crane"
and pronounces it a "tragedy" (*Q*, 88) [76]. The tragedy, of course,
is that Olsen has projected into his painting the very gaze that
thwarts Helga's ability to express herself creatively and sexually.
Modern portrait painters, unlike the realists who preceded them,
sought to capture more than the superficial facade of a subject; they
wanted to paint the inner workings of the psyche and the soul. * * *
Olsen believes he has captured Helga's sensual nature, which he
presumes she is suppressing by refusing his marriage proposal. Helga
attempts to disassociate herself from the painting as she always does
from situations that disturb her: "It wasn't, she contended, herself
at all, but some disgusting sensual creature with her features" (*Q*,
89) [77]. However, like Helga, the portrait is praised by critics enam-
ored with the primitive, and it "attracted much flattering attention
and many tempting offers" (*Q*, 89) [71].

Once Helga has returned to Harlem, her eroticized, mulatta body
is seen as primitive by the middle-class African American community. Anne Grey, now the newly married Mrs. Anderson, avoids
Helga, apprehensive at the thought that her new husband might also
encounter her. Lurking beneath the surface of intellectual interests
and polite behavior, Anne fears, is "a vagrant primitive groping
toward something shocking" (*Q*, 95) [81]. In an impulsive act that
appears to justify Anne's perception of Helga's appeal, Dr. Anderson kisses Helga shortly after her chilly reception from Anne. The
kiss encourages Helga to allow herself to finally act on the "ecstasy
which had flooded" her during their encounter (*Q*, 105) [88]. But
Dr. Anderson ultimately dismisses the kiss with a "trivial apology"
and "direct refusal," thus preventing Helga from fulfilling the
"desire" that "burned in her flesh with uncontrollable violence"
(*Q*, 109) [91]. In response to this rejection, she slaps him "savagely"
(*Q*, 108) [90]. Ironically, the "primitive" diction that describes both
the encounter and Helga's response to it suggests that the "true
Helga Crane" featured in Olsen's painting may not have been that
far off the mark (*Q*, 88) [76]. Together, the kiss and Dr. Anderson's
rejection precipitate Helga's religious epiphany and her subsequent repressive marriage to a Southern preacher. Unable to reconcile two seemingly oppositional aspects of mulatta identity, the
Jezebel and the madonna, Larsen's musings on the tragic mulatta as a
black female artist end as Helga's domestic responsibilities stifle
her creativity. Her potential for artistic or intellectual production
is subsumed beneath the reproductive duties of a wife.

* * *

The mulatta, as the representative of American anxieties of miscegenation, patriarchy, citizenship, and legal racial classification, is an icon whose shrine we both worship and scorn. An integral part of African American literary history and visual culture, she appears in a variety of media and artistic productions, a hidden national icon whose desirability disturbs us, even if her beauty, like Dorcas's light-skinned but "hoofmark[ed]" face in Toni Morrison's *Jazz*, is flawed.[7] We fear her allure yet are inevitably drawn to her, as Irene is drawn to Clare in *Passing*. The mulatta figure of the twenty-first century still has the potential to be tragic, but contemporary writers and scholars are attempting to mine the mulatta and her accompanying iconography for her transgressive potential, focusing on her capacity to traverse rigid class and race hierarchies. Avant-garde works such as Adrienne Kennedy's *Funnyhouse of a Negro*, or singer Laura Love's Afro-Celt folk-song "Octoroon," take the icon into new, global directions. However, even those who excise tragedy from the trope have to understand the historical and cultural context of its legacy. While the mulatta figure was a marketable fixture in Harlem Renaissance literature, visual art, and popular culture, she remains a contradictory figure, idealized on one hand and demonized on the other. Visual portraits and fiction about the mulatta often manifest these aspects simultaneously, but it is only through attending to the dialogue that occurs between visual renderings and fictional portrayals of the mulatta that the collaborative nature of these artistic endeavors is rendered intelligible. Continued probing into both the obvious and circuitous visual and literary intersections during the Harlem Renaissance exposes a fertile interdisciplinary plain in the Afro-modernist landscape. By placing Larsen's novels in conversation with Motley's paintings, the complex contours of what some might consider an overwrought trope can be examined in a new light, and Larsen's writing can be understood as a fundamentally dialogic undertaking, as interartistic as it is intertextual.

7. Toni Morrison, *Jazz* (New York: Knopf, 1992), 130.

Nella Larsen: A Chronology[*]

1868   Mother, Mary Hensen (spelled Hanson in some accounts and Hensen in others), born.

1890   July 1, marriage license issued to Mary Hensen (white; Danish) and Peter Walker (black; West Indian).

1891   Mary Hensen marries Peter Larsen/Larson, according to census records. D gives date as March 7.
        April 13, Nella is born Nellie Walker in Chicago (listed as born in New York in some sources and as born in 1893 and 1892 in others) to Mary Hansen Walker ("white") and Peter Walker ("colored"). Nella's birth certificate lists her as "colored."

1892   June 21, sister Anna ("Lizzie") Larsen is born. D gives this birthdate as 1893. Anna is listed as "white."

1895   Nella travels to Denmark with her mother and her sister Anna, according to F and H.

1898–   D surmises that Nella may have spent these years in the
1900   Erring Women's Refuge for Reform on Chicago's South Side, placed there to help the rest of the family pass for white. H reports, however, that on April 19, 1898, Nella sailed from Denmark to New York with her mother and sister, on the SS *Norge*.

1898–99 Begins school at a private kindergarten, then at Moseley and moves with her family to 201 22nd Street in Chicago, according to H. According to F, they live first at 325 22nd Street.

1901   According to D, Larsen is enrolled in Colman Primary School as Nellie Larson in September by Peter Larson, who lists himself as "Father." H gives the date of her Colman enrollment as 1903.

1903   According to H, Nella enters seventh grade at Colman Primary School. The family moves to 4538 State Street.

---

[*] Compiled primarily from Larsen biographies by Thadious Davis (D), George Hutchinson (H), and Charles Larson (L), as well as from a recent chronology by DoVeanna Fulton (F). As there is significant disagreement among Larsen's principal biographers about even some basic facts of her life, variant versions of her biography are noted as abbreviated above, when possible.

1905   Nella is enrolled as Nellye Larson by Peter Larson, "Parent," in the Wendell Phillips High School.

1907   The Larsens purchase a home on West 70th Place. According to D, Peter Larson changes his name to Larsen. Nella enrolls in the Fisk Normal School in Nashville, Tennessee, as Nellie Marie Larsen, according to H and as Nella Larsen according to D.

1908   According to H, the Fisk faculty vote not to invite Nella to return after her first year; D suggests she completed only one semester. F writes that she, and some teachers, are expelled for violating dress codes.

1908–12   D calls these the "mystery" years and suggests that Nella may have spent them in Chicago in an illicit interracial relationship. According to H, Nella sailed to Denmark at least once and perhaps twice during these years and is listed on ships' manifests as returning from Denmark to New York in both 1909 and 1912. In Denmark she audits courses at the University of Copenhagen.

1912   Enters Lincoln Hospital and Home Training School for Nurses in May.

1915   Nella is licensed as a Registered Nurse under the name Nella Marian Larsen on May 1 and attends graduation on May 13. In October, accepts position of Head Nurse at Tuskegee Institute Training School for Nurses, starting work in October according to D and early November according to H. (This experience becomes the basis for descriptions of "Naxos" in her novel *Quicksand*.)

1916   Mary, Peter, and Anna Larsen relocate to 6418 Maryland Avenue in Chicago. In August, attends annual meeting of the National Association of Colored Graduate Nurses. On October 10, resigns from Tuskegee and, according to H, is released immediately from her duties, although she requested a month's time. According to D, returns to Lincoln Hospital as a visiting nurse.

1916–18   According to F, returns to Lincoln to teach courses in pharmacology and nursing history.

1918   According to L, Nella works for New York City Department of Health. According to H, she sits for the "Healthy Drive nursing exam" and works for Health Department's Bureau of Preventable Diseases. According to D, Nella is appointed District Nurse in New York Department of Health and also is professionally active in a visiting nurse association dedicated to working with the Circle for Negro War Relief. Nella and Elmer Imes meet in late summer or early fall.

1919   Nella Marian marries Elmer Imes on May 3 in the chapel of Union Theological Seminary. According to D, they move to Imes's apartment in Staten Island. H locates them at 984 Morris Avenue in the Bronx.

1920   Publishes "Three Scandinavian Games" and "Danish Fun" in *The Brownies' Book* in June and July.

1921   According to D, Nella and Elmer move to 51 Audobon Avenue in Jersey City. H locates them living in Harlem at 34 W. 129th Street, apartment 17, that same year, in January. From May to September, Nella volunteers to organize New York's first "Negro Art Exhibit," which took place from August 1 to October 11. According to D, Nella resigns from the Board of Health on September 15. H dates the resignation as October 4. According to H, Nella becomes "substitute assistant" at the 135th Street Branch of the New York Public Library (NYPL) in September. D dates this assignment as beginning in January of 1922.

1922   Larsen family moves to California, and Mary Larsen sells the house on Maryland Avenue. According to D, Mary does not join the family there until 1928.

1923   In June, Nella receives her library certificate and attends commencement on June 8. On July 1, returns to the 135th Street Branch of the NYPL as Assistant Librarian, Grade II, according to D. According to H, she takes the NYPL exams in October and passes, then begins work in November at the Seward Branch of the NYPL in the Children's Division. Becomes a regular at many Harlem Renaissance gatherings where she meets Walter White, Carl Van Vechten, Fania Marinoff, Donald Angus, and others. In May, Nella's review of *Certain People of Importance* is published in *The Messenger*.

1924   According to D, Nella is promoted to Children's Librarian at the 135th Street Branch.

1925   Takes leave of absence from NYPL in October and resigns in January of 1926, when her leave expires. Joins a Gurdjieff group organized by Jean Toomer.

1926   Publishes "The Wrong Man" and "Freedom" in *Young's Magazine* (January and April) under the name Allen Semi. In September, *Opportunity* publishes her review of *Flight*.

1927   According to D, Peter Larsen dies sometime between January 1927 and fall of 1928. In March, following revisions, Knopf formally accepts *Quicksand* for publication. In April, Nella and Elmer move to 236 W. 135th Street, apartment 5A.

1928   *Quicksand* is published by Knopf in March and is
             awarded the Harmon Foundation's Bronze Award for
             Literature in December. In May, Nella and Elmer
             move to the famous Dunbar Apartments, living at
             2588 Seventh Avenue, apartment 6N. In April, Eddie
             Wasserman hosts a large book party for her. In May,
             favorable reviews of *Quicksand* begin to appear, and
             the NAACP hosts a tea for Nella that, according to H,
             is rescheduled to May 20 and, according to D, Nella
             could not attend because of illness. By July, there are
             signs of problems in the Imeses marriage. By fall,
             Nella completes a draft of *Passing*, which is accepted
             by Knopf.

1929   In January, publishes a review of *Black Sadie* in *Oppor-
             tunity*. In March, according to D, Nella goes back to the
             library for five months for extra income and does so
             again, briefly, in October. According to H, these periods
             are somewhat shorter. In April, *Passing* is published;
             Nella is honored by a tea hosted by Blanche Knopf. Nella
             speaks at "Authors' Night" at the St. George Playhouse
             in Brooklyn with Walter White on April 14. In May,
             Elmer accepts an appointment as Head of the Physics
             Department at Fisk University, to begin in winter of
             1930. In November, Nella applies for a Guggenheim Fel-
             lowship. In December, the NAACP publishes an excerpt
             from *Quicksand* in its Benefit Concert program booklet.

1930   Publishes "Sanctuary" in *Forum* in January and is
             accused of plagiarism. In March, receives the Guggen-
             heim Fellowship. In May, goes to Fisk to join Elmer.
             Sometime in late summer or fall, Nella confronts Elmer
             about his affair with white, fellow Fisk professor Ethel
             Gilbert.

1930   Travels to Spain on her Guggenehim. D dates her
             departure as September 9. H locates her leaving on the
             SS *Patria* on September 19. While overseas, lives in
             Spain and France and works on *Mirage*.

1931   In January, requests an extension of her Guggenheim
             Fellowship. By March, a romance with Norman Cam-
             eron has begun to sour, and in April, Nella leaves Spain
             for France. In Paris stays first at the Hotel Paris-Dinard
             then moves, in July, to an apartment at 31 bis rue Cam-
             pagne Première. In late summer or early fall, is informed
             that Knopf has rejected *Mirage*. In fall, returns to Spain
             with Dorothy Peterson, and in November they travel to
             North Africa and then back to Spain again.

1932   In January, returns to New York and moves, in late February (H) or March (D), into brownstone apartment at 53 W. 11th Street. During this time, she is ill with pleurisy. In April (D) or May (H) joins Elmer at Fisk (L has him teaching at Vanderbilt at this time). In June, returns briefly to New York. In July, renews her passport and writes Dorothy Peterson that she is working again on *Mirage*. In September, Nella and Imes move into a new home in Nashville. In the fall, Nella is friendly, perhaps romantically, with Tom Mabry.

1933   In the summer, collaborates with Edward Donahoe, also a possible romance. Over spring and summer, Nella and Elmer's marriage deteriorates further, and Nella either falls or jumps out of a window of their home, inciting further scandal. Nella divorces Elmer on grounds of "cruelty," on August 30, in Davidson County, Tennessee. In September, travels briefly to Chicago before returning to New York, where she stays with Dorothy Peterson before taking an apartment on the Lower East Side. In October, the *Baltimore Afro-American* reports on the Larsen/Imes divorce and subsequently on the Larsen/Imes/Gilbert love triangle. In December, Nella lists her address as the Manual Training School at Bordentown and later takes over Dorothy Peterson's apartment at 320 Second Avenue. In December, Nella also works with the Independent Writers' Committee Against Lynching as Assistant Secretary.

1934–37 Friendships with her former friends continue to diminish; some express concern about her.

1940   Moves from 320 Second Avenue to 315 Second Avenue.

1941   Elmer dies on September 11. Nella runs into old friends on the street, sparking rumors about possible drug or alcohol abuse.

1942   June 17, Nella attends a memorial birthday celebration for James Weldon Johnson at the 115th Street Branch Library.

1944   February 14 is appointed Chief Nurse at Gouverneur Hospital.

1951   Mary Larsen dies in Santa Monica Hospital in September.

1954   Applies for a Social Security card in January. Resigns from Gouverneur Hospital in the spring but is rehired as Night Supervisor in the fall.

1956–57 According to F, is promoted to Supervisor over head nurses.

1959   In October, Nella writes a will naming her friend Alice Carper as beneficiary.

1960   Nella is mugged in front of the hospital and suffers a broken arm.

1961   In March, the City of New York tells Gouverneur to stop accepting patients.

1962   Accepts position as Supervisor of Nurses at Metropolitan Hospital, New York.

1963   In February, Nella is scheduled to begin working as the Night Supervisor in the Psychiatric Ward. In April, travels to Santa Monica to see her sister Anna, who refuses to acknowledge her. In June, found to be past legal retirement age, Nella is forced to take a three-month leave and works her last shift on June 22. On September 12, Nella is officially listed as retired.

1964   March 30, Nella is discovered dead in her apartment by the building supervisor. Her funeral is arranged by Alice Carper and takes place on April 6 at the Miles Funeral Home. Nella is buried in the Carper family plot. On April 7 the *New York Times* reports Nella's death. According to F, her death is listed as a heart attack, occurring on March 29, Easter Sunday.

Selected Bibliography[†]

• Indicates works included or excerpted in this Norton Critical Edition.

LARSEN'S WORK

Larsen, Nella. "The Author's Explanation." [Letter Explaining the Circumstances under Which "Sanctuary" Was Written]. *Forum* April 1930: supl. 41–42.

———. *The Complete Fiction of Nella Larsen*. Ed. Charles R. Larson. New York: Anchor Books, 2001.

———. "Correspondence." [on Walter White's *Flight*.] *Opportunity* (September 1926): 295.

———. "Danish Fun." *The Brownies' Book* (July 1920): 219.

• ———. "Our Book Shelf [Review of *Black Sadie*. By T. Bower Campbell]." *Opportunity* (January 1929): 24.

———. "Playtime: Three Scandinavian Games." *The Brownies Book* 1 (June 1920): 191–92.

———. *Quicksand*. Ed. DoVeanna S. Fulton. Boston: Bedford St. Martin's, 2017.

———. *Quicksand*. Ed. Thadious Davis. New York: Penguin Books, 2002.

———. *Quicksand and Passing*. Ed. Deborah E. McDowell. New Brunswick: Rutgers UP, 1986.

———. "Review of *Certain People of Importance* by Kathleen Norris." *Messenger* V (May 1923): 713.

• ———. "Sanctuary." *Forum* 83 (January 1930): 15–18.

———. "The Wrong Man." *Young's Realistic Stories Magazine* 51 (1926): 3–9.

REVIEWS OF *QUICKSAND* AND NOTICES

"12 Negroes Honored for Achievement." *New York Times*, January 3, 1929: 12.

"19 Negro Physicians on Hospital Staff." *Hamilton Daily News*, February 27, 1930: 8.

† By Hanna Musiol, with help from Lauren Kuryloski and Sarah Payne.

"Activities among Negroes." *Oakland Tribune*, February 24, 1929: T9.

The Associated Press. "Writers to Appeal to Roosevelt." *New York Times*, December 5, 1933: 3.

• Bennett, Gwendolyn B. "The Ebony Flute." *Opportunity* (May 30, 1928): 153.

• "Bids for Literary Laurels." "[Review of *Quicksand*. no author]." *Chicago Defender*, May 12, 1928: A1.

• "Book a Week." *Baltimore Afro-American*, May 15, 1928: 6.

"Books for Vacation." *Chicago Defender*, July 1928: A2.

"Books on the Race." *Chicago Defender*, April 25, 1931: 15.

"Books Recently Added to the Library." *Pittsburgh Monthly Bulletin*, (June 1928): 321.

• Bradford, Roark. "Books: Mixed Blood." *New York Herald Tribune*, May 13, 1928: 522.

• Brascher, Nahum Daniel. "Random Thoughts." *Chicago Defender*, September 30, 1933: 11.

De Haven Tracy, Morris. "Books of the Week." *Montana Standard* [Butte], April 28, 1929: 4.

Du Bois, W. E. B. "The Sorrow Songs." *The Souls of Black Folk*. Ed. Henry Louis Gates Jr. and Terri Oliver Hume. New York: W. W. Norton and Company, 1999, 154–64.

• ———. "Two Novels." *The Crisis* (June 1928): 202, 211.

• Fauset, Arthur Huff. "*Quicksand*." *Black Opals* (June 1928): 19–20.

• Gordon, Barefield. "The Quest of Life." *Chicago Defender*, August 25, 1928: A1.

• Gordon, Eugene. "Negro Fictionist[s] in America." *Saturday Evening Quill* 2 (April 1928), 18–19.

"Guggenheim Fund Makes 85 Grants" *New York Times*, March 24, 1930: 28.

• G. W. K. "New Novels." *New Statesman* (2 June 1928): 259–60.

• Hayden, Katharine Shepard. [Review of *Quicksand*]. *Annals of the American Academy of Political and Social Science* 140 (November 8, 1928): 344–45.

• "[H]onor Author of 'Quicksand' at Tea." *Chicago Defender*, 26 May 1928: 11.

• H. W. R. "*Quicksand*: A Story of the Revolt of a Negro School Teacher." *Boston Evening Transcript*, June 20, 1928: 2.

"In *Opportunity*." *Chicago Defender*, 5 Jan. 1929: A1.

"Intimate Talk on Theatre." *New York Times*, December 6, 1928: 35.

Jacobs, George W. "Negro Authors Must Eat." *The Nation* (June 12, 1929): 710–11.

• Johnson, Charles S. "An Opportunity for Negro Writers." *Opportunity* (September 1924): 258.

Johnson, James Weldon. "Since Lincoln Freed the Negro." *Billings Gazette*, February 11, 1934: 2–3, 15.

"[Larsen, Nella. *Quicksand*. Knopf]." *Monthly Bulletin of Carnegie Library of Pittsburgh* (June 1928): 321.

• Latimer, Margery. "Nella Larsen's 'Quicksand.'" *Book World*, July 22, 1928: 7M.

• Locke, Alain. "1928: A Restrospective Review." *Opportunity* (January 1929): 8–11.

• Matthews, T. S. "What Gods! What Gongs!" *The New Republic*, May 30, 1928: 50–51.

• "Miscegenation? Bah!" *New York Amsterdam News*, May 16, 1928: 16.

• Mortimer, Raymond. "New Novels." *The Nation and Athenaeum* [London], June 23, 1928: 397.

"A Mulatto Girl" *New York Times Book Review*, April 8, 1928: 16–17.

• "The New Books." *Saturday Review of Literature*, May 19, 1928: 895–96.

• "New Books and Reprints." *Times Literary Supplement*, July 26, 1928: 553.

"Novelist Here." *Chicago Defender*, September 23, 1933: 4.

"Novelist Secures Guggenheim Prize." *Chicago Defender*, March 29, 1930: 1.

"[Obituary—No Title]." *New York Times*, April 7, 1964: 35.

• Ovington, Mary White. "Book Chat." NAACP Press Release, August 3, 1928.

• Parsons, Alice Beal. "Three Novels." *The Nation*, May 9, 1928: 540.

"*Quicksand*, by Nella Larsen." *The World Tomorrow* (November 1928): 474.

• R. H. A. [*Quicksand*, by Nella Larsen]. *The Canadian Forum* (1928): 730.

• Root, E. Merrill "Ebony Hour-Hand, Pointing Midnight." *Christian Century*, October 18, 1928: 1261–62.

• Schuyler, George S. "Views and Reviews." *Pittsburgh Courier*, April 14, 1928: 2, 8.

• "Selections from the New Spring Fiction." *Manitoba Free Press*, June 4, 1928: 12.

• Thurman, Wallace. "High, Low, Past and Present." *Harlem* (November 1928): 32.

• Walton, Eda Lou. "*Quicksand*, by Nella Larsen." *Opportunity* (July 1928): 212–13.

"Who's Who." *Opportunity* (January 1929): 25.

• Yates, Ruth L. "[Review of *Quicksand*]." *Pittsburgh Courier*, May 26, 1928: 20.

QUICKSAND BIBLIOGRAPHY

Ahad, Badia Sahar. "The Anxiety of Birth in Nella Larsen's *Quicksand*." *Freud Upside Down: African American Literature and Psychoanalytic Culture*. Urbana: U of Illinois P, 2010. 39–59.

Anisimova, Irina. "Masks of Authenticity: Failed Quests for the People in *Quicksand* by Nella Larsen and *The Silver Dove* by Andrei Belyi." *Comparatist* 32 (2008): 175–92.

Baggett, Marybeth Davis. "Narrating the Gaze in Nella Larsen's *Quicksand*." *Griot: Official Journal of the Southern Conference on Afro-American Studies, Inc.* 31.2 (2012): 66–76.

Balshaw, Maria. "'Black Was White': Urbanity, Passing and the Spectacle of Harlem." *Journal of American Studies* 33.2 (1999): 307–22.

Bande, Usha. "'Only Connect' and the Failure to Connect: A Comparative Study of Anita Desai's Sita and Nella Larsen's Helga." *Notes on Contemporary Literature* 25.2 (1995): 5–7.

Barbeito, Patricia Felisa. "'Making Generations' in Jacobs, Larsen, and Hurston: A Genealogy of Black Women's Writing." *American Literature: A Journal of Literary History, Criticism, and Bibliography* 70.2 (1998): 365–95.

Barnett, Pamela E. "'My Picture of You Is, after All, the True Helga Crane': Portraiture and Identity in Nella Larsen's *Quicksand*." *Signs* 20.3 (1995): 575–600.

Barnhart, Bruce. "Rhythmicizing the Novel: Temporal Taxonomies from Larsen to Hemingway, Stein to Hughes." *Jazz in the Time of the Novel: The Temporal Politics of American Race and Culture*. Tuscaloosa: U of Alabama P, 2013. 152–209.

Beemyn, Brett. "A Bibliography of Works by and About Nella Larsen." *African American Review* 26.1 (1992): 183–88.

Bender, Bert. "Harlem, 1928: The Biology of the Black Soul and the 'Rising Tide of Rhythm.'" *Evolution and "the Sex Problem": American Narratives During the Eclipse of Darwinism*. Kent: Kent State UP, 2004. 244–97.

Berg, Allison. "Fatal Contradictions: Nella Larsen's *Quicksand* and the New Negro Mother." *Mothering the Race: Women's Narratives of Reproduction, 1890–1930*. Urbana: U of Illinois P, 2002. 103–32.

Bone, Martyn. "*Den Sorte*: Nella Larsen and Denmark." *Afro-Nordic Landscapes: Equality and Race in Northern Europe*. New York: Routledge, Taylor & Francis Group, 2014. 208–26.

———. "Intertextual Geographies of Migration and Biracial Identity: *Light in August* and Nella Larsen's *Quicksand*." *Faulkner and Formalism: Returns of the Text*. Ed. Annette Trefzer and Ann J. Abadie. Jackson, MS: U of Mississippi P, 2012. 144–62.

Brickhouse, Anna. "Nella Larsen and the Intertextual Geography of *Quicksand*." *African American Review* 35.4 (2001): 533–60.

Calloway, Licia Morrow. "Elite Rejection of Maternity in Nella Larsen's *Quicksand* and *Passing*." *Black Family (Dys)Function in Novels by Jessie Fauset, Nella Larsen & Fannie Hurst*. New York: Peter Lang, 2003.

Capo, Beth Widmaier. *Textual Contraception: Birth Control and Modern American Fiction*. Columbus: Ohio State UP, 2007.

Carby, Hazel V. "The Quicksands of Representation." *Reconstructing Womanhood: The Emergence of the Afro-American Woman Novelist*. New York: Oxford UP, 1987. 163–75.

Chandler, Karen M. "Nella Larsen's Fatal Polarities: Melodrama and Its Limits in *Quicksand*." *CLA Journal* 42.1 (1998): 24–47.

Christian, Barbara. "The Rise and Fall of the Proper Mulatta." *Black Women Novelists: The Development of a Tradition, 1892–1976*. Westport, CT: Greenwood Press, 1980. 35–61.

Clark, W. Bedford. "The Heroine of Mixed Blood in Nella Larsen's *Quicksand*." *Identity and Awareness in the Minority Experience: Past and Present*. Ed. George E. Carter and Bruce L. Mouser. La Crosse: Institute for Minority Studies, U of Wisconsin-La Crosse, 1975. 225–38.

Clemmen, Yves W. A. "Nella Larsen's *Quicksand*: A Narrative of Difference." *CLA Journal* 40.4 (1997): 458–66.

Cohen, Paula Marantz. "Creative Plagiarism." *Chronicle of Higher Education* 59.9 (2012): B11–13.

Craig, Layne Parish. "'That Means Children to Me': The Birth Control Movement in Nella Larsen's *Quicksand*." *Gender Scripts in Medicine and Narrative*. Ed. Marcelline Block, Angela Laflen, and Rita Charon. Newcastle upon Tyne, England: Cambridge Scholars, 2010. 156–77.

———. "'That Means Children to Me': The *Birth Control Review* in Harlem." *When Sex Changed: Birth Control Politics and Literature between the World Wars*. New Brunswick, NJ: Rutgers UP, 2013.

Cutter, Martha J. "Sliding Significations: Passing as Narrative and Textual Strategy in Nella Larsen's Fiction." *Passing and the Fictions of Identity*. Ed. Elaine K. Ginsberg. Durham, NC: Duke UP, 1996. 75–100.

Dagbovie-Mullins, Sika A. "From Naxos to Copenhagen: Helga Crane's Mixed Race Aspirations in Nella Larsen's *Quicksand*." *Crossing B(l)ack: Mixed-Race Identity in Modern American Fiction and Culture*. Knoxville: U of Tennessee P, 2013. 27–50.

Davis, Sara. "The Red Thing: Fabrics and Fetishism in Nella Larsen's *Quicksand*." *Skin, Culture, and Psychoanalysis*. Ed. Sheila Cavanagh, Angela Failler, and Rachel Alpha. New York: Palgrave Macmillan, 2013. 90–114.

Davis, Thadious. *Nella Larsen, Novelist of the Harlem Renaissance: A Woman's Life Unveiled*. Baton Rouge: Lousiana State UP, 1994.

Dawahare, Anthony. "The Gold Standard of Racial Identity in Nella Larsen's *Quicksand* and *Passing*." *Twentieth Century Literature: A Scholarly and Critical Journal* 52.1 (2006): 22–31.

Dean, Sharon, and Erlene Stetson. "Flower-Dust and Springtime: Harlem Renaissance Women." *Radical Teacher: A Newsjournal of Socialist Theory and Practice* 18 (1980): 1–8.

DeFalco, Amelia. "Jungle Creatures and Dancing Apes: Modern Primitivism and Nella Larsen's *Quicksand*." *Mosaic: A Journal for the Interdisciplinary Study of Literature* 38.2 (2005): 19–35.

Dittmar, Linda, and Suzanne W. Jones. "When Privilege Is No Protection: The Woman Artist in *Quicksand* and *The House of Mirth*." *Writing the Woman Artist: Essays on Poetics, Politics, and Portraiture*. Philadelphia: U of Pennsylvania P, 1991. 133–54.

Doyle, Laura. "Transnationalism at Our Backs: A Long View of Larsen, Woolf, and Queer Racial Subjectivity in Atlantic Modernism." *Modernism/Modernity* 13.3 (2006): 531–59.

———. "Liberty, Race, and Larsen in Atlantic Modernity: A New World Genealogy." *Geomodernisms: Race, Modernism, Modernity*. Ed. Laura Doyle and Laura Winkiel. Bloomington: Indiana UP, 2005. 51–76.

———. "Queering Freedom's Theft in Nella Larsen." *Freedom's Empire: Race and the Rise of the Novel in Atlantic Modernity, 1640–1940*. Durham, NC: Duke UP, 2008. 393–412.

duCille, Ann. "Blues Notes on Black Sexuality: Sex and the Texts of Jessie Fauset and Nella Larsen." *Journal of the History of Sexuality* 3.3 (1993): 418–44.

———. "'The Bourgeois, Wedding Bell Blues of Jessie Fauset and Nella Larsen." *The Coupling Convention: Sex, Text, and Tradition in Black Women's Fiction*. New York: Oxford UP, 1993. 86–109.

Dunbar-Nelson, Alice. "Woman's Most Serious Problem." *The Messenger* 9.3 (March 1927): 73; 86.

Elkins, Marilyn. "Expatriate Afro-American Women as Exotics." *International Women's Writing: New Landscapes of Identity*. Ed. Anne E. Brown and Marjanne Goozé. Westport, CT: Greenwood Press, 1995. 264–73.

English, Daylanne. "W. E. B. Du Bois's Family Crisis." *American Literature: A Journal of Literary History, Criticism, and Bibliography* 72.2 (2000): 291–319.

———. "Selecting the Harlem Renaissance." *Critical Inquiry* 25.4 (1999): 807–21.

———. *Unnatural Selections: Eugenics in American Modernism and the Harlem Renaissance*. Chapel Hill: U of North Carolina P, 2004.

Esteve, Mary. "A 'Moving Mosaic': Harlem, Primitivism, and Nella Larsen's *Quicksand*." *The Aesthetics and Politics of the Crowd in American Literature*. Cambridge, UK: Cambridge UP, 2003. 152–71.

———. "Nella Larsen's 'Moving Mosaic': Harlem, Crowds, and Anonymity." *American Literary History* 9.2 (1997): 268–86.

Favor, Martin. "A Clash of Birthrights: Nella Larsen, the Feminine, and African American Identity." *Authentic Blackness: The Folk in the New Negro Renaissance*. Durham, NC: Duke UP, 1999. 81–110.

Federmayer, Eva. "Theory and Practice: Nella Larsen's Novels in the Hungarian Classroom." *Americana: E-Journal of American Studies in Hungary* 8.2 (2012).

Fleissner, Jennifer. *Women, Compulsion, Modernity: The Moment of American Naturalism*. Chicago: U of Chicago P, 2004.

Fleming, Robert E. "The Influence of Main Street on Nella Larsen's *Quicksand*." *MFS: Modern Fiction Studies* 31.3 (1985): 547–53.

Gallego, Mar. "'Ain't I a Woman' and a Mother?: Sexuality and Motherhood in Nella Larsen's *Quicksand* and *Passing*." *Passing Novels in the Harlem Renaissance: Identity Politics and Textual Strategies*. Münster, Germany: LIT Verlag, 2003. 121–52.

Gates, Henry Louis Jr., and Nellie Y. McKay. "Nella Larsen." *The Norton Anthology of African American Literature*. New York: W. W. Norton and Company, 1997.

Gebhard, Ann O. "The Emerging Self: Young Adult and Classic Novels of the Black Experience." *The English Journal* 82.5 (September 1993): 50–54.

Gilbert, Sandra, and Susan. M. Gubar. "Nella Larsen." *The Norton Anthology of Literature by Women. The Traditions in English / Volume 2, Early Twentieth Century through Contemporary*. New York: W. W. Norton and Company, 2007. 360–443.

Godfrey, Mollie. "Rewriting White, Rewriting Black: Authentic Humanity and Authentic Blackness in Nella Larsen's 'Sanctuary.'" *MELUS* 8.4 (Winter 2013): 122–45.

Goldsmith, Meredith. "Edith Wharton's Gift to Nella Larsen: *The House of Mirth* and *Quicksand*." *Edith Wharton Review* 11.2 (1994): 3–5, 15.

———. "Shopping to Pass, Passing to Shop: Bodily Self-Fashioning in the Fiction of Nella Larsen." *Recovering the Black Female Body: Self-Representations by African American Women*. Ed. Michael Bennett, Vanessa D. Dickerson, and Carla L. Peterson. New Brunswick, NJ: Rutgers UP, 2001. 97–120.

———. "Shopping to Pass, Passing to Shop: Consumer Self-Fashioning in the Fiction of Nella Larsen." *Middlebrow Moderns: Popular American Women Writers of the 1920s*. Ed. Michael

Bennett and Vanessa D. Dickerson. Boston: Northeastern UP, 2003. 263–90.

Gosselin, Adrienne Johnson. "Beyond the Harlem Renaissance: The Case for Black Modernist Writers." *Modern Language Studies* 26.4. Colonizing Theory (1996): 37–45.

Gray, Jeffrey. "Essence and the Mulatto Traveler: Europe as Embodiment in Nella Larsen's *Quicksand*." *Journal of Transnational American Studies* 4.1 (2012): 257–70.

———. "Essence and the Mulatto Traveler: Europe as Embodiment in Nella Larsen's *Quicksand*." *Novel: A Forum on Fiction* 27.3 (1994): 257–70.

Hampton, Gregory J. "Beauty and the Exotic: Writing Black Bodies in Nella Larsen's *Quicksand*." *CLA Journal* 50.2 (2006): 162–74.

Hardwig, Bill. "'A Lack Somewhere': Lacan, Psychoanalysis, and *Quicksand*." *Soundings: An Interdisciplinary Journal* 80.4 (1997): 573–89.

• Harrison-Kahan, Lori. "'Structure Would *Equal* Meaning': Blues and Jazz Aesthetics in the Fiction of Nella Larsen." *Tulsa Studies in Women's Literature* 28.2 (2009): 267–89.

Hart, Jamie. "Who Should Have the Children? Discussions of Birth Control among African-American Intellectuals, 1920–1930." *The Journal of Negro History* 79.1 (Winter 1994): 71–84.

Haviland, Beverly. "Passing from Paranoia to Plagiarism: The Abject Authorship of Nella Larsen." *MFS: Modern Fiction Studies* 43.2 (1997): 295–318.

Hobbs, Allyson. "Searching for a New Soul in Harlem." *A Chosen Exile: A History of Racial Passing in American Life*. Cambridge: Harvard UP, 2014. 175–216.

Hochman, Barbara. "Love and Theft: Plagiarism, Blackface, and Nella Larsen's 'Sanctuary'." *American Literature* 88.3 (2016): 509–40.

Hoeller, Hildegard. "Race, Modernism and Plagiarism." *African American Review*, 2006. 421–37.

Hostetler, Ann E. "The Aesthetics of Race and Gender in Nella Larsen's *Quicksand*." *PMLA: Publications of the Modern Language Association of America* 105.1 (1990): 35–46.

Howard, Lillie P., and Victor A. Kramer. "'A Lack Somewhere': Nella Larsen's *Quicksand* and the Harlem Renaissance." *The Harlem Renaissance Re-Examined*. York: AMS, 1987. 223–33.

Hutchinson, George. "Nella Larsen and the Veil of Race." *American Literary History* 9.2 (1997): 329–49.

———. "*Quicksand* and the Racial Labyrinth." *Soundings: An Interdisciplinary Journal* 80.4 (1997): 543–71.

———. "Subject to Disappearance: Interracial Identity in Nella Larsen's *Quicksand*." *Temples for Tomorrow: Looking Back at the*

Harlem Renaissance. Ed. Geneviève Fabre, and Michel Feith. Bloomington: Indiana UP, 2001. 177–92.

———. *In Search of Nella Larsen: A Biography of the Color Line.* Cambridge: Harvard UP, 2006.

Jenkins, Candice M. "Decoding Essentialism: Cultural Authenticity and the Black Bourgeoisie." *MELUS* 30.3 (2005): 129–54.

John, Caresse A. "Strategic Ambivalence: A Feminist Standpoint Theory Reading of Nella Larsen's Novels." *Feminist Formations* 23.1 (2011): 94–117.

Johnson, Barbara, et al. "The Quicksands of the Self: Nella Larsen and Heinz Kohut." *Female Subjects in Black and White: Race, Psychoanalysis, Feminism.* Berkeley: U of California P, 1997. 252–65.

Kaiser, Laurie. "The Black Madonna: Notions of True Womanhood from Jacobs to Hurston." *South Atlantic Review* 60.1 (January 1995): 97–109.

Karl, Alissa. "Consumerism, Race, and Rationalization in Nella Larsen's *Quicksand.*" *Modernism and the Marketplace: Literary Culture and Consumer Capitalism in Rhys, Woolf, Stein, and Nella Larsen.* New York: Routledge, 2009. 113–39.

Katz, Deborah. "The Practice of Embodiment: Transatlantic Crossings and Black Female Sexuality in Nella Larsen's *Quicksand.*" *Race and Displacement: Nation, Migration, and Identity in the Twenty-First Century.* Ed. Maha Marouan and Merinda Simmons. U of Alabama P, 2013. 43–56.

Kelley, Joyce. "Transdermal Excursions in Larsen, Rhys, and Hall." *Excursions Into Modernism: Women Writers, Travel, and the Body.* Farnham, Surrey: Ashgate Publishing, Ltd., 2016.

Klimasmith, Elizabeth. "Paradoxes of Intimacy: Mobility, Sociology, and the Function of Home in *Quicksand.*" *At Home in the City: Urban Domesticity in American Literature and Culture, 1850–1930.* Durham, NH: U of New Hampshire P, 2005. 191–211.

Knadler, Stephen. "Unsanitized Domestic Allegories: Biomedical Politics, Racial Uplift, and the African American Woman's Risk Narrative." *American Literature* 85.1 (2013): 93–119.

Kocher, Ruth Ellen. "Consequences of Character: Ruth Ellen Kocher on Nella Larsen." *Poets and Writers* 30.1 (2002): 44–48.

Labbé, Jessica. "'Too High a Price': The 'Terrible Honesty' of Black Women's Work in *Quicksand.*" *Meridians: Feminism, Race, Transnationalism* 10.1 (2010): 81–110.

Lackey, Michael. "Larsen's *Quicksand.*" *Explicator* 59.2 (Winter 2001): 103–06.

———. "No Means Yes: The Conversion Narrative as Rape Scene in Nella Larsen's *Quicksand.*" *African American Atheists and Political Liberation: A Study of the Sociocultural Dynamics of Faith.* Gainesville: UP of Florida, 2007. 73–95.

Larson, Charles. *An Imitation of Things Distant: The Collected Fiction of Nella Larsen.* New York: Anchor Books, 1992.

———. *Invisible Darkness : Jean Toomer & Nella Larsen.* Iowa City: U of Iowa P, 1993.

Larson, Kelli A. "Surviving the Taint of Plagiarism: Nella Larsen's 'Sanctuary' and Sheila Kaye-Smith's 'Mrs. Adis.'" *Journal of Modern Literature* 30.4 (2007): 82–104.

Lay, Mary M. "Parallels: Henry James's *The Portrait of a Lady* and Nella Larsen's *Quicksand*." *College Language Association Journal* 20 (1977): 475–86.

———. "Henry James's *The Portrait of a Lady* and Nella Larsen's *Quicksand*: A Study in Parallels." *The Magic Circle of Henry James: Essays in Honour of Darshan Singh Maini.* New York: Envoy, 1989. 73–84.

Lemert, Charles. "The Queer Passing of Analytic Things: Nella Larsen, 1929." *Dark Thoughts: Race and the Eclipse of Society.* New York: Routledge, 2012. 197–220.

Lewis, David L. Ed. "Nella Larsen." *The Portable Harlem Renaissance Reader.* New York: Viking, 1994. 409–85.

Lewis, Jenene. "Women as Commodity: Confronting Female Sexuality in *Quicksand* and the *Awakening*." *MAWA Review* 12.2 (1997): 51–62.

Lewis, Vashti Crutcher, and Harry B. Shaw. "Nella Larsen's Use of the Near-White Female in *Quicksand* and *Passing*." *Perspectives of Black Popular Culture.* Bowling Green, OH: Popular, 1990. 36–45.

Lockridge, Aisha Damali. "Helga Crane: Failed Transnational Diva." *Tipping on a Tightrope: Divas in African American Literature.* New York: Peter Lang, 2012. 22–40.

• Lunde, Arne, and Anna Westerstahl Stenport. "Helga Crane's Copenhagen: Denmark, Colonialism, and Transnational Identity in Nella Larsen's *Quicksand*." *Comparative Literature* 60.3 (2008): 228–43.

Lutes, Jean Marie. "Making Up Race: Jessie Fauset, Nella Larsen, and the African American Cosmetics Industry." *Arizona Quarterly: A Journal of American Literature, Culture, and Theory* 58.1 (2002): 77–108.

Macharia, Keguro. "Queering Helga Crane: Black Nativism in Nella Larsen's *Quicksand*." *MFS: Modern Fiction Studies* 57.2 (2011): 254–75.

Mafe, Diana. "Self-Made Woman in a (Racist) Man's World: The 'Tragic' Lives of Nella Larsen and Bessie Head." *English Academy Review* 25.1 (2008): 66–76.

McDougald, Elise Johnson. "The Task of Negro Womanhood," *The New Negro*, ed. Alain Locke (New York: Touchstone, 1997): 369–82; originally published as "The Double Task: The Struggle of the Negro Women for Sex and Race Emancipation," *Survey Graphic* (March 1925): 698–91.

• McDowell, Deborah E. "'That Nameless . . . Shameful Impulse': Sexuality in Nella Larsen's *Quicksand* and *Passing*." *Black Feminist Criticism and Critical Theory*. Ed. Joe Weixlmann and Houston A. Baker Jr. *Studies in Black American Literature*: 3. Greenwood, FL: Penkevill, 1988. 139–67.

———. *Quicksand and Passing*. New Brunswick, NJ: Rutgers UP, 1986.

McLendon, Jacquelyn Y. *Approaches to Teaching the Novels of Nella Larsen*. New York: The Modern Language Association of America, 2016.

———. "Self-Representation and Art in the Novels of Nella Larsen." *Redefining Autobiography in Twentieth-Century Women's Fiction: An Essay Collection*. Ed. Janice Morgan, and Colette T. Hall. New York: Garland Publishing 1991. 149–68.

———. "Social Nightmare in *Quicksand*." *The Politics of Color in the Fiction of Jessie Fauset and Nella Larsen*. Charlottesville: UP of Virginia, 1995. 71–93.

Monda, Kimberly. "Self-Delusion and Self-Sacrifice in Nella Larsen's *Quicksand*." *African American Review* 31.1 (1997): 23–39.

Moxley, Jennifer. "Things. Things. Things." *There Are Things We Live Among: Essays on the Object World*. Chicago: Flood Editions, 2012. 67–71.

Moynahan, Sinead. "Beautiful White Girlhood?: Daisy Buchanan in Nella Larsen's *Passing*." *African American Review* 47.1 (Spring 2014): 37–49.

• Musiol, Hanna. "Cosmopolitan Intimacies in Nella Larsen's *Quicksand*," in *Creoles, Diasporas, Cosmopolitanisms: Creolization of Nations, Cultural Migrations, Global Languages and Literatures*. Ed. David Gallagher. Dublin and Palo Alto: Academica Press Bethesda, 2011. 461–78.

Muzak, Joanne. "'The Things Which Money Could Give': The Politics of Consumption in Nella Larsen's *Quicksand*." *Agora: An Online Graduate Journal* 2.1 (Winter 2003): 1–18.

Norris, Margot. "Female Transmigration in James Joyce's 'Eveline' and Nella Larsen's *Quicksand*." Ed. Helen Maxson and Daniel Morris. *Reading Texts, Reading Lives: Essays in the Tradition of Humanistic Cultural Criticism in Honor of Daniel R. Schwartz*. Newark: U of Delaware P, 2012. 81–95.

Orlando, Emily J. "Irreverent Intimacy: Nella Larsen's Revisions of Edith Wharton." *Twentieth-Century Literature* 61.1 (2015): 32–62.

Piep, K. H. "Home to Harlem, Away from Harlem: Transnational Subtexts in Nella Larsen's *Quicksand* and Claude McKay's *Home to Harlem*." *Brno Studies in English* 40.1 (2014): 109–121.

Pines, Davida. "Love and Politics of Marriage in Nella Larsen's *Quicksand* and *Passing* and Zora Neale Hurston's *Their Eyes Were Watching God*." *The Marriage Paradox: Modernist Novels and the Cultural Imperative to Marry.* Gainesville: UP of Florida, 2006. 76–92.

Plakkoottam, Alphy J. "Racial and Gender Discrimination in Fiction by Afro-American Women." *Indian Journal of American Studies* 20.1 (1990): 11–19.

Prettyman, Quandra. "Visibility and Difference: Black Women in History and Literature—Pieces of a Paper and Some Ruminations." *The Future of Difference.* Ed. Hester Eisenstein and Alice Jardine. New Brunswick, NJ: Rutgers UP, 1990. 239–46.

Rabin, Jessica G. "'The Mixedness of Things': Nella Larsen." *Surviving the Crossing: (Im)Migration, Ethnicity, and Gender in Willa Cather, Gertrude Stein, and Nella Larsen.* New York: Routledge UP, 2004. 207–13.

Ramsey, Priscilla. "Freeze the Day: A Feminist Reading of Nella Larsen's *Quicksand*." *Afro-Americans in New York Life and History* 9 (1985): 27–41.

Ranson, Portia Boulware. "They Call Me *Mrs.* Imes, But What Do I Call Myself?" *Black Love and the Harlem Renaissance (The Novels of Nella Larsen, Jessie Redmon Fauset, and Zora Neal Hurston): An Essay in African American Literary Criticism.* Lewiston: Edwin Mellen Press, 2005. 39–56.

Rayson, Ann. "Foreign Exotic or Domestic Drudge? The African American Woman in *Quicksand* and *Tar Baby*." *MELUS* 23.2 (1998): 87–100.

Redding, Saunders Jay. "Emergence of the New Negro." *To Make a Poet Black.* College Park, MD: McGrath Publishing Company, 1939. 92–125.

Reddy, Chandan. "Nella Larsen's *Quicksand*: Black Literary Publics During the Interwar Years." *Freedom With Violence: Race, Sexuality, and the US State.* Durham, NC: Duke UP, 2011. 90–133.

Reverby, Susan M. [Hallowed Ground]. Unpublished.

Rhodes, Chip. "'Writing up the New Negro': The Construction of Consumer Desire in the Twenties." *Journal of American Studies* 28.2 (1994): 191–207.

Roberts, Kimberley. "The Clothes Make the Woman: The Symbolics of Prostitution in Nella Larsen's *Quicksand* and Claude McKay's *Home to Harlem*." *Tulsa Studies in Women's Literature* 16.1 (1997): 107–30.

Roffman, Karin. "Nella Larsen: Librarian at 135th Street." *From the Modernist Annex: American Women Writers in Museums and Libraries.* Tuscaloosa: U of Alabama P, 2010. 67–102.

———. "Women Writers and Their Libraries in the 1920s." *Institutions of Reading: The Social Life of Libraries in the United States.* Ed. Thomas Augst and Kenneth Carpenter. Amherst: U of Massachusetts P, 2007. 203–30.

Rosenblum, Lauren M. "'Things, Things, Things': Nella Larsen's *Quicksand* and the Beauty of Magazine Culture." *Communal Modernisms: Teaching Twentieth-Century Literature and Culture in the Twenty-First-Century Classroom.* Ed. Emily M. Hinnov, Laurel Harris, and Lauren M. Rosenblum. New York: Palgrave Macmillan, 2013. 50–61.

Rottenberg, Catherine. "Begging to Differ: Nella Larsen's *Quicksand* and Anzia Yezierska's *Arrogant Beggar*." *African American Review* 41.1 (2007): 87–98.

Rutledge, Gregory. "From Tragic Mulatto to Grotesque Racial Horror: Epic/Exceptionalism and Larsen's *Quicksand*." *Journal of African American Studies* 20.1 (2016): 75–98.

Sasa, Ghada Suleiman. "'It Had Begun, a New Life for Helga Crane': Helga Crane as Femme Fatale in Nella Larsen's *Quicksand*." *The Femme Fatale in American Literature.* Amherst NY: Cambria Press, 2008. 117–140.

Saunders, James Robert. "The Attractive Trap: Helga Crane's Journey to Pleasant Green." *The Wayward Preacher in the Literature of African American Women.* Jefferson, NC: McFarland, 1995. 9–42.

Scheper, Jeanne. "The New Negro *Flaneuse* in Nella Larsen's *Quicksand*." *African American Review* 42.3 (2008): 679–95.

Scruggs, Charles. "Sexual Desire, Modernity, and Modernism in the Fiction of Nella Larsen and Rudolph Fisher." *The Cambridge Companion to the Harlem Renaissance.* Ed. George Hutchinson. Cambridge, UK: Cambridge UP, 2007. 155–69.

• Sherrard-Johnson, Cherene. "'A Plea for Color': Nella Larsen's Iconography of the Mulatta." *American Literature* 76.4 (2004): 833–69.

Silverman, Debra B. "Nella Larsen's *Quicksand*: Untangling the Webs of Exoticism." *African American Review* 27.4 (1993): 599–614.

Simon, Zoltan. "From Lenox Avenue to the Charlotteborg Palace: The Construction of the Image of Europe by Harlem Renaissance Authors." *B. A. S.: British and American Studies/Revista de Studii Britanice si Americane* (4)2 (1999): 105–12.

Solomon, Samuel. "'The Necessity of Reading and Being Read': Barbara Johnson and the Literary Politics of Narcissism." *Differences: A Journal of Feminist Cultural Studies* 21.3 (2010): 97–111.

Stringer, Dorothy. "'Anyone with Half an Eye': Blackness and the Disaster of Narcissism in *Quicksand*." *Not Even Past: Race*

Historical Trauma and Subjectivity in Faulkner, Larsen and Van Vechten. New York: Fordham UP, 2010. 66–87.

Tanner, Laura E. "Intimate Geography: The Body, Race, and Space in Larsen's *Quicksand*." *Texas Studies in Literature and Language* 51.2 (2009): 179–202.

Tate, Claudia. "Desire and Death in *Quicksand*, by Nella Larsen." *American Literary History* 7.2 (1995): 234–60.

Tenorio, Samantha. "Women-Loving Women: Queering Black Urban Space during the Harlem Renaissance." *UCI Undergraduate Research Journal*. XIII (2010): 33–44.

Terry, Jennifer. "City Space: Claims, Cosmopolitanisms and Dwelling: Dionne Brand, Patrick Chamoiseau, C. L. R. James, Nella Larsen, Andrea Levey, Claude McKay, John Edgar Wideman." *Shuttles in the Rocking Loom: Mapping the Black Diaspora in African American and Caribbean Fiction*. Liverpool: Liverpool UP, 2013. 174–215.

Thornton, Hortense E. "Sexism as Quagmire: Nella Larsen's *Quicksand*." *College Language Association Journal* 16.3 (1973): 285–301.

Tolliver, Willie. "The Wings of the Furies: Teaching Nella Larsen and the American Literary Tradition." *Teaching American Literature: A Journal of Theory and Practice* 5.2 (2012): 32–51.

Wagner, Johanna M. "(Be)Longing in *Quicksand*: Framing Kinship and Desire More Queerly." *College Literature* 39.3 (2012): 129–59.

Walker, Rafael. "Nella Larsen Reconsidered: The Trouble with Desire in *Quicksand* and *Passing*." *MELUS* 41.1 (2016): 165–92.

Wall, Cheryl A. "Passing for What? Aspects of Identity in Nella Larsen's Novels." *Black American Literature Forum* 20.1–2 (1986): 97–111.

———. "Nella Larsen: Passing for What?" *Women of the Harlem Renaissance*. Bloomington: Indiana UP, 1995. 85–138.

Wegmann-Sanchez, Jessica. "Rewriting Race and Ethnicity across the Border: Mairuth Sarsfield's *No Crystal Stair* and Nella Larsen's *Quicksand* and *Passing*." *Essays on Canadian Writing* 74 (2001): 136–66.

Weinbaum, Alys Eve. "Racial Masquerade: Consumption and Contestation of American Modernity." *The Modern Girl Around the World: Consumption, Modernity, and Globalization*. Durham, NC: Duke University Press, 2008. 120–46.

West, Elizabeth J. "Transformed Religiosities: Africanity and Christianity in Nella Larsen's *Quicksand* and Zora Neale Hurston's *Jonah's Gourd Vine* and *Their Eyes Were Watching God*." *African Spirituality in Black Women's Fiction: Threaded Visions of Memory, Community, Nature, and Being*. Lanham, MD: Lexington Books, 2011. 149–75.

Whitted, Qiana. "'A Loveless, Barren, Hopeless Western Marriage':
Spiritual Infidelity in the Fiction of Nella Larsen and Alice Walker."
*"A God of Justice?": The Problem of Evil in Twentieth-Century Black
Literature*. Charlottesville: U of Virginia P, 2009. 77–108.

Williams, Bettye J. "Nella Larsen: Early Twentieth-Century Novelist
of Afrocentric Feminist Thought." *College Language Association
Journal* 39.2 (1995): 165–78.

Williams, Erika R. "A Lie of Omission: Plagiarism in Nella Larsen's
Quicksand." *African American Review* 45 (2012): 205–16.

Zackodnik, Teresa C. "Commodified 'Blackness' and Performative
Possibilities in Jessie Fauset's *The Chinaberry Tree* and Nella
Larsen's *Quicksand*." *The Mulatta and the Politics of Race*. Jackson,
MS: UP of Mississippi, 2004. 115–55.

Zafar, Rafia. "A New Negro, A New Woman: Larsen, Fauset, Bonner." Ed. Sacvan Bercovitch, and Cyrus R. K. Patell. *The Cambridge History of American Literature*. Cambridge, UK: Cambridge
UP, 1994. 317–25.

Ziarek, Ewa Plonowska. "The Enigma of Nella Larsen: Letters,
Curse, and Black Laughter." *Feminist Aesthetics and the Politics
of Modernism*. New York: Columbia UP, 2012. 193–27.

DISSERTATIONS

Abdur-Rahman, Samira. *Sites of Instruction: Education, Kinship and
Nation in African American Literature*. Diss. Rutgers The State
University of New Jersey. 2014.

Ahad, Badia Sahar. *"Wonders of the Invisible World": Psychoanalysis
and Border Identities in the Novels of Nella Larsen, Ralph Ellison
and Danzy Senna*. Diss. University of Notre Dame. 2004.

Aid, Katherine. *Making Scenes: Transnational Politics in Performance, 1890–1939*. Diss. University of Pennsylvania. 2014.

Alexander, Torin. *What Meaneth This? A Postmodern "Theory" of
African American Religious Experience*. Diss. Rice University.
2010.

An, Jee. *"There Was a Whole Lot of Grayness Here": Modernity, Geography and "Home" in Black Women's Literature, 1919–1959*. Diss.
The University of Chicago. 2003.

Aronowicz, Yaron. *Fascinated Moderns: The Attentions of Modern
Fiction*. Diss. Princeton University. 2013.

Bash, Rachel. *Standing at the Precipice: Restrained Modernism in the
Fiction of E. M. Forster, Nella Larsen, and Elizabeth Bowen*. Diss.
University of Oregon. 2014.

Bianchi, Cristina. *(De)constructing Identities: Self-Creation in Women
Writers of the Harlem Renaissance*. Diss. University of Ottawa
(Canada). 2002.

Blockett, Kimberly Denise. *Traveling Home/Girls: Movement and Subjectivity in the Texts of Zilpha Elaw, Nella Larsen and Zora Neale Hurston*. Diss. The University of Wisconsin, Madison. 2003.

Broaddus, Virginia. *Sowing Barren Ground: Constructions of Motherhood, the Body, and Subjectivity in American Women's Writing, 1928–1948*. Diss. West Virginia University. 2002.

Brown, Judith. *Violent Fascinations: Reading Glamour in the Fictions of Modernism*. Diss. Tufts University. 2002.

Byron, Lindsay. *Modernism from the Margins: Unruly Women and the Politics of Representation*. Diss. Georgia State University. 2014.

Cunningham, Anne. *The Feminine Aesthetic of Failure: Negative Female Subjectivity in the Modern Novel*. Diss. State University of New York at Stony Brook. 2014.

Dagbovie, Sika. *Black Biracial Crossings: Mixed-race Identity in Modern American Literature and Culture*. Diss. University of Illinois at Urbana-Champaign. 2004.

DeFrancis, Theresa. *Women-Writing-Women: Three American Responses to the Woman Question*. Diss. University of Rhode Island. 2005.

Fanetti, Susan. *The Mirthful Medusa: The Transgressive Act of Writing Women in the Works of Edith Wharton, Willa Cather, Nella Larsen, and Zora Neale Hurston*. Diss. Saint Louis University. 2004.

Feikema, Denise Karachuk. *School Days and Family Ways: Education in African American Literature, 1903–2005*. Diss. University of Connecticut. 2010.

Feldman, Denise. *The Exotic Other and Feminine Virtue: Dilemmas of African American Female Self-Representation in the Novels of Jessie Fauset and Nella Larsen*. Diss. St. John's University. 2009.

Fiero, Erin Ponton. *Signifying on Sigmund: Harlem Renaissance Women Speak Back to Psychoanalysis, Neurasthenia, and the "Fathers" of Modern Psychology*. Diss. St. John's University. 2015.

Fisher, Laura R. *Pedagogies of Uplift: Reform Institutions and U.S. Literary Production*. Diss. New York University. 2012.

Fisher, Lydia. *Domesticating the Nation: American Narratives of Home Culture*. Diss. University of Washington. 2000.

Francis, Conseula. *(Re)making a Difference: Theorizing Experience and Racial Individuality in Twentieth-Century African American Literature and Literary Theory*. Diss. University of Washington. 2002.

Francis, Terri. *Under a Paris Moon: Transatlantic Black Modernism, French Colonialist Cinema, and the Josephine Baker Museum*. Diss. The University of Chicago. 2004.

Franks, Matt. *Queer Eugenics: Modernism and the Politics of Uplift*. Diss. University of California, Davis. 2014.

Gautier, Amina Lolita. *Encoding Vision, Envisioning Race*. Diss. University of Pennsylvania. 2004.

Germana, Michael. *Standards of Value: United States Monetary Policy and the Negotiation of Racial Difference in American Literature, 1834–1952*. Diss. The University of Iowa. 2006.

Gradisek, Amanda R. *Passing Figures: Fashion and the Formation of Modernist Identity in the American Novel*. Diss. The University of Arizona. 2009.

Gueye, Khadidiatou. *Mapping the Liminal Identities of Mulattas in African, African American, and Caribbean Literatures*. Diss. The Pennsylvania State University. 2006.

Hanlon, Christopher. *Pragmatism and the Unconscious: Language and Subject in Psychoanalytic Theory, Pragmatist Philosophy, and American Narrative*. Diss. University of Massachusetts Amherst. 2001.

Hildebrand, Molly. *Mind the Gap: The Visual Arts, the Reader-as-Viewer, and Identity Critique in Early Twentieth-Century American Women's Writing*. Diss. Tufts University. 2015.

Hinnov, Emily. *Choran Community: The Aesthetics of Encounter in Literary and Photographic Modernism*. Diss. University of New Hampshire. 2005.

Hiro, Molly. *The Forces of Feeling: Sympathy and Race in American Modernity*. Diss. The University of California, Los Angeles. 2005.

Hodge, Deckard. *Expatriate Modernisms: Border Crossing in the 1920s*. Diss. University of California, Riverside. 2005.

Hudson, Jenise Shree. *Keeping it Together: Reading Affect and Strong Black Womanhood in Larsen, Hurston and Shange*. Diss. Florida State University. 2016.

Jenkins, Candice. *Cultural Infidels: Intimate Betrayal and the Bonds of Race*. Diss. Duke University. 2001.

John, Caresse A. *Narrating Choices: The Significance of Technique in the Work of Sarah Orne Jewett, Willa Cather, Nella Larsen, and Zora Neale Hurston*. Diss. Northern Illinois University. 2008.

Karl, Alissa. *Modernism and the Marketplace: Literary Cultures and Consumer Capitalism, 1915–1939*. Diss. University of Washington. 2005.

Koch, Lisa. *"Indecent Exposure": American Women Writers, the Body, and Public Performance*. Diss. University of Maryland, College Park. 2000.

Kramer, Elizabeth Brooks. *Freedom Reconceived: Reinscribing the Erotic in African American Protest Literature, 1845–1930*. Diss. University of California, Berkeley. 2000.

Labbé, Jessica. *"No Room for Her Individual Adventure": The American Woman's Journey Narrative in the Works of Edith Wharton and Nella Larsen*. Diss. University of South Carolina. 2007.

Lamm, Kimberly. *Composing and Contesting the Space of Visibility: Literary and Visual Portraiture in Nineteenth- and Early Twentieth-Century American Culture.* Diss. University of Washington. 2007.

Lee, Julia. *Almost American: Cross-Racial Representations in African American and Asian American Literatures, 1896–1937.* Diss. University of California, Los Angeles. 2005.

Mafe, Diana. *Mixed Bodies, Separate Races: The Trope of the "(Tragic) Mulatto" in Twentieth-Century African Literature.* Diss. McMaster University (Canada). 2008.

Manora, Yolanda. *A Someone like the Dreamer: Relationship, Community and Consciousness in 20th-Century African American Women's Novels.* Diss. Emory University. 2002.

Mays, Andrea Louise. *Revisioning Reality: Normative Resistance in the Cultural Works of the Lincoln Motion Picture Company, Nella Larsen, and Allan Rohan Crite, 1915–1945.* Diss. The University of New Mexico. 2014.

McCray, April Letitia. *Unholy Matrimony: Marriage and Identity in Twentieth Century African-American Women's Fiction.* Diss. The Florida State University. 2011.

McMullen, Liv. *Privilege and Pain: Problems of Gender, Class and Race during the Harlem Renaissance.* Diss. Villanova University. 2007.

Moore, Steven T. *Black Rage in African American Literature before the Civil Rights Movement: Frederick Douglass, Harriet Jacobs, Charles Chesnutt, Nella Larsen, Richard Wright, and Ann Petry.* Diss. University of Nebraska. 2008.

Musiol, Hanna. *"Objects of emancipation": The Political Dreams of Modernism.* Diss. Northeastern University. 2011.

Nakachi, Sachi. *Mixed-Race Identity Politics in Nella Larsen and Winnifred Eaton (Onoto Watanna).* Diss. Ohio University. 2002.

O'Brien, Alyssa Joan. *Gendered Disidentification in the Fiction of James Joyce, Virginia Woolf, and Nella Larsen: A Modernist Aesthetic of Mobility.* Diss. University of Rochester. 2001.

Pabst, Naomi. *Always a Little Different: A Politics of Blackness.* Diss. University of California, Santa Cruz. 2000.

Pan, Arnold. *The Space for Race: The Minority Demographics of United States Modernism.* Diss. University of California, Irvine. 2007.

Peters-Golden, Rebecca. *Modern Gothic Realism: How America Became Generic.* Diss. Indiana University. 2011.

Pickens, Roxane. *Dark Play: Notes on Narrative Festivity, Identity, and Interactions with African Americans in the U.S. Jazz Age.* Diss. College of William and Mary. 2014.

Rabin, Jessica. *Surviving the Crossing: (Im)migration, Ethnicity and Gender in Trans-National America*. Diss. Emory University. 2000.

Robinson-Whitted, Qiana. *African-American Literature and the Crisis of Faith*. Diss. Yale University. 2003.

Roffman, Karin Sabrina. *Museums, Libraries, and the Woman Writer: Edith Wharton, Marianne Moore, and Nella Larsen*. Diss. Yale University. 2004.

Rosen, Jody. *People Don't Want to Marry Me. People Want to Marry Me. I Don't Want to Marry People: Marriage-Plot Subversion through Repetition in Anglo-American Fiction of the 1920s*. Diss. City University of New York. 2007.

Rosenblum, Lauren. *Smart Ladies Sit Still: Women, Modernism and Photography*. Diss. State University of New York at Stony Brook. 2012.

Rudisel, Christine. *"A Lack of Acquiescence": The Women Writers and Uncanonized Texts of the Harlem Renaissance*. Diss. City University of New York. 2004.

Sasa, Ghada. *The Femme Fatale in American Naturalism*. Diss. Indiana University. 2006.

Schmidt, Suzanne. *"Crafting" the Race House of the Domestic Individual: Political Subjectivities, Hierarchy and Value in the Crafting and Do-It-Yourself Labors of Domestic Fiction, 1850–Present*. Diss. University of Washington. 2014.

Sengupta, Satarupa. *Citizenship and Expatriation in United States Women's Fiction, 1868–2004*. Diss. George Washington University. 2006.

Shaw-Thornburg, Angela. *Reading and Writing African American Travel Narrative*. Diss. Rutgers The State University of New Jersey. 2006.

Sheehan, Elizabeth Mary. *Modes of Dress and Redress: Aesthetics, Politics, and Fashion in Transatlantic Modernism*. Diss. University of Virginia. 2011.

Sherrard, Cherene Monique. *Imagining the "New" Mulatto: Ideology and Iconography in the Literature of the Harlem Renaissance*. Diss. Cornell University. 2000.

Stringer, Dorothy. *"Dangerous and Disturbing": Traumas and Fetishes of Race in Faulkner, Larsen, and Van Vechten*. Diss. State University of New York at Albany. 2003.

Sweeney, Jennifer Francis. *Narrating the Sartorial: Reading Fashionable Resistance in the Literary Archive*. Diss. State University of New York at Binghamton. 2016.

Tenerelli, Polyxeni. *Hybridity, Monstrosity, and Women's Voices in Black and Greek Fiction*. Diss. Harvard University. 2007.

Ulmer, Tisha. *Independent Women: Black Women as Consumers in Literature Written from Slavery to the Harlem Renaissance.* Diss. City University of New York. 2010.

Urban, Monica Bowerman. *Fashion Sense: Surfaces, Aesthetics, and Urban Space in U.S. Literature and Culture, 1843–1928.* Diss. University of Miami. 2016.

Wahaltere, Sidra Smith. *Novel Identities: Black Female Self-Authorization in Late Nineteenth- and Early Twentieth-Century African American Fiction.* Diss. Tufts University. 2006.

Walker, Karen. *The Art of Resistance: Reappropriating Community in American Women's Literature, 1898–1987.* Diss. The University of Arkansas. 2010.

Walls, Charles. *Acts of the Imagination: Racial Sentimentalism and the Modern American Novel.* Diss. Columbia University. 2005.

White, Hope. *Love in Spite of Their Trouble: African-American Women Writers and a Romantic Tradition.* Diss. The University of Alabama. 2004.

Williams, Erika Renée. *The Art of the Aesthete: Aesthetics, Subjectivity, and Ethics in the "New Negro" Writings of Alain Locke, William Edward Burghardt Du Bois, and Nella Larsen.* Diss. University of Pennsylvania. 2005.

Wood, Jennifer. *The New Black: Sartorial, Corporeal and Sexual Politics in the Harlem Renaissance.* Diss. Yale University. 2009.

Zellmer, Jill. *Valuing Female Friendship: The Ethics of Intimacy in American Women's Novels from 1870–1990.* Diss. University of Wisconsin, Milwaukee. 2003.